FOR LIBERTY AND JUSTICE

A BIOGRAPHY OF BRIGADIER GENERAL WŁODZIMIERZ B. KRZYŻANOWSKI, 1824-1887

BY

JAMES S. PULA

ETHNIC HERITAGE STUDIES CENTER
UTICA COLLEGE

PUBLISHED BY THE

ETHNIC HERITAGE STUDIES CENTER

AT

UTICA COLLEGE

ISBN 0-9660363-9-5
Ethnic Heritage Studies Center
Utica College
1600 Burrstone Road
Utica, N.Y. 13502

For Haley Lynch

JAMES S. PULA

James S. Pula graduated from New York Mills High School in 1964. He received a baccalaureate degree at SUNY-Albany, an M.Ed. degree in administration from the University of Maryland, and M.A. and Ph. D. degrees in history from Purdue University. The author and editor of over a dozen books and more than fifty articles, most dealing with ethnic and immigration history, two of his books have been honored with the Oskar Halecki Prize for the best book published each year on the Polish experience in America, and another received the Gambrinus Prize offered by the Milwaukee County Historical Society for the best book on Wisconsin history. He has also been honored with the Miecislaus Haiman Award for distinguished contributions to the field of Polish American history, the Distinguished Service Award from the American Council for Polish Culture, and several other professional awards. The editor of the scholarly journal *Polish American Studies* since 1982, he is currently Professor of History at Purdue University.

Table of Contents

Acknowledgement vii

Introduction ix

1. "The Son of a Foreign Land"
   From Childhood in Poland to a New Life in America 1

2. "Free Men Are Brothers"
   Organizing a Regiment and Leading it at Cross Keys 19

3. "I Fights Mit Sigel"
   The Second Bull Run Campaign 49

4. "For Liberty and Justice"
   Winter in Camp and News From Poland 73

5. "A Hell of a Fix"
   The Chancellorsville Campaign 95

6. "A Portrait of Hell"
   The Gettysburg Campaign 113

7. "The Most Distinguished Feats"
   The Chattanooga and Knoxville Campaigns 145

8. "Veteran Volunteers"
   Furlough and Frameup 163

9. "A Most Splendid Officer"
   The Final Months of the War 185

10. "Those Who Were Faithful"
    The Reconstruction Era 197

11. "I Feel That I Have Done My Duty"
    Special Agent, United States Treasury 211

12. "Without Injury to His Dignity"
Life in San Francisco 223

13. "Wounds Which Do Not Heal"
A Return to Federal Service 235

14. A "Genial and Loyal Spirit"
Twilight Years and Beyond 255

Appendices
A. Honors Received by Krzyżanowski 273
B. Report on the Battle of Cross Keys 274
C. Report on the Second Battle of Bull Run 275
D. Report on the Battle of Chancellorsville 278
E. Itinerary of Krzyżanowski's Brigade During the Reopening of the Tennessee River 281
F. Krzyżanowski's Staff officers 282

Endnotes 283

Bibliography 319

Index 327

ACKNOWLEDGEMENTS

Were it not for the kind assistance of a great many people this work could not have been attempted. I owe an exceptional debt of gratitude to my parents—Winifred S. Pula and Stanley J. Pula—who helped in so many ways it would be impossible to enumerate them all. Particular appreciation also goes to Joseph Wieczerzak who read my initial manuscript and made many excellent suggestions; to Ludwig Ziarnik who translated original documents from Polish and Russian; to Jaroslaw Lyktey who translated material on Carl Schurz from the original German; and especially to my father, Stanley J. Pula, for translating Gen. Krzyżanowski's memoirs and other materials from the original Polish.

Special thanks for aid "above and beyond the call of duty" go to Katherine Robinson and Cheryl Knodle of the Purdue University Inter-Library Loan Office; Josephine L. Harper, Reference Curator of the State Historical Society of Wisconsin; Robert G. Carroon, Curator of Research Collections, Milwaukee County Historical Society; James J. Sullivan, Curator of the Military Museum of the State of New York; Richard Sommers of the U.S. Army Military History Institute Archives in Carlisle Barracks, Pennsylvania; Jan Lorys and Leonard Kurdek of the Polish Museum of America in Chicago; William M. Lamers; Józefa Rzewska, Curator of the Archives of the Polish National Alliance; Donald Woods, University of Wisconsin-Milwaukee; Rev. Donald Biliński, OFM, Curator of the Polish Museum of America; David A. Keough, Pamela A. Cheney, R. Hackenburg and Michael Winey of the U.S. Army Military History Institute; Jane Kedron of the Polish Institute of Arts & Sciences of America; Jay Willard of the California Historical Society; Frances D. Miller of the Union College Library; Margaret Key of the Bowers Museum; John Heiser of the Gettysburg National Military Park; James Gandy of the New York State Military Museum in Saratoga, New York; Adele Chwalek of the Mullen Library at the Catholic University of America; Robert B. Roesler, Curator of the Greenfield Historical Society, WI; Melanie Yolles of the Manuscript and Archives Division of the New York Public Library; and the following members of the staff of the National Archives—Albert Blair, Steele Hill, Michael Meier, Michael Musick, Angie van Dereedt, James Walker and Philip R. Ward.

I would also like to express my appreciation to M. B. Biskupski, Stanley R. Burleson, W. L. Damkoehler, Robert T. Ewens, Mary A. Geiger, Donnabelle Gerhardt, Joseph H. Gillis, Carmen Gonzalez, Steven Gunther, James A. Huston, Robert J. Kadlec, Walter J. Karwowski, John C. Leitzmann, Robert D. Medley, Steven Miske, Dennis R. Moore, J. E.

Morley, Margaret Paulus, Joseph Piekarczyk, Sr., Charles Rothlauf, D. JoAnn Schiefelbein, Russell Scott, Erv Seeger, John F. Stover, Fred Turk, Alicja Wegner, Alfred Wickesberg and Joseph W. Zurawski.

Other organizations that provided assistance included the Biblioteka Narodowy, Warsaw, Poland; the Boudoin College Library & Archives, Brunswick, Maine; the Gettysburg National Military Park; the Indiana State Library; the Indiana State Historical Society; the Library of Congress; the Massachusetts Historical Society; the Milwaukee County Historical Society; the Milwaukee Public Library; the Milwaukee Turners Foundation, Inc.; the National Archives and Record Service in San Francisco; the New-York Historical Society; the New York Public Library; the New York State Library & Archives; the New York State Military Archives; the Ohio Historical Society; the Oneida County Historical Society; the Polish Arts and Cultural Foundation; the Polish Institute of Arts & Sciences of America; the Polish Studies Program and Archives at Central Connecticut State University; the State Historical Society of Wisconsin; the U.S. Army Military History Institute; the William L. Clements Library, University of Michigan; and the Wisconsin Veterans Museum.

INTRODUCTION

Biography is the essence of history for it examines the hopes and fears, the circumstances and events, the acts and motivations that animate people in any given historical setting. By studying the lives of individuals one may better understand not only the actions of a single human being, but the effects of those inexorable events that dominate the time in which the individual lives.

Throughout the panorama of American existence, historians and biographers have concentrated on the themes of decisive events and "great men" whose decisions have changed the course of history. John F. Kennedy's *Profiles in Courage* is but one example of a variety of works that examine the determination of America's foremost political leaders. These were men whose acts and decisions molded the course of American history. Yet, they did not act alone. Behind them were thousands of political supporters and individuals upon whom fell the task of implementing the directives of the nation's leaders. Certainly those leaders exhibited courage of conviction; yet, there is a dramatic difference between the courage of the politician, arguing his case in the lush halls of Congress, and the courage of the politician's pawn, the anonymous blue-clad infantryman standing exposed to hostile shot and shell in an open field north of Gettysburg. Assured of his place in history regardless of the outcome of his rhetoric, the legislator risks only re-election and a lucrative salary. The nameless infantryman, the neglected man in American history, risks his very life.

Among those who contributed substantially to the material and cultural progress of the United States were millions of immigrants who came to the shores of North America to begin a new life. Usually with little but the few possessions they brought with them, they became Americans by the choice of their own free will, not by the geographical chance of their birth. They came because they wanted to, because they valued the freedoms and opportunities America had to offer. They brought with them unique bits of knowledge and culture that they added to the mosaic of modern American society.

One of those immigrants was Włodzimierz Bonawentura Krzyżanowski. A son of Poland, steeped in her traditions and culture, he was exiled because of his participation in the democratic and patriotic Polish revolt of 1846. He arrived in the New World without fanfare, with neither resources nor a knowledge of the English language. Over the course of many difficult years he rose from the depths of poverty to a position as a leading citizen in the large ethnic community of Washington, D.C. Krzyżanowski was not a "great man" in the sense of someone who shapes and defines policies that alter the course of human events; rather, he was an idealist who possessed the determination and courage of his convictions to risk all that he had in the pursuit of the goals he valued. It was through the efforts of Krzyżanowski, and those like him, that policies were implemented.

Though more prominent than most immigrants, Krzyżanowski's life reflects the hopes and aspirations of that group of rugged individuals who risked everything in the hopes of finding freedom and liberty. Although this work is intended to explore the life and contributions of one man, it is also hoped that it will shed light on the ethnic subculture—virtually untouched by the major American historians—through which the protagonist walked.

SECOND EDITION

The first edition of this work, based on my doctoral dissertation at Purdue University, was published by the Polish American Congress Charitable Foundation in 1978. Since that time I have occasionally run into additional information on the general, including original materials from archives or private collections in the United States and Poland that was unavailable at the first writing. Some of that information explains more fully and accurately significant instances in the protagonist's life such as his participation in the abortive Mierosławski Insurrection in Poland, the failure of his nomination as brigadier general in the spring of 1863, and his life as a Special Agent for the U.S. Treasury following the war. This, and the urging of several friends and colleagues, led to the preparation of this second edition of the general's biography in an attempt to update and make more complete the story of the intersection of his life with the times in which he lived.

— CHAPTER ONE —

"THE SON OF A FOREIGN LAND"

FROM CHILDHOOD IN POLAND TO A NEW LIFE IN AMERICA

> In the epic struggle of the human race to govern itself Poland for centuries has been the champion of freedom. Through stress and storm whether her sun shone brightly or suffered long through temporary eclipse, she has ever fought to hold aloft the torch of human liberty.
>
> Because we hold this ideal of liberty in common, ours has been a long and unbroken friendship with the people of Poland. From the days of our struggle to achieve Nationhood, unbroken by any rift through the century and a half of our life as a Nation, the American people and the people of Poland have maintained a friendship based upon this common spiritual ideal.
>
> ... It is a high privilege to bear witness to the debt which this country owes to men of Polish blood. Gratefully we acknowledge the services of those intrepid champions of human freedom ... whose very names are watchwords of liberty and whose deeds are part of the imperishable record of American independence. Out of the past they speak to us to bid us guard the heritage that they helped to bestow.[1]

A eulogy of the statesman Ignacy Paderewski? A memorial, perhaps, to the Revolutionary War leaders Kazimierz Pułaski and Tadeusz Kościuszko? No. These words, spoken by President Franklin D. Roosevelt in 1937, refer to another Pole who, like those before and after him, fought for the freedom of both his native and his adopted lands. Who was this man? It is best we begin in the small village of Rożnowo, in the province of Wielkopolska, Poland.

The date of July 8, 1824, passed into Western history with little to mark its existence. On a nobleman's estate near Rożnowo in the Grand Duchy of Poznań, however, the day was one of joy for Stanisław and Ludwika Krzyżanowski. On that day, in the home of her father, Stanisław Pągowski, Ludwika gave birth to a baby boy who received the Christian names Włodzimierz Bonawentura. Though a cause for great rejoicing, the new baby was

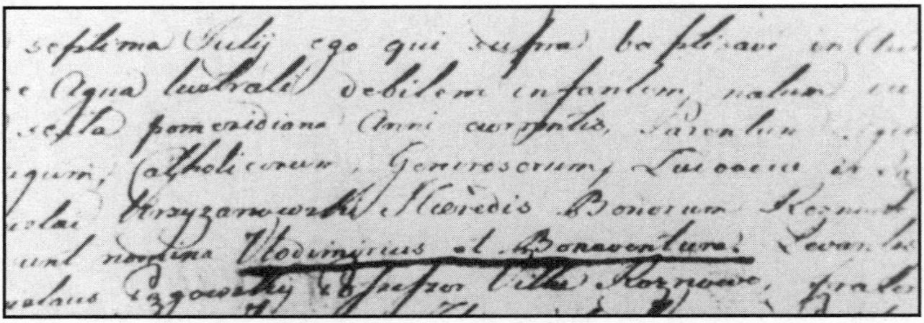

Krzyżanowski's birth notice. *Courtesy of Henry Archacki.*

---

afflicted with such ill health that his concerned parents had him baptized at home rather than risk the journey to the church. Nevertheless, his health and strength gradually improved to that of a normal child.[2]

Though born the son of a land owning noble, the new child arrived into circumstances that presented him with no riches save the treasured memories of the past. The Krzyżanowski family had long been prominent in Polish political and historical records. The child's grandparents, Jakub and Antoinette Krzyżanowski, minor nobles residing near Długie in the Kujawia district of Poland, brought into the world three sons and a daughter. The girl, Justyna Krzyżanowska, married French émigré Michel Chopin, becoming the mother of Fryderyk Chopin, the child prodigy and world-renowned national composer of Poland. The three sons—Stanisław, Bogumil, and Bonawentura—all fought for Polish independence under the banners of Napoleon Bonaparte.[3]

In Poland, partitioned into three zones of occupation by Austria, Prussia and Russia, the Napoleonic Wars brought hopes of an independent Poland to the minds and hearts of ardent patriots like Stanisław Krzyżanowski. But just as Napoleon's reign signified a period of hope for Poles, it also brought sorrow and despair. Stanisław suffered through the torturous rigors of Napoleon's Russian debâcle as a quartermaster-general. He endured the agonizing defeat of the last hope for Polish independence, only to return home to a wife who suddenly became ill and died in 1819. With four children to care for, Stanisław quickly remarried, choosing as his bride the sister of his former wife. Ludwika bore him four additional children, bringing the family total to eight. Young Włodzimierz was the third offspring of Stanisław's second marriage.[4]

Though rich in memories, the family was poor in financial resources. Debts incurred during the wars remained unpaid, while the cost of maintaining such a large family depleted the sparse income. Threats of foreclosure constantly beset Stanisław Krzyżanowski until 1826 when his principal creditors—Wolff, Falk, and Levin Koenigsberger—began legal proceedings to recover the debts due them. No longer able to support his family, or to stave off the demands of his creditors, Stanisław was finally forced to redeem his debts by selling his modest estate to Fabron Koszutski in 1827. Valued at some 86,000 thalers, the lands and buildings returned a mere 57,000 thalers because of the prevailing buyers' market and the need to satisfy his debts of 56,000 thalers quickly. No doubt the burden of this string of political and economic reverses contributed to Stanisław's death on July 29, 1830.[5]

The death of the head of the family left the Krzyżanowskis in financial ruin. In addition to these problems, the spirit of revolt again drove Poland to action against its' oppressors. First Uncle Bogumil, then brother Nemezy left to fight in the November Insurrection. With its failure both men were condemned to prison after their arrest by authorities at the Brodnica border station. The deep and lasting influence this experience had on young Włodzimierz's life can be seen in a letter he wrote to his family in Poland a half-century later in 1881:

> You mention the celebration of our unfortunate revolution in 1830. Instead of celebrating a holiday, we should be holding mourning services. I remember this unfortunate epoch despite the fact that I could not evaluate events since I was only six years old. We lost the flower of our young generation. Our intellectuals were banished to exile, and the thousands who remained behind wept over them. Our country was filled with sorrow. Mothers were forever separated from their sons. How many similar mistakes did we commit?[6]

In the midst of this grave situation Ludwika struggled to keep her family together. She sought support from her relatives, but none could offer succor enough to sustain the family as a single group. Finally, in desperation, she took her daughter Stanisława and her youngest son, Edmund, to live with relatives in the Congress Kingdom. Little Włodzimierz, who was of course too young to comprehend the causes of this separation from his mother, was sent with his step-brother and step-sisters to the home of an aunt named Szefer in Poznań. The move, for him, proved a lasting trauma. Though his aunt and his in-laws apparently treated him well, he never recovered from the loss of his mother's loving presence. Instead, he spent the rest of his life in a quest for the lost companionship and familial love of his youth.[7]

Włodzimierz's aunt was a pleasant, affectionate woman who did what she could to fill the void of maternal love in his life. She, along with her daughter Emily, always occupied a special place in his heart. However, as a

Church of the parish of St. Catherine in Rożnowo. *Courtesy of Henry Archacki.*

child Włodzimierz was not particularly healthy. This, coupled with his separation from his mother, must have weighed heavily on his mind, no doubt causing him to be more pensive and introverted than the normal child. His experiences during his early years may, in fact, account for the development of what appears to be a high degree of human sensitivity in his adulthood. As he grew older he corresponded frequently with his brother Edmund, attempting all the while to bridge the gulf of distance separating him from his mother and his homeland.[8]

"A Rash Pursuit of a Vision"

Life for Włodzimierz in Poznań progressed at a peaceful, "snail-like" pace until the year 1844 when he enrolled as a student in the Department of Mathematics and Technology at the Lycée of St. Mary Magdalene in that city. By the time he entered school the oppressions and restrictions aimed at Poles in the occupied Grand Duchy of Poznań were somewhat ameliorated by the ascension of the moderate Frederick William IV to the Prussian throne on June 7, 1840.[9] While Galicia and the Congress Kingdom suffered under the iron rule of Metternich and Paskievich, the Grand Duchy emerged as the center of Polish culture and education. Indeed, the western borderlands of the former Polish state became a haven for the romantic and idealistic thought of philosophers like Karol Libelt, Bronisław Trentowski, and August Cieszkowski; scholars such as Edward Raczyński and Titus Dzialyński; as well as literary figures including Ryszard Berwiński, Franciszek Morawski, and Stanisław Kozmian. Due to this influx of liberal idealists, Poznań became a hotbed of Polish revolutionary scheming. In 1843 the movement became international when a committee in the Grand Duchy established close, lasting ties with the Democratic Society in Paris.[10]

Into this atmosphere of patriotic and democratic fervor stepped Włodzimierz Krzyżanowski at the age of twenty-one. Nurtured on stories of the past glories of Poland, and on the exploits of his own family in defense of a Polish national state, he already possessed a strong belief in loyalty to the fatherland which drew him into close alliance with a circle of plotters who advocated the use of harassing tactics against the occupying powers. The democratic spirit of the revolutionaries further impressed his youthful ideals with a sense of freedom that was to accompany him for the rest of his life, shaping his future with decisive effect. By 1844, with youthful abandon for a cause he never doubted, Krzyżanowski was firmly committed to the movement for Polish liberation. As he later wrote, "the hope for a better future, which flashed before us like a meteor, enchanted us, intoxicated us, and carried us away. ... I loved my native land and all it stood for. I dreamed; I soared above the clouds; I went blindly where I was told, not reflecting over the consequences of such a rash pursuit of a vision."[11]

The year 1846 was, in Poland, a prologue to the traumatic upheavals that swept across Europe in 1848-49. The center of this emerging "Springtime of Nations" was Poznań, where a revolution was planned for February 1846 under the leadership of Ludwik Mierosławski. The plan that Krzyżanowski hoped would free his homeland called for the formation of a peasant army under the leadership of émigré officers, patriotic intelligentsia, and liberal gentry. Encouraged to action by the 1845 celebrations commemorating the anniversary of the November Insurrection, Mierosławski arrived in Poznań in December to take charge of the planning. The plotters drafted a proclamation designed to liberate the peasantry, abolish class inequities and institute other democratic reforms. The three severed portions of Poland were to rise simultaneously, but disaster struck a fatal blow before the movement could get underway when an informer betrayed the conspirators and the details of their plan to the authorities. On the eve of the proposed insurrection, Mierosławski and many other Poznań leaders found themselves under police arrest.[12]

In Russian-occupied Poland the revolt was also abortive. Only in the Free City of Kraków were the revolutionaries able to establish a new gov-

Ludwik Mierosławski.
Courtesy of the Polish Museum of America in Chicago.

ernment. From there, the rebellion spread into the Galician countryside, showing early success. It ended only when the Austrian authorities succeeded in motivating the Ruthenian peasants against the Polish land owning nobility before a revolutionary proclamation of emancipation could be circulated throughout the countryside. Austria used the revolt as a pretext for annexing Kraków, while in Krzyżanowski's area of Poznań the Prussians retaliated with a series of trials before a special tribunal. These legal proceedings implicated 254 people, many of them tried in absentia. Eight of the accused received death sentences, while most of the others were condemned to varying prison terms.[13]

Political refugees flocked from Poland to havens in other European nations, much as they did after previous revolts. They became such a potent force in other revolutionary movements that in 1848 Karl Marx noted that "the cause of Poland's liberation became inseparable from revolution and Pole and revolutionary became a synonym."[14] Among those forced into exile were the prominent as well as the not so prominent. In the former category was Jan Tyssowski, the dictator of Kraków who later became a successful American citizen. Another was Dr. Leopold J. Boeck, a confederate of Lajos Kossuth, Sorbonne professor, and American Educational Commissioner at the Universal Expositions in Vienna and Philadelphia. In the latter category was Włodzimierz Krzyżanowski.

With the failure of the Mierosławski Insurrection, Krzyżanowski's relatives managed to raise enough money to secure his passage out of Poznań and start him on his way in search of another life in the New World. But the youth's exit from his homeland was nevertheless fraught with danger. A letter from the Royal Magistrate at Szamotuly to the Honorable Ritter und Elder von Beurmann, Royal Chief Magistrate of the Province of Posen [Poznań] indicates the hasty and secretive nature of his escape, just one step ahead of the authorities.

> It has come to my attention that a stranger is kept in hiding at the manor house of the landowner von Swinarski and when I ordered an investigation, he was already gone. Herr von Swinarski was not to be found either and no pertinent information could be gained; therefore a suspicion of concealment of a politically criminal person caused a further pursuit in the matter. It was found that this was a certain Wladimir von Krzyzanowski who left Radzyn in the direction of Bamblin, Oborniki, where he was staying at the residence of the landowner von Dobrzycki wherefrom he again left toward an unknown destination. The landowner von Dobrzycki explained von Krzyzanowski's situation at a hearing on the 11th day of this month. Your Honor, I want to present this report, obedient to your wishes, and leave it up to you as to what extent a further tracking of von Krzyzanowski might be in order.[15]

Despite his youth, or perhaps because of it, Krzyżanowski was not frightened at the prospect of leaving home. The lure of the unknown cast its spell upon him, while his youthful idealism prompted visions of great adventures and successes to be found across the sea. He left to seek his fortune. He left to take advantage of the freedoms offered by North America's fountain of liberty. Grief did not enter his mind, for he felt certain that he would soon return to his family and friends in Poznań.[16]

Escaping from Poland, Krzyżanowski traveled overland to Hamburg where he booked passage on a ship bound for New York. After purchasing his ticket, a few hours remained before his scheduled departure. Reassured by his safe escape from the Prussians that a lucky star must surely be guiding his future, he decided to use the hours before his departure to begin amassing his fortune through the medium of the local game of chance. Too late he found his star to have been in a state of eclipse, for he left the game only after losing his remaining money.[17]

Abandoned by his sense of confidence, distressed by the loss of his funds, Krzyżanowski wandered about the streets of Hamburg wondering what would become of him. As he meandered along the roadways the moon passed from in front of his star as quickly as it had appeared. An old friend of the family suddenly materialized from amid the crowd of strange faces. The young traveler confessed his plight to the friend, who lent him additional funds on the promise that Krzyżanowski's family would repay the loan.[18]

With money again in his pocket, he boarded the vessel that would carry him to a new life. Quietly he stood at the ship's rail watching the crowd gather to bid a pleasant voyage to those journeying on the seas. First the dock, then the buildings, and finally the shoreline faded from view. Sadness gripped tightly about him. He pictured his family fading farther and farther behind him with each passing minute. He became acutely aware, as well, that taking an ocean voyage definitely did not resemble standing on the shore or going on a short pleasure cruise. In every direction he turned his eyes met forbidding sky and endless leagues of water. Not unlike another later Polish traveler, Joseph Conrad, Krzyżanowski developed an instant respect for the extraordinary strength and will it took for men to make their living fighting the vastness of the ocean. The powerful open sea emphasized to him, as no other experience had, the insignificance and vulnerability of man.[19]

The voyage was not a pleasant one. Constant winds rocked the small ship from stem to stern, starboard to port, halting only briefly to begin a new assault from a different direction. White-capped waves pounding against the hull were the traveler's constant companions, with the only reward being the colorful daily sunrises. Krzyżanowski's only solace was the thought that had he undertaken the voyage a generation earlier the ordeal would have been reckoned in terms of weeks rather than days.[20]

The long solitude of the open sea at last provided him with an opportunity to collect his thoughts and reflect upon his future following the hurried flight from Poznań. He looked at himself. What he found was not the brightest prospect for the future that a young man could wish. He suddenly realized that he was alone, without substantial funds, skills, or even letters of introduction. He could not even speak a word of the language used by the inhabitants of the new land where he hoped to find freedom, liberty, and good fortune enough to recover what he had lost in Europe. He looked to the United States as a nation that succeeded in obtaining freedom, tolerance, equality and brotherhood for its citizens by uniting all of the classes of European society. Yet he also thought longingly of his home in Poznań. The deepening anguish he felt at leaving behind all he knew was tempered only by the hope of an eventual return to the life he longed for in his native land.[21]

"A Vortex of Unknown Power"

After an eternity of endless sea the long awaited cry of "Land Ho!" echoed from the ship's masts. The joy of finally sighting land quickly changed to a feeling of despair in the mind of the Poznań émigré. Flat roofs and massive buildings, broken only by the protruding forms of factory chimneys and disheveled streets, presented a drab waterfront greeting to the expectant immigrant. Surely, he thought, the city's faceless panorama would not inspire any of Europe's famous artists.[22]

No crowds gathered to greet the vessel as they did in European ports. Thus the loneliness the newcomer felt upon his arrival was magnified all the more. Deposited on the docks, alone and lost, he felt "like a tiny atom thrown into a vortex of unknown power." Looking back on his arrival in a letter to his family in Poland in 1881, he described his feelings at the moment of arrival in this strange new land.

> I had no parents to protect me from misfortune, no brother and sister who could aid me. No one spoke the language which I heard from my mother's lips. I suffered alone, nursing my misfortune with tears of sorrow, hoping that something would turn up to rescue me from the depths of despair.[23]

Alone on a foreign shore, with no letters of introduction, he found himself unable to communicate with anyone. Fearing the worst, he called out for help in his native language. No doubt he felt his ears mistaken, but luck indeed shone on him once again. Someone answered him in phrases he could readily understand. His plea struck the ears, and the sympathies, of a Polish carriage driver of several years residence in New York.[24]

Thankful for the sympathies of a fellow Pole, Krzyżanowski explained his dilemma in detail. It was a joyous meeting on the part of both parties. Eager for news from *Stary Kraj*—the "Old Country"—the carriage driver invited Krzyżanowski home to meet his wife and children. The family opened their home to the new arrival until he could make his own way in his new surroundings.

These first weeks in New York were a very depressing period in Krzyżanowski's life. Uprooted from his homeland, he had lost all that was familiar to him on his entrance into a completely new society and culture. Lacking a knowledge of the national tongue, he met with disappointment in his attempts to find a steady job. In a letter to his cousin Emily he lamented that "everything was foreign to me, there was no hand to shield me from distress, there was no heartbeat of brothers or sisters which would have echoed mine, there was no language which I had heard from my mother since the days of the cradle. I suffered through my distress with the hope that something better would grow, and I watered it with my tears and I suffered."[25]

To relieve his despair, and satisfy his hosts, Krzyżanowski spent endless hours discussing recent developments in Poland. After he mastered enough English so he could make his way about the city he satisfied his own curiosity by exploring what he later referred to as the "American Babylon." Though well acquainted and pleased with the Constitutional guarantees of liberty and equality in America, he was at first bewildered by the constant movement about him. It was not at all like the peaceful, well-ordered existence customarily found in Poznań. Though enormous in size, New York did not create a favorable impression on the Pole for he could not help but note how the grand palaces of the wealthier sections of the city contrasted sharply with the deteriorated residences in the poorer neighborhoods. The walls of the city were covered with a myriad of placards and advertisements; even the finest streets were dotted with holes where a man could easily break a leg.[26]

With little to do but think of his homeland, the lonely exile spent endless hours studying English and making contact with other Polish exiles in America. One of these was Henryk Kałussowski, a veteran of the November Insurrection in 1830-31 who arrived in American in 1842, settling in Washington, D.C., where he gained employment with the U.S. government. Maintaining an active interest in Polish affairs, he was a founding member of the Association of Poles in America [Stowarzyszenie Polaków w Ameryce] in 1842 through which he nurtured ties with Polish exiles in Europe, becoming a frequent correspondent to Polish periodicals and the acknowledged leader of the Polish group in America. In 1852, with the influx of émigrés from the revolutions of 1846 and 1848, he helped organized the Democratic Society of Polish Exiles in American [Towarzystwo Demokratyczne Wygnańców Polskich w Ameryce] with its headquarters in New York.[27] It is no doubt through these activities that Kałussowski and Krzyżanowski met, becoming correspondents and friends. Most likely it was through his association with Kałussowski that Krzyżanowski became interested in a proposal to found a colony of Polish exiles in the western farmlands of Virginia. Journeying there to join other Poles in the project, he soon became disillusioned when very few of his countrymen arrived to join him, and the few that did soon began to melt away, leaving him even more isolated than he had been in New York. The 1850 United States Census listed him a "farmer" living in Cabell County, Virginia [today West Virginia], on real estate he owned that was valued at $100. In the same district, census records recorded several Germans and Swiss along with fourteen-year-old Witold Kałussowski, probably Henryk's son, John Kruszewski with his wife and two children, and Anna Lucknoski [probably Lukomski] and her three children.[28]

Henryk Kałussowski.
Courtesy of the Polish Museum of America in Chicago.

Soon, Krzyżanowski was writing to Kałussowski of his desire to return to Washington, D.C. On New Year's Day, 1852, he wrote to his friend "From the Woods" to inform him that he was trying to return to Washington but, although he had received \$5.00 from Aleksander Bielaski and \$2.00 from Kałussowski, he had to pay taxes and that left him with too little money to afford the trip. He continued:

> …none of your letters made such an impression on me as the last one dated Dec. 15, which I received yesterday; you accuse me of not writing to you and rejecting your propositions, but you do not understand the situation and did not consider whether I could write. A month ago I received your letter with \$5.00 from Bielaski and \$2.00 from you. I answered it immediately and mailed it through the Post Office. Since Witold's departure I have not been in Guyandotte. It pains me that you did not receive that letter

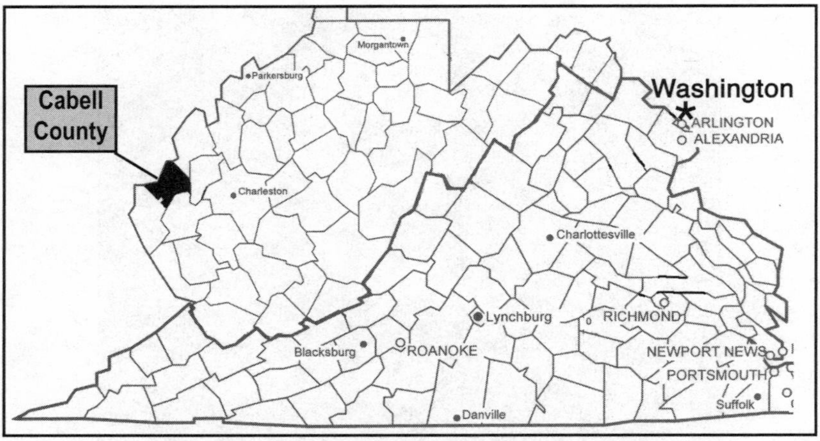

A map of Virginia showing the location of the planned Polish colony along the Ohio River in what is today West Virginia.

---

because if you had you would have no suspicion as to why I did not travel to Bielaski. My sincere intention was and is to come to you and what Bielaski sent me will be paid back. So far my circumstances have not permitted me to do what I wrote you in my last letter. I had to pay tax from whatever I had for the trip and so I had only $8.00 for the journey, not enough to reach Washington.I also had an urgent need to buy a suit of clothes, otherwise I would have had nothing to wear. This meant that from the $8.00 only $1.00 would be left for transportation. You write that I should sell your belongings which are still in my possession and use the proceeds for travel; you also wrote that I should bring bedding and it is my intention to do so. There are also your chairs, the kettle, curtains and some small items. It is impossible to sell those things, nobody has any money, so I am trying to sell a cow and some produce to have enough for the trip, but it is like trying to get something from a stone, so with what can I travel? You say that you do not know if you insulted me; oh no, Dear Henry, if I still can call you that, if I had anything against you I would write to you straightforwardly and not through a parenthesis.

You are surely convinced that I would do everything in my power for you, because I know that you did, and are still doing much for me. My biggest desire from the time I met you was to remain near you to spend the difficult moments of a homeless wanderer close to a real friend, and you have proven yourself to be one. For this reason I remained in Virginia, although I might have gone elsewhere to make some money, but when I saw that I could be useful to your son in case of the death of Mrs. Leha I stayed here. From the beginning when you proposed that I come to Washington I immediately made a decision; however, without means it was difficult and remains so. As soon as I can sell the cow and whatever else to have enough for the trip, I shall move right away.

Dear Henry, please explain to Bielaski not to be mad at me if I disappointed him, it is not my fault. Also, I am asking you to write me immediately when you receive my letter, I will be waiting to see if you received it. You did not write anything about Witold, Mrs. Leha and about our people from the Duchy.[29]

Although he longed for a letter from Kałussowski and a return to the friendlier atmosphere of Washington, he continued to be frustrated by letters that either went astray or were delayed in delivery. Further disappointment came in the form of other Poles who borrowed funds from Krzyżanowski that were not repaid. Although this may have been a legitimate request for assistance, it is also quite possible that the young Pole was swindled by a fellow countryman he tried to assist. On February 16 he wrote to Kałussowski to explain his situation and plead for help:

Dear Henry, new sorrows and misfortunes are coming toward me every day. I was hoping that we would see each other soon, but it was not to be. I had the $10.00 for the journey to Washington; however, Koniuszewski appeared wanting the constable to intervene against the shoemaker in Guyandotte. He asked for $10.00 and so I gave it to him. Koniuszewski expected to get some money every day and I was sure he would give it back. Soon, however, Koniuszewski began getting cold feet. I did not want to press him, although I could not explain his attitude, when all of a sudden I met Mass on the road. He was polite, and the next day I met him and Koniuszewski. I did not want to get involved; nevertheless, I understood what was going on. The following day he reproached me for allowing Lange to be in a position where he would starve to death, and while he was making a scene I told [illegible] to repay his debt to Koniuszewski. He made out a note for $586.00 for a year, which Mass guaranteed. But no mention was made about what he owed me, so they picked up their belongings and left for Cyorcy[?] where the sheriff was to find a job for him. I was left alone in Korzy[?] without any means to get out of here. I saw Dodd thinking that I might get the money for the trip; but that, too, was in vain. I really do not know what to do, I am in the greatest despair. Henry, you are the only one I have confidence in and so, please, have mercy and send me the money for the journey to Washington. I will pay you back the first thing after I find a job. Please do not abandon me this time and help me, otherwise I may go crazy. I can not stay here any longer so please write me as fast as you can so I know what to do with myself. The time of planting is approaching and I do not want the neighbors to make inquiries why I am not cultivating the soil. It would make a bad impression if I would tell them that I am leaving Virginia, otherwise I would have to stay. I hope to get an answer from you within 3 weeks. I will wait impatiently.[30]

His impatience to leave the backwoods of Virginia was only heightened by the maddening delays in mail delivery. From Guyandotte on March 8 he wrote:

> I do not know if my letters are reaching you since you are asking me in your letters for an answer and what I intend to do when I get to Bielaski. I wrote back several times and I would love to come if I had the means. Three weeks ago I wrote you extensively and anticipated that the letter had reached its destination, since there are no obstacles on the roads. That is why I am not writing about it now; secondly, my hand is very weak with grief. I am the only Pole left here and I have no means to move about. Others have more luck getting help, but I have to live in this forest without help, barely keeping afloat and on the verge of going crazy. As if destiny did not persecute me enough, my disappointments continue. You are the only one to whom I can open my heart. I have no one else to share my misery and poverty. You are not writing about Witold; what is he doing? He is not writing either, even when I was as good to him as I was to myself. Now I must stop. Dear Henry, my hand does not want to lead the quill anymore.[31]

"The Greatest Happiness I Could Find Outside My Own Fatherland"

The last Pole to leave the failed colony, Krzyżanowski eventually managed to reach Washington and the friendly camaraderie of its small émigré community. Though disillusioned and penniless, with the assistance of his fellow immigrants he was able to acquire enough proficiency in English to complete his training and qualify as a civil engineer in New York. With a new profession before him, he accepted a position that led him to the Midwest. Krzyżanowski journeyed west along the old Erie Canal route through central New York. Traveling north along the Hudson River, he soon arrived at the port of Albany that was kept busy trans-shipping freshly cut timber south to New York City. Heading west from Albany, he passed through the rustically appealing Mohawk Valley, where the majestic pines and firs of Northern New York reminded him of his homeland. When he came upon acres and acres of cleared land deprived of its vegetation by what he termed "human greed," he felt a deep sense of loss.[32]

Passing through Utica, Syracuse and Rochester, the traveler soon reached the banks of the Niagara River, the western terminus of the old Erie Canal. From there he left his train to make a short excursion to the famous waterfalls that have lured the curious since the time of the early French explorers. The Niagara Falls created a lasting impression on Krzyżanowski. He was mesmerized by mists rising hundreds of feet into the air forming a

Alexander Bielawski.
A wartime sketch courtesy of the U.S. Army Military History Institute.

multi-colored rainbow. He was awed by the overpowering roar of the water, a feeling not unlike that which overcame him on his ocean voyage to New York.[33]

From Niagara Falls, Krzyża-nowski journeyed west crossing Pennsylvania, Ohio and Indiana to the sprawling meat and grain center at Chicago. Much impressed with the huge expanse of his adopted home-land, he nevertheless felt a sense of sadness and despair at the newness surrounding him. He felt there was a great wealth to be taken from the sparsely populated areas of the Old Northwest, which seemed to cry out for settlers. His finances were more secure now that he was employed in constructing the rapidly-multiplying Midwestern railroads, but emotional security eluded him. He was a man without a country who had lost his old culture, yet still felt uncomfortable with his new environment. He longed for the familiar voices of his lost youth, for the gentle touch of his mother, for the reassuring companionship of friends and relatives.[34]

It was probably during his long sojourn in the West, or possibly even earlier in New York, that the lonely immigrant became acquainted with General Ward Benjamin Burnett, a fellow engineer. A graduate of the United States Military Academy and hero of the Mexican War, Burnett introduced the Pole to his twenty-one year old niece Caroline Mathilda Burnett. Young Caroline exposed Krzyżanowski to a dimension as yet unknown to him. She gave him love, attention, encouragement, and an importance which his life had not yet known. This newfound companionship soon soothed his sullen temperament, shattering the barrier of doldrums behind which he hid.[35] "I saw a star," Krzyżanowski wrote, "which in my distress lit my way, this light warmed my heart so that I could feel a new life enter it. I found the greatest happiness I could find outside of my own fatherland."[36] Marriage followed a brief courtship in 1854, followed by the birth of a son, Joseph, in New York in 1855. The family then settled in Washington, D.C., boarding with Caroline's father Enoch Burnett at 351 8th Street West, and working in the Burnett's pottery business. By 1860, Krzyżanowski and his wife operated their own pottery shop, specializing in glass and earthenwares, located at

383 7th Street West, only a few steps away from their lodging.[37]

For the first eight years after his arrival in America Krzyżanowski was preoccupied with trying to exist in his new environment, and with trying to promote his career. During that period he was unable to explain much of what was taking place around him. He likened himself to a fly falling into the inner machinery of a great clock. He could see all of the gears and wheels turning, producing a constant hum of activity and noise, each cog fitting into another so that the whole mysteriously functioned as a unit. He saw the movement and the result, but he was unable to comprehend the meaning or intricacies of all the different cogs and gears. Now that he had at last settled down, now that he was no longer inhibited by his moroseness, he had an opportunity to deliberate the meaning of his travels and his first impressions of America.[38]

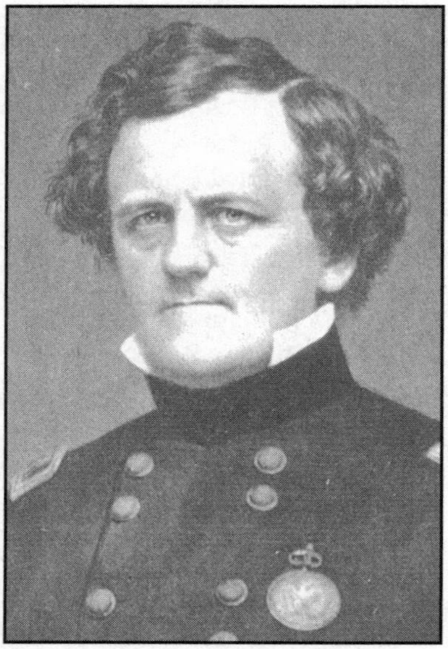

Ward Benjamin Burnett
Courtesy of the National Archives.

As he reflected upon his eight years in the United States he was impressed by the tremendous growth of such a comparatively young nation. Himself a devout advocate of the powers of a good education, he credited the huge strides made by the infant nation to the continual search for knowledge among its populace, the poorest citizen of which could not get along without his daily newspaper. He was struck by the equality of education present in the Northern states through which he traveled, as well as the toleration extended to divergent religious convictions. Coming from a nation that was largely Roman Catholic, but also harboring people of many diverse faiths, Krzyżanowski was particularly interested in the great proliferation of sects and Utopian societies. Their existence was, he reasoned, only one of the many results of the magnanimous Constitution.[39]

Business activities and his new wife occupied most of Krzyżanowski's time in the first months after his marriage. Gradually, as his home became more settled, his mind again turned to his homeland. From Washington he frequently wrote home to his family in Poland. He joined the local Turnverein, a Germanic brotherhood where he found camaraderie among fellow refugees from the European revolutions of 1848. There, in addition to participating in a regular program of calisthenics to keep himself physically fit, he began to develop into a leader among his fellow exiles.[40]

With his finances well-established and his wife to encourage him, Krzyżanowski gradually developed a keen interest in the political debates within his adopted country. His liberal ideals led him into the camp of the infant Republican Party in 1854, two years after its founding. By 1857 his oratorical skill and political prominence were such that he gained election as chairman of the local District of Columbia Republican Society. He was one of twelve local citizens who successfully petitioned the President to appoint Ward H. Lamon as Marshall of the District of Columbia, and in the spring of 1861 he was elected a member of the Republican Association of Washington, D.C., representing the German Association in that city. Such vocal support of Republican candidates for office made him much in demand as a speaker.[41]

The Republican Party first appealed to Krzyżanowski because of its opposition to the doctrine of States' Rights espoused by the Southern Democrats. Since he worshiped the American Constitution with its protection of personal freedoms, he concluded that the best way to guarantee the continued effectiveness of that document was to secure the strength of the federal government charged with enforcing its provisions. To have the individual states exerting their authority over that of the federal government, he reasoned, only served to weaken that government. A government thus weakened likewise undercut the principles upon which it stood.[42]

No doubt he likened this situation to that of the old Polish system where the ill-advised *liberum veto* provided that a single negative vote could void any constructive attempts to aid the people at the expense of the nobles or any other special interest group. If the American states could choose which federal statutes to obey and which to reject the central government would be as ineffective as the Polish *Sejm* [Senate] became. As long as the Republicans opposed the advocates of state supremacy, Krzyżanowski would support their candidates.

Much in demand as a speaker at various political and social functions, especially in the immigrant community, Krzyżanowski developed into an accomplished orator. The new resident of America spoke kindly of George Washington's refusal to become king of the United States. Similarly, he exhibited great pride in the efforts of his countryman Tadeusz Kościuszko to establish schools for Africans in Virginia. To Krzyżanowski's mind, there was no question whatsoever that the seeds of disunion were sown by the owners of the vast Southern estates whose aristocratic way of life rested on a foundation of human slavery. To him, the very existence of this dehumanizing system within the United States rendered the Constitution little better than hypocrisy.[43] In Poland he fought for nationalism and democracy. In the

United States he upheld these views in his opposition to States' Rights and in his open espousal of the abolitionist principles of Northern Republicans. "The institution of slavery," he later wrote, "could not exist in a country dedicated to personal liberty."[44] The course of American political life soon provided him with an opportunity to convert his words into action.

— CHAPTER TWO —

"FREE MEN ARE BROTHERS"[1]

ORGANIZING A REGIMENT AND LEADING IT AT CROSS KEYS

It was a crisp November 6, 1860, when Americans made their way to polling places to select the next president of the United States. To Krzyżanowski, the choice was obvious. As a Republican activist and avowed anti-slavery advocate, Krzyżanowski wholeheartedly supported Abraham Lincoln for the difficult job of leading the American Republic in defense of its principles of freedom and national unity against the threatening cancer of States' Rights. Indeed, throughout the campaign he spoke to small meetings of like-minded immigrants and others who favored the candidate that to them represented freedom and hope. Southern leaders, just as determined to defend their cause as Krzyżanowski was to promote his own, reacted to Lincoln's anti-slavery associates in a spirit of self-defense of their principles not unlike the feelings the Pole reserved for what he viewed as a Southern conspiracy aimed at bringing about the demise of the republic. The Lincoln victory that reassured Krzyżanowski, fulfilled all the predictions of doom that Southern statesmen continually warned their constituents would come to pass. The South had lost control of the House of Representatives early in the nation's history. It had lost control of the U.S. Senate with the admissions of several free states during the 1850s. Now the presidency, what it considered its last hope for preventing federal legislation from being enacted against its best interests, would be passing into the hands of a president whose party platform and leaders were avowedly anti-slavery. Seeing their last hope for critical influence on the federal government slip from their grasp, Southerners felt compelled to defend their way of life in the only manner they believed left to them—secession.

As the stream of Southern reaction grew into a river of secession, the North, preparing for the worst, began to arm volunteers in the event a resort to force proved necessary. The need for these citizen-soldiers was most keenly felt in the nation's capital where the very seat of federal government lay surrounded on all sides by slaveholding states. One of those who sensed the seriousness of the situation was Włodzimierz Krzyżanowski. Caught in the outpouring of emotional patriotism rampant in Washington, driven equally by a sense of gratitude to his adopted country and memories of his boyhood in Poland, the transplanted patriot enlisted as a private in the local militia on April 11, 1861, along with men from two Washington *Turnverein* who organized a company of sharpshooters for the defense of the city. Some eighty strong under the leadership of Capt. Joseph Gerhardt, the men were armed with what the *Daily National Republican* described as "long range rifles." As part of this early wave of volunteers, Krzyżanowski was on duty when president-elect Lincoln arrived in Washington, D.C., and later participated as part of the guard called out for service during the inauguration ceremonies. Yet, not everyone thought Krzyżanowski's rush to the colors was a wise idea. Fellow exile Henryk Dmochowski wrote to Henryk Kałussowski on April 18: "I am sad about what you are writing about Krzyżanowski. But then, he may succeed."[2]

It was April 11, 1861. In the early light of the following morning Southern artillery shells fell on Fort Sumter. With the outbreak of hostilities Krzyżanowski found his unit assigned to guard duty at the White House. For nine dramatic days he stood in the midst of America's greatest stage as the leading actors in the drama about to unfold scurried to and from conferences, reporting new developments and receiving urgent instructions. Though his off-duty hours were few, once the president issued his famous call for 75,000 volunteers on April 15 the Pole spent many hours encouraging others to enlist. With the assault on the Massachusetts militia by Southern sympathizers in Baltimore on April 19, a new sense of urgency animated Krzyżanowski's activities.[3]

His task was not difficult. War fever bordering on frenzy gripped the North, causing a massive rush to the colors. Krzyżanowski perceived about Washington a change in public attitudes. He attributed it to the fact that while Fort Sumter surrendered under full military honors, with the garrison intact, the Baltimore riots actually spilled the blood of the Massachusetts patriots. Fort Sumter, he felt, awakened the nation. The mob action in Baltimore provided the spark that drove the people to action.[4]

By April 22 the active immigrant enrolled sufficient volunteers to form "Krzyzanowski's Company," officially known as Company B, Turner Rifles, 8th Battalion, District of Columbia Militia, consisting of three lieutenants, five sergeants, four corporals and fifty-eight privates including two drummers. On the same date, the unit mustered into service with the Pole as its commanding officer. Though he attributed his captaincy to the government's search for men with even the most meager military experience, it is more likely that his recruiting achievements qualified him for his commission since the government at that time rewarded those who recruited volunteers with commissions appropriate to the number of men they enlisted.[5]

Krzyżanowski as a captain in the District of Columbia Militia.
Courtesy of Mikel Uriguen.

A less formal photograph of Krzyżanowski early in the war.
Courtesy of Donald Irving.

A new sense of pride overcame Krzyżanowski as he swore his oath of allegiance. He could not resist the opportunity to draw his men into line and deliver a short oration of his thoughts and hopes.[6] Perhaps this sense of pride resulted from his new rank; yet he could have attained rank without first enlisting as a private. Probably his feelings stemmed from the knowledge that he was again actively engaged in promoting the causes that necessitated his flight from Poznań—the ideals of liberty and patriotism.

Quite possibly it was also during April 1861 that the captain acquired the nickname "Kriz" from his fellow officers, whose attempts to pronounce his name no doubt proved an embarrassing struggle. One newspaper account, commenting on the difficulty in pronouncing his surname, described him as being "of unfavorable patronymic but undoubtable patriotism." Kriz adapted well to life in the military. His former wanderings prepared him for the nomadic existence of an army on the move. He enjoyed the impressive drills the troops had to master. He performed his official duties with the utmost of alacrity and diligence.[7] Most of all, he found a new home in the army; he developed a close kinship with his fellow soldiers which served to some degree as a substitute for the companionship he longed for as a youth. The Civil War gave his life new purpose beyond his own being. He mused, in fact, that the old saying about every Polish noble being born with a sword must indeed be true. But then, it was still the spring of 1861. War was still an adventurous life of bright new uniforms, blaring brass bands, and the sighs of lovely young ladies.

As the war began to accelerate, the government called for 500,000 volunteers to defeat the Confederacy by the end of the year. About May 10, no doubt through the influence of political friends, the War Department offered Krzyżanowski a commission in the Regular Army. He refused because he believed he owed it to the men whom he recruited to share with them any dangers their three months of service might bring. In fact, when his duties permitted, he continued his recruiting activities. In a speech he delivered in Baltimore during the election campaign of 1860, he boasted that the American flag was no more deeply loved than by her adopted sons.[8] In his actions he expended every effort to prove his point.

Company B was assigned to the defenses of Washington, but occasionally ventured into the countryside as it did on April 23 and 25 when it marched to Annapolis Junction to keep the road open for reinforcements moving into the capital. In May the company paraded on the 10th, marched in a grand parade of the militia on the 13th, and took part in the procession in honor of the death of Col. Elmer Ellsworth on the 27th. The local press noted that they presented "a very creditable appearance." From Camp C. M. Clay on June 18, Krzyżanowski published in the *Daily National Republican* a brief note of appreciation and solicitation for the support of his company.

> Company B, Turner Rifles, Captain Krzyzanowski, tender herewith their heartfelt thanks to the citizens of the Northern Liberties for the bountiful supply of eatables and other refreshments furnished them, on Saturday last, at their camp. This kindness will ever be remembered by the company. Such of the citizens who may wish further to extend their good will toward the Rifles, in furnishing them provisions, &c., will please leave such at their armory, Green's Row, Capitol Hill, or at the captain's store, Seventh street, where they will be thankfully received.[9]

The immigrant captain's baptism of fire occurred during an expedition to Rockville between June 10 and July 7. With the battalion commander, Major Gerhardt, absent in Washington, as senior captain, Krzyżanowski led about 200 men of Companies A and B to Great Falls where they took up position on the Maryland side of the Potomac River opposite a larger force of Confederates. Early on the morning of the 7th the rebels fired several volleys across the river into the militia, but Kriz opened fire, driving them to cover with no known losses on either side. Later, about 4:00 P.M. in the afternoon, the enemy, reinforced by a strong cavalry unit, launched an attack on Krzyżanowski's position, but the captain again held his ground, killing eight of the rebels. Two members of Company B—Privates Martin Ohl and Henry Richs, both of Capitol Hill—were mortally wounded, the first mem-

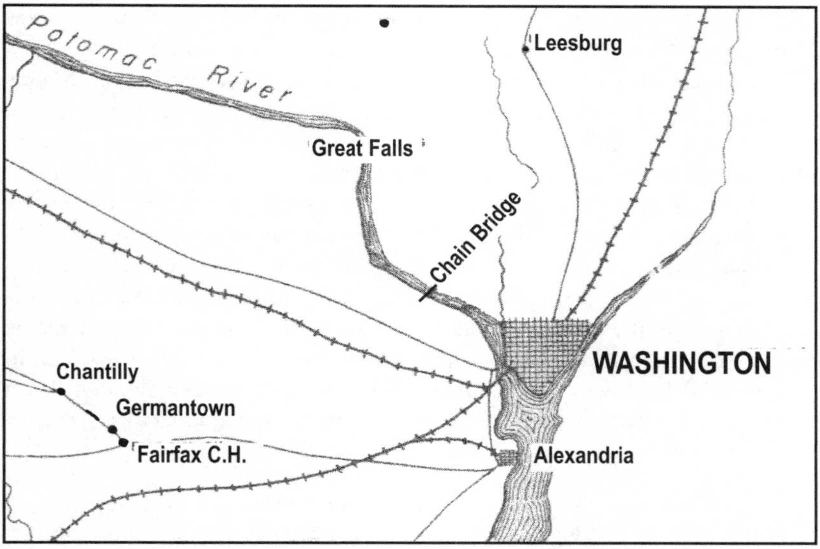

Location of the skirmish at Great Falls.
Adapted by the author from an original map.

bers of the District of Columbia Militia to lose their lives during the war. Kriz later joined Charles Uhlman to create a subscription to support the widow and young child of Private Ohl. With this single action behind it, the company mustered out at the conclusion of its service on July 22, 1861.[10]

"No Talents, However Small, Were Overlooked"

During the summer of 1861 the recruiting of volunteer regiments by state authorities became widespread. Commissions were offered to men who could fill out the muster rolls of companies and regiments. Because it desired to retain the services of men whom it had already trained, the government offered Kriz a commission as major, which he accepted on the expiration date of his service with "Krzyzanowski's Company." Humbly he commented: "no talents, however small, were overlooked."[11] The government's hopes were fulfilled as the swift promotions spurred him to greater achievements.

One of the primary recruiting areas in the nation was New York City where the large population and the weekly influx of immigrants proved a constant source of volunteers. Fixing his sights on this target, Kriz first secured a commission from Secretary of War Simon Cameron, dated August

20, 1861, to raise an infantry regiment to be called the "United States Rifles." He then asked the aid of a friend in approaching New York's Governor Edwin D. Morgan. Ward H. Lamon wrote to the Empire State's chief executive in support of Krzyżanowski's request to raise a regiment in New York City, noting that the major was "a gentleman of standing in Washington and wields a potent influence in certain Quarters here."[12]

With his interests thus promoted, Kriz opened a recruiting office at No. 239 Broadway in New York. From there he contacted other men interested in raising troops, utilizing friends from his earlier days in the city, and combed the ethnic areas of the metropolis. Although he conducted his recruiting activities primarily in the Manhattan area, his advertisements appeared in newspapers as distant as *Der Deutsche Correspondent* in Baltimore.[13] Nor were the interests of perspective recruits ignored. With some foresight he published the following appeal that appeared in *The New York Times*.

> It is a notorious fact that the supply of hospital stores, surgical instruments, bandages, lint, and all such articles which contribute to the comfort of the sick and disabled, and mitigate the horrors of war, that are furnished by the Government, are totally insufficient. You would, therefore, secure the warmest thanks of the sick and disabled, whose numbers have increased greatly in consequence of the sudden change in the weather, by permitting a small space in your valuable and widely circulated journal, for an appeal to the well-known patriotism and the tender hearts of the ladies of New York, to ask them to contribute such hospital stores, bandages, night shirts, lint, and such other necessities as their charity and benevolence would prompt them to bestow. The wife who has attended the sick bed of a beloved husband, the kind sister who has relieved the pains of a fond brother, and the anxious mother who has kept watch over, perhaps, an only child, administering to all their comforts, will not be appealed to in vain. Contributions, or money, which will be applied to the purchase of such articles, will be thankfully received by Col. Krzyzanowski, at the headquarters, or by the surgeon of the regiment, Dr. T.R. Staehli, at his residence, No. 4 Harrison-street.[14]

Among the many acquaintances that Kriz made during his recruiting activities was John Carleton, Master of Eureka Lodge No. 243 of the Free and Accepted Masons. Through his efforts, Krzyżanowski became interested in the secret order, perhaps as another means of securing acceptance into American society. On October 7 Brother Carleton proposed Krzyżanowski's name for initiation and membership. A committee charged with examining his candidacy reported favorably two weeks later and, following the payment of a $25.00 fee, the initiate passed to the Fellowcraft Degree "in due and ancient form." As his regiment neared completion, and its departure for the front became imminent, the Masonic Order passed a special wartime dispensation which allowed the new member to rise to "the Sublime Degree of Master Mason in due and solemn form."[15]

By the time Krzyżanowski first became associated with the Masons he was already deeply involved in recruiting, yet his efforts to enroll volunteers did not proceed without some difficulties. On one hand, he came under criticism from some fellow Poles for his close association with the German community in America. An anonymous letter in the London publication *Demokrata Polski* accused him of favoring Germans over Poles in organizing his regiment. "Although Mr. Krzyżanowski is a Pole by birth, through upbringing and opinion he has so incarnated himself into the Germans, that he must be recognized only as a true German. … He did not willingly give Poles places in his regiment, perhaps because he had served in the Imperial Guards and had been a Prussian lieutenant."[16] Since the letter was published anonymously, it is not possible to determine the motives behind it, but clearly Krzyżanowski worked with a number of Poles, offering many positions as officers in his new unit. Some accepted, while others chose to enroll in other regiments where the prospects for higher rank or future advancement may have appeared brighter. Krzyżanowski's openness to working with and assisting his fellow Poles is attested to in a letter Henryk Kałussowski penned to a fellow exile in 1862. In part, it read:

> The situation of this country in the near future does not seem to promise much. As you know, many of our countrymen joined one side or the other; not many were successful except Krzyżanowski who gained a good position and continues on his way up. He is already a colonel and is in charge of a brigade. Such a position brings influence for the good of his compatriots. With his help, Dr. [Robert] Thomain, a native of the Ukraine, became a chief physician with the rank of major. Godf[ried] Mass from Warsaw, a former volunteer in the Polish Army, is a captain and an organizer in Yonkers, north of New York. Aleksander Małuski is a captain, and [Karol] Barwicki, a second lieutenant in the 58th [New York]. [Edward] Antoniewski is to become a captain in that same unit, while Kulinski and Szwarcenberg are suppliers [probably meaning "sutlers"] of the brigade.[17]

Interestingly, in another letter written after the war, Kałussowski also speaks of Krzyżanowski having served in the Imperial Guards. "Krzyzanowski became a general," Kałussowski wrote, "by convincing the Yankees that he served in the Imperial Guard and was an officer in the Prussian 9th Regiment."[18] No documentary evidence to confirm this has yet come to light.

Another problem Krzyżanowski encountered was the competition from rival officers seeking to lure men to fill their own regiments. As early as September 4 Kriz wrote to Kałussowski to inform him of suspicions he harbored that an acquaintance was attempting to influence Burnett to support establishment of a rival recruiting camp. Speaking of Luigi Tinelli who was active in recruiting for the 39th New York, to be known as the "Garibaldi Guard," Kriz wrote: "Yesterday while I was at the camp Tynelli came and left a letter which I am sending to you. I think that letter seems to indicate his own selfish prospects for Burnett to provide another camp for him etc. You know better how to judge this."[19] In his attempt to fill the ranks of his regiment, Kriz sought to encourage men who had already recruited others to merge their groups with his, no doubt promising commissions to the other recruiters based on the number of men they provided. This was a frequent practice as competing recruiters attempted to fulfill the requirements for completing their regiments, the standard size of which was approximately 1,000 men. On September 6, apparently after receiving a letter from Kałussowski, Kriz wrote to his Washington friend:

> I spoke with Kazinski after receiving your letter regarding Burnett. Kazinski mentioned that they might be ready to make a decision if Gen. Burnett would help with the reimbursement of all their expenses from the beginning of their organization; he read the petition directed to the President and was to give me an answer yesterday, but so far there is no answer; now to avoid being blamed I am writing hastily that I am willing to join as I said in Washington, explain to the General that as soon as he obtains the authorization it will be easy to get people. Tynelly is also entering into the general's service, so there is a beginning, he should not give up hope and work, instead, so we will reach our goal. That young captain who we saw at Burnett's met me on the street on Monday and promised to return the same day, but so far he did not. Please write to me as fast as you can and tell me how things are going, our recruitment is going well.[20]

Recruiting took on new urgency that same day when Kriz read the New York newspapers. A new directive of the War Department invested in state governors the authority to complete the organization of units within their states, including the power to combine incomplete units if necessary. On September 7, Kriz again write to Kałussowski to express his concern and ask his friend to assist him by obtaining letters of recommendation he could present to the governor.

> Yesterday's papers published an order of the War Department, that all people who organize regiments under the authority of the Secretary of War are being ordered to report to the Governor of New York and they will remain under his command. Being a foreigner here, I need to look for recommendations for the Governor so that he will not attach us to another reg-

iment. I received a recommendation from Washburn [Elihu B. Washburne] from Illinois, Leski [probably Władysław Leski] obtained one from Sedgwick [Charles B. Sedgwick] from New York. I would like you to ask Gen. Burnett to send me a recommendation as soon as possible, because I have to travel to Albany. Please try your best, see what you can do.[21]

In a further attempt to solicit the support of Burnett, Kriz sent him a telegram promising to provide his regiment for a brigade the general was attempting to form. That Kriz was clearly concerned and pursuing every avenue that might help activate his regiment can be seen in his next letter to Kałussowski.

I received your letters and immediately sent a telegram to Burnett that I am joining his brigade with the permission of the War Department. I really cannot understand that Burnett does not yet have his authorization. I did not send the petition to the President. When I spoke with other people everybody seemed to have a different proposition. Tynelli's letter appeared to be sufficient for him. I wrote you that I am ready to go with Burnett in view of the order. Thomas was here visiting with Gen. Artur and he told me that he is in no position to make a decision regarding myself, therefore I am going to see Governor Morgan today. I am taking my recommendation letters from Washborn [Washburne] from Illinois and Sachwick [Sedgwick] from N.Y. to the Governor. I do not think that it would be profitable to be attached to the State of New York. However, the great influence Burnett has here would also be useful. I requested today in a telegram that he answer and let me know how things stand. Please try and work on it so that we can be together with Burnett, which would be a splendid idea. Podbielski is here and sends his regards. Please mail my letter to Danne of the *Tribune* so that they might help us in the press."[22]

While Krzyżanowski continued to bolster his position by calling upon his friends and political connections for support, he also had to fend off the attempts of others to lure away his recruits. Additionally, yet another difficulty arose with the pending expiration of his commission for forming a regiment. Authorization to form units was granted for a specific period of time, and with the large number of regiments being formed in New York City those with commissions vied with one another to attract volunteers, sometimes lengthening the time it took to fill each unit. He explained these threats to Kałussowski on September 12:

I received your letter dated September 10, 1861. I am happy that Burnett's enterprise is going well. My recruiting is coming very well; however, today I suffered a great misfortune. A man who was to become a captain, but was not yet sworn in, and another who had been sworn in as a lieutenant, created a commotion in my regiment. During the night when there were not many on watch, they abducted 90 men. I already found out where they are and I took out as U.S.W. [United States Warrant?] on the civilian who wanted to become a captain; he will be sent to prison. I am reporting the lieutenant, and where the other officers from the regiment went, to the Adjutant General in Washington and I believe that they will receive their just reward. Now I beg you to ask Burnett to secure for me a time extension. My time expires on the 18th day of this month, which is next Wednesday. I hope to complete my undertaking. I am awaiting your immediate reply.[23]

On September 16, Krzyżanowski appealed directly to Governor E.D. Morgan of New York for an extension of the time allotted him for the formation of his regiment.

In presenting herewith an official recommendation from the War Department for the extension of my time for organizing the Regiment of United States Rifles, I beg leave to submit to Your Excellency's favorable consideration some of the causes which impeded the formation within the specified time.

My Commission from the War Department which is dated August 20th, I received at New York only on the 23rd, this takes away already *three days* of my time.

Again, I was expecting, and I believe I had reason to expect, support and cooperation from Republican quarters, but I could not well desire the support of the party until Colonel [Rudolf] Rosa's [46th New York] Regiment was fully organized as he was already patronized by the party. And as Colonel Rosa commenced to organize his Regiment about six weeks before I received my commission, I was therefore fully expecting the departure of Rosa's Regiment some time ago, when I could rely upon the cooperation of the party.

Nevertheless my Regiment would have been far more advanced towards its completion were it not for the affair at Camp Scarsdale, which for the whole of last week completely paralyzed the recruiting in my Regiment.

The long delay in *receiving orders* for the return of the deserters to their duty, and for the arrest and punishment of the officer who was *party* and *originator* of the mutiny (and which is imperative not only for the good military discipline of these men, but also as an example for other Regiments) has injured my Regiment considerably; and only through the most arduous and untiring exertions on the part of myself, of Lt. Colonel Leski, and of my officers, we have so far succeeded to bring the whole again into order, to be able now to report to Your Excellency, that I shall muster into the service, within the next couple of days a considerable number of men, and that I have the best prospects for the future, and still more so after the departure of Colonel Rosa's Regiment. In conclusion I beg leave to call Your attention to the fact, that mine is the most recent, and that all other Colonels have received an extension of time.[24]

About this time, Gov. Morgan contacted Col. Eugene A. Kozlay to inform him that the men from Krzyżanowski's incomplete regiment would be consolidated with Kozlay's men to form a single full regiment with Kozlay as colonel and Krzyżanowski as lieutenant colonel. When Kriz learned of this threat he went with great concern to speak with Kozlay. What transpired next was recorded by Kozlay in his diary:

> Kryzanowski was too much terrified and asked me to save him. I did so. I stated to the Governor that I don't need his men, nor do I intend to take away his chances of becoming a colonel. That I have nine companies mustered in and the tenth one ready to be mustered. The Governor accepted my proposition, and thereby Kryzanowsky was saved.[25]

By the 21st, Krzyżanowski's persistent efforts, supplemented with a large dose of political influence from his friends, led him to feel better about his prospects. Once again writing Kałussowski, he explained:

> As far as we are concerned, our operations are moving smoothly, we overcame many difficulties, a letter from [Ward] Lamon and the Ministry helped us a lot. Those gentlemen are politicians; with Washborn from Illinois I went to the Governor. Gen. Wallbrige was alone calling on Leski. We embarrassed them so much that they, that is Morgan and Gen. Hillhaus [Thomas Hillhouse, adjutant general for New York City volunteers], told us that they will leave us alone in our endeavors and so we are working accordingly. I have much to thank my friends Lamon, Wood, Washbir [Washburne] and others for their true friendship. With influence we also received English rifles which no other regiment is getting outside of Washington and so in our office we already have weapons, uniforms and everything else needed for the soldier. As soon as he is sworn in, he is being clothed, equipped with arms and then transferred to our camp on 45th Street by the river. This is a very nice place; the men are very satisfied. Dear Henry, if something can be done with Goodwin it needs to be done fast in order to forestall any moves that are coming out daily from Gen. Thomas and to make sure that we are organizing for his [Goodwin's] brigade and having that way a secure assignment they would not dare mix in with anything, talk to him so I know how things stand.[26]

The situation continued to be fluid, with new recruiting offices opening all the time and increased pressure being placed on new recruits to jump from one unit to another. To advance his own prospects, Kriz continued to call upon his friends for support, while at the same time lobbying with other recruiters to attach their men to his unit. At the same time, he grew increasingly concerned about the lack of a response from General Burnett to his proposal that his new unit join the brigade Burnett was forming. On October 3 he wrote to his Washington confidant:

Capt. Gustavus Adolphus Schmager. A Prussian piano maker – 38 years old, blue eyes, dark hair, 5'7". *Courtesy of the New York State Military Museum.*

Quartermaster Henry Kern. A Prussian soldier – 36 years old; blue eyes, light hair, 5'4". *Courtesy of the New York State Military Museum.*

2nd Lt. John Beutel. Wurtemburg – 40 years old, grey eyes, brown hair, 5'5". *Courtesy of the New York State Military Museum.*

Corp. Martin Beutel. Clerk – 19 years old, grey eyes, brown hair, 5'5". *Courtesy of the New York State Military Museum.*

> I received your letter and feel bad about the manner Burnett is treating you. I cannot understand Mr. B. A week ago I sent a telegram asking for an answer as to what to do, but up to now there is no response. I do not intend to waste too much time in a delusion of our linkage, however if I leave things the way they are, they may attach me to Blenker. I am writing to you before my visit with Tynelli and Schöning [Col. Emil Schoening, 52nd New York]. I do not know when I can see them, one cannot always find them. Tynelli came to me last week and told me, that he will be in Washington this week, he may be there already. He joined up with some regiment. Schöning is embarrassed because his officers are up in arms. He is to be sworn in this week. Our recruitment is going well, we now have 3 sworn-in companies, one not as yet sworn-in in Albany and we are to get one in Syracuse also. We do have agents in Boston, Lowell, Providence and Hartford. Here the Swiss had a meeting with the leading merchants participating to organize a Swiss company for our regiment, yesterday evening their committee came to see me, stating that they decided in a gathering to organize a company and asking me if we want to accept them, they handed me a resolution which they agreed upon. Last night they had another meeting to discuss my decision of acceptance and elected Leski and myself to be committee members. It appears as if they would deliver a company. I hope that in 18 days we will be ready to march. Try to see Burnett and ask him what he intends to do and to give us a fast answer. I believe that if we join up with him, he will not dare to deny us our assignment and will give the promised commissions, I do not know about Tynelli. I think that because he joined another regiment, all the staff positions may be filled. Małuski traveled to Canada but I do not know where to, he left his belongings with me and was to write me right away, so far I have no letter from him. I do have a letter which Domanski brought and which I will forward to him as soon as I know his whereabouts.[27]

By this time, Krzyżanowski's recruiting campaign had already succeeded in enlisting some 400 volunteers. Though a substantial number, it remained less than half the number necessary to fill out the ranks of a full regiment. Because of the shortage of men at the front, state authorities, encouraged by the War Department, began combining incomplete regiments into units that could be quickly readied for action. Before long, these consolidations effected the Pole's organizing efforts. Unable to complete their units in the allotted time, the state merged Col. Julian Allen's "Polish Legion," Col. Edward Lutz's "Humboldt Yaegers," and Col. Theodore Lichtenstein's "Gallatin Rifles" with Col. Frederick Gellman's "Morgan Rifles," the latter being so named in an appeal to the sensitivities of New York's governor. As demands for more troops rose in Washington, additional pressure on state authorities led to the further consolidation of the Morgan Rifles with Krzyżanowski's "United States Rifles" to form the 58th New York Volunteer Infantry. The former unit supplied six companies, A-F, while

Sergt. Teodor Guenzert.
Wurtemburg, farmer – 31 years old, brown eyes, dark hair, 5'8". *Courtesy of the New York State Military Museum.*

Anthony Tegethoff.
Company H, 58th New York, he later served in the Signal Corps. *Courtesy of Gil Barrett.*

Krzyżanowski's recruits formed companies G, H, I and K.[28] Since the Morgan Rifles already consisted of four separate units, the largest single portion of men in the regiment were those recruited by Krzyżanowski.

The colonelcy of the new regiment went to the man who raised the most troops. The rank and file consisted of a myriad of different nationalities making it truly international in character. German names such as Jacob Eitel, Peter Kampf, Adolph Baum and Valentin Mueller dominated the muster rolls, along with Polish names like Wiktor Wyborny, Piotr Wątroba, Jan Szumowski and Andrzej Siemon. Jean Baptiste Meunier was a native of France, while scores of others represented Hungary, Russia, Austria, Italy, Switzerland, Holland, Denmark, Ireland, Sweden, Scotland, Belgium, and England.[29] According to the editors of *Naród Polski*, the 58th New York was "built around a hard core of freedom fighters—men like its commanding officer, Colonel Krzyżanowski, who had struggled for freedom in Europe and who knew the full value of the deep underlying cause which they instinctively lay beneath the simple cause of American union." Even the correspondents of the English-language press noted the uniqueness of the regiment while it was forming: "It is rather remarkable that this is the only regiment which does not embrace within its ranks English, Irish or Scotch, but is composed of men who have fought and are descendants of those who have

Krzyżanowski as colonel of the 58th New York Volunteer Infantry.
Courtesy of the Polish Museum of America in Chicago.

taken part in the European continental wars. The 58th is made up of Italians, Germans, Poles, French, Danes and what no other regiment can boast of, that has left for the seat of war, Russians form a strong part of the Corps. Strictly speaking, it is a Continental European Regiment."[30]

Apparently known first as the Morgan Rifles, the regiment increasingly came to be referred to as the Polish Legion. Legend has it that the name was chosen in honor of five of its captains who served in the Polish Legion during the Hungarian Uprising of 1848. On closer observation, however, we find that of the five only Bogumił Mass was one of its original captains. Karol Barwicki entered as a private, Aleksander Małuski joined in 1862 and Ludwik Galeski did not become a member until 1863. There is no record of the fifth man, Ludwik Biski, ever enrolling in the regiment.[31] Thus, while records list the name Polish Legion as the official moniker of the unit, another reason for this must be found. Possibly it resulted from a combination of deference to the commanding officer—who may have become personally attached to the name—and a tribute to the Poles in the regiment whose homeland still lay subdued by foreign powers.

The new colonel began to muster his troops into the service in his encampment at Turtle Bay on October 27. As state troops, the men were issued regulation uniforms and United States Model .577 caliber Enfield rifles weighing 8.88 pounds and measuring 55.75 inches. If there was anything unique about the uniforms of Krzyżanowski's men it was their headgear. The rank and file preferred small black caps for service, while the officers outfitted themselves in fur hats for dress occasions and standard forage caps for field duty.[32]

By the beginning of November anxiety for action motivated the colonel, the officers, and the enlisted men alike. Though as yet incomplete, the Federal authorities enthusiastically greeted the activation of the 58th New York because General George B. McClellan's persistent calls for more men left the capital devoid of many of its defenders. Thus, with orders in hand, Krzyżanowski led his men through the streets of New York toward their embarkation point at the railway station. A new brass band furnished the pomp of martial music. Flags donated by the officers' wives gently rose and fell above the heads of men whose pride in their spotless blue uniforms and glittering accouterments was very much in evidence. A newspaper correspondent reported that "The men are a fine soldierly-looking set of fellows, and well disciplined. During their march down Broadway they were loudly cheered." From the sidewalks and windows lining the route of march shouts of encouragement and approval were punctuated by the kisses and bouquets of elegantly clad young ladies bidding luck and farewell to their heroic knights. It was November 7, 1861. For these 862 men it was the beginning of a new life from which many would not return.[33]

WAR BECOMES REALITY

Through the windows of the Camden and Amboy coach Krzyżanowski saw crowds rushing to greet the train as it passed through even the smallest of villages. As the hours passed, and the nation's capital drew closer, the number of people attracted to the train increased. The mood of the well-wishers also changed, becoming visibly more excited, subtly more apprehensive. Shouts of encouragement penetrated the walls of the coach, while the men gloried in praise for deeds as yet undone.

While the men of the Polish Legion reveled in the gaiety of a thankful reception by the population of Washington, their colonel journeyed to the War Department to report his regiment's readiness for service. Although the disaster of Bull Run stood fresh in people's minds, and the need for additional combat troops grew more acute by the day, the apprehension in the capital was not strong enough to abate the prevailing prejudices of the times. Because the 58th New York was predominantly a regiment of immigrants and second-generation Americans, the authorities considered it a "foreign" regiment and segregated it into organizations of similar composition.

Colonel Henry Bohlen, the son of a prominent Philadelphia merchant, led the brigade to which Krzyżanowski found his men assigned. The other two regiments, the 74th and 75th Pennsylvania, the latter of which Bohlen outfitted at his own expense, were German to the core. The division commander was General Ludwig Blenker, himself a German immigrant. Almost exclusively comprised of immigrants and their sons, Blenker's Division became known rather condescendingly throughout the army as the "German Division."[34]

Joining the army in November, Krzyżanowski's first experience was that of the monotony of an army in winter quarters. Continuous, repetitious maneuvers and tactical lessons consumed much of his time, as did the filing of the voluminous reports so vital to the sanity of a well-entrenched military bureaucracy. Regimental contests and the intoxicating music of German brass bands provided welcome relief from the drudgery of everyday routine. Frequent visits to fellow officers served as occasions for friendly festivity and a renewal of interest in the intricacies of card playing. Krzyżanowski received letters regularly, and the close proximity of his camp to Washington allowed him to spend an occasional day with his beloved Caroline.[35]

While the winter encampment brought drill, boredom and a genius for inventing new means of entertainment, it also gave Kriz his first insight into the reality of what the war would be like. Crippling diseases reached epidemic proportions in the crowded, poorly kept camps around Hunter's Chapel, Virginia. Returns for February 6, 1862, showed that over five percent of the 2,250 men in the brigade were sick enough to be confined to the

Brig. Gen. Ludwig Blenker.
Courtesy of the National Archives.

Brig. Gen. Heinrich Bohlen.
Courtesy of the Library of Congress.

Major Gen. John Charles Frémont.
Courtesy of Library of Congress.

Brig. Gen. Julius Stahel.
Courtesy of the Library of Congress.

hospitals. Krzyżanowski's regiment, the second smallest in the division, led the list with 8.92 percent of its men sick in hospital beds. The problem became so extensive that an additional regiment, the 54th New York, had to be added to the brigade to bolster its strength.[36]

By late March, 1862, impatience motivated Krzyżanowski and his men to hope for the beginning of the spring campaigns. Tired of the boredom of camp life, the colonel and his officers feared that the men would grow careless or ill if they languished about their disease infested camps much longer. Everyone voiced anxious hopes that the army would march out to meet the enemy. The signs of spring only served to stir their blood to action.

Action came in the form of "Stonewall" Jackson, while a new commanding officer arrived in the person of John C. Frémont. Coming East with a reputation for lack of tact and a quick, heated temper, the man who had been the Republican presidential nominee in 1856 bitterly complained about the small size of his command. To sooth Frémont's ruffled ego, Krzyżanowski found himself marching with the rest of Blenker's Division to the aid of the Western explorer whose headquarters was in the Shenandoah Valley.[37]

General McClellan, who commanded the army outside Washington, opposed this weakening of his command to reinforce Frémont, but the decision was final. Krzyżanowski and his men reflected the same deep sense of loyalty that most of McClellan's troops honored him with during the war. But the circumstances of the transfer excited Kriz and his compatriots as they would no other division of McClellan's army. Krzyżanowski looked upon Frémont as one of the great patriots of American history. He heartily endorsed Frémont's unilateral proclamation of emancipation for slaves in Missouri which caused an embarrassed President Lincoln to relieve the general from his earlier post. To the colonel, and the men of his Polish Legion, the war was one of freedom versus slavery. To them, Frémont deserved the highest esteem for striking the first blow at the Southern slaveholding aristocracy which plunged the nation into the bloody fratricidal conflict they sought to end.[38]

Reinforced by Battery I, 1st New York Light Artillery, known as Wiedrich's Battery, Bohlen's brigade began its long trek to the Shenandoah Valley on April 5, 1862. Two days later at Salem, Virginia, a heavy spring snowstorm blanketed Krzyżanowski's command, clogging the roadways and drenching the men with an icy-cold dampness that seemed made for no purpose other than bestowing misery and sickness. The troops' misery was only heightened by the government's neglect to provide them with foul weather gear. Their colonel ordered them into a nearby woods where they built fires and obtained some small protection from the piercing winds and alternating rain and snow.[39]

The men's misery was captured in the diary of Private Leonhard Schlumpf:

> April 2, 1862: It was very cold and we had no extra clothes and no tents to sleep in. So during the day we have to march hard and at night sleep in the open, and how cold is it. We get only 1/2 food rations.
>
> April 7, 1862: Marched to Salem. We stayed here for 4 days, but not one of us will ever forget these 4 days! As we arrived late it started to snow. It snowed the whole night and the following day. We had to stay and rest in the open without any shelter from snow and cold. Overcome by extreme exhaustion many of us lay down and fell asleep. In the morning we were found half frozen in the snow and had to be taken to a hospital. Our trials were hard and we suffered much as no food provisions could be sent to us. The roads are muddy and we find ourselves in the middle of the Blue Ridge Mountains, cold & hungry. We are forced in order not to starve to death to find our own food in farms, sometimes 4-5 miles out of our way. When we do find such a farm we plunder it for what is edible.[40]

Again on the following day, April 8, Kriz had to lead his men through weather which alternated between driving rain and snow, turning the roads into an impassable mire. The inadequate provisions provided by the commissary officers for the march gave out, adding hunger to the dampness and cold. Under such conditions renewed epidemics of emaciating diseases such as chronic diarrhea, dysentery, typhoid fever and bronchitis ravaged the ragged ranks. Laboring westward in this wretched condition, betrayed as well by faulty government maps, Krzyżanowski's men had to feed themselves off the countryside, gaining in the process little respect and few friends among the native Virginians. In desperation foraging became widespread as men combed farms along the way for food and wood to make fires, so widespread that the term "Blenkered" became a verb synonymous with unrestrained foraging and pillage.[41]

After two weeks of fatiguing marches in this unseasonably inclement spring weather, which left scores of men in the hospitals and reduced the entire division to an abject state of physical exhaustion, Kriz finally led his command into Winchester, Virginia, on April 18. The once rigid discipline and commanding appearance of the troops were gone, ruined by extreme exposure and lack of sufficient essential items such as wagons, tents, shoes, knapsacks, blankets, overcoats and food. Gen. Rosecrans, sent by the War Department to investigate the situation, reported that the command arrived in Winchester "destitute," with "no tents, no shelters, no shoes, no clothes, no forage, no subsistence, no horse shoes or nails & inadequate transportation consisting of train teams which had reached them from time to time with provisions." Morale suffered as both officers and men felt abandoned

Gen. Ludwig Blenker and the officers of Blenker's Division.
#1 Julius Stahel; #2 Ludwig Blenker; #3 Prince Felix Salm-Salm; #4 Adolf von Steinwehr; #5 Wladimir Krzyżanowski; #6 Eugene Kozlay. *Photo courtesy of the National Archives and Record Service. Identifications courtesy of Janet Kozlay.*

by the government they were trying to protect. Whole regiments acquired these neglect complexes, while developing in the process ill-tempers to match these feelings.[42]

Though Krzyżanowski received some time to refurbish his troops, there was a general lack of much of the needed equipment even at Frémont's headquarters. When the regiment left Winchester in the first week of May many of its men stayed behind, medically incapable of continuing without further hospitalization and rest.

Stalking Stonewall Jackson's elusive "foot-cavalry" was not an easy task. Marching first toward Romney, Krzyżanowski led his men laboriously up and down the rugged mountain faces of the Blue Ridge. The difficult terrain, the cold, damp, foggy weather, and the elusiveness of the enemy combined to convince many soldiers they were being abandoned in a useless pursuit of a non-existent enemy. Krzyżanowski found that his gravest problem became the maintenance of morale in the face of such seemingly hopeless adversity. It was no small task as he too felt betrayed by his superiors, whom he felt abandoned the immigrant soldiers to their fate. So poorly were the troops equipped that at one point they had to borrow an axe from a nearby farmhouse to repair a partially destroyed bridge. At the south branch of the Potomac River Kriz had to improvise a rope across the waters so his troops could ford the swollen stream using the rope for support against the swift current.[43]

On June 1 the leading elements of Frémont's army ran into the Southern rear-guard at Strasburg, but a rain storm terminated the skirmish before Krzyżanowski became involved. The downpour continued all night. The next morning, however, the Polish Legion marched up the Shenandoah Valley under a hot sultry sun. Though welcomed at first, the sudden heat quickly began to take its toll on regiments now conditioned to the cold, damp weather of the previous weeks. Worn out infantrymen began to drop out of the ranks all along the line of march. They trudged through Mt. Jackson in a torrential downpour on June 4, searching once again for something to eat because the supply wagons could not move along the muddy roads or cross the rain-swollen rivers.[44]

Wiedrich's Battery duelled with rebel gunners at Union Church on June 6. Kriz could not get forward in time to participate in a sharp skirmish two miles beyond Harrisonburg on the following day, but the weather finally moderated and the men came alive with the anticipation of combat.

Krzyżanowski rose early on June 8. His men were in line by 6:00 A.M. About 8:30 Frémont's army of 12,000 ran into part of Jackson's Southern army consisting of 6,500 men under General Richard S. Ewell. The brigade commanded by General Gustave Paul Cluseret drove in Ewell's pickets, but Frémont remained uncertain as to how many men he faced and became reluctant to commit his force to an assault on Ewell's strong defensive position located on a ridge behind a small creek.[45]

Frémont arranged his army with Gen. Robert C. Schenck's brigade on the far right, with Gen. Robert H. Milroy, Col. Gustav Paul Cluseret, Gen. Julius Stahel and Col. Heinrich Bohlen following in order to the left. Gen. Adolf von Steinwehr's brigade remained in reserve. The Federal assault began with an artillery barrage at 10:00 A.M., but Frémont only ordered a single brigade forward, a force too large for a reconnaissance and much too small to have any real chance of fracturing the Confederate line.[46]

From his position on the left flank of Frémont's army, Kriz watched as Stahel's troops advanced down a small hill, crossed an open field in perfect order, and closed on the Southern defenses. As Stahel moved within fifty yards of the Confederate troops, the ridge exploded in a sheet of flame and smoke. Volley after volley of deadly lead tore through the helpless blue ranks, killing and maiming scores at a time. In ten minutes Colonel Franz Wütschel's 8th New York lost 220 of its 600 men.[47]

While Krzyżanowski stood watching the destruction of Stahel's force Colonel Bohlen began shifting his units to meet the expected counterattack. Companies I and K of the 75th Pennsylvania rushed off to defend Wiedrich's exposed battery. The 58th New York and 74th Pennsylvania received orders to cover the escape of the refugees from Stahel's shattered formation.[48]

Krzyżanowski quickly moved his regiment forward into the middle of a large rye field bordered on the right by a small woods. Briefly he stood studying the gently undulating terrain, broken here by a creek, there by a woods. Quickly his eyes sought out a position that offered some hope of protection for his men. Advancing one company as skirmishers, he stationed the remainder of his men behind a rail fence at the edge of the woods, hoping to take advantage of not only the fence but the woods as well.

Peering intently from behind the fence rails Kriz watched his retreating comrades hastening back across the green Virginia fields. Confederate artillery shells casually arced across the sky and fell randomly among Stahel's harried bluecoats, compounding their disorganization. It was a strange, unrealistic scene. Some men running, some walking. A shell fell in one place severing arms and legs, while a hundred yards away men walked slowly, seemingly unaware of the tragedies about them. Krzyżanowski felt briefly as if he were viewing a theatrical performance, as detached from the action as the audience is from the stage.

Reality reappeared quickly in the form of Captain Louis Schirmer, one of Frémont's artillery commanders, who hurried forward to plead for Krzyżanowski's support so that he could move a section of guns forward to protect Stahel's withdrawal. Kriz unhesitatingly promised his full support. Schirmer moved his guns forward and soon silenced the most deadly of the Southern artillery fire.[49]

In the advancing Confederate lines, Brig. Gen. Isaac Trimble ordered the 16th Mississippi and 21st Georgia to advance, while the 15th Alabama swung right to take the Union artillery in flank, placing it on a direct path toward the skirmish line of 58th New York. Trimble, accompanying the 15th Alabama, divided it into two parts. Lt. Col. John Teutlin took one battalion to attack the 58th's skirmish line on a hill, while Col. James Cantey took the other battalion to advance directly on the guns.[50]

In a few minutes Krzyżanowski's pickets reported that the expected Confederate counterattack was under way. In the distance Southern infantry could be seen following the remnants of the Northern assault back toward the Federal batteries. The situation was critical. If the enemy infantry gained the Union artillery it could turn the left flank of Frémont's entire army, threatening to cut the federals off from their line of retreat.

Someone had to act quickly or two batteries would be overrun and the Northern position outflanked. With no sword at his disposal, Krzyżanowski seized a bayonet in one hand, yelling for his men to advance on the enemy. With their commander waving his ersatz sword and shouting encouragement the Polish Legion moved forward. Supported by fire from the 74th

Drawing of the Battle of Cross Keys by Edwin Forbes.
The approximate position of the 58th New York in support of an artillery battery is indicated by the number 4 just above the battery between the trees to the right of the center and identified with an arrow.

Pennsylvania on their left, bayonets fixed, Krzyżanowski's men ran headlong into the surprised Alabamians, broke them, and pursued the retreating rebels for some one hundred yards.[51]

While his men cheered and fired on the retreating enemy in their front, Kriz spotted two fresh Confederate regiments—Trimble's 16th Mississippi and 21st Georgia—making their way through the woods to the right of his position, firing into his flank as they approached. Rebel marksmanship soon began to take a toll on the nearest companies who suffered the loss of several men killed and wounded. If he remained very long in this exposed position Krzyżanowski knew that casualties would uselessly mount and he might well be cut off from his own lines. Looking out over the fields he could see no more of Stahel's refugees. Carefully, so as not to cause confusion, he gathered his wounded, faced his men about, and retired slowly toward Frémont's front line. His surprise assault, together with a gallant stand by Colonel Eugene Kozlay's 54th New York several hundred yards to the right, checked the Confederate advance until Stahel's men could be rallied and the Federal flank stabilized.[52]

Although the Northern line remained intact, losses were heavy. Frémont's command lost 684 men to only 288 Confederate casualties. Most of the losses were in Stahel's unfortunate brigade which lost 398 men. Capt.

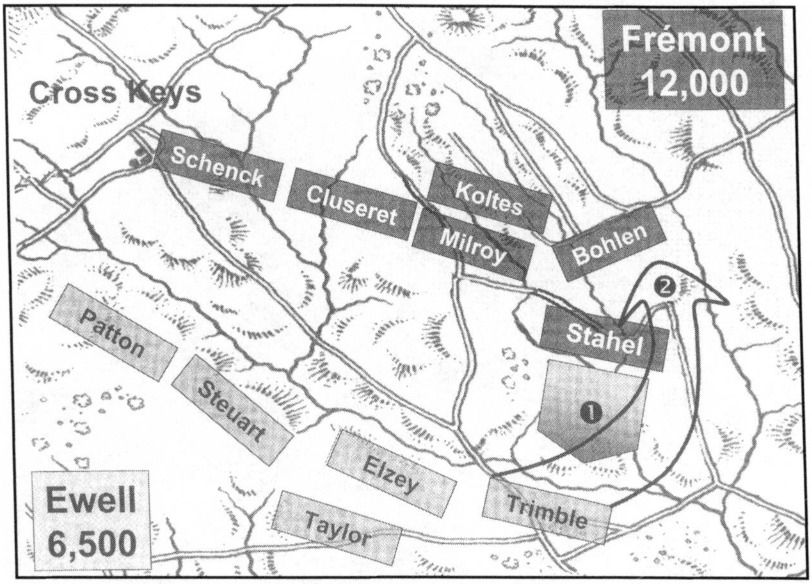

The "Polish Legion" at Cross Keys.

1. Stahel's brigade advances, only to be driven back by Trimble's Confederates.
2. Trimble counterattacks and is met by Bohlen's Brigade including the 58th New York—the "Polish Legion"—preventing the Federals from being outflanked.

Schirmer, fearing that the line might not hold, ordered Wiedrich's battery to the rear. Bohlen protested, but Frémont concurred with the artillery captain. Fearing that his left flank would to be turned, the army commander ordered a general retreat. Krzyżanowski and the other regimental commanders were shocked. They could not believe the order. Stahel's brigade suffered heavily, but most of the troops fought well. Indeed, most of the rebel losses occurred in the regiments facing the brigades of Bohlen and Stahel.[53]

The following day the Polish Legion fought a brief skirmish at the Port Republic ford on the Shenandoah River. Marching back down the valley, Kriz and his men felt a new sense of depression. Krzyżanowski believed Frémont performed miracles by getting his worn-out army into action at all. He feared that because of Stahel's repulse the commanding general had lost faith in Blenker's division. Although Krzyżanowski's regiment received praise for fighting with "great gallantry," some newspapers reported that the blame for Frémont's defeat lay in the poor showing of the "foreign" troops. Those on the field that day knew better, but that was of little solace to men who knew these ugly rumors might well reach the ears of friends and loved ones at home.[54]

This allegorical miniature by the artist Arthur Szyk depicts in fanciful style Col. Krzyżanowski leading his men forward against the Confederates at the Battle of Cross Keys. *Courtesy of the Kościuszko Foundation, New York City.*

ANALYSIS

The Union campaign against Stonewall Jackson in the Shenandoah Valley was a series of disasters, one following closely on the heels of another. Mismanagement, miscommunication and missed opportunities characterized the disjointed Northern efforts to maneuver multiple forces against a fast-moving, elusive foe who succeeded in fighting battles against individual units before they could unite against him. Typical of the way in which the campaign went was the Battle of Cross Keys on June 8, 1862. Although he outnumbered his opponent, Gen. John C. Frémont, perceiving himself to be outnumbered, moved cautiously. With his troops arrayed for battle, he sent forth to attack the Confederates only a brigade, more fitting to a reconnaissance in force than a serious assault. With no prior reconnoitering of the enemy position, and no supports readily on hand, the Northerners blundered into a killing frontal attack which was easily repelled. From that point on, the Confederates held the initiative while Frémont attempted only to hold his position.

Northern blunders were legion, and typical of the early campaigns in the east: overestimation of enemy strength, tentative moves, easy relinquishment of the initiative and failure to commit the bulk of the troops on hand to serious action.

Although Union generals collectively failed to perform well during the campaign, the troops generally fought bravely when committed. Among the regiments in Blenker's Division, the privations of their march across Northern Virginia to the Shenandoah Valley left many dead, disabled or debilitated. The cool damp weather of the early campaign compounded the problem, yet when brought to battle at Cross Keys the men performed well.

There have been few detailed analyses of the battle on June 8, and fewer still that provide anything but a passing reference to Krzyżanowski and the 58th New York. Unfortunately, one of the few to do so was Robert K. Krick, a Southern apologist whose *Conquering the Valley: Stonewall Jackson at Port Republic* is yet the latest in a long line of studies recognizable by their adulation of the mythic powers of Jackson, Lee and the other leaders of the "Lost Cause." Krick's portrayal of anything Union is quite the opposite of the reverence he reserves for the rebels. He informs readers, for example, that Kriz "wound up in a field of rye, mightily confused, wondering where the enemy were, and what he was to do."[55] A look at Krzyżanowski's report on the battle paints a different picture.

> After the arrival of my regiment near the field of battle to the left of the battery of the First Brigade, I received your [Gen. Bohlen's] orders to move to the right, when Brigadier-General Stahel asked me to come up to his assistance. I at once formed my regiment into line, being in column by

> division, and advanced to the place indicated by General Stahel. I was at that time in the middle of a large rye field, skirted by woods immediately on the right of the battery and in front of my regiment, into which direction I moved in line up to and just beyond a fence at the outskirts of these woods, looking for the troops I was to assist and for the enemy. On the right of my position was another open field, on the opposite side of which I saw a column move by the flank toward the left of our lines, and upon a hill I perceived a battery opening fire toward our right. In order to find out whether I was on the left I sent one company out as skirmishers to keep up the connection on that side and by throwing them a little forward to give information of the enemy's advance.[56]

Far from appearing "confused" and not knowing "what he was to do," the report reflects an officer attempting to carry out his orders. He arrived in the position he was directed to by his brigade commander, only to be moved to a new location by Gen. Stahel. Upon arriving at the location designated by the general, he did not see the troops he was supposed to support, but did observe a column of troops moving off toward the left of the Union line and a battery opening fire on the right. To find out whether he was on the Union left he sent out a company of skirmishers to maintain connection and to move forward and, as military people would say, "feel" for the enemy. Given the circumstances, his actions were entirely reasonable and designed to apprise himself of exactly where the Union and Confederate forces were so that he could carry out his mission and avoid any unpleasant surprises. Aside from not knowing exactly where friendly and enemy units were, a typical circumstance for any commander moved to a new and unfamiliar part of a battlefield, Kriz appears to have moved, deployed and prepared his troops as any competent officer would.

Not satisfied with his effort to belittle the competence of yet another Union officer, Krick then engages in a series of *ad hominem* attacks in which he refers to Kriz as immodest, "histrionic" and "excitable." And what is the evidence of this? Krick asserts that to Kriz "the affair seemed like a veritable Armageddon. He later referred to his regiment's role as 'the massacre at Cross Keys,' though he reported only seven men killed."[57] The reference here is to Krzyżanowski's memoirs in which, reflecting on the campaigning in 1862, he says: "The marches in the Blue Ridge Mountains, plus continuous battles with the Southerners, gave us no respite. In contrast to our former forced idleness we were now asked to bear continuous difficulties. I cannot begin to name the battles we fought. This year was very disappointing. After the massacres at Cross Keys and Richmond, it was climaxed by our defeat at Bull Run."[58] Quite clearly, Kriz is *not* speaking about his regiment's role at Cross Keys but rather about the Union defeats in the Shenandoah Valley and around Richmond, the latter of which he did not even participate in. However one wishes to translate the original—the "horrible slaughter," the "dreadful killing," or the "massacre"—his intent was clearly a reference to the great killing that occurred in these campaigns. Nor was he alone in this. Casualties during even the early Civil War battles surpassed anything in the previous American experience, anything most people had imagined this war might be like. Comments on the severity of the fighting and the extent of the casualties were commonplace at the time, as any historian of the Civil War should have known.

Krick continues, sarcastically commenting that the bayonet charge Kriz led was "a feat unconfirmed by any observer, which evidently transpired entirely in his own fevered imagination."[59] Yet, in Gen. Bohlen's report on the engagement we find the following: "...the Fifty-eighth [NY] marched gallantly ahead, supported by a section of Captain Schirmer's battery, which disabled the enemy's pieces placed on a hill on the right of the regiment. The Fifty-eighth met the enemy and drove him back at the point of the bayonet." Bohlen goes on to say: "From the report of Captain Schirmer, whose guns were supported by the Fifty-eighth Regiment, this regiment behaved with great gallantry, under the command of Colonel Krzyzanowski."[60] This would, of course, tend to support Krzyżanowski's version of events, or at least show that Krick was incorrect in stating that no one else observed the advance.

Next, Krick takes issue with the fact that if the Union left had been turned Frémont's army would have been in serious jeopardy. Yet, anyone with even a passing knowledge of Civil War tactics is aware that the flank of an army is a weak spot vulnerable to enemy attack. Several entire books have been written about the 20th Maine's defense of the Union left flank at Gettysburg and how important that position was to the stability of the entire Northern position. The celebrated movement of Krick's hero Stonewall Jackson at Chancellorsville had as its primary purpose positioning the Confederates for a flank attack on the Union position. But here Krick belittles the obvious—that if Bohlen's brigade, including the 58th New York, had given way on the Union left the entire position would have been in jeopardy. "The histrionic Colonel Krzyzanowski," Krick writes, "was sure that the fate of free men everywhere hung in the balance."[61] If there were ever "histrionics," this is a good example. In none of his writings did Kriz ever state anything remotely resembling what Krick's vivid imagination conjures up.

Aside from the small skirmish at Great Falls in July, 1861, when he was a captain in the District of Columbia Militia, Cross Keys was the first time that Kriz had been under fire during the war. It was the first time that he led a regiment into a major engagement, and the first time his regiment "saw the elephant," as Civil War soldiers referred to their baptism under fire. Under the circumstances, both he and it performed well, gaining the recognition of their brigade commander and others on the field. To be sure, Cross Keys was dwarfed by Shiloh, the Seven Days, and battles yet to come—Second Bull Run, Antietam, Chancellorsville, Gettysburg and the killing fields of the Overland Campaign. But this early in the war, and in this campaign, Cross Keys was as deadly to its participants as any other battlefield was to its. In it Krzyżanowski behaved like a professional, commanding his regiment with skill and honor.

— Chapter Three —

"I Fights Mit Sigel"

The Second Bull Run Campaign

Laboring slowly down the Shenandoah Valley at the head of his dispirited troops, Krzyżanowski soon found even the gentle rains that mitigated the humidity of the afternoon served as nothing more than a cruel example of the proverbial "double-edged" sword. Evening showers beat down the dust along the roads, cooled off the heat of the afternoon, and made morning marches in mid-June crisp and pleasant. Afternoon rains covered the dusty roads with a muddy paste that spattered men's faces and sucked at their feet, making a simple day's march into an ordeal of physical strength and endurance. Provisions ran out. Horses quickly wore down, becoming useless. Not a few of the men had to walk barefoot for want of shoes.[1]

Neglected, fatigued, the attitude of the troops reflected a range of emotions from severe depression to a high point of cautious hope. Most of the men echoed their colonel's despair concerning the army's failure. Doubts about their own abilities began to haunt the enlisted men and officers alike. Depressed, discouraged, but not defeated, Kriz led his destitute regiment into Middletown on June 17. Despondently he looked about for something to rekindle the hopes that animated his men only a few weeks earlier. His gaze fell upon a new officer in camp—Franz Sigel.

Undoubtedly one of the more charismatic figures of the entire war, Sigel's reputation as an early and prominent member of the conspiracies that exploded into the revolutions of 1848 circulated widely among immigrant communities before the war. At the beginning of hostilities in 1861 he served under Gens. Nathaniel Lyon and John C. Frémont, soon becoming one of only six foreign-born officers during the entire war to attain the rank of major general. Highly regarded by the rank-and-file under his command, the near fanatical allegiance displayed to him among the immigrant communities manifested itself in the proud rallying cry of the German regiments—"I fights mit Sigel."[2]

Sigel's arrival brought instant hope to Krzyżanowski and his battered troops. Sagging spirits revived as officers and enlisted men alike rallied to the image of a dedicated comrade from earlier campaigns for liberty. These

Major Gen. Franz Sigel.
Courtesy of the Library of Congress.

Major Gen. John Pope.
Courtesy of the National Archives.

renewed hopes were further buoyed by the confirmation of rumors, toward the end of June that the army was being reorganized. In from the West came victorious John Pope, the laurels of New Madrid and Island No. 10 still fresh about him, to command the newly created "Army of Virginia." The First Corps of this new army, which included Blenker's old division, was entrusted to the command of Franz Sigel.[3]

Another change that encouraged Kriz occurred in the command of Blenker's division. When the "German Division" first came into existence its members enjoyed the flamboyant military flair of their commander. They respected him as a soldier, a solid disciplinarian in the Old World tradition. Gradually, over the course of the campaign, Blenker's image began to sour. Krzyżanowski and the other philosophical democrats became embittered by Blenker's acceptance on his staff of German nobles and adventurers, such as Prince Felix zu Salm-Salm, whose philosophical outlook rested on decidedly aristocratic ideals. An intense rivalry developed between Blenker's followers, on the one hand, and the liberal following of Sigel and other revolutionary émigrés on the other. Within the division respect for Blenker nearly disappeared, with Colonel Schimmelfennig laconicly characterizing his commanding officer as nothing more than a "bum." Outside the division a vicious newspaper campaign against Blenker developed in the German-language press. Karl Heinzen, the radical editor of the *Pionier*, led the attack. His editorials accused the hapless general of financial irregularities, including the licensing of sutlers at $100 per month for his own profit.[4]

Major Gen. Carl Schurz.
Courtesy of the U.S. Army Military History Institute.

Col. Eugene A. Kozlay.
Courtesy of the U.S. Army Military History Institute.

Under the realignment that occasioned the formation of the Army of Virginia, Blenker found his division dismembered. He retired, a broken man, to a farm in New York where he died in November, 1863. In his place came Carl Schurz, the German revolutionary who led the assault on the Seigsburg arsenal in 1848 and later rescued the revolution's spiritual leader, Gottfried Kinkel, from a Berlin prison. An active Republican, Schurz campaigned over 21,000 miles on Lincoln's behalf in 1860. In his famous "Doom of Slavery" speech delivered in St. Louis on August 1 of that year, he asserted that slavery was a question of morality, and was doomed by the progress of the modern world. That blight on freedom, he promised, would not survive a Republican victory. Although many Germans saw in Schurz a rival to the popularity of Franz Sigel, and thus remained cool toward him, the troops loved him because of his outspoken views, his humanitarianism, and his efforts to secure governmental attention to their needs.[5]

Schurz's new division came into existence by splitting Bohlen's battle-tested brigade to form the nuclei of two new brigades. The first of these units, under Bohlen's command, included the 74th Pennsylvania, 61st Ohio, 8th West Virginia, and Independent Battery F, Pennsylvania Light Artillery. The second brigade consisted of the 54th and 58th New York, 75th Pennsylvania, and Battery L, 2nd New York Light Artillery, known as Roemer's Battery. Command of this new unit went to Colonel Wladimir Krzyżanowski. Not everyone was happy. With the defeat and the anticipation of reorganization, political maneuvering between officers to promote their claims to command abounded. Col. Eugene A. Kozlay of the 54th New York confided to his diary:

> ... our Pole friend Krizanowsky being the senior in the rank, is assigned to the Command.... All right. Let him have his share of Republican plunder also. I cannot protest against the appointment, because he is senior Colonel in this brigade, but the best portion of the arrangement is that Schimmelfenning, being the most senior, he was taken out of our brigade, because if this is not done, then the Comd must have been given to him. But to gratify Krizianowsky, they put aside Schimmelfenning. I am the junior, therefore I have no part in the intrigue, and unfair political movements. ... I certainly will not mix myself into the Brigadier quarrel. Let Schimmelfennig and Krizianowsky fight out amongst themselves.[6]

Cheered by the arrival of Sigel and Schurz, as well as the opportunity for a brief, well-deserved rest, Kriz led his brigade back up the Shenandoah Valley on July 6, 1862. The atmosphere was a veritable furnace as the sun beat down mercilessly through a cloudless blue sky. Dust stuck fast to thousands of sweating bodies jammed into the narrow roads. Throats parched and choked. Long rows of luxurious cherry trees, their branches hanging low under the weight of blood-red fruit, lined the route of march. At every rest stop men rushed over wooden fence rails to fill their knapsacks with the delicious, moist delicacies.[7]

Krzyżanowski's brigade camped along with the rest of the First Corps at Sperryville on July 12. Kriz immediately ordered his officers to conduct stiff drills to recapture the discipline and alacrity the troops exhibited prior to their ordeal in the Shenandoah Valley. The presence of Sigel and Schurz breathed new life into the army, while the universal joy at leaving the Valley far behind made the officer's tasks much easier.[8]

With the failure of General McClellan's Peninsula Campaign against Richmond, the Army of Virginia received orders to move east to protect Washington until the Army of the Potomac completed its withdrawal from the York Peninsula and arrived in the capital. General Pope conducted a hasty review of Sigel's Corps on August 7 before ordering it off toward Culpeper to unite with the army's other two corps under Generals Nathaniel P. Banks and Irwin McDowell. Marching through intense mid-afternoon heat which reached 100° in the shade, Krzyżanowski soon arrived at the Hazel River where he encamped for the night.[9]

Kriz rose early on August 9. He had his men ready to move by 5:00 A.M., but they remained in position under the direct orders of General Pope throughout the early morning hours. Shortly after 9:00 A.M. orders arrived for the brigade to march at once to Cedar Mountain where Banks' Corps was engaged with Stonewall Jackson.[10]

The colonel put his men in motion at once. Long lines of infantry rushed off down the dust enveloped roads in stifling 100° temperatures. The sun's rays beat cruelly down upon the exposed columns through a cloudless sky. Thick clouds of dirt kicked up by thousands of marching feet hung about the soldiers like an endless fog. It stuck to their clothing and faces, creating an impression not unlike a column of marching coal miners fresh from a day's labor.[11]

Marching rapidly despite the punishing sun, Krzyżanowski arrived at Culpeper about 4:00 P.M. Instantly he formed his panting command into a line of battle as General Milroy's leading brigade beat off a charge by Southern cavalry. Beaten infantry from Banks' Corps streamed past them toward the rear, spreading rumors of imminent disaster. Kriz advanced onto the field, but Milroy's arrival already tipped the delicate balance of the contending forces and the Southern army began to disengage and retreat. Krzyżanowski pursued Jackson as far as the Robertson River where his brigade encamped as the advance element in Pope's army.[12]

DUELING ALONG THE RAPPAHANNOCK

August 16 dawned bright, cool and clear. Shortly after dawn Krzyżanowski led his brigade out of their camp, turning down the road leading to the Rappahannock River. Thus began a desperate race to the Rappahannock to prevent the Southern army from crossing the river to gain a position between Pope's force and Washington. The movement began a period of three weeks which found the brigade continually on the move, skirmishing, and listening to the boom of artillery. It culminated in three fiercely contested, bloody battles—Groveton, Second Bull Run, and Chantilly.[13]

The fierce summer heat returned on August 19. Reaching his goal ahead of Jackson's Confederate veterans, Krzyżanowski allowed his weary men to take advantage of the Rappahannock's welcome waters to wash their dust-caked faces and refresh themselves. Kriz led his brigade into Rappahannock Station on the 21st, where he met McDowell's Corps, closing the Federal defensive line on the northern bank of the river. Artillery duels and heavy skirmishing broke out all along the line during the next forty-eight hours as the Southern army tried to uncover a weakness in the Northern defenses that would allow it to cross the river and march on Washington.[14]

August 22 found the two armies feeling their way northward along their respective banks of the Rappahannock. Lee's Southern forces pushed on in the hope of crossing the river ahead of Pope, while the Northern infantry labored to keep in front of Lee and prevent his crossing. A sharp skirmish developed at Freeman's Ford between Confederates and Bohlen's brigade. Kriz detailed Roemer's battery along with the 75th Pennsylvania to support Bohlen in this inconclusive fight which cost the general his life.[15]

While the rest of Schurz's division battled Southern troops at Freeman's Ford, Krzyżanowski pushed northward with his two New York regiments, determined to foil any further attempts by Lee to cross the river ahead of Pope's army. At Fox's Ford he ran into Jubal Early's whole brigade of infantry already going into position astride Pope's line of march. The situation loomed critical not only for Krzyżanowski's outnumbered infantry, but also for Pope's entire army. Early held Fox's Ford. He need only defeat Krzyżanowski for Lee to have his sought after avenue to Washington.[16]

Clearly outnumbered, with Schurz's division embroiled in the affair at Freeman's Ford, Kriz realized an assault would be futile. Instead he devised a ruse to contain Early's Confederates until help arrived. Quickly he rushed the Polish Legion and the Schwarze Jäger into line-of-battle facing Fox's Ford. By maneuvering so as to make it appear that his two regiments were but the leading elements of a larger force, the colonel bluffed Early into believing that a major assault loomed near. Southern infantry ceased crossing and went into position to receive an attack that Krzyżanowski possessed no power to actually deliver. Jackson's wing of Lee's army was clearly ahead of Pope, but fast action and hard marching by Krzyżanowski and the other "foreign" officers kept him from crossing the river in force.[17]

The following day, August 23, the two armies continued to move north along the river. Sharpshooters fired across the sparkling waters. Artillerymen lobbed shells through the sky in seeming aimlessness. Occasionally a man fell from the ranks, a casualty of this constant probing. In the Polish Legion fate dealt a losing hand to Private Edward Gehrlein.[18]

Krzyżanowski arrived at Farquier White Sulphur Springs on the 24th to find Confederate infantry entrenched along the river, threatening to cross. Kriz formed his brigade for action as Southern artillery opened fire. Strange missiles shrieked across the sky making a shrill, piercing squeal as they fell toward their targets. A missile struck the carriage of one of Roemer's guns, smashing it to bits. The unnerving sounds came from ten-inch pieces of railway iron wrapped in wire which rebel gunners used because constant action exhausted their supply of solid shot.[19]

Amid the clamor of batteries going into position, and the unearthly scream of railway iron, Kriz ordered the 58th New York forward. Confederate skirmishers wounded Sergeant John Volkhardt and Private Friedrich Schnepper, but the Polish Legion pressed forward, pushing the skirmishers back across the river.[20]

Once again on the 25th Krzyżanowski came under fire. This time Southern infantry attempted to force a crossing at Waterloo Bridge. For five consecutive days Lee tried to place his troops across the Rappahannock. On each occasion Krzyżanowski, along with the rest of Sigel's corps, thwarted the attempt. After his repulse at Waterloo Bridge, Lee determined to gamble on a dangerous plan. He could see no alternative other than losing his opportunity to crush Pope before the arrival of McClellan.[21]

Lee dispatched Jackson on a long, circuitous flanking march to cut the Federal supply lines along the Orange and Alexandria Railroad. Marching swiftly without support, Jackson fell upon the huge Northern railway center and supply depot at Manassas Junction. The booty read like a commissary list for an entire campaign. Whatever could not be eaten or carried off felt the fury of Southern destruction. Only dismembered tracks, smashed engines, ruined freight cars, and burned and looted supply dumps remained for Federal forces to reclaim.[22]

Stunned, Pope rushed toward Manassas Junction determined to bring Jackson to a stand before Lee arrived to reunite his army. Kriz led his men off quickly in the vanguard of Sigel's corps. Near Warrenton, and again near Gainesville, he paused to brush aside Confederate skirmishers. On August 28 Krzyżanowski's scouts sighted Jackson's columns of rebel infantry, but Pope misinterpreted this as a Southern retreat. He ordered Sigel's corps off toward Centreville.[23]

That evening found Krzyżanowski's tired brigade laboring eastward along the dusty Virginia roads. For nearly two weeks it alternately marched, fought or listened apprehensively to the nearby sounds of artillery fire. With dusk settling in the men marched quickly toward Centreville. Soon news arrived that Jackson was back near Manassas Junction where they sighted him earlier in the day. A battle developed as the Northern troops encountered Southern positions in the evening twilight. Kriz quickly faced his weary command about, retracing his steps toward the enemy. Suffering from lack of sleep and fatigue, the men had no provisions because the supply wagons, as usual, floundered about far behind the front lines. Darkness descended before the colonel halted his brigade for the evening. Despite the close proximity of the enemy, the men slept soundly.[24]

AUGUST 29, 1862

While the exhausted infantrymen of Krzyżanowski's brigade lay beneath the stars, oblivious for the moment to the events of the day, Generals Pope and Jackson planned their strategies for the coming day. The generals made momentous decisions that night, sealing the fate of thousands of those who enjoyed the last sleep from which they would awake. Recognizing an opportunity when he saw one, Pope decided to attack Jackson's troops before the rest of Lee's army arrived on the field. In the early morning hours of August 29 he ordered Sigel's corps and Reynold's division to attack Jackson to prevent his escape. His orders to Sigel commanded the I Corps to attack Jackson and bring the Southern forces to a stand. But Pope also cautioned Sigel not to press the issue if he found himself confronted by superior numbers. Pope planned to utilize the divisions of Ricketts and King in the assault also, but they were not available that morning because their commanders moved them during the night without orders.[25]

And what of Jackson? The wily Virginian harbored no thought of retreat. He had Pope confused. Jackson determined to hold his men in defensive positions until Lee arrived with the remainder of the Confederate army to administer the *coup-de-grâce* to Pope's army. Jackson established his lines west of Groveton behind an embankment of the Manassas Gap Railway, as perfect a defensive breastwork as an officer could ask for in the field. From left to right the troops consisted of veterans of the Valley Campaign and the Peninsula successes, the divisions of Gens. Ambrose P. Hill, Richard S. Ewell (under Alexander R. Lawton), and Jackson (under William E. Starke). Cavalry brigades protected each flank. Some two miles in length, the position contained almost 25,000 troops deployed in depth in three lines, supported by forty guns.[26]

Krzyżanowski rose before dawn to prepare his command for the tasks they would be called upon to perform that day. As he walked about the campfires greeting his men their plight showed all too clearly. Although the huge Federal supply base at Alexandria swarmed with troops and supplies, Krzyżanowski's men remained destitute of even the most basic items. General William B. Franklin, the commander at Alexandria, and a McClellan supporter, steadfastly refused to forward food or ammunition until Pope provided an escort! And what was the result of this absurd requirement? On the morning of what would be the last day in the lives of many, Krzyżanowski's men nibbled on a few remaining crackers. They washed these down with a little coffee diluted with generous quantities of water to make it stretch so that everyone could have a few precious ounces.[27]

About 5:00 A.M. orders arrived at Krzyżanowski's headquarters. Within half an hour the men of his brigade, their near-empty stomachs rumbling in discomfort, fell into line, ready for action. To the right of Kriz stood Bohlen's old brigade, now led by Colonel Alexander Schimmelfennig. Turning to his left, Kriz saw the men of Brig. Gen. Robert H. Milroy's veteran brigade going into line. The brigades moved forward slowly, forded Young's Branch, pausing briefly to realign their ranks. A cheer went up from thousands of throats as the tall, lean figure of Carl Schurz rode past to inspect the lines, but officers swiftly restored silence so as not to alert the enemy.[28]

Col. Alexander Schimmelfennig.
Courtesy of the Library of Congress.

Brig. Gen. Robert H. Milroy.
Courtesy of the Library of Congress.

Krzyżanowski placed the 75th Pennsylvania and 58th New York in line of battle, with the 54th New York in reserve. Roemer's battery unlimbered in an advantageous position on a small hillock a short distance behind the lines. As his troops moved forward toward the woods masking the railway embankment containing Jackson's troops, Krzyżanowski noticed a gap developing between Schurz's two brigades. He sent the 54th New York to the right to close the opening. To cover his advance he ordered skirmishers forward into the woods under Captain John G. Schmidt of the 54th New York and Lieutenants Gustav Stoldt of the Polish Legion and Reinhard Gerke of the 75th Pennsylvania.[29]

On the opposite side of the woods, behind the formidable embankment, stood Gen. Maxcy Gregg's brigade of 1,500 veteran South Carolinians with five companies advanced as skirmishers. Krzyżanowski's skirmish line plunged cautiously into the woods from the east. The men advanced some 200 yards when exploding muskets suddenly shattered the early morning stillness. Captain Schmidt directed an effective fire on the enemy, forcing Gregg to order Major Edward McCrady forward to support the skirmish line with his 1st South Carolina Infantry. By the time the regiment descended the embankment and entered the woods Krzyżanowski had his two New York regiments in position to receive the Confederates. A thunderous volley shook the woods, smashing into the Southern unit, throwing it into disorder. Caught in this fire, which McCrady described as "severe," the South Carolinians narrowly escaped being captured en-masse. Quickly they

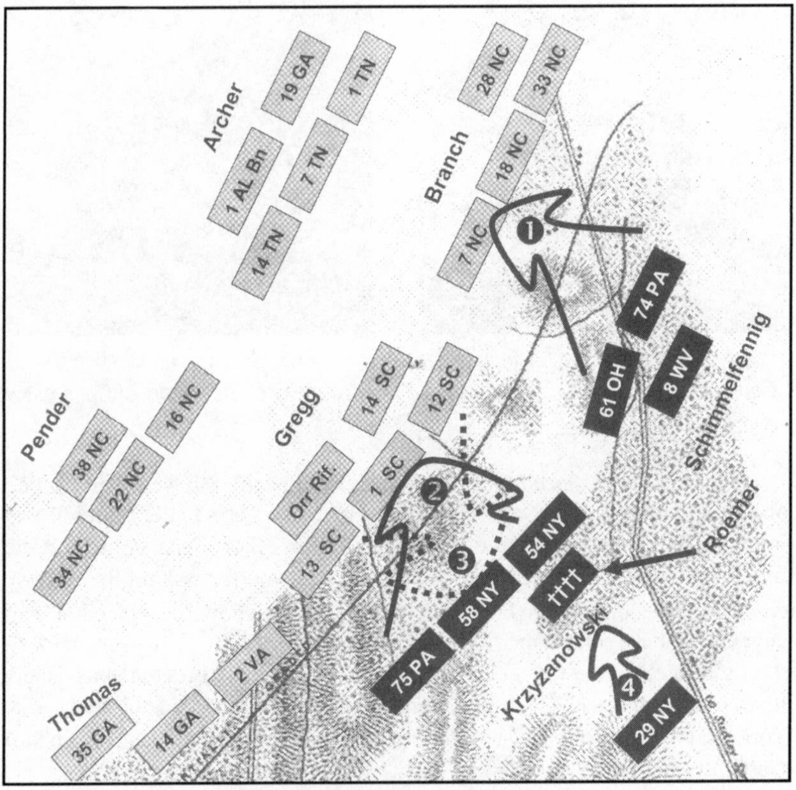

Second Battle of Bull Run, August 29, 1862.

1. Schimmelfennig's Brigade attacks and drives across the railroad embankment into the fields beyond.
2. Krzyżanowski's Brigade attacks Gregg's South Carolina Brigade.
3. Gregg's Brigade counterattacks (dotted arrow). Fighting takes place through the woods until Krzyżanowski drives Gregg from the railroad embankment.
4. The 29th New York moves forward to reinforce Krzyżanowski.

turned, rushing back toward the safety of the railway position.[30]

Victorious Union hurrahs echoed through the woods, but the battle was only beginning. Gregg reacted quickly to the rude rebuff of his advanced regiment, ordering Col. Dixon Barnes with his 12th South Carolina forward to stabilize the line. Entering the woods on the flank of Krzyżanowski's regiments, Barnes opened a devastating enfilading fire that cut through the blue ranks from end to end. Their lines already disordered due to the dense woods, the New Yorkers found themselves caught in a small hollow which exposed them all the more to the enemy's fire. In the midst of the turmoil Captain Schmidt rushed about trying to restore order until shot through the side and thigh, wounds that later cost him his leg.[31]

Stunned by the sudden assault of Confederates upon their flank, caught at a disadvantage while reforming, the advanced ranks of the two Northern regiments recoiled back in confusion. Krzyżanowski ordered the 75th Pennsylvania, as yet unengaged to the left of the New Yorkers, to strike the Confederate flank and dispatched orders for Roemer's battery to join the fray. Then he and his staff waded in among the disorganized blue ranks to restore order. Slowly the men began to reform while skirmishers covered their retreat with accurate fire from their Enfields.[32]

At the east edge of the woods Captain Jacob Roemer rushed his artillerymen into position on the crest of a sloping hill some 800 yards away. Roemer's military philosophy was simple. Make the first shots count. If they did not, he often cautioned, the enemy gained courage.[33]

Roemer placed two of his guns in the open, nestling the other three pieces out of sight in a small wooded area to his right. No sooner did his guns unlimber than Confederate infantry burst from the woods. Sensing victory within their grasp, the South Carolinians raced across the open ground toward where the section of guns stood naked on the hilltop. They hesitated briefly as the two pieces fired, then rushed forward with triumphant rebel yells to claim their prizes.[34]

From the woods to their left a third gun blasted their ranks with double-canister. A fourth gun dealt out more death and destruction, then a fifth. The surprised Southern lines turned as one, fleeing toward the woods as the first two guns, now reloaded, sent another wall of canister screaming after them. Cheering New Yorkers lined their flanks, pouring volley after volley into the mass of grey fugitives. A hurrah went up from the Empire State Germans as they charged back into the woods after the Confederate fugitives.[35]

Nervously, Gregg committed Colonel Oliver Edwards' 13th South Carolina to stem the retreat. Edwards slammed into the flank of the 58th New York causing some disorder, but Krzyżanowski learned the art of war quickly. This time he was ready. Aided by the conspicuous efforts of Captain Alexander Małuski, Kriz realigned his companies, spreading skirmishers out

Capt. Jacob Roemer.
From his *Reminiscences.*

behind trees to fight Indian fashion while he reorganized the remainder of the regiment into a tactical reserve. The Polish Legion wavered, but did not break.[36]

Under Krzyżanowski's direction Colonel Franz Mahler rushed his 75th Pennsylvania into action on the left of the embattled New Yorkers, outflanking the Carolina soldiers and rendering their existence tenuous. Ordered by Gregg to push the Federals out of the woods, Major McCrady found that Krzyżanowski's troops "rendered it impossible for the First to advance; indeed, it was all we could do to hold our own position."[37]

The situation grew desperate on both sides of the firing line. The 1st New York of Gen. David B. Birney's brigade arrived on the right of Krzyżanowski, but the 12th South Carolina counterattacked and broke the new regiment. The retreat of the 1st New York left the flank of Krzyżanowski's 54th New York exposed, forcing it to fall back, but Schurz ordered the 29th New York from Koltes' brigade in to stabilize the line. Before Kriz could relax, Lt. Colonel J. Foster Marshall led "Orr's Rifles," another unit from the Palmetto State, into action. But the Rifles had no more success than its sister regiments. Krzyżanowski's riflemen took a terrible toll of officers among the South Carolina units. The rebels soon gave up any thought of pushing their antagonists from the woods. They contented themselves with defending against the deadly Northern volleys sweeping the woods. Slowly the ranks of gray infantry moved backward, retiring behind the railway embankment for protection against federal marksmanship.[38]

The retreat of Gregg's hard-pressed infantry left Krzyżanowski firmly in possession of the woods leading up to the railway embankment. With this, the two antagonists paused briefly to regroup and care for their wounded. A host of closely guarded Southern prisoners started for the rear. Under interrogation some of these men readily boasted to Krzyżanowski and Schurz that they would have the last laugh of the day. Longstreet's whole corps was expected on the field to reinforce Jackson in just a few hours! Kriz dispatched this alarming information at once via courier to Generals Sigel and Pope.[39]

Col. Franz Mahler.
Courtesy of the U.S. Army Military History Institute.

Krzyżanowski ordered that the wounded of both sides be cared for as well as could be done under the circumstances. The colonel detailed as many men as he could spare to help the casualties to the rear. As he stood in the woods with death and destruction all about, he stared in amazement at the number of prisoners from the 1st South Carolina, and at the dozens of men from that regiment who lay amid the underbrush maimed and dying.[40]

To Captain Roemer, on the far side of the woods, "it seemed as if more dead bodies and wounded men were brought out than there had been living sent in."[41]

Federal reinforcements in the form of General Philip Kearny's division began to arrive near the field around 10:00 A.M., but halted behind the lines and did not immediately became engaged. Seeking to make use of these new troops before Longstreet arrived to reinforce Jackson, General Sigel ordered Schurz and Kearny to cooperate in an assault on the railway embankment. To aid in the difficult task Sigel sent Schurz a pair of cohorn guns called "grasshoppers" because of their strange appearance when readied for action.[42]

Schurz's division advanced shortly after noon. Schimmelfennig's brigade quickly drove in Gen. Lawrence O. Branch's North Carolina troops, carrying the embankment on the left of the Confederate line. Pushing beyond the railroad to the Cushing Farm, Schimmelfennig found himself caught in a crossfire of canister and musketry from Jackson's reserves. Unable to advance any further without support, the brigade fell back to the embankment where it prepared to defend its prize. Sigel sent urgent messages to Gens. John Reynolds and Philip Kearny for support, but his pleas went unanswered.[43]

While Schimmelfennig moved forward on the federal right, Krzyżanowski, supported by the two "grasshoppers," advanced through the tangled underbrush toward Gregg's position. As Kriz watched his troops advance, the colors of the 54th New York fell to the ground. William Rauschmuller picked them up and rushed for the embankment. Confederate fire reverberated through the woods. Lieutenant Adolf Beer died amid the underbrush. Sergeant Herman Voigt, Corporal Adolf Derndringer, and a dozen others fell wounded at the base of the embankment. Still the regiment staggered on, clawing its way up the steep eastern slope toward the Confederate line.[44]

Capt. Roderick Theune.
75th Pennsylvania Infantry.
Courtesy of the U.S. Army Military History Institute.

To the left of the Schwarze Jäger, Major William Henkel led the Polish Legion out of the woods and through the brambles. Sergeant Frederick Sautter fell with a painful wound near the edge of the woods. Confederate fire hit Corporals William Bertsch, Henry Klein and Albert Zetsche who lay bleeding on the ground. Private Christian Elder rushed from the woods, fought his way through the tangle of vines, and reached the foot of the embankment. He went no further. Musket balls shattered his left arm and right hand.[45]

Caught among the undergrowth by a withering fire from Confederate defenders, Krzyżanowski saw his men begin to waver. The assault began to lose its momentum. Quickly he rushed in among the men of his old regiment, exhorting them onward. Infected by the spirit of Krzyżanowski's pleas, Major Henkel called for his men to follow him as he clamored up the side of the slope. A minié ball struck Corporal Andrzej Siemon who fell lifelessly at the base of the breastwork. Another whistled past Kriz, slashing its way into Captain Roderick Theune of the colonel's staff. Still another bullet tore into Major Henkel who, despite his wound, refused to leave the field.[46]

Desperate, sanguinary fighting took place all along the railroad, but slowly, with Kriz urging them on, the three Northern regiments evicted the Palmetto State defenders. Realizing that the attack could go no further, Kriz made plans to defend the embankment purchased at such a high cost in human suffering. Part of Gen. Edward L. Thomas's Confederate brigade rushed toward the railway position in a haphazard attempt at a counterattack, but well-aimed volleys from the Union infantry soon tore the heart out of the attack.[47]

It was a cloudless, suffocating August day. Krzyżanowski's men enjoyed no food or drink since the crackers and coffee-flavored water they consumed around 5:00 A.M. Clothing stuck to their sweating bodies. Exposed

Capt. Alexander Małuski.
58th New York Infantry.
Courtesy of the U.S. Army Military History Institute.

flesh vanished beneath a thick coating of dust and gunpowder. For six continuous hours the brigade fought and died. Krzyżanowski feared the scanty ammunition remaining would not be sufficient to withstand a determined enemy assault on his exhausted troops. He looked about for signs that Kearny might advance to his aid, but to no avail. The fresh Federal troops remained relaxing behind the lines with no intention of helping Sigel and his "foreigners."[48]

For two long hours during the intense afternoon heat Kriz made his way about his regiments, aligning the defenses and encouraging his men to hold on. Firing continued as sharpshooters sought to eliminate anything that moved. Krzyżanowski's troops fought off several half-hearted efforts to evict them. Finally, shortly before 3:00 P.M., Federal reserves moved forward to relieve Schurz's hard-pressed men.[49]

As soon as the relief forces arrived, Krzyżanowski led his men to the rear for a well-earned rest. They passed through the woods, pausing here and there to remove the body of a dead comrade. Silently they trudged past Roemer's battery, appearing to the artillerymen more dead than alive. A quarter of a mile from the woods where the desperate fight began they stopped to make camp for the night. A small creek bubbled nearby. The exhausted men eagerly fell to their knees, scooping up water by the handful to wet parched lips and mouths. They rinsed the dirt and powder from their faces, and they rested. A few crackers remained, along with a preciously small amount of diluted coffee. They sat quietly contemplating the horrors of the day, devouring their meager fare as if it were a Thanksgiving feast.[50]

Carl Schurz stood with his brigade commanders, Krzyżanowski and Schimmelfennig, surveying the field in the waning hours of the evening.

> The stretchers coming in dreadful procession from the bloody field, their blood-stained burdens to be unloaded at places where the surgeons stand with their medicine chests and bandages, and their knives and unrolled sleeves and blood-smeared aprons, and by their sides ghastly heaps of cut-off legs and arms—and, oh! the shrieks and wailings of the wounded men as they are handled by the attendants, and the beseeching

eyes of the dying boy who, recognizing me, says with his broken voice: "Oh, General! can you not do something for me?"—and I can do nothing but stroke his hands and utter some words of courage and hope, which I do not believe myself.[51]

There were quite a few men who could recognize Carl Schurz that evening: men like Corporal Henry Klein who lost his left forearm, or Corporal William Bertsch who lost his left leg. Those who survived the chaos of the day slept on the battlefield among the dead bodies of men with whom they shared crackers and coffee but a few hours before.[52]

ANALYSIS

For eight hours Sigel's "foreigners" fought their way back and forth through the woods. They climaxed their assaults by carrying, and holding, the formidable railroad position defended by the highly touted veterans of Stonewall Jackson's corps. Kearny, Reynolds and Hooker dragged their feet all day. When they finally launched their attack late that afternoon, Gregg, reinforced by Jubal Early's command, handily repelled their efforts. These Federal units, which one historian called "two of the best combat divisions in the army," retreated in less than thirty minutes. Schurz took and held the embankment with no more than eight regiments. Kearny and Hooker, who together could employ about thirty regiments, abandoned the same position.[53]

Sigel's men did well. Krzyżanowski's men fought all morning, and most of the afternoon, gaining praise from those present on the field. Krzyżanowski's assault on Gregg's brigade proved so severe that Colonel McGowan, who wrote the battle report for the South Carolinians, assumed that he faced the major portion of Sigel's whole corps! Of the 1,500 men from the Palmetto State who fought with Gregg's brigade on August 29, 613 were killed or wounded. And that figure does not include men listed as captured or missing! Losses proved so severe that the 1st and 12th South Carolina each lost over fifty-four percent of their men as casualties. Most of these were shot down by Krzyżanowski's brigade because Early's brigade relieved most of Gregg's men before the attack of Kearny and Hooker in the late afternoon. The significance of Krzyżanowski's accomplishments on August 29 is further evidenced by the report of Confederate Colonel E.P. Alexander who admits that Gregg received help from Thomas' brigade prior to 10:30 A.M., and from part of Branch's brigade once Kriz occupied Gregg's original position.[54]

In his thoroughly researched book on Gregg's brigade, McCrady, who led the 1st South Carolina in the battle, stated clearly that Schimmelfennig was not opposed by elements of Gregg's brigade, but by the 7th, 18th, and 37th North Carolina regiments of Branch's brigade. He further states that General Lane, with the 28th and 33rd North Carolina, covered the woods beyond Gregg's position before 10:00 A.M. Speaking of the fighting in the woods that morning, McCrady verified that "In this affair the four regiments suffered severely, and lost some of our very best men."[55]

AUGUST 30, 1862

Kriz awoke before dawn on August 30 to prepare for another day's work. For his men there remained a chance to sleep a little longer as Sigel's corps found itself placed in reserve. Pope's plan envisioned a frontal assault calculated to smash the center of Jackson's line before the arrival of Longstreet. To carry out this plan the commanding general stripped his flanks of defenders to provide weight to his assault. Scouts brought in alarming intelligence that Longstreet's advance elements were even then arriving on Jackson's right, but Pope shrugged this off, leaving only Gen. John F. Reynold's division to guard against this eventuality.[56]

Pope's attack began about 2:30 P.M. Led by General Daniel Butterfield, a division of Gen. Fitz John Porter's corps advanced across the fields toward the railway. Volley after volley ripped the blue ranks. In just a few minutes time Porter's entire corps came streaming to the rear, past Krzyżanowski's position in much disorder. Ill-timed and ill-prepared, Pope's movement proved a complete failure.[57]

While the remnants of Porter's corps filed to the rear, a Confederate battery to the left of Reynold's division began firing shells across the federal lines, into the position held by Schurz's division. One solid shot that landed amid the Polish Legion tore off Private Peter Hoefer's head, splattering blood and brains for yards around. Here and there men fell wounded, but the troops held their ranks despite the frustration of being unable to reply to those shooting at them.[58]

Pope ordered Gen. Nathaniel C. McLean's brigade to reinforce Reynolds' division on the exposed left flank. On his own initiative, Sigel sent Julius Stahel's brigade off to support McLean. The reinforcements arrived at the same time as Longstreet's Confederates. Rebel infantry swept over Gen. Gouveneur K. Warren's out-manned brigade, scattering the infantry and capturing a four-gun battery. As Reynolds' division fell back exposing McLean and Stahel to simultaneous assaults from both front and flank. If the left of the line collapsed Longstreet could capture the bridges across Bull Run, trapping Pope's army against the stream with little hope of escape. Sigel sensed the situation immediately. He sent Milroy's brigade to support Stahel's left, and John Koltes' brigade to aid Milroy. For each

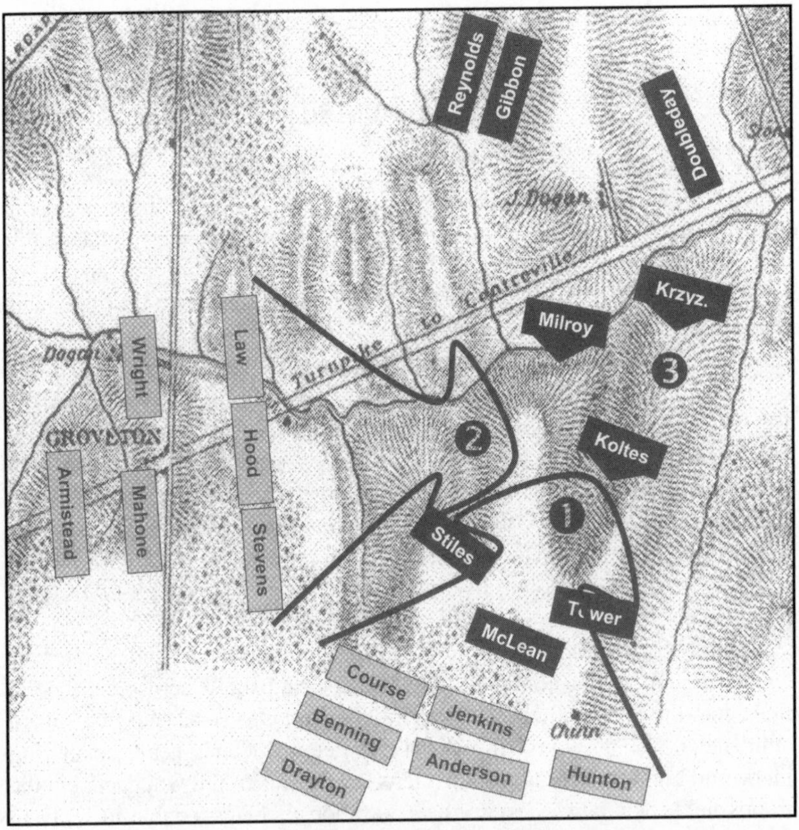

Second Battle of Bull Run, August 30, 1862.

1. Two Confederate divisions attack the lightly held flank of Pope's army.
2. Two additional Confederate divisions envelop the flanks of the three Federal brigades trying to hold Pope's flank on Chinn Ridge.
3. Additional Federal forces, including Krzyżanowski's Brigade, are thrown in piecemeal in an attempt to hold Pope's flank against the Confederate veterans of Gen. James Longstreet's Corps.

Northern brigade that arrived, fresh Confederates joined the fight. Still acting on his own authority, Sigel dispatched Krzyżanowski to prolong the line and prevent its being turned. Kriz was the last hope—no more units remained uncommitted.[59]

Kriz moved out immediately, following in the footsteps of Stahel, Milroy and Koltes. His men pushed forward at the double-quick. It was well they did for the situation deteriorated steadily. Gallant Colonel Koltes died leading his brigade into position. Lt. Colonel Johann Klüfisch fell severely wounded at the head of his 68th New York. Two color bearers in the regiment died, and after the battle survivors counted thirty-six holes in the regimental colors. In the face of this terrible fire, Koltes' troops took their place on Stahel's left.[60]

Kriz joined the fight just in time to meet a column of Confederates threatening to outflank Koltes' left. Southern marksmen poured a deadly fire into the leading regiment—the 54th New York. Lieutenant Emil Haberkorn died in those first minutes along with several of his men. Kriz ordered his other regiments forward to support the Schwarze Jäger. Edwin Wertheimer, a Jewish officer in that regiment, grabbed a fallen company guidon while urging his men to advance. The whole brigade followed, charging up a small slope toward the Southern skirmishers. Gaining the crest of the hill, Krzyżanowski's veterans found themselves flanked on both ends of their line but nevertheless repulsed the Confederate assaults with a series of volleys at close range.[61]

Fresh Southern infantry ran up the hill toward the brigade, but the immigrant riflemen met them with another volley that covered the ground with dead and wounded. In the forefront of the fight, the 75th Pennsylvania suffered severely. Colonel Franz Mahler and Lt. Colonel August Ledig fell wounded. Adjutant William Bowen and Lieutenant William Froelich hastened about shouting encouragement until both met their deaths.[62]

Over in the Polish Legion casualties also mounted. A minié ball shattered Sergeant Frederick Schneapper's hand, while another sliced through the stomach of Private Nicholas Buhr. Dr. Rudolf Neuhaus served as a physician with the Baden revolutionaries in 1848. While administering aid to the injured in skirmishes along the Rappahannock he received several minor wounds himself. At the front as usual, three bullets found their mark, incapacitating the brave physician. The troops carried him from the field, his army career at an end. Confederate lead found John Offen, Jean Baptiste Meunier, Jacob Pauly, Hermann Elling and Christopher Kehr. They were lucky. For Jacob Giessinger, Caspar Handlin and Henry Hoffman this day would be their last.[63]

Staff officers galloped about behind the lines, animated with the frenzy of the moment. In the midst of the turmoil rode Colonel Krzyżanowski, issu-

Col. John Koltes.
Courtesy of the U.S. Army Military History Institute.

Major Stephen Kovacs.
Courtesy of the U.S. Army Military History Institute.

ing orders and shouting encouragement to his men. Soon Confederate sharpshooters turned their attention to these conspicuous targets. Lieutenant Max Schmidt fell from his saddle with a gunshot wound in the right thigh. Bullets tore into Krzyżanowski's horse. The stricken animal loosed a shrill whine, raising briefly into the air before plunging to the ground. The colonel fell down hard upon his head, momentarily pinned by the struggling animal. Stunned, dizzy, his head throbbing, Kriz struggled to his feet to continue the fight.[64]

For long minutes that seemed an eternity the brigade slugged it out with Southerners in their front until the rebels finally withdrew to try another tactic. Within minutes a new Confederate flanking movement developed farther to the left. Though still dazed from his close brush with death, Kriz immediately perceived the danger. Yelling orders to the nearest units, he promptly managed the difficult maneuver of changing front under fire. With part of his command faced about, he directed them down a wooded slope to prevent the Union line from being attacked from the flank and rear.[65]

A sharp fight broke out as Southern infantry tried to force its way through the ravine to the Federal rear. For fifteen minutes muskets blazed at close range, with the 75th Pennsylvania again in the forefront of the fray. Sergeant Robert Jordan, formerly an officer in Schleswig-Holstein, moved his regiment's colors forward, shouting to his comrades to follow until he fell, still clutching the flag in his lifeless hands. Sergeant John Emleben picked up the fallen banner, only to be wounded himself.[66]

The two forces fought each other to a standstill. Kriz stood amid his embattled infantry, holding his critical position with dogged determination. Finally, troops appeared on the left. It was the brigade of General George L. Hartsuff dressed in bright blue uniforms. Slowly the Confederates withdrew up the ravine in the face of this new pressure. Krzyżanowski sensed an opportunity to catch the rebel force in a crossfire. He dispatched a message to Hartsuff imploring him to advance and close the trap. Hartsuff refused.[67]

Though reinforcements arrived to strengthen the left, Krzyżanowski knew the situation remained critical. Just how desperate it really was he could only guess. Enveloped in thick clouds of smoke, the defenders of Chinn Ridge grew fewer and fewer with each passing moment. Colonel Koltes lay dead among the bodies of so many of his men. Colonel Fletcher Webster, the son of the famous statesman and orator Daniel Webster, fell lifeless among the remains of his command. A bullet shattered General Schenck's right arm. General Zealous B. Tower, Colonel Franz Mahler, and a host of other officers had to leave the field with serious wounds. McLean's brigade lost well over 400 men. Koltes' lost over one-third of those taken into action.[68]

Federal artillery batteries supported their infantry as best they could, but ammunition grew scarce and casualties mounted alarmingly. In Roemer's battery a shell fragment killed Sergeant Adam Wirth. Another struck Captain Roemer in the leg. Twelve men and twenty-two horses were casualties, causing Roemer to wonder if he could save his battery with the few remaining animals.[69]

Under the combined assault of the Confederate divisions of Gens. John Bell Hood, Richard H. Anderson, James Kemper and David R. Jones, supported by the brigades of Nathan G. Evans and Cadmus Wilcox, the federal lines began to waver, with Kriz finally being outflanked by Henry Benning's Georgians. Sigel did the only thing possible under the circumstances. He ordered a retreat to Henry House Hill, scene of the worst fighting at First Bull Run. Covered by Schimmelfennig's brigade and Dilger's battery, the Northern regiments extricated themselves from the Chinn Ridge position only with great difficulty. Confederate infantry pressed them closely all the way to Henry House Hill where Sigel's men joined the regulars of Gens. George Sykes and Robert C. Buchanan in repulsing Longstreet's further attempts to dislodge them.[70]

Darkness put an end to the fighting around 8:00 P.M. Krzyżanowski led the survivors of his brigade into camp between Young's Branch and Bull Run. Orders arrived detailing Roemer's battery and the Schwarze Jäger to another part of the field. Everyone else promptly fell asleep. The colonel rested with his men, his head still wracked with pain from his fall.[71]

Capt. Frederick Tiedemann.
75th Pennsylvania Infantry.
Courtesy of the U.S. Army Military History Institute.

Nicholas Buhr.
Company D, 58th New York Infantry, wounded in the stomach.
Courtesy of George Buhr.

During the night Pope decided against a renewal of the fighting and ordered a retreat across Bull Run. About 1:00 A.M. Schimmelfennig's troops, Sigel's rear-guard, burned the last wooden bridge across the stream and moved off toward the northeast on the road to Centreville. Behind him Schimmelfennig left a rain-swept battlefield where all that remained to indicate the late Federal presence were corpses, thousands of wounded, a few cavalry patrols, and Krzyżanowski's command. Somehow, amid the confusion of the retreat, Kriz failed to receive any order to move out.[72]

About an hour after Schimmelfennig destroyed the last bridge over Bull Run, a cavalry patrol awoke Krzyżanowski to report Pope's withdrawal. The colonel went off in the middle of the rain storm to find Schurz or Sigel. When he arrived at the hospital the generals occupied the previous evening he found only a few physicians tending seemingly endless rows of wounded. Unable to locate any superior officers to confirm the retreat, Kriz returned to rouse his troops. Officers scurried about getting their men in line. Hastily the regiments marched off through the mud along the road to Centreville. At the Bull Run they slipped, clawed and fell down the steep banks into the cool waters. With great difficulty the tired men waded across the stream alongside the destroyed bridge, thus becoming the last federal infantry to leave the battlefield.[73]

On they marched through the rain, the mud, and the darkness. Krzyżanowski led his men into the Federal camp near Centreville around 6:00 A.M. They arrived to find that while they fought and died on Chinn Ridge some mysterious "higher authority" removed all of the property of the 58th New York from the wagon trains and burned it.[74]

ANALYSIS

Krzyżanowski's brigade served with particular distinction throughout Pope's campaign. The culminating battles of the campaign were soldier's battles, face to face fights between regiments and brigades where the tactical decisions rested not with the famous generals, but with brigade and regimental commanders. In this test of courage General Schurz praised Kriz highly for standing fast in the face of repeated enemy assaults. The brigade's determination near Groveton resulted in the capture of a strong defensive position.

At Second Bull Run, Krzyżanowski's brigade was the last unit to arrive on Chinn Ridge. In the words John J. Hennessy's *Return to Bull Run*, the best treatment of the engagement to date, "By the time Krzyzanowski arrived atop the ridge there was no hope of salvaging anything already lost; he could hope only that a few more minutes might be gained." According to Hennessy's analysis, "Krzyzanowski fell back in good order to the northeast base of the ridge."[75] In this hopeless position, the steadfastness of Krzyżanowski's troops helped save Pope's army by delaying the Confederate advance, thereby denying them early possession of the bridges over Bull Run, the only escape routes of the Federal army.

In his official reports General Schurz made particular mention of Krzyżanowski's courage. The colonel, in turn, noted in his own report the services of several junior officers. The brigade suffered heavy casualties, 372 according to the *Official Records*. But this figure should no doubt be much higher. Roemer's battery, for example, is listed as suffering only two wounded during the entire campaign. We know that at Second Bull Run alone the battery suffered fourteen wounded, including one mortally.[76]

Krzyżanowski believed that Pope should not be blamed for the Federal failures in Northern Virginia. To him, it appeared Pope did as well as could be expected with the forces at his disposal. President Lincoln agreed, but the Chief Executive sensed the low morale of the army. He knew that he needed a popular figure with exceptional administrative ability to revive the spirit and efficiency of the army. Lincoln disliked McClellan's uncooperative attitude, but "Little Mac" possessed all the other qualities he felt the service needed. Reluctantly he relieved Pope of his command and united the two Northern armies under the command of George McClellan. To

Krzyżanowski the change appeared unwarranted, but he harbored no negative feelings about the possibility of serving under the ever-popular McClellan. His immediate concern, aside from the welfare of his men, rested with the future of the brigade. Sigel's corps was an unwanted, orphaned unit. What might become of it? Would it be transferred intact, or would it be broken up? A great prejudice against Sigel's "foreigners" surfaced throughout the eastern armies. Newspaper correspondents and senior officers alike ascribed sole responsibility for any reverses to Sigel's beleaguered corps. Kriz knew this, as did every man in his command. They could only ponder the alternatives while they awaited the decisions of the policy makers in Washington.[77]

— CHAPTER FOUR —

"FOR LIBERTY AND JUSTICE"

WINTER IN CAMP AND NEWS FROM POLAND

The flap on the hospital tent drew back admitting a crisp breeze that ruffled the still air. A sharp ray of sunlight invaded the haze. Through the brief opening stepped the tall, mustachioed figure of a Union soldier. Colonel Krzyżanowski belonged to that circle of officers who looked upon their men as individuals, not nameless pawns. After the guns grew silent he often sought out the wounded of his command, hoping that his soft gray eyes and sympathetic demeanor might reassure them that someone cared. To many it served as their only consolation for giving to their country the only thing they possessed—their lives.

Dozens of men from the brigade lingered on the verge of death during that grim September. They awaited only the inevitable end to their suffering. Throughout the fall men struggled for life, only to fall victim to infection, disease, or exhaustion. Those whose last breath came amid the anonymity of the crowded, impersonal field hospitals deserved every kindness the living could bestow upon them. In an era of limited medical knowledge and disgracefully poor sanitary conditions, these unfortunates usually spent their remaining days in protracted pain and misery.[1]

To those more fortunate than their suffering comrades, the early days of fall offered a chance for recuperation following the grueling marches and brutal battles they recently endured. Throbbing headaches prevented the colonel from enjoying these hours of solitude. Aggravated, no doubt, by the anguish of his recent experiences, the gnawing torment of these recurring pains made his daily routine one of mental and physical exasperation. Evenings found him a restless insomniac.

During this troubled period Kriz enjoyed the good fortune of having his command attached to the defenses of Washington. Leaving his brigade in the capable hands of Major Stephen Kovacs, a former compatriot of the European revolutionary Lajos Kossuth, the colonel used his sick leave to visit his wife in Washington. The rest, coupled with Caroline's loving care, proved to be just the antidote required for what the physicians diagnosed as a concussion suffered at Second Bull Run.[2]

Col. Wladimir Krzyżanowski.
Courtesy of the Library of Congress.

Upon his arrival in the nation's capital Kriz sought spiritual as well as physical restoration. He did not miss the opportunity to take Caroline to Sunday Mass. Seated toward the back of the church, the couple probably expressed in terms of utmost sincerity their thanks for a happy reunion following the dangerous tribulations of the past months. They listened intently as the priest prayed for the souls of those whom the newspapers reported as slain on the recent battlefields. One can only imagine the chilling sensation of shock that must have overcome them as the priest began to eulogize Colonel Wladimir Krzyżanowski![3]

Reorganization and Renewal

While the men of Krzyżanowski's brigade manned the defenses of Washington, the Army of the Potomac, instilled with a new sense of vitality by George McClellan, marched off to keep its rendezvous with Robert E. Lee on the banks of Antietam Creek. Although the brief rest rejuvenated the worn bodies of Krzyżanowski's men, their spirits proved more difficult to revive. Their problems reached much deeper than those of the other Northern troops. Their morale ebbed to its lowest point yet. Many blamed themselves for the recent reverses in the Shenandoah Valley and Northern Virginia, a view all too readily confirmed by Northern editors seeking a convenient scapegoat for recurrent federal failures.[4] Snubbed by the War Department, belittled by the press, the only reaction that Krzyżanowski's men could make was the silence of discouragement and despair. They suffered much that summer. They endured hardships they never before thought possible. They met the best troops the enemy could muster. They fought them a dozen times from Cross Keys to Second Bull Run. They pushed on when their bodies weakened. They fought, they bled, they died—and, they lost.

There were those who blamed General Frémont. Kriz did not. There were those who openly delighted in the downfall of frequently pompous John Pope. Kriz did not. On the contrary, he commented that both men performed admirably with the limited forces at their disposal.[5] From colonel down through the ranks to private, the men of the brigade offered no excuses. As the colors of fall turned into the stark landscape of winter, they bore their disappointment in the tortured silence of self-doubt.

When the Army of the Potomac marched off toward Antietam it left more behind than the settling dust of its lengthy columns. In its wake were three army corps assigned to garrison the defenses of Washington. This force included the Eleventh Corps, a unit created by a new army reorganization on September 12. The new corps included most of the men previously attached to the First Army Corps in Pope's Army of Virginia. The commander of the

Eleventh Corps, Franz Sigel, found himself the senior officer present, but commanding the smallest of the three corps. In addition, he fell subject to the overall command of General Samuel P. Heintzelman, his junior in rank. Quite naturally Sigel protested these indignities. But he reserved his most vehement objections for the neglect shown by the War Department to his troops. With many of his men in a beggarly state, he pursued his protests over the heads of those who chose to ignore his appeals. He even wrote to the president, expounding on the shortages of men, horses, artillery, and all types of equipment. With an army corps that numbered only 5,000 men, devoid of many of the basic military necessities, it is no wonder Sigel and his men felt neglected and dispirited.[6]

As a result of the consolidation of the armies recently commanded by Pope and McClellan, Kriz found himself commanding the Second Brigade, Third Division, Eleventh Corps. For the colonel and his men, it was the first ray of happiness to penetrate their morose dispositions in quite some time. Fate, they felt, finally smiled on the "foreign" regiments. They were not to be broken up. Rather, Franz Sigel would serve as their leader, with Carl Schurz as their division commander.

Krzyżanowski's counterpart within the Third Division was Colonel Alexander Schimmelfennig, commander of Schurz's First Brigade. The two colonels presented a study in contrast. Schimmelfennig possessed a thorough knowledge of formal military tactics obtained while earning a captaincy in the highly-regarded Prussian Army. Kriz, on the other hand, exhibited a temperament more suited to the inspiration of troops in the front lines. A veteran of the European revolutions, Schimmelfennig usually dressed haphazardly in old uniforms, which only served to make his small stature all the more obvious. Despite a reputation for an asocial, laconic temperament, his fellow officers thought highly of him because he was not a "complainer." He spoke kindly of everyone except aristocrats and adventurers. He possessed an eternal optimism despite a continuous affliction with chronic dyspepsia, sprained ankles, smallpox, and chronic diarrhea.[7]

In contrast to Schimmelfennig's expertise and precision, Krzyżanowski maintained a more flexible, extroverted personality. Kriz preferred to be at the front with his troops, exhorting them through personal example. Most formally trained officers chose to direct their brigades from behind the lines where they believed they achieved more effectiveness in controlling the flow of events. While their styles and personalities differed considerably, Krzyżanowski and Schimmelfennig shared the common bonds of devotion to the cause of a united American nation, and a fierce hatred of all vestiges of autocracy. November brought personal satisfaction to these two officers whose paths crossed amid the exigencies of war when each was nominated for a brigadier general's star.

The failure of the Union Army to win a decisive victory, combined with the neglect and condemnation of the immigrant troops, fostered in Krzyżanowski a sense of deep despair. Throughout this period of adversity, however, he never lost hope that the cause he embraced would eventually triumph. Gradually, his disposition improved. Caroline once again proved an effective antidote for his depression. Rested and rejuvenated, mentally as well as physically, his disposition began to acquire new determination in appreciation of the honor of the president's nomination. But this personal compliment was of little consequence compared to new, exhilarating news that made his heart rejoice with newfound vigor. At long last Lincoln moved to eradicate the "peculiar institution."

Krzyżanowski viewed the Emancipation Proclamation as a noble act, the first positive step toward freedom for millions of human beings. It renewed his zeal for the task before him. He could now look upon past endeavors in the reality of positive achievement. All of the sacrifices were not in vain. Indeed, he saw in the president's declaration the first real punishment the South received for initiating the armed conflict that tore the nation asunder. To those who questioned the legality of the move, or denounced it as only a partial measure, Kriz addressed ready answers in sup port of Lincoln's new policy. The president, Krzyżanowski reasoned, clearly had the right, in time of war, to confiscate the property of men who took up arms against their country. It was equally clear to Kriz that Lincoln had no right to act in such a fashion in states that remained loyal to the Union. Lincoln proceeded correctly from this legal standpoint. Kriz also believed the president's action would have positive results. To abolish slavery in the Deep South, the very seat of the current rebellion, would certainly lead to its demise in the more peripheral areas of the border states. No question remained in Krzyżanowski's heart, no reservation crossed his mind. To him, Lincoln's plan appeared a model of wisdom and legality.[8]

Cheered by this new development, Krzyżanowski at last began to see some positive changes in the condition of his troops. Their collective disposition slowly improved. Their enthusiasm grew with the arrival of reinforcements. Kriz greeted the new troops warmly despite a necessary reorganization of his brigade. The veteran 54th and 68th New York regiments left to reinforce the First Brigade, First Division. In their place came two new regiments, the 119th New York and 26th Wisconsin. Despite their lack of experience, they proved a welcome addition to the brigade. Not only did they double the size of the command, but they were well suited to its ethnic composition.[9]

Colonel Elias Peissner led the 119th New York, composed in part of German immigrants. A revolutionary compatriot of Lola Montez, Peissner formerly taught Latin and German at Union College in Schenectady, New

Recruiting poster,
119th New York Volunteer Infantry.
Courtesy of the U.S. Army Military History Institute.

Col. Elias Peissner,
119th New York Volunteer Infantry.
Courtesy of the U.S. Army Military History Institute.

York. A Republican of long standing, he served as an influential delegate to the National Convention that nominated Abraham Lincoln. In 1861 he published a spirited defense of the Northern political position titled *The American Question in its National Aspect*.[10]

Formed under the spirit of the German Republican movement of 1848, the 26th Wisconsin claimed Franz Sigel as its "patron saint." The men in its ranks rejoiced at the opportunity to serve under Sigel, and many were past acquaintances of Carl Schurz who claimed Wisconsin as his home state. Organized in an area of German settlement in Milwaukee and the surrounding counties, the regiment contained an interesting balance of young, robust, eager men with older, calmer men who first learned their discipline in the Old Country.[11]

Dark-haired, blue-eyed William Jacobs, a Milwaukee banker, served as the regiment's colonel. From colonel to private, the 26th Wisconsin may well have been the most literate regiment in the service at that time. Bankers, lawyers, printers, and publishers served in the ranks as well as in commissioned grades. The surgeon, Dr. Franz Hübschmann, played an instrumental part in writing Wisconsin's constitution in 1846. Captain Bernhard Domschcke, an Abolitionist newspaper editor, collaborated with radical Karl Heinzen as an author of the "Louisville Platform" in 1854. This uniquely liberal document denounced all racial and class privileges, attacked slavery,

Col. Wilhelm Jacobs,
26th Wisconsin Volunteer Infantry.
Courtesy of the Milwaukee County Historical Society.

Recruiting poster,
26th Wisconsin Volunteer Infantry.
Courtesy of the State Historical Society of Wisconsin.

and refuted the Fugitive Slave Laws. A more typical example was Adam Muenzenberger, former secretary of the Greenfield, Wisconsin, Burger-Verein. Muenzenberger worked as a simple shoemaker before he enlisted in 1862 because, tradition has it, the local church needed the bounty money for repairs. During his stay in the army he wrote a series of poignant letters to his wife which opened the lives of the men in his company as no novelist could.[12]

Krzyżanowski looked upon these new arrivals as a physical indication that the maligned "foreigners" would indeed receive a chance to fight again. Immediately he organized daily drills at Arlington Heights, the brigade's campsite that lay across the river from Washington. In anticipation of the long winter, the men built log cabins. As a diversion they fashioned pipes and chess pieces out of scraps of wood or Virginia red clay. They did all of this while still performing extensive patrol duties throughout the countryside of Northern Virginia. Lieutenant Emil Koenig of the 58th New York, for example, brought back valuable information concerning Confederate movements in the vicinity of Rappahannock Station on October 3.[13]

Despite all of these activities, the days at Arlington Heights were ones of relative calm. The security of this life ended October 23 when Kriz received orders to move his brigade south in search of the enemy. Cautiously he moved his regiments along the Bull Run hills, avoiding the open fields to

Capt. Bernhard Domschcke,
26th Wisconsin Volunteer Infantry.
Courtesy of the Milwaukee County Historical Society.

either side. Patrols constantly probed the countryside, seeking signs of Confederate activity. Danger lurked in many seemingly innocent surroundings. Despite their vigilance, two patrols from the Polish Legion met with misfortune. At Union Mills Sergeant Gottlieb Friedlander and five privates found themselves surrounded by Confederate cavalry. Similarly, while probing on the outskirts of Manassas Junction, Captain Frederick Braun ran into a Southern ambush. Kriz brought his brigade forward to seize the latter town, an important rail center, but not before Braun and eleven of his men capitulated.[14]

The brigade camped at the railroad crossing, using it as a base of operations until November 2. Pushing further into the Virginia countryside, Krzyżanowski led his men through the hostile hamlets of Fairfax Court House, Thoroughfare Gap, New Baltimore and Gainesville. As they marched through Haymarket, Virginia, Southern sympathizers lining the streets hurled abuses upon the passing troops. Always equal to the occasion, Krzyżanowski's Wisconsin regiment strode through town singing the strains of a rousing song whose chorus contained the words: "In the South, in the South, where the German guns explode and the rebels fall."[15]

The command arrived at Centreville, their new home, on November 18. Compared to his service in previous campaigns, Kriz found plenty to be thankful for at this new base. Normal meals consisted of crackers, salt pork and bean soup. Every other day supplies of wheat bread and fresh beef arrived, which did much to keep up the good humor of all concerned. Sickness still proliferated, but the mortality rate declined substantially from the previous spring. Because the camp was located along a major rail line, news from home arrived regularly. Corporal Muenzenberger and his friends in the 26th Wisconsin read with unrestrained glee accounts of the draft system being instituted in their home state.[16] "We have a great laugh at the simpletons who laughed at us because we volunteered," he mused in a letter to his wife. "Please let me know who was drafted if you can find out so that I can laugh at their lot the way they laughed at mine."[17]

Sergt. Adam Muenzenberger,
26th Wisconsin Volunteer Infantry.
Courtesy of William Lamers.

Krzyżanowski stayed at Centreville with his command until December 9 when orders arrived for them to move farther south to support Burnside's troops around Fredericksburg. The following day he moved his brigade off toward Stafford Court House. The winter nights grew cold. The ground froze in the evening, only to thaw into a nearly impassable quagmire of mud the following morning. Wagons bogged down so that supplies fell far behind, but the troops were at least able to draw twenty crackers and six tablespoons of coffee per man as they passed through the railhead at Brook's Station. Five days of mud and cold found the brigade at its destination on December 14.[18]

Although Krzyżanowski's headquarters at Stafford Court House rested close to Fredericksburg, his brigade remained in reserve during the calamitous bloodbath perpetrated at the foot of Marye's Heights by General Ambrose Burnside. Despite their absence from combat in this Northern disaster, the men under Krzyżanowski's command still had to spend much of their time during December digging graves for former comrades. Diseases swept the cold, damp camps, claiming a weekly toll of dead and disabled. The troops expended much time in making their quarters more comfortable. To pass the time they whittled pipes for regimental contests, or engaged in various multi-regimental events. Many of the officers studied military manuals, read novels or played chess.[19]

The year ended with a flourish of pageantry because December 31 happened to be the date on which the bimonthly muster occurred. Officers and men donned their finest apparel. Dark blue jackets formed solid lines above light blue trousers. Sunlight glistened off polished brass buttons. Bright flashes rebounded from officers' swords as their owners raced about issuing commands. Easily recognizable amidst the strutting humanity were the round fur hats worn by officers of the Polish Legion. The piercing echo of brass bands shattered the cold, clear December air. One by one the colorful flags of New York, Pennsylvania and Wisconsin surged before the wind as the regiments passed smartly in review, determined to impress observers with the soldierly expertise of their precision movements. Compliments flew in all directions, with most being reserved for the regiment generally acclaimed the best in the corps—the 26th Wisconsin.[20]

Naturally much of the praise directed at the Sigel Regiment fell upon the shoulders of its brigade commander. The men from Wisconsin heartily approved. Though new to his command, they developed a fond attachment to Krzyżanowski. They regarded him as a just, conscientious, considerate officer. Speaking of Kriz in a letter to his wife, Adam Muenzenberger commented that he "behaves himself well. He is liked by everyone. Every morning he visits the hospital."[21]

Krzyżanowski fought too hard in Poland and America against the special privileges of aristocratic upper classes to indulge in those prerogatives himself. Even in the army, where the privilege of rank had been ingrained from time immemorial, he sought to alleviate the sufferings of the infirmed and brighten the days outlook for the common soldier. The men in the ranks noted his sense of fairness toward them, even when their grievances involved other officers.[22]

The colonel's compassion elicited respect, camaraderie and determination from the brigade's rank and file. Through their zeal to succeed, the men molded themselves into what observers acknowledged to be the best-drilled brigade in the corps. The praise they received proved a just reward, yet their commander felt the need of some personal touch to show the men his gratitude for their efforts. That night, New Year's Eve, he saw to it that each member of his command received a large drink of whiskey to celebrate the holiday. On New Year's Day he strained his meager resources further by procuring for each man three tablespoons of flour, their first since arriving in Virginia. They did not waste it. They spent the day cooking pancakes, singing songs, engaging in contests, and thoroughly enjoying the rare wartime opportunity for a celebration.[23]

Yet, not everyone in the brigade was happy with his commanding officer. Adjutant Theodore A. Dodge of the 119th New York disliked foreigners in general, and his brigade commander in particular. Writing in his diary he sketched his own version of the New Year's events:

> Some Captain had kept his Company up and cheered the New Year as it came in. At the same time there began the most outrageous discharge of fire arms—many men, as I suppose, had let their allowance of grog get the better of them, and were venting their superfluous *spirits* in utter disregard of all military rule. It actually went so far that whole volleys were fired by the excited Dutch soldiery before it was stopped. This morning Col. and officers went to wish Krzyzanowski "Many happy returns of the Day" [and] were rewarded with some hot punch brewed out of such wretched whiskey that I got a severe headache from it. However, the intention was hospitable, but it was my habit of using *good* liquor when I use any that

> made it disagree with me. *That* could not be put down to Col. K's account. This same Col. K is a crockery-dealer at home; & while he is off to the Wars, Madame K keeps up said business. She comes out here occasionally, at which times she is Madame La Généralé at home however she is Mistress Crockery. I have never had the happiness of seeing her. Of my immediate Brigade Commander I will not speak, having the Articles of War in my memory, but I may state that he has the reputation of being an old Bear. ...
>
> Col. Krzyzanowski had another dinner today, to which our 3 field officers were invited. As usual they had all which goes to constitute a good dinner. Col. K is a great hand at getting good things out here.[24]

Dodge's critique notwithstanding, this period of holiday merriment served as a bright spot amid an otherwise dull and depressing winter. Following his ignoble defeat at Fredericksburg, Burnside attempted to recoup his lost laurels by turning the Confederate left flank upriver from the scene of his recent rebuff. He should have attempted the maneuver as his initial movement of the campaign. By now, even the weather conspired to preclude such an attempt. Never one to let the voice of reason stand in his way, Burnside determined to press on with his second reckless attempt at generalship.

Reluctantly, Krzyżanowski led his men out of their camps in the midst of what can only be described as a torrential downpour. They staggered on amid the cascading waters and deepening mud for three full days. The overflowing creek beds sometimes forced men to wade along up to their belt buckles in accumulated slime. Field pieces parked on firm ground for the evening sank hub-deep into the mud by dawn. So firm was nature's vice-like grip that often all the horses of an entire battery were required to recover a single mired piece of ordnance. These conditions led one exasperated officer to request "50 men, 25 feet high to work in mud 18 feet deep."[25] On January 23, Adjutant Dodge described the situation in his diary: "It seems that Mud is really King. He sets down his foot and says 'Ye shall not pass,' and lo and behold we cannot. But Mud wields more despotic sway these last two days than ever I saw him wield before. The horses sink into Mud up to their Bellies, and it is said down near the river you sometimes have to put sticks under the mules Necks to prevent their being engulphed [*sic*] in the very slough of despond. How inspirited and confident the men feel in their leaders you can well imagine."[26]

The ultimate failure of this desperate, face-saving attempt by a humiliated general led to still another new army commander. In the interim period Krzyżanowski's brigade enjoyed three months of comparative quiet. Drill followed upon drill, day after day, until some of the men began to wonder whether the exercises were really for their benefit or that of the officers.

Adjutant Theodore A. Dodge.
119th New York Infantry.
Post-war photo courtesy of MOLLUS.

Although food presented little problem during this time, the men became quite disgruntled when the end of the year arrived without them having received any pay for several months. Kriz took the payroll problems to his superiors, but with only moderate results. At the end of January the troops received two and one-half months of their back pay. The one problem that neither Kriz nor anyone else could solve was the constant mud-producing rain which made even routine activities a loathsome burden.[27]

Nevertheless, military routines had to continue and there were even occasions for celebration. In February, the Eleventh Corps observed George Washington's birthday with a 68-gun salute. To mark the occasion, Kriz invited his brigade's officers to join him for speeches and whiskey punch. A petition was also circulated to be sent to President Lincoln pledging the loyalty and devotion of the brigade's officers. Adjutant Dodge suspected other motives, as he explained in his diary:

> Col. K had a paper dawn up which he wished us all to sign, assuring the President of the firm determination of this Brigade to stand by the Country, to put down the Rebellion, in spite of Traitors who circulated pamphlets etc. etc.; he has given it to Col. Peissner, who will I suppose have it read at Officers Meeting and signed by those who choose to do so; and then it will be sent to the 75th Penn. Col. K is fishing for a Brigadier Generalship, and this I suspect is a fine new bait.[28]

Then, on the following day:

> The address to the President which Col. Krzyzanowski wished us to sign was debated upon yesterday evening at an Officers' meeting, and was strongly opposed by some of the Officers, the Q.M. [Dodge's father] among others, on the ground of its political tendencies. A Resolution was passed to recommend the Document to Col. Peissner, who had received it from Col. K, with the desire that he should take it back to Col. K and ask him to change it. This was successfully done. The Colonel and Q.M., at Col. Krzyzanowski's request, remodeled it and then it was signed by all

our Officers who were present.[29]

On March 2 another occasion for celebration arrived in the form of Carl Schurz's birthday. Krzyżanowski hosted a dinner in his commander's honor,[30] but the pleasant distraction of these events diverted the men's attention only momentarily from the gloomy spring rains and the otherwise monotonous drill, guard mounting and other camp activities.

POLAND IN REVOLT

In contrast to the dismal physical surroundings produced by the weather, the spring of 1863 brought to Krzyżanowski and his fellow Poles the exhilarating mental uplift of a new Polish insurrection. Thoughts of returning to aid his native land in her hour of need rushed through his head. Some Poles did, in fact, resign to take up the old cause in Europe. Once the spontaneous outburst of emotionalism gave way to reason, Kriz realized the impracticality of such a course. The reality of how little he could achieve so far from home became apparent. He likened his dream of returning to Poland to the wings of Icarus that pulled the mythical hero ever upward until the reality of the sun's rays melted the wings, hurling Icarus to the ground. While some Poles followed their hearts toward Poland, Kriz reasoned that he might be of more service by working within the context of his influential position in the United States to aid his embattled fatherland.[31]

According to the U.S. Census, there were, in 1860, 7,298 people scattered throughout the United States who claimed to have been born in Poland. Krzyżanowski, in cooperation with other Polish leaders, hoped to collect from these immigrants financial contributions to be forwarded to the Polish revolutionaries. On March 14 a number of Polish exiles, joined by other friends of Poland, met at the Steuben Hall in New York to discuss ideas for aiding their homeland. Roman Jaworowski, who, before the year was out, would found *Echo z Polski* [Echo from Poland], the first Polish-language newspaper in America, gave the main address, with the concluding formal presentation being a reading of the Manifesto of the National Government from Warsaw dated January 22, 1863. By the time the lengthy meeting concluded, the delegates decided to organize a committee to implement their program of propaganda and philanthropic work. As initially constituted, the new "Polish Central Committee in the United States" [Komitetu Centralnego Polskiego w Stanów Zjednoczonych] included on its membership rolls many of the foremost Polish exiles then residing in North America. Among them, in addition to one Wodzimierz Krzyżanowski, were Dr. Henryk Kałussowski, Colonel [later General] Joseph Kargé, Captain Aleksander Małuski of the Polish Legion, Captain [later Major] Aleksander

Major Alexander Raszewski,
31st New York Volunteer Infantry.
Courtesy of the U.S. Army Military History Institute.

Brig. Gen. Józef Kargé.
Courtesy of the U.S. Army Military History Institute.

Raszewski of the 31st New York, and ten other prominent individuals. Although the new group established contacts with similar groups in London and Paris, it clung to the belief that its time would be best spent in aiding its revolutionary patriots through influencing favorable response in the United States toward Poland, thus increasing the possibility of accomplishing its goal of soliciting financial support.[32]

During the Polish revolts of 1831 and 1846 Americans showed themselves to be actively sympathetic toward the cause of Polish liberation. The American people readily advanced financial backing, and then accepted into their midst the unfortunate exiles of those ill-fated movements. In 1863 the circumstances of international diplomacy conspired to negate previous American tendencies to aid a nation struggling to throw off the yoke of oppression. In 1863 the Union lay on the verge of destruction. Defeat after defeat brought home to people in the North the vivid reality of war, destruction and death. During 1863 the Union fought for its very life in what appeared, after Fredericksburg, to be its darkest hour. Everyone in the nation, politician and factory worker alike, perceived the desperate situation that existed.

In this time of utmost peril, across the ocean from North America, England and France showed little desire to prevent their subjects from aiding the Southern war effort. At a time when many in the North openly feared

English or French military intervention on the side of the Confederacy, a single voice in Europe spoke out in support of the beleaguered Federal government. The voice was that of Mother Russia. The Czar feared English or French intervention on behalf of the Polish revolutionaries. In seeking possible allies against this threat his gaze turned to North America. He dispatched his fleets to call on American ports, probably so they would not be blockaded in Russian ports in the event the English or French chose to act.[33]

Regardless of his true purpose, most Northern leaders looked upon the Czar's actions as indicating support for them at a time when they badly needed it. This view appeared confirmed because the Czar, in 1861, issued his own emancipation proclamation freeing the Russian serfs. As a result of this complex and unusual series of circumstances the great bulk of the American people became lost in a wave of cordiality directed toward Czarist Russia. Naturally these sentiments worked to the detriment of the programs envisioned by Krzyżanowski and his compatriots on the Polish Committee.

Since he was actively engaged with his responsibilities in the Union Army, Kriz was unable to participate fully in the Committee's efforts. However, it has been estimated that there were at least forty Polish émirgés living in Washington at the time, including the most active of the committee leaders, Henryk Kałussowski, so Krzyżanowski had ample opportunity to interact with fellow Poles and assist in whatever capacity his military duties allowed. One important contribution was his friendship with Franz Sigel and Carl Schurz, both of whom issued impassioned pleas to their fellow Germans on behalf of the Polish revolutionaries. Despite these efforts the activities of the Polish Committee netted a mere $16,000 by the end of the year. Half of the total came from San Francisco where that city's residents, somewhat divorced from the turmoil engulfing the east, entertained a more realistic appraisal of the Czar's claims. Toward the end of 1863 Horace Greeley noted in the *New York Tribune* that the cause of Poland appeared "queerly out of fashion in America."[34] It certainly did.

The Polish Committee also attempted to rally Poles living in the Confederacy to the cause of the new Polish revolution. That these efforts met with no success against the background of the American Civil War should be no surprise. When Romuald Jaworowski wrote to the Poles in New Orleans to solicit their aid, Stanisław Wrotnowski responded: "We had a meeting but after considering the circumstances in which Louisiana found itself, we judged it necessary to put aside our efforts for Poland for a later and more peaceful period. You are not aware, my dear countryman, that the consequences of the constant battle of civilian authorities in the state, the clashes of armies in the fields in this vicinity, make success unlikely in presenting the interest of a distant country about whom one has barely a name as information."[35]

The Polish Committee chose the anniversary of the 1830 revolt, in November, to attempt a final appeal on behalf of its suffering homeland. In an open address entitled "To the Land of the Free and the Home of the Brave," they called upon freedom-loving Americans to rally to the support of Poland. In New York the German and Irish newspapers responded favorably. But the majority of Americans still failed to realize either the underlying Czarist motivations or the possibility that the Polish Insurrection might distract England and France from future attempts to aid the Confederacy. Caught up in the more immediate problem of its own self-preservation, America turned a deaf ear to pleas from the Polish freedom fighters.[36]

"We Cannot Confirm...."

Frustration at the lack of support for the Polish revolutionaries was not the only disappointment Krzyżanowski faced in the spring of 1863. Another series of events led to more personal melancholy. The chain of events began on October 28 when Carl Schurz nominated Colonels Schimmelfennig and Krzyżanowski for promotion to brigadier general.

> Col Alexander Schimmelfennig, 74th Pa. Vol., formerly an officer in the Prussian and Schleswig-Holstein Armys, commissioned as Col. of the 74th Pa. Vol. In July 1861 distinguished himself greatly in the fight at Freeman's Ford Aug. 22nd, '62, commanded the 1st Brigade 3rd Division of Gen. Sigels Corps since that day distinguished himself very much in the battles of Bull Run Aug. 29th and 30th and is now in command of the Brigade.
>
> This promotion for a Brigadier Generalship was petitioned for by Gen's Sigel and Schurz.
>
> Col. Wladimir Krzyzanowski, 58th N. Y. Vol. Served as a private, lieutenant, captain and major in the three months service, was commissioned as Col. of the 58th N. Y. in November 1861, was put in command of the 2nd Brig. 3rd Div. Gen. Sigels Corps in July 1862 and distinguished himself greatly by his bravery in the battles of Bull Run Aug. 29th and 30th 1862. This promotion was petitioned for likewise.[37]

On November 29, President Lincoln, aware of the excellent work done by Krzyżanowski and Schimmelfennig, and wishing to advance their ranks in keeping with their status as brigade commanders, nominated them for positions as brigadier generals.

Unfortunately for the two deserving men, their nominations quickly became entangled in the machinations of a Congressional committee. There a vociferous block of anti-Lincoln men, combined with several anti-immigrant members of the former "Know-Nothing" party, conspired to deny a positive recommendation on confirmation. The mutual animosity between Generals Halleck and Sigel precluded any assistance that Halleck might have rendered. Instead, he used his influential position as general-in-chief to lobby against consideration of any "foreigners" for promotions.

Carl Schurz addressed pleas on behalf of the two nominees to several influential government officials. They included an old friend from Illinois who resided in the White House. In his letter to the president, Schurz stressed the argument that both of his brigade commanders proved their abilities to lead men on several fields of battle. He pointed out that the men deserved promotions based on past performance, rather than upon the conjecture of future achievement. Both of the officers, he insisted, were among the very best in the service.[38]

Writing during the period of extreme despair which followed the long list of Federal defeats in 1862, Schurz enumerated the problems he encountered in dealing with bigoted officials, such as General Halleck, whose prejudices blinded them to actions which might be taken for the good of the army. He concluded with an appeal for simple justice.

> For once, let the personal prejudices, which may be at work to put an able general and good troops upon the shelf and to frustrate a promising plan be overruled. Try us! for you must try something. Try us, and I am confident, we shall not disappoint your expectations. I advised you to dismiss every unsuccessful general without delay. Try us fairly, and we claim no exemption from this rule.[39]

After considerable delay the names of the two colonels finally appeared before the Senate for confirmation. There, the presiding official intentionally hissed and choked as he stumbled through the consonants of the men's names, mocking their pronunciation. As the laughter increased with every contortion of the speaker, a voice rose amidst the commotion to proclaim the verdict of the distinguished Senators: "We cannot confirm the nomination of a man whose name no one can pronounce."[40]

Although Carl Schurz sarcastically commented that Krzyżanowski's promotion was denied because no one could pronounce his name, it is clear there were other reasons for the rejection. Following his nomination, Kriz came under suspicion of having defrauded the government of funds by claiming reimbursement for recruiting expenses incurred for men who had not joined his regiment. The charges stemmed from the incident when some of his recruits were lured away by agents of another regiment, leading Kriz to prefer charges against the ringleaders in question. When an investigation was launched into the charges, Kriz was able to provide evidence that the expenses had actually been paid, as well as additional evidence of the circumstances surrounding the enrollment of the men in question into another

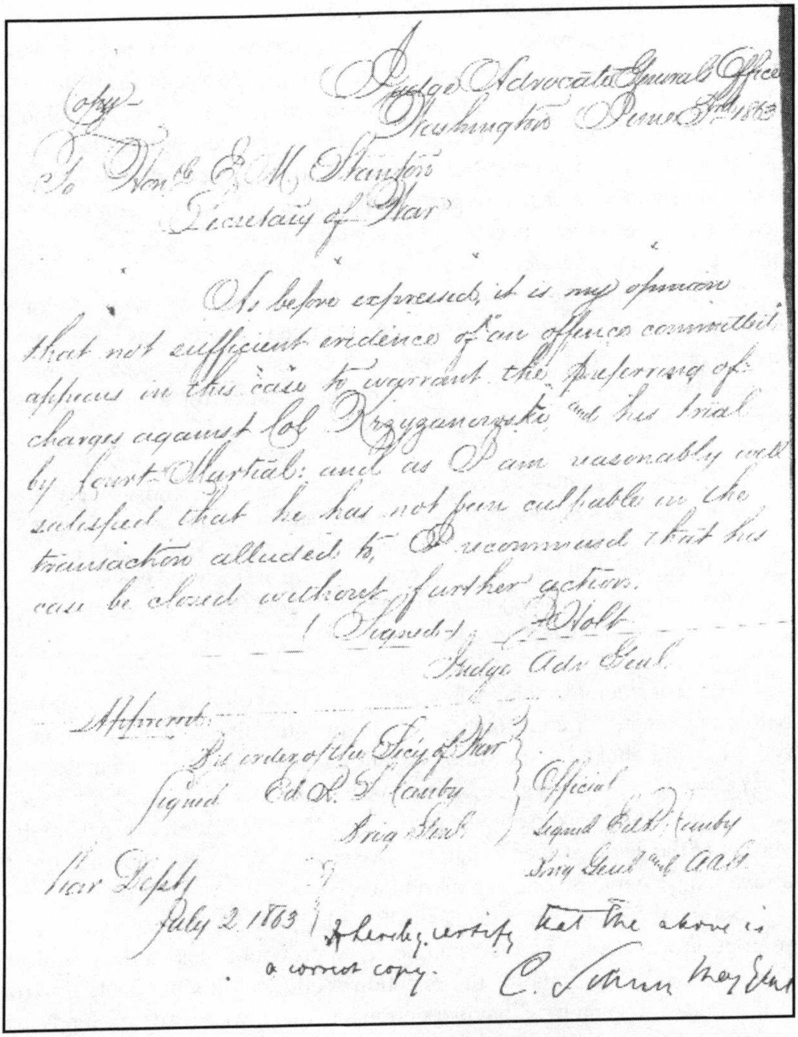

Copy—

Judge Advocate General's Office
Washington June 3rd 1863

To Hon. E. M. Stanton
Secretary of War

As before expressed, it is my opinion that not sufficient evidence of an offence committed appears in this case to warrant the preferring of charges against Col. Krzyzanowski and his trial by Court-Martial: and as I am reasonably well satisfied that he has not been culpable in the transaction alluded to, I recommend that his case be closed without further action.

(Signed) J. Holt
Judge Adv. Genl.

Affirmed:
By order of the Secy of War
Signed Ed. R. S. Canby
Brig. Genl.

Official
Signed Ed. R. S. Canby
Brig Genl. & A.A.G.

War Dept.
July 2, 1863

I hereby certify that the above is a correct copy.
C. Schurz Maj. Genl.

Letter from Judge Advocate General Holt to Secretary of War Edwin Stanton confirming his belief that Krzyżanowski is "not culpable" of the charges against him. *Courtesy of the National Archives.*

regiment. On June 3, 1863, Judge Advocate General Joseph Holt wrote to Secretary of War Edwin M. Stanton confirming that his investigation found that Kriz "was not culpable in the transaction alluded to, I recommend that his case be closed without further action."[41] Although exonerated, the initial charges preferred against him no doubt cost Kriz the promotion to a brigadiership recommended by his commanding officers and the president.

Lincoln, seeking to assuage the offended dignity of the immigrant troops who only recently performed so well, summoned the influential Secretary of War to his office.

"The only point I make," Lincoln explained, "is there has got to be something done that will be unquestionably in the interest of the Dutch, and to that end I want Schimmelfennig appointed."

"Mr. President," Stanton replied, "perhaps this Schimmel-what's-his-name is not as highly recommended as some other German officers."

"No matter about that," replied the President. "His name will make up for any difference there might be, and I'll take the risk of his coming out all right."[42]

The appointment of Schimmelfennig to the rank of brigadier general proved to be no mistake. Neither did it prove to be of any consolation to Colonel Krzyżanowski. Following the president's nomination, Kriz temporarily received the courtesies due a brigadier general. When the Senators failed to confirm him, however, he reverted to the rank of colonel on March 4, 1863. It is easy to understand how a man, under these circumstances, might become bitter over the discrimination that thwarted his advancement. There were many who resigned over lesser slights than this obvious affront hurled at the Polish colonel. It is a tribute to both men that the circumstances that rewarded one while denying the other impaired neither their friendship nor their ability to work together in the field. It is to Krzyżanowski's further credit that he never thought of abandoning his principles. He chose to continue in pursuit of those principles. "As a son of a foreign land," he wrote, "I fought for an ideal, for liberty and justice."[43]

When reports that Krzyżanowski's nomination was finally going to the Senate for confirmation reached the army's campgrounds, and before news of the rejection arrived, the officers from throughout the Eleventh Corps went to Kriz's tent to congratulate him on what they certainly felt would be his promotion. According to Theodore A. Dodge, the nativist adjutant of the 119th New York, Kriz treated them "liberally" to claret. "We each congratulated him separately, as we entered his tent," Dodge confided to his diary, "and, after having seated ourselves and having been supplied with Cups of wine, the new fledged General arose to return thanks. He made an 'Oration' in point of modulation of voice and action, but as wretched a 'speech' as one can imagine a Polish Jew to make on point of sentiment or language. Still to ordinary German ears it was an 'oration,' and American ears were at its close suddenly startled by: 'Three cheers for our General, hip, hip, hurrah!!' from Capt. Von Bories."[44] Despite Dodge's feelings, the party went on with many toasts to the new general's health and a seemingly enjoyable time for everyone except the diarist.

Within a few days, however, news of the Senate's failure to confirm Krzyżanowski's promotion arrived in camp. "The news has come today that Gen. Krzyzanowski; who was felicitated and fêted on his appointment as General, has passed thro' a reconsideration & been rejected," Dodge wrote in his diary on March 16, "much to the delight of the Q.M., who thoroughly despises him."[45] Yet, the matter did not rest there. Upon hearing of the failure of Krzyżanowski's nomination to be confirmed, the officers of his brigade drew up a petition to the President of the United States. It read:

> Having heard with feelings of profound regret that the confirmation of Wladimir Krzyzanowski, Colonel of the 58th Regt, N.Y.V., as Brigadier General had been annulled by the Senate, We, the Officers of the 2d brigade, 3d Division, 11th Corps, Army of the Potomac, most urgently desire that you will, so far as in your power lies, exert yourself to have such annulment cancelled.
>
> The unexpected news of this action on the part of the Senate has cast a gloom over the soldiers of his command that can only be dispelled by the actual knowledge of his confirmation.
>
> Exiled from his native land, because he dared to battle for truth, liberty, justice, and right, Col. Krzyzanowski, early grasped his sword to do battle for American liberties.
>
> A man of great Military knowledge and experience, he entered the ranks of freedom as a private and tendered his life a sacrifice for the great principle for which we are now battling.
>
> America owes to Poland a debt of gratitude.
>
> Then in the name of those great patriots Kosciuski [*sic*] and Pulaski, in the name of the soldiers to whom Col Krzyzanowski has, by his soldierly qualifications and gentlemanly bearing, endeared himself, and in the name of gratitude, patriotism, and true valor, we ask for his Confirmation.
>
> The want of time alone prevents our sending to you the signatures of every member of his Command.
>
> With the utmost confidence in your discretion we remain, ….[46]

The petition was signed by sixty-seven officers of the 75th Pennsylvania, 26th Wisconsin, and 58th New York regiments. However, not everyone was displeased with the failure of Krzyżanowski's nomination. In the 119th New York, Adjutant Dodge, whose diary and writing betray significant antiforeign bias, confided another scenario for the petition's origin.

> Today another of those miserable petitions came round for signature. It originated in this manner; Lieut. Col. Matzdorf, of the 75th Pa., when he

heard of K's confirmation as Brig. Genl., congratulated him in these words—"If you, Sir, had not been confirmed I would have resigned my commission"—now that the Senate of the United States have refused to confirm him, this valorous Officer must do something, Accordingly *he* gets up a Petition, ostensibly, but really the petition savours of Col. K's own Clerk's pen. The officers of the 75th sign it, and then those of the 58th, and then it comes to us,—the "independent" Regiment. The officers hold a meeting, whereupon Col. P. said to them "P. 220 Revised Regulations forbids such a proceeding" (which in effect it does) "petitions have several times brought us into trouble & therefore I am opposed to it." Accordingly this is indorsed on the petition and it is sent back with a note as follows: "Col. P. and officers respectfully decline signing this paper." We are not liked in the Brigade and no wonder. They abuse us and we have sometimes a chance to retaliate. Anyhow the Petition was a manifest absurdity: "America owes a debt of gratitude to Poland," and more such twaddle.[47]

Lt. Col. Alvin Matzdorff, 75th Pennsylvania Volunteer Infantry, and author of a petition seeking Krzyżanowski's promotion to brigadier general. *Courtesy of the U.S. Army Military History Institute.*

Despite Dodge's feelings, Krzyżanowski's friends continued to lobby on his behalf through petitions and personal appeals. One of the latter was a letter penned by Carl Schurz to Secretary of War Edwin M. Stanton:

> Permit me to address you once more on behalf of Col. W. Krzyzanowski, comdg my 2d Brigade. I have learned now by good authority, that the charges on the ground of which his nomination for a Brigadier Generalship was rejected in the Senate, have been found entirely without foundation and withdrawn. I learn also that his reappointment was recommended by the officers who investigated his case. I would therefore respectfully represent, that the great wrong and injury done this brave and deserving officer by the action of the Senate on the ground of unfounded

> accusations cannot be repaired but by his reappointment. As a man of character and honor he would seem to have a right to expect this reparation as a simple act of justice. I would respectfully add that, aside from the reparation due him, his bravery, irreproachable conduct and soldierly qualities fully entitle him to promotion. He has been in command of his brigade now for a whole year and has won the affection and confidence of his soldiers as well as the approval of his superiors in the highest degree. Permit me, then, to ask for his reappointment as an act of justice due him in every respect.[48]

For now, however, Kriz received a fifteen-day leave of absence to return to Washington to see his family and, no doubt, to meet with fellow Poles about the situation in Poland. Upon his return, he received another ten-day leave on April 10.[49] In the meantime, events began to be set in motion that would lead to his next serious test in command of his brigade.

— Chapter Five —

"A Hell of a Fix"

The Chancellorsville Campaign

Friday, April 10, 1863. Only two days remained before the war entered its third year. The rising sun illuminated a cold, clear morning over the Virginia countryside. A biting wind stung Colonel Krzyżanowski's ears as he walked down the ranks of his assembled brigade. Next to his men, drawn up in formal order, stood Schimmelfennig's brigade. Beyond that, rows and rows of troops comprising the remainder of the Eleventh Corps. Across the wide, wind-swept field stood a solitary reviewing stand that contained a host of high-ranking officials and governmental dignitaries. Krzyżanowski paused, looking toward the assembled entourage. His eyes hesitated momentarily, examining the stern features of the new commanding general, Joseph Hooker. Quickly Kriz moved his gaze to the center of attraction on the podium, the thin, towering profile of the President of the United States.[1]

Lincoln spent several days examining the revitalized Army of the Potomac. He conferred extensively with blond, blue-eyed Joseph Hooker, his choice as a replacement for Ambrose Burnside following the Fredericksburg debâcle. A son of Massachusetts, Hooker possessed an abundance of self-confidence that often led him to criticize superiors and subalterns alike. He joined the army with a reputation as a connoisseur of the fairer sex, a notoriety whose luster never diminished despite the other adversities of war. Although some were quick to criticize these quirks of personality, Lincoln saw in Hooker a man who performed as well on the battlefield as he did in his social endeavors. The president hoped the same drive and devotion that won Hooker the nickname "Fighting Joe" would infuse an aggressive, winning spirit into the whole army.[2]

As far as the troops were concerned, "Fighting Joe" began the way a general should begin. He set a priority on improving food supplies, after which he managed to procure new uniforms and foul weather gear for the veteran units whose original issue of these basic commodities long ago wore out. These reforms, combined with the establishment of a furlough system, led to an improvement in morale and a corresponding decline in the desertion rate. In the Eleventh Corps, however, a new change in field commanders somewhat offset the effects of many of these positive alterations.[3]

Exasperated by a series of rebuffs from the War Department, Franz Sigel finally tendered his resignation. While this move caused considerable relief in Washington, it generated much chagrin within the Eleventh Corps. This disappointment turned to consternation when the War Department named Sigel's replacement. Carl Schurz acted as the corps' interim commander, everyone naturally assuming that his promotion would become permanent. Instead, the authorities assigned General Oliver Otis Howard to lead the Eleventh Corps. This meant that Schurz reverted to his divisional command. Schimmelfennig, who commanded Schurz's division in the latter's absence, found his authority reduced to that of his former brigade. To complicate matters even further, Howard brought with him Generals Charles Devens and Francis Barlow to replace Nathaniel McLean and Orland Smith, two very popular officers who returned to their former commands.[4]

By the time these changes took place the strength of the Eleventh Corps stood at nearly 13,000. Although only 5,000 of these could be counted as Germans or "foreigners," the new modifications in leadership affected the entire command. While the overall morale of the troops remained high, as evidenced by their maintaining the lowest desertion rate in the army, the troops acquired a personal dislike for their corps commander. They blamed him, rather unjustly, for the departure of Sigel and the reduction of Schurz, Schimmelfennig, McLean and Smith. Nor did Howard's peculiar personality engender any particular allegiance among the rank and file. At the age of thirty-four the Maine general possessed a spotless military record including habitual instances of daring that finally cost him an arm at Fair Oaks where he won one of the nation's first awards of the Medal of Honor.[5]

Beyond this distinguished service record, however, Howard possessed personal prejudices and intolerances that offended many members of his new command. A deeply religious man, the "native Americans" in the Eleventh Corps came to dislike his excessively pious attitudes and pronouncements. To the German free-thinkers his demeanor exuded a much despised clericalism. Throughout the corps, men gathered about their evening campfires to amuse themselves with witticisms revolving around such lines as "Boys, let us pray!" and "Tracts now, instead of sauerkraut!" Worse still, company and regimental officers found it impossible to elicit from their men that "spontaneous" cheer which traditionally greeted general officers as they rode before their troops.[6]

Suddenly the boom of guns echoed across the field as artillery batteries began a salute from right to left. Rapid staccato drumbeats pierced the deep bass tones of martial brass as the infantry bands struck up "Hail to the Chief." Hurriedly completing his inspection, Krzyżanowski assumed his place at the head of his brigade. Emotions filled him with a sense of excitement as unit after unit marched off to impress the President with their soldierly *élan vital*.[7]

Last in the long line of marchers came Schurz's division. Kriz waited patiently for the first brigade to file past before ordering his own men, the last in that long blue line, to move out onto the field. Stiffened with pride, the troops strode past the reviewing stand as the massed bandsmen sent strains of martial music surging through the wind. Drums, trumpets and fifes pierced the gloomy chill of the afternoon, bringing a smile to the lips of the Chief Executive. Lincoln loved the martial flair of the Eleventh Corps' German bands, generally acknowledged as the best in the service.[8]

Admiring looks of approval illuminated many a previously stoic face on the reviewing stand. With near unanimity the dignitaries singled out Krzyżanowski's command as the best appearing brigade, while the 26th Wisconsin won laurels as the best drilled regiment. Many officials echoed the sentiments of Noah Brooks who commented that "These men impressed us as the best drilled and most soldierly of all who passed before us during our stay."[9]

Lavish praises once again fell upon the colonel. Kriz felt justifiable pride in these men who, despite a history of repeated adversity, worked so hard to mold themselves into such a well-drilled unit. He formally thanked the men for their outstanding efforts. Later, he further honored the western regiment in his brigade by personally lauding it in the presence of Wisconsin's Governor Salomon who visited their camps on April 19. The governor, serenaded by former members of the Milwaukee *Sängerbund* with songs such as *In Der Heimat ist es Schoen* [It is Beautiful in Our Homeland] and *Das Treue Deutsche Herz* [The True German Heart], showed obvious signs of emotion. "In my whole life," he declared, "I have never been so proud of my German descent as I am now in the camp of the Twenty-Sixth Regiment."[10]

OUTFLANKING BOBBY LEE

The festivities now at an end, warmer weather beckoned the contending armies to renew their hostilities. Blessed with the largest, best equipped Union army to date, Hooker felt safe in promising to capture Richmond during his first campaign. Across the Rappahannock from the Federal camps, Robert E. Lee certainly had cause to worry. While the Northern army received continuous reinforcements during the winter months, his own Army of Northern Virginia mustered less troops to begin the third year of campaigning than it had the previous spring. With the limited forces at his disposal Lee would certainly be hard-pressed to hold his positions against Hooker's plan to put half his army across the upper Rappahannock, in posi-

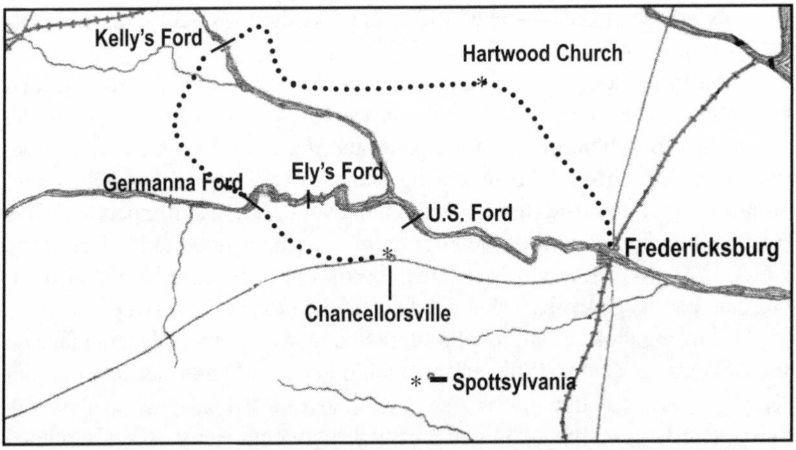

Map of the March of the Eleventh Corps to Chancellorsville (dotted line).

---

tion to cut off Lee's supply lines and threaten the rear of the Confederate army at Fredericksburg.

Hookers campaign began ominously on the rain-soaked morning of April 27, 1863. Krzyżanowski rose early, making sure that his brigade was in line by the announced starting time of 5:30 A.M. From their camps at Brooke's Station, the order called for them to proceed, in company with the Twelfth Corps, twenty-seven miles to Kelly's Ford on the Rappahannock. About 9:00 A.M., as Krzyżanowski passed through Grove Church, the intermittent rains developed into heavy thunderstorms. Pushing on toward Morrisville, the troops found the slippery road rapidly turning into a deep, muddy morass. Despite this adverse weather Krzyżanowski noted that the men's spirit remained high. Frequent interludes of laughter and singing helped relieve the fatigue of the march. Shortly after midnight on the morning of April 29, joined along the way by the Fifth Corps, the brigade crossed the rain swollen Rappahannock on a pontoon bridge at Kelly's Ford.[11]

Though he awoke after only a brief sleep, Krzyżanowski did not receive orders to continue the march until about 10:00 A.M. The column soon came under a brief artillery fire from two light guns belonging to Gen. J.E.B. Stuart's Confederate horse artillery. Federal cavalry quickly drove the nuisance away. The column continued south, reaching Germanna Ford on the Rapidan River about 4:00 P.M. Kriz rested his men briefly while scouts investigated the far bank to guard against surprise. Thus assured that no ambush awaited, the brigade crossed under a light rain around 11:00 P.M. On the far side of the stream the colonel posted a heavy picket line, then allowed his men to get some rest while the remainder of Hooker's troops crossed the waters.[12]

April 30 found Kriz and his troops on the move once again, reaching Locust Grove sometime near noon. There they halted, forming line of battle around the Chancellor House, located in a small clearing surrounded by a desolate wilderness of second-growth pine and scrub oak. Since leaving their camps, Krzyżanowski and his comrades-in-arms covered some forty-five miles along muddy, rain-swept roads, and crossed two major rivers. They arrived with manpower and spirits unabated, on the exposed left flank of Lee's position at Fredericksburg.[13]

Krzyżanowski's men fully realized the importance of their movement. Morale soared with the knowledge that they succeeded in catching the rebels off guard. From his headquarters at Falmouth, Hooker added to their jubilation by issuing General Order No. 47.

> It is with heartfelt satisfaction the commanding general announces to the army that the operations of the last three days have determined that our enemy must either ingloriously fly or come out from behind his entrenchments and give us battle on our own ground where certain destruction awaits him.
>
> The operations of the 5th, 11th, and 12th Corps have been a succession of splendid achievements.[14]

The following morning, May 1, Hooker ordered a general advance to press his advantage upon Lee's flank. At noon Krzyżanowski received orders to move his command toward the enemy. This was the moment they had waited for so long. Excitement animated the troops as they fell into line. The anticipation of combat shown in the tenseness of their faces. Eyes forward, the ranks gazed upon their colonel as he stood before them on his jet-black steed. Quickly, but calmly, he spoke to them, impressing upon them the importance of the task before them. The Eleventh Corps, he told them, would hold the position of honor on the right wing of the army. Theirs would be the position that the enemy would no doubt choose to attack. Then, ordering his men into columns to provide greater mobility and freedom of action, the colonel led them down the Plank Road to begin their work.[15]

About the time that Krzyżanowski began his movement, the leading Northern infantry ran into Confederate skirmishers at Tabernacle Church. A sharp fight quickly developed. Rather than press the issue, as his combat commanders urged, Hooker ordered a withdrawal. "The major general commanding," he explained, "trusts that a suspension in the attack to-day will embolden the enemy to attack him."[16]

By halting his advance at Tabernacle Church, Hooker forfeited an excellent opportunity to destroy Lee's army in detail. Furthermore, by relinquishing the initiative that his troops were keenly aware they possessed, he subjected his own men to the psychological effects of a check or repulse. General Darius Couch, watching the disappointed infantrymen marching back to their original positions, commented that "the observer required no wizard to tell him ... that the high expectations which had animated them only a few hours ago had given place to disappointment."[17]

Dawn on May 2 found the Eleventh Corps strung out for roughly one and one-half miles along the turnpike leading through the famed Wilderness area west of Chancellorsville. Devens' division held the extreme right, followed by Schurz and von Steinwehr. The men dug rifle pits and erected some light works facing south, but the far right flank appeared completely neglected. Indeed, the exposed flank lay protected by only two small regiments from Leopold von Gilsa's brigade of Devens' division.

Throughout the day reports arrived at the various Eleventh Corps divisional headquarters indicating Confederate infantry on the move. Dust raised by their columns became visible at many places along the Union line. From McLean's headquarters officers clearly observed, through clearings in the forest, Southern infantry heading off toward the southwest. General Daniel E. Sickles, commanding the Third Corps, now in line on the Eleventh Corps' left flank, sent a warning to General Howard as early as 9:00 A.M. Soon thereafter, at 9:30 A.M., a similar note arrived from General Hooker.[18] Some time during the day Capt. Theodore A Dodge in the 119th New York confided in his diary:

> Gen. Hooker passed about 8 a.m., riding down the lines. ... This moment news has come that the Enemy is making a demonstration on our Right flank. A Cavalry Officer has just passed with his Company, which has been driven back from its position on the picket line; he says they are 1/4 a mile from here. We are just alarmed by a very heavy Volley of Musketry on our Right, but nothing more has yet come of it. Severe cannonading is going on all the time.[19]

The reports multiplied during the afternoon, but Howard paid them no heed.

Hooker, besieged by a multitude of such reports, became convinced that his plan was succeeding. He interpreted the sightings as evidence that Lee knew his defeat was imminent. Obviously, Hooker reasoned, this was an attempt by the Southern general to escape toward Gordonsville. It all fit so well with his preconceived notion of the campaign that he dismissed any other possibilities from his mind. He ordered Sickles out to intercept Lee with the Third Corps, and required Howard to detach Barlow's brigade to support the move. Sickles rushed forward, only to find the quarry already beyond his reach. He contented himself with a brief rear guard action in which he made prisoners of a number of rebels from the 23rd Georgia who were guarding the rear of the Confederate column heading west.[20]

Robert E. Lee would have been the first to acknowledge the tenuous situation he found himself in that day. But Lee was never one to panic. Hooker viewed Lee's move as a precipitate withdrawal. In reality, what his men saw were 28,000 infantry commanded by Stonewall Jackson. Supported by 1,450 cavalrymen, 2,240 artillerymen, and 112 guns, Jackson planned to move southwest until such time as he could turn north undetected to fall upon the unprotected flank of the Union Army.[21] Hooker's belated half-measures only served to make Jackson's task that much simpler. Sickles' movement successfully isolated the Eleventh Corps from its nearest support by more than a mile of dense wilderness undergrowth. The committing of Barlow's brigade to support Sickles deprived the Eleventh Corps of its only tactical reserve. As the afternoon wore on, Howard's men thus became isolated, without support, in a potentially disastrous position.

Behind the lines of the Eleventh Corps General Schurz discussed the continuous stream of sightings with his brigade commanders. As he spoke, still more reports filtered in. Schimmelfennig reported them to the corps headquarters, only to be ordered to stop reconnoitering and hold his position. General Devens held a long-standing dislike for McLean, whom he replaced as divisional commander. When McLean arrived at Devens' headquarters he met with rebuff. When he persisted, Devens accused him of cowardice and ordered him back to his unit.[22]

At 2:30 P.M. opposing skirmishers ran into each other out beyond the right flank. Shots rang out. Neither Hooker nor Howard, nor even Devens appeared concerned. Carl Schurz was. He requested permission to place his entire division facing west toward the exposed flank. Howard refused. Instead of investigating, the commander of the Eleventh Corps retired for a nap.[23]

By 5:00 P.M. Jackson completed his movement. Out beyond the exposed Union flank he formed 31,690 men into three parallel lines that stretched for a mile on either side of the turnpike. Seventeen regiments stood in the first line, supported by nineteen in the second: a total of over 17,000 men about to strike 9,000 isolated troops in the Eleventh Corps. Behind these two lines, in reserve, stood some 12,000 men of A. P. Hill's division. Two hours of daylight remained as seventy-four Southern regiments moved slowly into position for their attack on twenty-three ill-prepared blue units.[24]

Along the turnpike, men of the Eleventh Corps lay about with stacked arms. Here and there they played cards, slept, or cooked their evening meals. Horses and beeves grazed lazily behind the lines. The sound of laughter rose from around the campfires. At the Hawkins Farm Colonel Krzyżanowski supervised the movements of two of his regiments, the 58th New York and 26th Wisconsin. He put them into position facing west, a move ordered by General Schurz despite Howard's earlier refusal of his request to do so. At the Dowdall Tavern General Schimmelfennig nervously scanned the terrain with his field glasses.[25]

"If they should come in on our flank," he confided to his aides, "we will be in a hell of a fix."[26]

Lt. Col. John T. Lockman. 119th New York Infantry. Shown here later as a general. *Courtesy of the U.S. Army Military History Institute.*

Suddenly the report of a musket echoed through the woods. Then another. Before anyone had time to move, a volley of thunder burst from the underbrush, spreading death before it. Thousands of high-pitched, wavering yells provided an eerie background punctuated by the rattle of musketry as George Doles' Georgians and Edward O'Neal's Alabamans sprang from the woods to engulf von Gilsa's hopelessly outnumbered regiments. Caught end-on, the Northern units had no chance to make a meaningful defense. Against a hurriedly prepared front of one or two regiments at a time, thousands of Confederates overlapped the beleaguered Federals so far that they threatened imminent encirclement to any who attempted a stand. All along the line Federal regiments found themselves stacked up like so many dominoes.[27]

In front of the advancing Confederate line surged a swirling, howling, cursing mass of non-combatants unwittingly caught up in the flight. The turnpike, the only avenue of escape, bulged with horses, wagons, mules and all of the other paraphernalia of an army corps in the field. Near the Dowdall Tavern this mass of hysterical animals and befuddled civilians tore into the 119th New York, smashing apart its neatly arranged ranks. Colonel Peissner, the old professor whose scholarly defense of Northern political principles placed him in the forefront of Abolitionism, rushed about trying to restore order amid the chaos. Miraculously he reestablished his lines in time to meet the Southern onslaught. Lethal volleys swept the clearing from both directions. The entire color guard was either killed or wounded. Two bullets struck the colonel in the head and side, the latter lodging near his spine. Lt. Emil Frost bent to help his colonel, but Peissner was in too much pain to be moved. "God take care of my poor wife and children," he moaned, then died. Lt. Colonel John T. Lockman took command as shot and shell dealt

Capt. Henry Schwerin
119th New York Volunteer Infantry
Courtesy of the New York State Military Museum.

death and destruction on all sides. A shell fragment sliced into Captain Henry Schwerin's right leg. He took out his handkerchief to bind the wound, but was then struck with a ball that shattered the bone beneath the knee. Eventually, gangrene would set in taking the captain's life. Another shell fragment struck Private Adolph Stahl in the head, causing him to suffer from epilepsy for the rest of his life.[28] Lt. Dodge described the fierce action in his diary on May 5:

> We have just displayed our Colors on our Breastworks. They are full of holes and covered with blood. The lance of one of the Colors was broken Saturday night. One of the most affecting sights I ever saw was in the Color guard the evening of our Fight. The Color Sergeant fell pierced by 3 balls. Corporal Carter of the Color guard seized the flag, when he also fell. Orderly Sergt. Carter (his Father) who was too ill to carry a Musket in the action, was just behind him. As his Son fell he rushed forward, seized the Colors with the exclamation "Poor Joe, poor Joe, come on Boys!" and carried them thenceforward and from the Field. The Color Sergeant and three Corporals fell. The Sergeant was a splendid young fellow. The Boys on the Color guard were all young men—every one of them fine, handsome and brave. Together as they lay there face to foe, it was a noble sight to look upon. … An Orderly Sergeant shot through body and lived only a few minutes left a wife and 4 children. When men fall fast around, one does not think of individuals; but a solitary example like this one, makes one feel sad. He was a fine fellow![29]

Its ranks in confusion from the chaos, the regiment desperately held its ground in the face of the rebel onslaught.

Farther north, at the Hawkins Farm, Krzyżanowski ordered his regiments into line of battle with the Polish Legion on the left and the Sigel Regiment to its right. The Hawkins Farm was an important position. Aside from being General Schurz's headquarters, it marked the only place along the axis of the Confederate advance where troops were deployed north of the turnpike to meet the assault. General Schurz ordered Kriz to command the position in person, signifying its importance. If it fell quickly, Confederate

Capt. Charles Pizzala
26th Wisconsin Volunteer Infantry
Courtesy of Marc and Beth Storch.

Lt. Karl Doerflinger
26th Wisconsin Volunteer Infantry
Courtesy of the Milwaukee County Historical Society.

infantry could swing in behind the embattled Federals along the turnpike, cutting off their avenue of retreat and capturing the artillery and baggage wagons. The line had to be held at least until this vital equipment could safely withdraw and the other units rally upon the reinforcements that were sure to double-quick to their rescue.

Krzyżanowski advanced one hundred men into the woods as skirmishers under Captain Charles Pizzala and Lieutenants Albert Wallber and Karl Doerflinger. Soon the Confederates appeared in force. By the time they reached the Union skirmishers the Southern line of battle overtook the skirmish line, merging the two into a single, massive, seemingly irresistible force. Pizzala's men fired, then fled for the perceived safety of their own battle line. A musket ball pierced the captain's skull, killing him instantly.[30]

Bursting out of the woods, Lieutenant Doerflinger found himself opposite the color guard of the Polish Legion. For a second his heart stopped as he glimpsed the barrels of their rifled muskets, poised, awaiting only the order to hurl forth messengers of death. He ran toward them, hoping they would recognize him. A bullet from his pursuers sliced apart the shoulder strap of his haversack. Half-way to the Union line he could hear the New Yorkers yelling for him to hurry up. Another shot dented his scabbard. With this incentive he felt sure that he annihilated all previous records for the sev-

Capt. Emil Koenig
58th New York Volunteer Infantry
Courtesy of the New York State Military Museum.

enty-five yard dash.[31]

Panting for breath, Doerflinger ran past the color-guard, turned left, and headed for his own regiment. Looking back on his experience at a later date he felt fortunate that "no kodaks or kodak-fiends existed in those days to perpetuate such interesting and often ludicrous events for the edification of posterity."[32]

Seconds after Doerflinger's escape the rebel line emerged from the woods. Captain Frederick Braun yelled for his regiment to fire. A sheet of flaming smoke greeted the Confederates, followed by a second and a third. Amid the shower of lead, a minié ball found Captain Braun as he sat atop his horse directing his regiment. This courageous officer, only recently returned from a Southern prison, fell to the ground mortally wounded.[33]

To Krzyżanowski, watching the New Yorkers battle against overwhelming odds, the fight appeared hopeless. One after another of the brave men fell. Private Stephen Bengel—wounded. Dr. Henry Root—wounded. Raked by fire from their unprotected left flank as well, men began falling in groups. Asbach, Kantzmann, Thiele and Handelbaum—all wounded. George Pfeffer suffered his third wound of the war. With barely 250 men in line to meet the massive gray tide, the gallant command absorbed the initial shock of the assault for several critical minutes.[34]

In an exposed position with no one to support their left flank, Kriz could ask no more of them. He sent word to Captain Emil Koenig to retire several paces beyond a small bluff that afforded some protection. Firing as it went, the Polish Legion responded. Slowly, they gave ground back to their new position. There they halted to support the left flank of the 26th Wisconsin.[35]

The crisis to his left thus momentarily resolved, Kriz turned his attention to the Sigel Regiment. The Badgers, fighting in their very first engagement, received simultaneous attacks on their front, and obliquely on their right flank. Skillfully placed by Colonel Krzyżanowski behind a small hedge, the regiment nevertheless enjoyed little cover. The tremendous

Lt. Albert Wallber.
26th Wisconsin Volunteer Infantry.
From *Germania und Abend Post.*

Capt. Frederick C. Winkler.
26th Wisconsin Volunteer Infantry.
From *Germania und Abend Post.*

numerical superiority of the Confederates made resistance a costly affair. One determined rush by the rebel infantry could not possibly have failed to annihilate the small regiment. But the unexpected resistance of these 471 men momentarily halted the advanced elements, causing the impetus of the assault to wane.[36]

The left flank of the Southern line overlapped Krzyżanowski's position by a quarter of a mile. All of his men were on the firing line. He had no reserves to meet the thrust. Deadly enfilading volleys raked the lines from the exposed right.[37]

Amid the turmoil Adam Muenzenberger rammed charge after charge into his musket, firing as fast as he could load. All about him his friends, relatives and neighbors in Company C crumpled to the ground. All of the officers fell dead or wounded. Sergeant Jacob Michel suffered a mortal wound. Louis Manz received a painful head injury. A quick glance to either side disclosed the broken, maimed bodies of men named Springling, Burkhard, Deany, Stirn, Bigalke, Luther, Weiss, Krueger, Beres, Fritz, Urich, Hermann and Koch.[38]

A musket ball smashed the shoulder of Private Lastofka. Three separate missiles struck Peter Lorsch. A minié ball shattered Friedrich Puls' knee, and another inflicted a painful wound on John Waskowicz. Company E lost twenty men. Thirty-two fell in Company G. The silence of death mingled

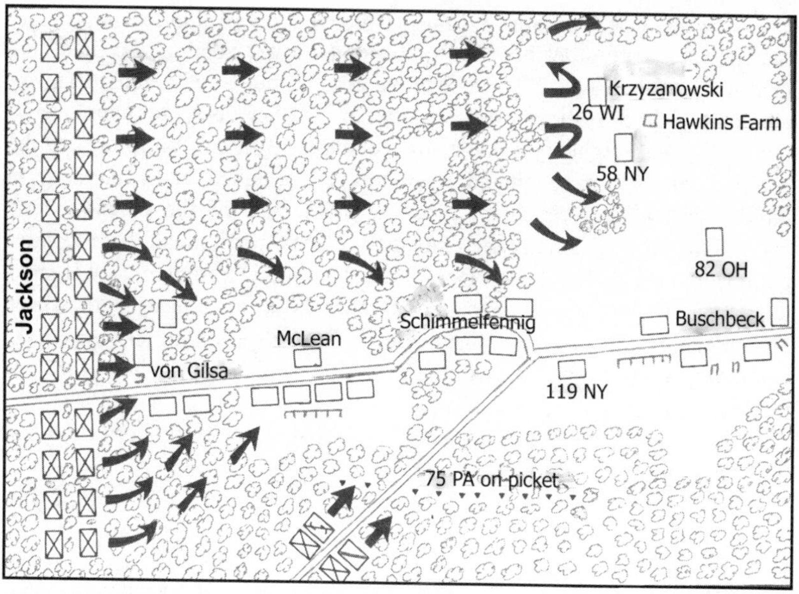

Map of the Battle of Chancellorsville, May 2, 1863, drawn by the author. Kriz held the far northern flank, which formed the right flank of the Union line during the attack. The 75th Pennsylvania was on picket duty and the 119th New York was in line between Schimmelfennig's and Buschbeck's brigades. Thus Kriz had only two of his four regiments available during the engagement.

---

everywhere with the cries of the wounded as the Confederates regrouped to press home their attack. Colonels Krzyżanowski and Jacobs rushed about amid the debris of battle issuing orders, cheering their men, and looking nervously over their shoulders for the help that never came.[39]

A ball passed through the neck of Adjutant Philip Schlosser's horse, but he controlled the animal long enough to reach down to rescue a private who was staggering about from a wound. A continuous stream of stretcher bearers carried the wounded to the Hawkins farmhouse. There they placed the injured on the bare floor, packed so tightly that the two available surgeons could scarcely move between them.[40]

Losses mounted to staggering proportions. Over one-third of the Badgers were already hit. Desperately seeking to hold his position, Kriz sent Lieutenant Louis H. Orlemann to General Schurz with an urgent appeal for reinforcements. There were none. Barlow's brigade was off chasing ghosts with the Third Corps and the remainder of the army still lay a mile away unaware of the fight taking place to the west. Mercifully, Schurz ordered the remnants of the two regiments to retreat.[41]

Krzyżanowski ordered Jacobs to face his men about. The Badger colonel refused to order his men to abandon the wounded on the field they paid for with their blood. It was a brave gesture, but Confederate skirmishers already fired at them from behind. Any further delay, perhaps even a minute or two, might spell doom for the whole regiment. With most of the company officers incapacitated, the men fired, reloaded, and fired again in rapid, mechanically repetitive motions. With time of the essence, Kriz spurred his horse in among the embattled infantrymen to lead them to safety. In Company K, Lieutenant Doerflinger lay on the ground, his ankle shattered by a musket ball. As he looked out over the scene of destruction where his company lost more than thirty men, his eyes focused on Krzyżanowski "galloping along leaning forward on his black steed under the hail of lead in the fashion of his Polish countrymen."[42]

"For God's sake, men," the colonel pleaded with the stubborn Badgers, "fall back."[43]

A good general, it is said, knows when to retreat. At Chancellorsville Krzyżanowski proved himself worthy of a star. While Kriz led his men in a hasty but orderly retreat, Lieutenant Doerflinger counted six distinct ranks of Confederates passing over him before he passed out. The tattered blue regiments moved slowly, pausing several times to fire on pursuers who kept at a respectable distance. About 400 yards to the rear they fell in with Buschbeck's brigade manning a shallow trench. There, for over half an hour, they exchanged fire with the rebels until this position also became flanked by the long Southern lines. Covered by Captain Hubert Dilger's Battery I, 1st Ohio Light Artillery, the retreat continued.[44]

Carl Schurz, accompanying Dilger's rear guard, walked slowly into the woods east of the embattled clearings. He glanced at his watch. It read 7:15 P.M. The Eleventh Corps fought against odds of well over three to one for more than two hours. Not a single man from another command came to its aid. Schurz turned to look at the battlefield. No one pursued them. Except for some skirmishers, the Confederate assault stopped at the Buschbeck line where the attackers halted in the gathering dusk to regroup their scattered ranks.[45]

The Battle of Chancellorsville did not end on May 2. Following Jackson's surprise attack, Hooker ordered the Eleventh Corps to the left flank of the army near the Rapidan River. For the next three days Krzyżanowski's men duelled with sharpshooters while the outnumbered but relentlessly aggressive Confederates succeeded in pushing Hooker's remaining corps from one position after another. Gradually the Federals found themselves driven closer and closer to the river. Finally, on the evening of May 5, Hooker ordered a general retreat back across the Rappahanock. To Kriz, the order was unfathomable. "Instead of receiving a command to attack, we were actually ordered to flee. The disorder and consternation of our soldiers, when ordered to throw themselves back across the Rappahannock, surpasses all imagination. What could have moved Hooker to this unheard of cowardly Retreat? What was the reason for this defeat and on whom does the blame fall?"[46]

The retreat began in great haste, under a drenching rain, on the morning of May 6. Alerted to the imminent move, Kriz formed his brigade into ranks at 1:20 A.M. They waited, wet to the skin, as minutes turned into hours without the arrival of their orders. Finally, at 6:00 A.M. the movement began. Ahead of them lay the long, muddy, rain-swept roads to Brooke's Station. Roads that they and their departed comrades so cheerfully traversed only a few days earlier.[47]

"All of the Papers Write Lies"

May 7 brought answers to the colonel's questions along with the beginning of a new trial for Kriz and his men. Not a physical exertion, but the more lasting pain of mental abuse. For the first time in quite a while recent newspapers circulated through the camps of the Eleventh Corps. Eagerly the men scanned the pages for some account of their desperate stand, some accolade for a job well done. Instead, their eyes fell upon shocking, incomprehensible stories describing in glowing detail how Schurz's men abandoned their positions behind prepared breastworks to rush in panic toward the rear. The *Daily National Intelligencer* in Washington, D.C., informed its readers that "to the disgrace of the Eleventh Corps be it said, the division of Gen. Schurz, which was the first assailed, almost instantly gave way. Threats, entreaties, and orders of commanders were of no avail. Thousands of these cowards threw down their guns and soon streamed down the road toward headquarters." The *New York Times* noted that the Germans ran too fast to suffer many casualties. It credited General Hooker's superb generalship with saving the bulk of the army. All over the North from Milwaukee and Indianapolis to Pittsburgh and New York, newspapers echoed the same sentiments.[48]

Stunned at first, reactions quickly turned to pain followed by anger. Invectives and blatant threats filled the air as newspapers passed from campfire to campfire. It was not the first time that journalists blamed the "foreigners" for a defeat—it happened frequently—but the maligned men always remained silent. Until now Kriz and his compatriots blamed themselves for not achieving better results. But Chancellorsville was different. Placed in a terrible position through the ineptitude of their commanding generals, the men fought desperately. They purchased crucial time with the blood of one-quarter of their number. Now, instead of praise, the newspapers castigated them more severely than ever.

Papers in hand, men appeared at the tents of their officers seeking some explanation. They received none, of course, for the officers felt as startled and appalled as their men. Schimmelfennig wrote a scathing letter of protest in which he attributed the stories to "the prurient imaginations of those who live by dipping their pens in the blood of the slain." Schurz complained to Hooker, maintaining that in fact the only fighting done on May 2 was by the "foreign" brigades of Krzyżanowski, Schimmelfennig and Buschbeck. When his protest bore no fruit he published a letter in *The New York Times* calling for a Congressional investigation.[49]

Swamped with complaints, Krzyżanowski passed along the protests of his men after adding his own endorsement. The effects of these callous charges must have made an indelible impression on a man as dedicated to the cause as the colonel. After the passage of a full twenty years, when he wrote his memoirs, he noted sarcastically that "'Fighting Joe' showed very little ability." Coming from the pen of one who consciously attempted not to hurt anyone by his reminiscences, one can imagine the deep resentment that he held even at that late date. In his view, Hooker completely lost his head, and with it an opportunity to exploit the confusion within the Confederate lines on the evening of May 2.[50]

Harangued with anathemas by not only the newspapers but General Hooker as well, few were willing to stand by the maligned "foreigners." Generals Darius Couch and Gouverneur K. Warren ventured the opinion that no troops placed in the positions of the Eleventh Corps could have held their ground. More to the point, General Abner Doubleday commented that the Germans were being made the scapegoat for the defeat. He called for justice to be done because the abusive censure could only injure the men's morale and *esprit-de-corps*.[51]

Theodore A. Dodge, adjutant of the 119th New York, commented in his diary on May 7: "I have seen a New York paper this a.m. and wish to state two or three facts. Three times was notice sent to General Hooker that the Enemy was turning our Right Flank, several hours before the attack commenced on Saturday night, but no answer, no reinforcements came."[52] On May 10 another entry noted: "Gen. Howard does not now stand by many pegs as high in my estimation as before the beginning of this month."[53]

Following the war, Dodge became a recognized author on military affairs, including among his publications an in-depth study of Chancellorsville. With the perception and insight of an established military scholar, he pointed to the real source of the defeat: the ineptitude of Joseph Hooker. Surely, he mused, the defeat of May 2 served as but a prelude to the fighting of the next two days. These later days witnessed the rare sight of "a slender force of 20,000 men who had been continuously marching and fighting for four days, pursuing in their own defenses an army of over sixty thousand men, while its commander cries for aid to a lieutenant who is miles away and beset by a larger force than he himself commands."[54]

Dodge's plea, like those of Schurz, Schimmelfennig, and the others, fell on deaf ears. Worse still, the men gradually came to ask the horrible question: "What are they thinking back home?" Day after day this single query plagued their minds.

"I deem it my duty as a husband and father," wrote Adam Muezenberger, "to write to you again and more particularly because the newspapers have published so much trash about the 11th Corps which no doubt disturbed you as well as others."[55]

Incensed by an article that appeared in the Milwaukee *Christliche Beobachter*, Charles Wickesberg wrote home to defend his comrades. "We stood firm," he insisted.

> And they say we ran away out of our trenches. I would like to see some trenches. We were standing in front of a bush.... All of the papers write lies. There are a few of those drunken scoundrels who have those things put into the paper. In time the truth will come out. ... It was all General Howard's fault. He is a Yankee, and that is why he wanted to have us slaughtered, because most of us are Germans. He better not come into the thick of battle a second time, then he won't escape.[56]

ANALYSIS

The stubborn stand of Krzyżanowski's small force bought the time necessary for the escape of the Federal artillery and the reforming of the remainder of the troops into a makeshift defensive line. Their stubborn resistance, together with that of Schimmelfennig's brigade, took the impetus out of the Confederate offensive, while denying to Jackson's men the objectives that they sought to achieve before dark. Following the campaign, General Schurz commended Kriz highly for the firmness with which he received the enemy and Gen. Howard included him in his report as an officer to be commended "for bravery, faithfulness, and efficiency in the discharge of duty." The same thoughts echoed in a letter from Howard to Hooker in late May: "The conduct of Colonel Krzyzanowski 58th N.Y. Vols. commanding the 2nd Brigade 3rd Division has been above reproach since I have been attached to the Corps."[57]

But the end was not achieved without great sacrifice. Looking at the after action reports of his regiments, Kriz no doubt found it difficult to conceal his grief at their losses. Thirty-one men did not respond to the roll call in the Polish Legion. Fifty-nine were absent from the 75th Pennsylvania. Peissner's gallant stand cost 120 casualties. The men from Wisconsin, under

Krzyżanowski's immediate command, lost 204. Indeed, of all the Federal regiments engaged at Chancellorsville during the next few days, the 26th Wisconsin ranked seventh in total casualties. Its fatality rate of eleven percent constituted one of the highest in the battle, a testimony to its dogged resistance.[58]

— Chapter Six —

"A Portrait of Hell"

The Gettysburg Campaign

Despondently, Krzyżanowski surveyed the results of a general roll call held on May 21, 1863. On paper his brigade contained 2,141 officers and men. In reality, only 1,205 reported as present and fit for duty. Nearly half of his command lay in hospitals suffering from the effects of wounds or disease. Some were recuperating at home while awaiting confirmation of their disability discharges. Furthermore, these grim figures did not reflect the scores of men who lost their lives on the deadly field at Chancellorsville. Despite this dejection over the losses his brigade suffered, Kriz felt motivated by a stronger emotion. The characterization of his men as cowards evoked in him a consuming sense of indignation. He, like those about him, remained adamant in his belief that the results of the fighting on May 2 were produced by the prejudiced and pusillanimous natures of Generals Joseph Hooker and Oliver Otis Howard.[1]

Soon after the roll call of May 21, Krzyżanowski received welcome reinforcements with the reassignment of the 82nd Ohio Infantry. The Buckeye regiment enlisted 931 men at Kenton, Ohio, on the last day of December, 1861. Veterans of many a battlefield, the 82nd Ohio lost its colonel, James Cantwell, at Groveton. After fighting as an unattached regiment assigned to Schurz's division at Chancellorsville, the unit now mustered only 350 men under Colonel James S. Robinson. Their addition lifted the active strength of the brigade to 1,555.[2]

Following his military *faux pas* at Chancellorsville, General Hooker moved his huge army into a defensive position to meet an anticipated follow-up assault by the Army of Northern Virginia. Realizing the folly of attacking Hooker's men in their prepared positions, General Lee decided upon a bold movement northward. The Southern commander reasoned that an invasion of the North itself might accomplish three goals. It would allow his legions to gather recruits in Maryland and much needed supplies in the rich farmlands of Pennsylvania. Such a move would certainly draw Hooker out into the open where he might be attacked with greater opportunity for success. Finally, a victory on Northern soil might convince many

Northerners that the war was hopeless, thus precipitating peace negotiations that would ensure an independent Southern Confederacy. Leaving a token force at Fredericksburg, Lee set his regiments in motion with the alacrity that had come to be the trademark of his campaigns. Striking northwest toward the Shenandoah Valley, then north toward the Potomac, Southern infantry easily outdistanced the snail-like movements of its ponderous adversary.

Initially, when Lee's strategy became apparent, Hooker proposed moving his army South. After overwhelming A. P. Hill's corps at Fredericksburg, he planned to continue south until he had Richmond in his grasp. Horrified at the thought of Lee's army romping through Maryland and Pennsylvania, as well as fearing for the safety of the capital, both Lincoln and Halleck vetoed the idea in no uncertain terms. Slowly, and with some aggravation, Hooker began moving west to follow Lee. At last realizing, on June 13, that Lee's objective was not the Shenandoah Valley but an invasion of the North, Hooker belatedly turned his columns north. The race for Pennsylvania was on.[3]

Tormented by a constant barrage of vicious anathemas heaped upon it by the press and by prejudiced troops from other corps, Krzyżanowski's brigade welcomed the opportunity to leave some of these mental scars behind. Never really considered a part of the original Army of the Potomac, the Eleventh Corps began to exhibit collective symptoms of the "Cinderella syndrome" due to the poor treatment accorded it in the aftermath of Chancellorsville. An aura of disappointment, compounded by thinly disguised and barely repressed feelings of anger and hostility, hung about the entire corps as it moved north.[4]

Krzyżanowski's brigade left Brooke's Station on June 12, marching via Hartwood Church and Catlett's Station to Centreville. "A Band of the First Brigade is playing merrily, and every one feels in good heart," noted Adjutant Dodge in the 119th New York. "Our Boys have marched well to day, despite the heat and dust, which are very aggravating." On the following day he wrote in his diary: "The Boys have marched splendidly. The road has been through a beautiful rolling Country, and mostly through woods so that the sun which has been somewhat shaded by clouds, is partly deprived of its powers."[5]

As the troops marched further north, clearing skies magnified the June heat. Virginia's roads turned into dust bowls that all but asphyxiated men marching at the rear of the columns. During their brief rest stops men broke ranks to assault nearby cherry orchards, ripping whole trees to the ground in the process. Plentiful strawberry and blackberry patches were left naked as the troops indulged themselves in these juicy, seemingly exotic treats.[6] Foraging was strictly prohibited, but Adjutant Dodge noted a strange proclivity of the local livestock for attacking Federal pickets. "The fact is that the animal creation about here are very pugnacious, and insist on attacking our picket line so often, that our boys are fain to bayonet them out of pure self defense. Of course there is no foraging done. Oh, no! only when Lambs, Chicken, Sheep and Calves will rush to an untimely fate: Quid faciendum?"[7]

Harassed now and then by Southern irregulars, Dodge noted the capture of three of "Mosby's Bushwhackers," one of whom bragged of slitting the throats of five Union stragglers. The captives, he noted, were at Gen. Howard's headquarters and would probably be executed.[8] Despite the bushwhackers, Krzyżanowski found his worst enemy to be the Army of the Potomac. Whenever his men met units from other corps along the crowded pathways, a predictably one-sided dialogue ensued.

"I fights mit Sigel," a man would remark, his tone of voice indicating no particular reverence for the proud rallying cry of the German-Americans.

"... und runs mit Schurz!" came the taunting conclusion of a fellow-conspirator farther back in the ranks.[9]

After two days of rest at Centreville Kriz led his brigade northward once more. Rumors circulated throughout the ranks as the columns pushed on along the winding roads. "Alas! for Staff Officers and rumors," commended Dodge. "They are on a par: the first don't know anything, the last always wrong." The farther north they went the clearer the skies, allowing the sun to blaze upon the marching men in unremitting fury. The suffocating heat engulfed the sweating men in a thick cloud of dust. The day's march was captured by the simple entries in Adjutant Dodge's diary for June 17: "Driest and hottest day on record! Drought through the land; springs all dried up; no water here where we halt for 2 hours for dinner. ... Oh! the heat! We are almost suffocated." Finally arriving at Goose Creek that evening, the men made the best of the shallow creek bed to cool off and cleanse their bodies of irritating coats of sticky paste.[10] His thirst finally quenched, Dodge took time to complete his diary entry for the day: "The march has been very severe. It has been fearfully hot and men and animals are almost worn out. I have had nothing to eat since noon, and feel very hungry withal. Luckily we are near water, which has been scarce all day and the boys are enjoying a good wash."[11]

The troops were allowed a few hours of extra relaxation on the morning of June 18, but Dodge felt this was not necessarily an advantage:

> Probably we shall wait until the sun is very high and hot, and then start off. There is a great lack of water about here. The men have suffered much the last two days march from want of it. It is a very hard duty (which falls to my lot) to stop the men falling our of ranks at wells we meet on the way. The water is poor anyhow and in the Canteens gets undrinkable. Many are the hard words that I get inwardly from the poor boys no doubt,

> and I do not wonder, nor blame them. Another hard duty is to keep those men in the ranks by threats when you can't do it by cheering them up. When you see a man almost exhausted it is very hard to force him on; cheer him up you can't, and I frequently have to ride them almost down, before I can get them forward.[12]

Several days of much-appreciated rest followed as General Hooker decided upon a course of action. The brief respite enabled the brigade's mail to catch up with it, cheering, at least temporarily, the mood of the troops. One exception was Adam Muenzenberger. His letter brought distressing news of the death of his son Ernst. Only a few months ago he opened a similar letter to learn of the death of another son. Twice within the space of a year tragedy entered his life. While his friends prepared to resume the march, he once again took up his pen in an effort to comfort his wife.[13]

"Whom the Lord loveth He chastiseth," Adam wrote. "Be comforted, dear. After the rain comes the sunshine."[14]

On June 24 Kriz marched his men to Edwards' Ford on the Potomac River. The following morning, amid great rejoicing, musicians struck up lively tunes while the regimental color guards unfurled their battle-torn flags. Cheerfully the men broke into song as they followed their colors across the undulating pontoons. "There is a curious swaying motion of a Pontoon bridge in crossing it, which would be apt to make some men giddy and sick," reported Adjutant Dodge.

> Something unsteady about it. The men have to march as unequally as possible in crossing for a steady tramp would break down the bridge. The country we are now passing through affords a rare contrast to Virginia. The land is fruitful and cultivated and the immense fields of corn (wheat) are a sight well worth seeing. The scenery of the banks of the Potomac of which we catch every now and then a glimpse is magnificent. … We just passed a delightful sight, actually two young ladies (whose home, we could see, a beautiful house in the distance), on horseback; pretty girls too they were, and I could not but sigh as I passed them and saluted them. Alas! for a good long talk with one of my lady friends. It would be the very most refreshing thing I know of. I wish I was a good enough sketcher to let you have some of the scenes we see. Such beauty as we pass is not seen everywhere.[15]

Delighted to leave Virginia's bloody soil behind them, they formed the first elements of the Army of the Potomac to cross back into Northern territory. Marching on, they passed through Jefferson, Maryland, to the lively patriotic tunes of the regimental bands. Arriving at Middletown about 4:00 P.M., the brigade was greeted by enthusiastic townspeople in a delightfully rich countryside. "The beauty of the scenery I cannot give you any idea of,"

Dodge wrote. "Plenty of water abounds.... Cattle and grain are seen on every side, and the Country people look very happy. All along the road groups of girls and boys watch the columns pass and occasionally one sees a refreshingly pretty face. In Middletown we were welcomed by the women with flags and handkerchiefs waving. It is the first Union town we have passed." The welcoming reception by the local residents gave the troops a new determination to rid the North of its Southern invaders.[16]

While Krzyżanowski led his men north with the renewed spirit that animates men fighting to defend their homes, another significant change took place. Piqued by his disagreements with the War Department, "Fighting Joe" gave up the fight. He asked to be relieved of command. Secretary of War Stanton, with Lincoln's hearty endorsement, eagerly accepted the request. On June 28, command of the army passed to George G. Meade, a sad-eyed Pennsylvanian with the stature and bearing of a clergyman. Not one to seek advancement at the expense of others, Meade protested that his appointment represented an affront to General John Reynolds, a personal friend and senior officer who led the First Corps. Reynolds, to his credit, lodged no complaint. With some misgivings, Meade applied himself to the enormous task of assuming command of an army on the eve of battle. Hooker departed with more vigor than he exhibited in any of his previous campaigns. The Eleventh Corps displayed anything but sorrow over his departure.[17]

Plodding along over the rain-soaked roads, Krzyżanowski brought his troops into Emmitsburg on June 29. The First Corps, marching in the wake of the Eleventh, soon arrived and encamped nearby. That afternoon the leading officers of the two army corps visited General Meade's headquarters to congratulate their new commander on his appointment. Ranged about his tent, they posed before a photographer to record the occasion for posterity.[18]

The bimonthly muster fell on June 30. The Eleventh Corps recorded 9,841 officers and men present for duty. Of all the corps in the army, only the Twelfth contained fewer. During the day Krzyżanowski dispatched fifty men of the 75th Pennsylvania to act as a guard for the reserve ammunition train and two companies of the 26th Wisconsin and a similar contingent from the 58th New York to serve as brigade pickets. The rest of Krzyżanowski's men made their camps on the grounds of the St. Joseph's College nunnery near Emmitsburg. "At Emmitsburg we pitched our camp in a grove adjoining the convent," wrote Capt. Alfred Lee of the 82nd Ohio:

> The beauty and tranquility of the place, so strikingly in contrast with the military tumult which suddenly invested it, are vividly remembered. The green lawns and scrupulously-kept gardens, the little cemetery with its methodical array of grassy graves and white crosses, the dainty chapel with its saintly group of gentle worshippers, all so eloquent of peace and repose, seemed to rebuke this rude interruption of armed battalions, and doubtless

yet constitute, in many memories, a pleasing picture, singularly at variance with the sanguinary experiences that so quickly followed.[19]

By evening rain clouds arrived to fill the atmosphere with dampness. Capt. Lee recalled:

> The evening of the 30th was wet and gloomy. As darkness fell, the soldiers sought the refuge of their shelter tents, and silence fell upon the camp, broken only by the tramp of sentinels and the heavy breathing of the sleepers. Late in the night, while I was yet writing letters by a flaring candle, a mounted orderly galloped to the colonel's quarters and delivered a message. The messenger's haste betokened something important, and soon afterward the sergeant-major came around to notify company officers to have their men up betimes, ready for an early movement.[20]

In the 26th Wisconsin, Adam Muenzenberger joined several of his friends in receiving Communion at the convent. Witnesses noted that the troops behaved themselves in exemplary fashion. Gathered about their campfires that evening, the men reflected over their lost comrades. They speculated on the battle about to be joined. The growing darkness provided an eerie background for *"Morgenrot,"* always a favorite song in the brigade. On this occasion it proved prophetic.[21]

Morgenrot, Morgenrot Leuchtest mir zum frühed Tod? Bald wird die Trompete blasen, Dann muß ich mein Leben lassen, Ich und mancher Kamerad!	Blush of Dawn, blush of dawn, Has my time on earth then gone? Soon the bugle will be blowing, Soon my life-blood will be flowing, Mine and many a comrade's too!
Kaum gedacht, laum gedacht, War der Lust ein End gemacht! Gestern noch auf stolzen Rossen, Heute durch die Brust geschossen, Morgen is das kühle Grab!	Scarce begun, scarce begun, Till the sands of life are run; Yesterday on horses flying, Now mid hail of bullets dying, Soon then in the cold, cold grave!
Ach wie bald, ach wie bald, Schwindet Schönheit und Gestalt! Strahlst du gleich mit deinen Wangen, Die wie Milch und Purpur prangen, Ach, die Rosen welken all!	Soon, alas, soon, alas, Lovely form and beauty pass; Cheeks today so proudly glowing, Boastful health and color showing! Roses wither soon and die!
Darum still, darum still Füg ich mich, wie Gott es will.	But be still, but be still, Life will go as fate may will;

Nun, so will ich wacker streiten,	So I'll try to bravely meet it,
Und sollt ich den Tod erleiden,	Even death and bravely greet it,
Stirbt ein braver Reitersmann!	Like a valiant cavalier!

JULY 1, 1863

Dawn made its appearance early on July 1. Before it grew old Captain Emil Koenig led the bulk of the Polish Legion off toward Creagerstown, on the road to Frederick, in search of Confederate marauders reported in the vicinity. At 8:00 A.M. the drowsy campsite became a hub of activity. A courier brought news that rebel infantry was on the outskirts of the small crossroads town of Gettysburg. Another rider brought news of skirmishing. General Reynolds was about to go into action, he said, and the Eleventh Corps should move forward to support the First.[22]

Activated by these reports, Kriz hastened his men into line and moved them off via the Taneytown Road. The route was two miles longer than the direct road, but the shorter route was crowded with the baggage trains of the First Corps that would have made progress very slow. A driving rainstorm quickly turned the earthen roads into a quagmire. Many of the men marched barefoot, their shoes having worn out on the tedious trek from Brooke's Station. Those with footwear slogged along, water soaking their shoes while the mud sucked at their feet in an effort to tear the coverings from them. They marched at a regular pace so as not to become exhausted, but forsook their normal ten minute break each hour. About 10:00 A.M. the brigade crossed the Pennsylvania state line, the 75th Pennsylvania "ruffling their drums, dipping their colors, and cheering as they stepped upon her soil." Adjutant Dodge in the 119th New York scribbled an entry into his diary as the troops pushed northward: "We have now crossed the Border and are in Pennsylvania. The marching is wretched and the atmosphere is so oppressively close that the men scarcely make any way at all, if we march ten miles to-day we shall do well." Through exceptional efforts, they would cover the thirteen miles to Gettysburg in less than five hours.[23]

At 10:30 A.M. Krzyżanowski's brigade reached Horner's Mill. Col. James S. Robinson of the 82nd Ohio remembered how the column soon

> halted a few moments to give the troops a rest. The rain came down in torrents. The soldiers prepared to make their accustomed tin cup of coffee, when through the heavy mists we were startled by the dull, thudding sound, which only issues from the mouths of cannon, but when first heard leaves us in doubt whether it may not be thunder. We listen. In a few seconds all doubts are put to rest....
>
> Aids came dashing along the line before we had time to fall in, with

Col. James S. Robinson,
82nd Ohio Infantry.
Courtesy of the Library of Congress.

Lt. Alfred Lee,
82nd Ohio Infantry.
Courtesy of the U.S. Army Military History Institute.

> pre-emptory orders to *double-quick* our commands on that hot July day. How little men on horseback reflect on such an occasion. If they had once marched in the ranks they would never have issued such a ridiculous order.[24]

The rain soon ceased, revealing a bright, sultry July day. Kriz pushed his men forward at the quick-step. The troops fought to maintain their footing in the slippery mud. From above, a now unshielded sun beat down upon them without mercy. Bernhard Domschcke in the Sigel Regiment considered it the most difficult and exhausting march he ever made. There were few who would have disagreed.[25]

Capt. Alfred Lee in the 82nd Ohio described the scene as the column struggled northward.

> An hour later the subdued booming of artillery far in front indicated for the first time since the Chancellorsville battle that hostilities were at hand. The detonations soon grew more distinct and rapid, and the column pressed yet more vigorously forward. The ranks were closed up, the hum of conversation ceased, and when the laggards, of whom there were always a few, began to drop out and make excuses for going to the rear, the provost-guard was cheered by their more sturdy comrades for driving them

> forward at the point of the bayonet. Hundreds of country-people, gathered by the roadside, dispensed food and drink and spoke words of encouragement to the hurrying soldiers. "God bless you, boys!" exclaimed these rustic patriots, whose seriousness showed plainly enough that they realized, vaguely, perhaps, yet profoundly, that a tremendous crisis was at hand.[26]

Spurring his horse on ahead of the laboring infantry columns, General Howard arrived near Gettysburg at 11:30 A.M. General Reynolds, he learned, was dead. As the senior officer present, Howard took command of the field from General Abner Doubleday, acting commander of the First Corps. Entrusting his division to the care of Schimmelfennig, Schurz hastened on ahead to get a first-hand look at the situation before his troops arrived. Upon reaching Cemetery Hill he found Howard, learned of Reynolds' death, and assumed command of the Eleventh Corps.[27]

Krzyżanowski's brigade came within sight of Gettysburg at 12:30 P.M. after covering the thirteen miles from Emmitsburg in only four and one-half hours. Gasping for breath, their feet already heavy with the weight of many miles, their ears picked up the rattle of musketry ahead, to the left of the village. Rushing toward the sound of the firing, Kriz raced his men the last mile into town at the double quick. Capt. Lee recalled how

> Along the slopes of these hills, and issuing sometimes from clumps of timber, spasmodic puffs of powder-smoke betrayed the positions of the rebel batteries. Nearer, and directly in front, the town of Gettysburg lay at the foot of the plateau. The First Corps, which was in advance, had filed out of the road, and was hastening into position beyond and to the left of the town. Descending by the Emmitsburg road, the Eleventh Corps followed rapidly, and pushed through the town, the appearance of which at this moment was one of magnificent confusion. The rush of artillery galloping to the front, the eager movement of infantry, the hurry-scurry of cavalry, the scamper of the terror-stricken inhabitants, the clatter of ambulances and other vehicles, all accentuated by the clatter of musketry and the thunder of cannon, constituted about as wild a scene of excitement as the tumult of war ever presents.[28]

The sounds of battle brought to some a new surge of energy. Adjutant Dodge in the 119th New York sensed his "blood surging faster, his pulse pounding loud enough to hear," and his nerves becoming more sensitive to the most subtle of nuances. Charles Wickesberg, in the Sigel Regiment, felt "wet as a cat and hungry as a wolf."[29]

Panting for breath, their faces streaming with sweat, the men entered the southern edge of town. Capt. Lee of the 82nd Ohio recalled "a tumult of excitement" against a background of "the clanging of sabres, the clatter of horses' hoofs, the gleaming of arms, the sweaty, excited countenances of the troops, the shouts of command, and the booming of the deep-throated guns. Groups of men and women, terror stricken ... stood showering upon us their benedictions. The prattling child joined the young maiden and the trembling matron in waving 'God bless you' to the soldiers." As they jogged through the hamlet citizens waved and cheered from their windows and porches. Some obliging samaritans rushed forward offering buckets of water for the men to quench their thirst. Here and there people held out loaves of bread or rolls to the famished soldiers. Two or three civilians ran forth with warm greetings for Lieutenant Henry Hauschildt, a former resident of Gettysburg now serving with the 75th Pennsylvania.[30]

As the regiments poured into town, Howard ordered Schimmelfennig's and Barlow's divisions to support the endangered right flank of the First Corps north of Gettysburg. Von Steinwehr's division, together with the reserve artillery, went into line on Cemetery Hill, a position that Howard determined to hold as a likely spot upon which to form the primary defensive works. Howard planned to hold the lines north and west of town as long as possible, then retreat to Cemetery Hill where the Twelfth and Third Corps, which were expected to arrive before nightfall, would form. The former, under Henry Slocum, lay at Two Taverns, some five miles south of Gettysburg. The latter, led by Daniel Sickles, was at Emmitsburg.[31]

North of the town Krzyżanowski formed his regiments into double column of companies in and around an orchard to the northeast of the Pennsylvania College. After dispatching Company H of the 119th New York to take possession of some buildings around the almshouse to prevent their use by Confederate sharpshooters, he rested his weary men briefly in the shade of an apple orchard while the first sergeants called the roll to the accompaniment of screeching shells exploding about them. To their left, the contest already raged with unremitting fury. With the sounds of battle growing closer by the moment, the infantrymen knelt in silent prayer. They were a resolute group of men. Only too well aware of the past abuses heaped upon them, they were determined to cleanse their record. Aware, as well, of the crucial significance of this invasion of the North, and the battle about to be joined, Kriz resolved to fight as never before.[32]

An artillery shell burst nearby. Then another. Confederate gunners on Oak Hill began finding the range. Krzyżanowski deployed his brigade in massed columns to the right of von Amsberg's brigade [formerly Schimmelfennig's]. Private Joseph Gillis, a musician in the 82nd Ohio, recalled marching "through an open field to a cluster of woods. We played the tune called 'The Yankees Are Coming.' It is a very quick piece and pretty. The rebs let go solid shot. The first went about three feet from the back drummer, and you ought to have seen him juke. Several came very close until we got to the woods. Then the Regt. was formed. The Col. said,

'Musicians to the Hospital, March.' I bid goodbye to the boys and left, and we just got about five or six rods to the rear when the 82nd went in on their nerve." Another Buckeye, Capt. Alfred Lee, described the scene: "The enemy's batteries completely swept the plain from two or three directions. The shells and shot howled, shrieked and plunged through the air like infuriated demons. There was no shelter, not even a stump or tree. Now a huge iron nugget plowed its way through the living mass, leaving in its track eight poor fellows torn and bleeding. The deadly 'thug,' and a submissive groan or two is all that is heard. Again and again the jagged fragments of iron sweep destructively through the ranks, but there is no wavering."[33]

At that moment Barlow's division arrived on Krzyżanowski's right, prolonging the line all the way to Rock Creek. Skirmishers from Krzyżanowski's brigade drove back the rebel skirmish line and the colonel dispatched some men to begin clearing the fence rails from their front to facilitate any future move in that direction. Shells from Carter's twenty-four gun Confederate artillery battalion on Oak Hill continued to fall about them. The rebel fire impressed Adjutant Dodge. It "was so accurate that shells were falling among and all around [us], causing considerable loss." Spooked by the turmoil, Dodge's horse "would not stand it" and "ran away with" the adjutant. Regaining control, Dodge dismounted and the mare ran away. Nearby in the 75th Pennsylvania a shell from a ten-pounder rifled gun killed one man and injured two others. The dead man was the one-time resident of Gettysburg, Henry Hauschildt.[34]

Dilger's and Wheeler's batteries clamored forward to bring their ten guns into play against the Confederates. Their fire brought some relief as they forced Carter's guns to change position, thus reducing their rate of fire. Adjutant Dodge took advantage of his regiment's position in reserve to pen another entry in his diary: "Shell are flying and bursting at a considerable rate. The Rebels are about half a mile off. The country is open and we can see everything. We see their Batteries are working hard. ... Our Corps is to hold this position of Gettysburg. God grant we may have Victory!"[35]

Schurz had less than 6,000 men north of Gettysburg, not enough to adequately fill the gap between the First Corps and Rock Creek. About 2:30 P.M. Barlow, without authorization, moved his division forward to take possession of a small rise known as Blocher's Knoll north of the almshouse. This forced Schurz to advance Krzyżanowski and von Amsberg, thus extending the gap between the First and Eleventh Corps to nearly a quarter of a mile.[36]

Krzyżanowski kept his men well in hand, pushing skirmishers forward to deal with sharpshooters from George Doles' Georgia brigade, the same unit that led Stonewall Jackson's assault at Chancellorsville, who were attempting to take possession of the county almshouse. Von Amsberg extended his thin line of skirmishers as best he could to connect with

Musician Joseph Gillis,
82nd Ohio Infantry.
Courtesy of Joseph H. Gillis.

Capt. Hubert Dilger,
Battery I, 1st Ohio Light Artillery.
Courtesy of the U.S. Army Military History Institute.

Krzyżanowski's left, with his own left located along the Mummasburg Road.[37]

Doles attempted to force a Federal withdrawal by exploiting the weakness of von Amsberg's right flank. As his Georgians advanced across the field, Kriz perceived the imminent danger. Quickly he dispatched the 75th Pennsylvania to deal with the threat. Colonel Franz Mahler, leading his Pennsylvanians forward, was nearly crippled when his mangled horse fell on top of him. He insisted upon remaining on the field to direct his troops. Under his steady leadership, a few effective volleys sent the attackers back across the fields in some disorder. Cheers went up all along the Federal line as the Confederates withdrew to reorganize. Spirits soared with the afternoon's successes, despite the precarious situation that still existed. Schurz's men had pushed Doles from his advanced positions, eased the pressure on the First Corps, and rebuffed Doles' attempt to push them back. Yet while the men congratulated themselves, the decisive event of the day began to unfold.[38]

Marching toward the sound of distant guns, Gen. Jubal A. Early's division of gray-clad infantry began to arrive on the battlefield about 3:00 P.M. Their arrival not only placed the Eleventh Corps at roughly a two-to-one disadvantage in manpower, but their positioning could not have been better for the rebels if planned well in advance. They arrived across Rock Creek, beyond the far right flank of the Eleventh Corps. It was Chancellorsville all over again.[39]

Jones' artillery battalion from Early's division placed twenty-four guns across Rock Creek from Barlow's exposed flank. Together with Carter's battalion on Oak Hill, these forty-eight guns caught the entire length of the Eleventh Corps lines in a terrific converging enfilade of exploding shells and deadly shrapnel.[40]

Shot and shell continued to tear into the thin blue ranks as Early sent Brig. Gen. John B. Gordon's Georgia brigade into action against Barlow. To Gordon's left, the brigades of Brig. Gen. Harry Hays and Brig. Gen. Robert Hoke (the latter under Col. Isaac Avery) threatened total envelopment of the Northern position. Behind them, Brig. Gen. William Smith's brigade waited to exploit their success. To the left, Doles' brigade renewed its assault with its battle lines replacing the earlier skirmishers. Taken at the same instant in flank and rear, nearly encircled, Barlow's embattled infantrymen remembered Chancellorsville. They gave ground grudgingly, even in the face of almost certain extinction.[41] A soldier in Gordon's brigade later paid testimony to their mettle when he wrote:

> We met the enemy at Rock Creek. We attacked them immediately, but we had a hard time in moving them. We advanced with our accustomed yell, but they stood firm until we got near them. They then began to retire in fine order, shooting at us as they retreated. They were harder to drive than we had ever known them before. Men were being mown down in great numbers on both sides.
>
> We drove them across a fence, where they stopped and fought us for a while. We advanced and drove them into and out of a deep road cut and on to the almshouse, where the Yankees stopped and made a desperate stand. Their officers were cheering their men and behaving like heroes and commanders of the "first water."[42]

Krzyżanowski had just ordered the fences torn down to facilitate movement east of the Carlisle Road when Early attacked Barlow's division in force. His ranks already tattered and torn by shot and shell, Kriz peered across the smoke-enshrouded fields at advancing lines of Confederate infantry enfilading the Union position on both flanks. Major Benjamin A. Willis of the 119th New York noted that Barlow's line was already beginning to waver when an order arrived from Schurz for Krzyżanowski to move to Barlow's aid. "It was evident that our brigade commander realized this new and dangerous situation of affairs," concluded Capt. Lee in the 82nd Ohio. "His face grew pale and distressed. To every mind, indeed, it was apparent that a great crisis had come—that the enemy must be met, and met at once." Kriz gave the order to advance, Capt. Lee describing the move:

> [T]he troops changed front, and a general advance of the line through the open fields began. Fences that might have served in the construction of a breastwork were thrown down in a twinkling, and absolutely nothing remained to screen our line from flank and front. The enemy's batteries swept the plain completely from two or three different directions, and their shells plunged through our solid squares, making terrible havoc. Yet the line swept steadily on, in almost perfect order. Gaps made in the living mass by the cannon-shot were closed again as quickly and quietly almost as though nothing in particular had happened, and the men were really less nervous under the ordeal of this fire than they had been during their inactive support of the artillery.[43]

Major Benjamin A. Willis, 119th New York Infantry, pictured here as a captain. *Courtesy of the U.S. Army Military History Institute.*

Quavering rebel yells pierced the roar of bursting shells as Doles' and Gordon's Georgians closed on the outnumbered blue defenders. To Capt. Lee, the scene was memorable:

> The gray lines of the Confederates now began to be unmasked from the ravine and to deploy themselves on the level surface of the plain. They belonged to Ewell's—formerly Stonewall Jackson's—corps, and were old acquaintances. Their movements were firm and steady, as usual, and their banners, bearing the blue Southern cross, flaunted impudently and seemed to challenge combat. On they came, one line after the other, in splendid array. Up to this time scarcely a musket-shot had been fired; but now our solid squares deployed, and the men were ordered to 'let them have it.' Quick as a flash the compliment was returned; bullets hummed about our ears like infuriated bees, and in a few minutes the meadow was strewn with arms and accouterments, with the wounded and the dead. The combatants approached each other until they were scarcely more than seventy-five yards apart, and the names of battles printed on the Confederate flags might have been read, had there been time to read them. Quickly our line became thinned to a mere shadow of its former self; and the field-officers, by the killing or disabling of their horses, were every one dismounted. The troops on our right were outflanked and driven back, and there being no reserves, no alternative remained but to withdraw.[44]

Lt. Col. David Thomson, 82nd Ohio Infantry. *Courtesy of the U.S. Army Military History Institute.*

Kriz spurred his horse back and forth behind the line, shouting orders and encouragement to his men. Amid the tumult of battle Kriz felt a sense of desperate helplessness. Tortured cries from the wounded penetrated the continuous bedlam of musketry. He could do nothing to aid their plight. Spurring his horse along the lines he yelled encouragement to those who could hear. Despite the urgency of the situation he could not help being struck by the peculiar picture of these men defying death in an obstinate stand against hopeless odds. Sweaty from the day's travail, the men appeared possessed by some animal-like thirst for blood. Motivated by revenge, blackened by the gunpowder, their bloodshot eyes painted a horribly grotesque picture, "a portrait of hell."[45]

In Doles' brigade a Georgian lifted his musket to his shoulder. Pointing it toward the Federal line, he pulled the trigger. Piercing the cloud of smoke that hung ominously over the laboring battle lines, the lead ball tore its way into Krzyżanowski's horse just as the colonel spurred his mount over an intervening fence. The stricken animal reared into the air, emitting a shrill scream of agony before plunging to the earth, its weight landing on Krzyżanowski's left side and chest. Pain shot through his body as he lost consciousness, blood oozing from his mouth and nose. Charles Stein, assistant surgeon in the Polish Legion, rushed to his colonel's aid where he immediately worked to relieve Krzyżanowski's impaired breathing. Carl Schurz arrived, bending gently over the fallen officer to ascertain the nature of his injuries. Nearby soldiers carried the unconscious colonel to the rear.[46]

With Krzyżanowski incapacitated, command of the brigade devolved on Col. Franz Mahler of the 75th Pennsylvania, himself already injured. Fighting on their home soil, the Pennsylvanians displayed an obstinate determination. Colonel Mahler, cheering his men under a severe fire despite his painful injuries, fell mortally wounded. Near him lay the lifeless body of Lt. Louis Mahler, the colonel's brother. Lt. T. Albert Steiger commanding companies I and K rushed to Col. Mahler's assistance despite the rain of death surrounding him. Carl Schurz, a longtime friend who served with

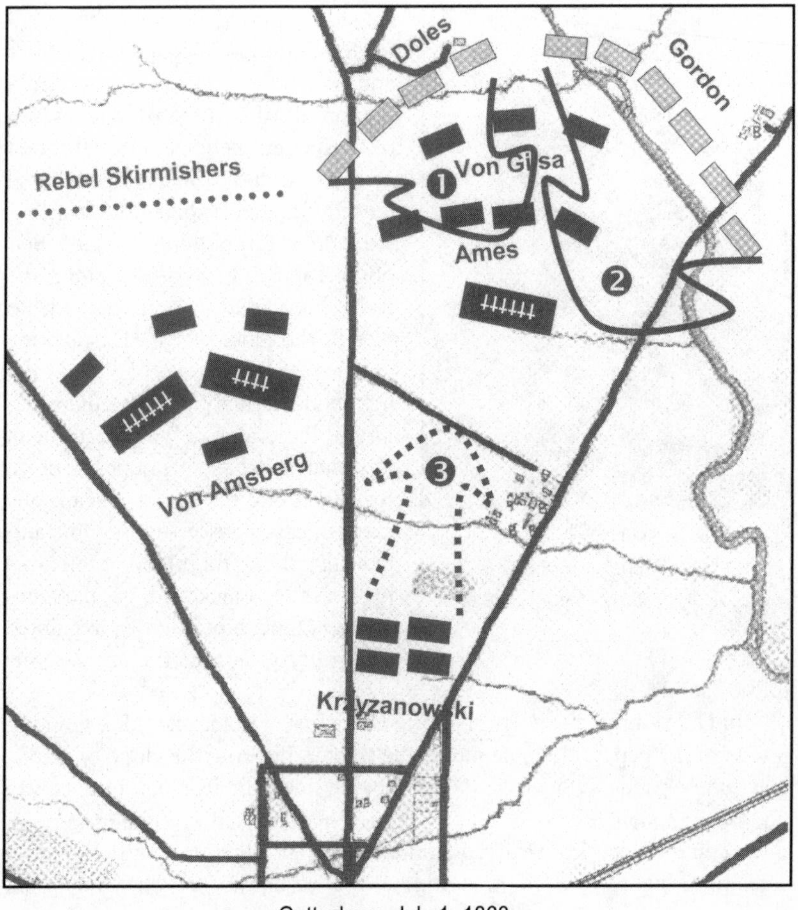

Gettysburg, July 1, 1863.

The Georgia brigades of Doles (1) and Gordon (2) attack Barlow's federal division comprised of Ames' and von Gilsa's brigades, overlapping their flanks and driving them back. Krzyżanowski's Brigade is ordered forward to their support (3).

Mahler at Festung Rastatt in 1849, bent over the injured officer to bid him a sad farewell, whereupon Steiger gently carried Mahler to the rear. The 75th Pennsylvania took 15 officers and 172 men into action on July 1, losing 8 officers and 129 enlisted men, a total of 137 casualties or over 73 percent of those in action. Major August Ledig rallied the survivors, eventually leading them to the relative safety of Cemetery Hill.[47]

The rapid transfer of command continued with Col. James S. Robinson the senior officer remaining. By this time Robsinson's horse had been shot

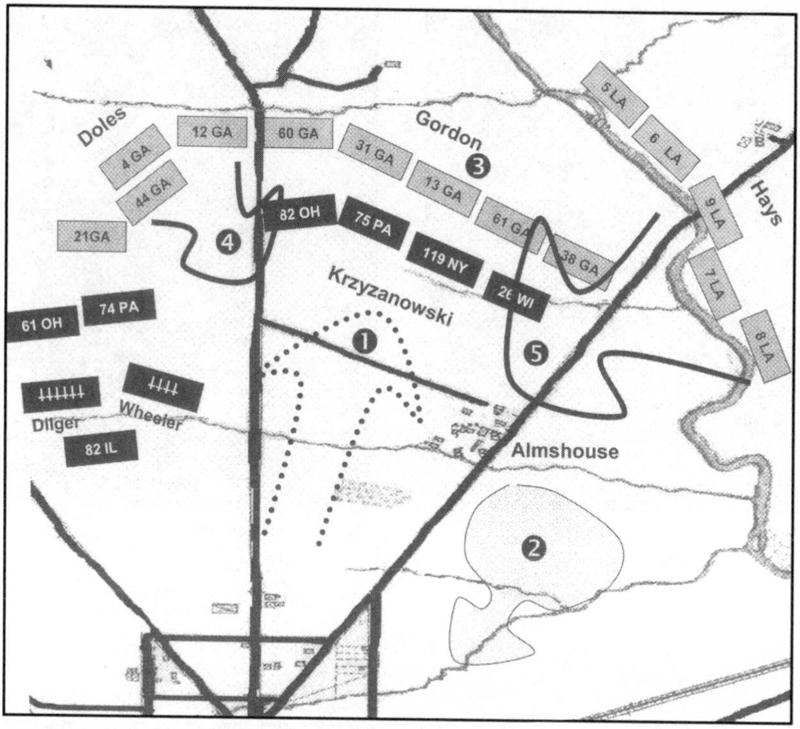

Gettysburg, July 1, 1863.

Krzyżanowski's Brigade moves forward (1) to support Barlow's Division, but it is already in retreat (2) before Kriz arrives. Gordon's Georgia brigade attacks Krzyżanowski's Brigade before Kriz can fully deploy (3). Doles' Georgians (4) attack Krzyżanowski's exposed left flank, while Hays' Louisiana brigade crosses Rock Creek (5) to strike the exposed right flank.

---

from under him, and all of the field officers in his 82nd Ohio had been unhorsed in the same manner. "From this point," Robinson explained, "we were gradually being pressed back by the power of overwhelming numbers. The men stubbornly contested every inch of ground. Our position was in every respect untenable." A 12-pound artillery projectile gruesomely dismembered the regimental adjutant. Lt. Philander C. Meredith and Lt. Henry Jacoby were killed and Capt. John Costin mortally wounded. A soldier standing next to 1st Lt. Stowell Burnham fell crying out "Oh, help me!" Burnham took the man's hand and he tried to struggle to his feet but could not. "Oh," groaned the man, "I'm gone! just leave me here." In another moment two musket balls found Burnham, snuffing out his life. Lt. Col.

Lt. Col. Hans Boebel,
26th Wisconsin Infantry.
Courtesy of Russ Scott.

Major Henry Baetz,
26th Wisconsin Infantry.
From *Germania und Abend Post.*

Capt. Franz Lackner,
26th Wisconsin Infantry.
Courtesy of the U.S. Army Military History Institute.

Sergt. Karl Wickesberg,
26th Wisconsin Infantry.
Courtesy of Alfred Wickesberg.

Thomson saw a shell fragment graze Sergt. Major Snow's cheek, "scratching it from the temple to the chin, back, cutting his ear and the side of his neck. That side swelled up immediately as though he had the mumps, yet he was not off duty. Several of our boys were torn to tatters, their blood and flesh scattered over their comrades. Yet these brave boys stood still and awaited for their turn patiently." The 82nd took 22 officers and 236 men into action on July 1. Only 3 officers and 89 men survived to rally around their colors on Cemetery Hill that evening, a loss of more than 64 percent.[48]

Amid the tumult, the men of the 119th New York quickly, methodically, fired volley after volley with the precision gained from past experience. Sergeant Louis Morell raised his ramrod to reload his musket. Two bullets struck him simultaneously, one passing through his body while the other destroyed his left eye. As he lay in agony upon the ground a third ball cut its way into his left thigh. Flying lead snuffed out the lives of Julius Frederici, Adam Hoesch, Thomas Hinterwald, Franz Hager, Gottlieb Dilpert and Heinrich Drober. Sharpshooters singled out the officers for special attention. Adjutant Dodge, an excellent gymnast and cricket player, felt the sledgehammer impact of a ball that shattered his leg bone and ankle, a wound that would cause the amputation of his leg two inches above the ankle. Colonel Lockman fell with a grievous wound. As he was carried from the field, Lt. Colonel Edward F. Floyd succeeded him in command of the regiment. Responding to the appeals of Floyd, aided conspicuously by Lieutenant Leopold Biela, the men held their positions. The 119th took 16 officers and 284 enlisted men onto the fields north of Gettysburg. By late afternoon it has lost 8 officers and 144 enlisted men, a casualty rate of 51 percent.[49]

On the right flank, the 26th Wisconsin was caught in a crossfire between Gordon's infantrymen and Jones' artillery firing from beyond Rock Creek. Lt. Colonel Hans Boebel lost a leg. Major Henry Baetz fell wounded. Command of the regiment passed to Captain John Fuchs who inherited a nightmare of whistling minié balls punctuated by exploding shells. The bullets appeared as thick as a hailstorm to Sergt. Charles Wickesberg, who felt the sting of a hostile missile upon his right wrist. Men fell by the scores, adding their names to the long list of maimed: Frank Benda, John Kunkel, Frank Suchara, August Puls, John Simonek, Frank Rezac, Henry Lew, John Swoboda and Charles Grochowski. They were lucky. Many never recovered: Friedrich Rohrig, Philip Berlandi, Friedrich Zuehlsdorff, François Stopples, Andreas Pfau, Joseph Zbitowsky, George Chalaupka.[50] Barely half the regiment survived, yet not a German nor a Pole, not a Hungarian nor a Czech lay dead upon the field. They were all, in the truest sense of the word, Americans.

A small contingent of the Polish Legion, shielded somewhat by the Badgers and part of Barlow's division, nevertheless suffered proportionally

National colors carried by the 26th Wisconsin Volunteer Infantry at Gettysburg.
Courtesy of the Wisconsin State Military Museum.

with "several wounded and 3 missing." Although the bulk of the regiment remained on detached service under Captain Koenig, the color guard gave a good account of itself. Leading his men, Captain Gustav Stoldt received a mortal wound. Other casualties included Jacob Eitel, Rudolph Asbach, Henry Thumann, Paul Linsbach, William Ottmer and George Rodder.[51]

Everywhere along the Union line, now flanked on both ends, confusion mounted in proportion to casualties and changes in command at the brigade and regimental levels. With more Confederates arriving by the minute, the situation deteriorated from hopeless to suicidal. Schurz sent a desperate plea for a brigade to halt Early's envelopment of the Union right. A similar note arrived at Howard's headquarters from General Doubleday whose First

Corps became flanked on the left by Pender's division. Howard had only two brigades in reserve. He did not want to risk losing Cemetery Hill so he sent word to the two beleaguered corps to retreat, rallying upon his position. Howard then ordered one of his reserve brigades forward to cover the withdrawals.[52]

Schurz fell back to the almshouse to shorten his lines and avoid encirclement by the brigades of Hays and Hoke. There the Eleventh Corps rallied until again outflanked. Retiring to the outskirts of town, it was holding its own against renewed Southern efforts when it received Howard's order to retreat. Col. Robinson reported that by the time his men reached the outskirts of town, they were "in perfect order and without confusion. The enemy was on our right front, right flank and in our rear. No troops could have fought better than the Eleventh Corps soldiers that came under my observation. They yielded only to the superior force of the enemy. They fought at a great disadvantage, but they fought well." But for Robinson the fight was over. Directing his men, a Confederate ball slashed through his right shoulder, passing through his body to emerge on the left below the neck. The fight was also over for Capt. Alfred E. Lee who lay in a wheat field near the Carlisle Road, shot through the hip. "I too felt the sting of a bullet," he wrote, "and fell benumbed with pain. It was an instantaneous metamorphosis from strength and vigor to utter helplessness. The man nearest me, being called to for assistance, replied by a convulsive grasp at the spot where a bullet that instant struck him." Lt. Col. David Thomson of the 82nd Ohio assumed command of the brigade as the senior officer present. Thomson's horse was shot three times, while the lieutenant colonel was hit twice "but only slightly hurt."[53]

As the remnants of Schurz's division entered the outskirts of town, the general's gaze fell upon Krzyżanowski. Carried from the field earlier, he had slowly revived, but his breathing continued to be difficult, each convulsion of his chest bringing a torment of agony. Nevertheless, once revived he struggled to rejoin his command. Schurz suggested that he go to the hospital, but Kriz refused. Later that evening, the symptoms persisting, Schurz would again suggest to Kriz that he retire to the corps hospital, but the colonel refused to leave his post. The Pole would suffer from the effects of the injury for the rest of his life, his later acquaintances commenting on his frequent pains and the difficulty he had gaining his breath after but little exertion.[54]

Closely pressed by the surging gray infantry, disengaging proved difficult for the battered Northern units. Riding at the head of one of Krzyżanowski's regiments as it entered town, Captain Alexander Małuski of the 58th New York, brigade aide-de-camp, became a target for rebel sharpshooters. One ball struck a front leg of his horse, while another struck his *portmanteau*, breaking the personal items it contained, flattening a watch and lodging in the watch's back cover. "Another four inches higher and it would have pierced my body," wrote Małuski. "Thanks to Providence I stayed alive."[55] Krzyżanowski's other aide-de-camp, 1st Lt. E. Washington Brueninghausen of the 119th New York, fell wounded while rallying the troops at the outskirts of town.[56]

Krzyżanowski's brigade was the last to enter town from the north, covering the retreat of the other units. At the foot of Washington Street the remaining survivors of the 119th New York beat back repeated assaults, allowing men and equipment to escape capture. In the center of town, at the public square, Krzyżanowski's men supported a section of guns from Dilger's omnipresent battery as it blasted away at rebel pursuers.[57]

The Eleventh Corps retreated into Gettysburg in relatively good order considering the circumstances. Confederate General Gordon later marveled that any of the Federals escaped from the precarious salient they initially held. Once the units reached town, however, order began to disintegrate. The two retreating corps came together in the middle of town, the confusion being heightened by several dead-end streets. Few officers knew where the various streets led. Captain August von Cleodt and Lieutenant William Moore surrendered several men from the 119th New York surrounded in one such cul-de-sac. In the Polish Legion Lieutenant Edward Kundel fell victim to another. A contingent of men from the Sigel Regiment led by Captain Domschcke found themselves similarly trapped. The unfortunate captives included luckless Adam Muenzenberger. Charles Wickesberg fared better. Wandering about the unfamiliar streets, blood gushing from his injured wrist, he attracted the attention of a sympathetic citizen. Rushing from her house, she dragged the wounded soldier into her home. There she gently washed his wound, bandaged it, and fixed him a hearty supper.[58]

Caught in similar circumstances, General Schimmelfennig vaulted over a high fence and secreted himself in a small woodshed to avoid capture. For three days he listened to the sounds of battle, emerging only upon hearing a band playing "Yankee Doodle" on July 4.[59]

Schimmelfennig's immobilization leads to the obvious question of who assumed command of his division. Howard relinquished command of the field to General Hancock later that evening. Schurz then reverted to command of his old division as Howard assumed command of the Eleventh Corps. The interim included the crucial time when the retreating army rallied on Cemetery Hill. Who directed the units of Schurz's division during this critical period? Who rallied the various commands, pieced them together, and placed them in positions to hold the vital hill? As the senior officer present, it had to be Krzyżanowski. Proof of this comes from Carl Schurz who noted that he suggested to Kriz while the two were on Cemetery Hill that evening that the Pole retire to the hospital. According to Schurz, the Pole declined, remaining on duty. Further, Lt. Col. Thomson's correspondence makes it clear that he remained in command of the brigade during this crucial period, without doubt because Kriz commanded the division.

One of the first regiments to reach Cemetery Hill was the 17th Connecticut of Barlow's division. Catching sight of its approaching flag, General Howard spurred his mount toward the color-bearer. Grasping the tattered standard, he placed it upon a stone wall as a guide for the men to rally upon.[60]

Krzyżanowski's regiments began to arrive about 4:45 P.M. The colonel directed them into position along a stone wall below the gatehouse to the cemetery from which the hill derived its name. With Schimmelfennig among the missing, it was probably at this point that Krzyżanowski assumed command of the division, with Lt. Col. Thomson of the 82nd Ohio temporarily commanding the brigade. Kriz rushed about rallying troops, seeking to create the strongest possible defensive line along the hill. From below, the makeshift positions appeared strong. The Confederate brigades needed time to reorganize and redeploy, but the rapid approach of darkness mitigated against a renewed Confederate assault. The hours that the Eleventh Corps purchased with its blood precluded any Southern attempts on Cemetery Hill that evening.[61]

Losses were severe. Every one of Krzyżanowski's regimental commanders lay among the casualties. Kriz was knocked unconscious and badly shaken, both of his aides wounded. Quietly, sergeants went about calling the roll.

Frederick Wendler
Matthias Rasemann
Emil Trost
Otto Trumpelmann
George Engelhard

Over one-half of all those present on the firing line that afternoon did not answer to their names.

James Austin
George Adams
Jacob Coles
William J. Sill
Julius Frederici

The loss was not in vain. Northern troops held Cemetery Hill, the key to the battlefield.

That night Krzyżanowski's survivors slept under the open sky surrounded by the cemetery's grave markers. A profound silence hung about the recent battlefield, broken only by the beating of horses hoofs and the dull tramp of new troops moving into position.

JULY 2, 1863

Dawn found Krzyżanowski kneeling with his men behind the stone markers in the cemetery. With less men than would normally fill out a full-size regiment, Kriz occupied the strategic center of the battlefield. The position held vital importance because artillery posted on the hill could command the entire Federal line spread out to the left along Cemetery Ridge. To the right lay Culp's Hill where the Union flank rested against Rock Creek. Despite its significance, Cemetery Hill remained probably the weakest point along the Northern lines throughout the three-day battle. Not only did it form a salient, notoriously weak for defensive purposes, but excellent positions surrounded it from which Confederate batteries could direct an enfilading crossfire. A sunken road, in addition, gave attacking forces adequate cover to well within 500 yards of the hill.[62]

Throughout the morning and early afternoon Krzyżanowski listened to the sounds of battle echoing down the line from the Round Tops where Union and Confederate infantry were locked in a desperate struggle for possession of the dominant feature on the Union left. From the outlying buildings of Gettysburg, including a church steeple, Southern sharpshooters trained their weapons on Federal officers moving about Cemetery Hill. Twelve volunteers from Schurz's division, their rifles fitted with Swiss made telescopic scopes, silenced the rebel snipers.[63]

Shortly after 3:30 P.M., fifty-five guns from A. P. Hill's corps began shelling Cemetery Hill. Although firing at extreme ranges, the gunners proved quite accurate. Shells began bursting all over the hill, some causing considerable damage to horses positioned on the reverse slopes, while others exploded with enough force to crack the headstones in the cemetery. A rain of shrapnel fell upon the Polish Legion, killing Krzyżanowski's adjutant, Lieutenant Louis Dietrich, and Private Louis Krause. The men crouched nervously behind the stone walls and grave markers, seeking what little protection they offered. Still the incoming barrage sought them out, wounding Daniel Hecht, Sebastian Vassoldt and others. Snipers also took a toll, mortally wounding Capt. Edward Antoniewski and wounding two others. Amid the cacophony of bursting shells and ricocheting fragments they gradually became aware of a new, comforting sound. Incongruously out of place, the rhythmical strains of waltzes and polkas drifted their way across the plain from some unseen Confederate band. Intended, no doubt, to relieve

The Confederate bombardment of Cemetery Hill on July 2, 1863.
From *Gettysburg Centennial.*

the tensions of sweating artillerymen, the ironically appropriate tunes calmed the frayed nerves of Krzyżanowski's infantrymen.[64]

As the sun set near the horizon, Confederate infantry fell upon Culp's Hill. While this attack progressed, the brigades of Hays and Hoke, the latter under Colonel Isaac E. Avery, formed into lines out of sight of the Federals near Gettysburg. Using the town, a small ridge, and the growing darkness as cover, they approached within a few hundred yards of the Northern lines. Suddenly, they burst upon the outmanned troops of Ames and von Gilsa at the foot of the hill. The defenders fought stubbornly, but the rebels were able to pierce the line in at least one place large enough for several score to rush the artillery at the top of the hill.[65]

Pausing briefly to reform their lines, the Confederates surged up the hill. At the crest lay six guns of Ricketts' battery along with four belonging to Wiedrich's German battery from Buffalo, New York. Led by the 6th North Carolina, Avery's men headed for Ricketts' battery. Alongside them Hays' famed "Louisiana Tigers," recognizable in their zouave uniforms, followed the 9th Louisiana toward Wiedrich's position. Retreating up the slope ahead of this host, Ames and von Gilsa rallied behind the batteries. The gunners, however, could not depress their muzzles enough to bear on the advancing enemy lines.[66]

The Tarheels achieved their objective despite the death of Colonel Avery. Hays' Tigers burst into Wiedrich's emplacements, only to be met by gunners determined to defend their pieces with their bare hands if necessary.

"This battery is ours!" shouted a triumphant zouave.

The attack of the "Louisiana Tigers" on Cemetery Hill as drawn by Alfred A. Waud. *Courtesy of the Library of Congress.*

"No," replied a German gunner as he brained the intruder with his sponge-staff, "dis battery is unser!"[67]

The 7th and 8th Louisiana poured into Ricketts' battery, seizing the three left hand guns with a loud cheer. They succeeded in spiking one of the pieces in the face of fanatical resistance by men employing swords, hand-spikes, rammers and even rocks. The attackers gained the guns, but in the growing darkness of July 2 a few determined men fighting with everything from clubbed muskets to fence posts succeeded in holding them for a few critical moments.[68]

During that time, the sounds of battle reached Colonel Krzyżanowski at his headquarters beyond the cemetery gatehouse. Unaware of the source of the commotion, he only knew that something was amiss. Most of his survivors stood on the picket lines, or occupied positions on the outskirts of town to discourage Southern snipers. Ranged about him were considerably less than 400 men, members of the 58th and 119th New York regiments. Nevertheless, Kriz did not hesitate for an instant. Mustering his two skeleton regiments into line, he ordered the men to fix bayonets. As he turned to lead them forward, General Schurz ran toward him accompanied by his aide, Captain Julius Szenowski. Schurz brought an order from Howard to ascertain the source of the trouble.[69]

Accompanied by Schurz and Szenowski, Kriz led his men off into the growing darkness at the double-quick. To the surprise of everyone, they

Capt. Michael Wiedrich,
Battery I, 1st New York Light Artillery.
Courtesy of the Buffalo and Erie County Historical Society.

arrived at Wiedrich's battery to find a general melêe in progress. Kriz knew that firing a volley was impossible. To fire into the tightly packed masses of struggling men would indiscriminately strike down friend and foe alike. Without halting to form conventional lines he led his men into the batteries to engage the zouaves in a rarity, hand-to-hand combat.[70]

By now, darkness had descended with the setting sun. Occasionally a bright flash illuminated the area as a pistol or musket blasted away at point-blank range. In the vanguard of Krzyżanowski's attack, the 119th New York engaged in a life or death brawl with an enemy often difficult even to identify. Bayonets slashed and jabbed. Musket butts became lethal clubs in the hands of maddened warriors. For brief moments that seemed an eternity, the issue remained in doubt. Imperceptibly at first, the defenders gradually expelled the Tigers from the emplacements. In his official report of the action, Major Benjamin A. Willis of the 119th New York wrote to Kriz: "It is needless for me to say, Colonel, for you led us in person, with what alacrity the regiment responded and with what determination it moved forward, and with what courage it met the foe, drove him back, saved the position, and thus secured the whole Army from irreparable disaster."[71]

Suddenly it was all over. The zouaves broke, escaping down the hill from whence they came. No longer did the shrill rebel yell pierce the evening calm. Now deeper tones resonated from the throats of jubilant gunners. Low, steady Union "hurrahs" drifted through the night as Krzyżanowski and Ames, along with Carroll's "Gibraltar" brigade, newly arrived as reinforcements from Hancock's Corps, pursued the fleeing Confederates down the slope.[72]

Back in town Michael Jacobs, professor of mathematics at Gettysburg College, wrote in his diary:

> The rebels returned to our street at ten p.m., and prepared their supper; and soon we began to hope that all was not lost. Some of them expressed their most earnest indignation at the foreigners—the

This photograph of the cemetery gatehouse was taken by Timothy O'Sullivan shortly after the battle ended. The dirt piled in the foreground was a hastily prepared revetment for some of the guns of Wiedrich's Battery. Krzyżanowski's troops counterattacked from behind and slightly to the right of the gatehouse to clear the battery on the evening of July 2, 1863. *Courtesy of the Library of Congress.*

> Dutchmen—for having shot down so many of their men. This led us to believe that the Eleventh Corps, of whom many were foreign Germans, and whom, on the previous evening, they tauntingly told us they met at Chancellorsville—had done their duty and had nobly redeemed their character.[73]

CONCLUSION AT GETTYSBURG

The early morning hours of July 3 offered little opportunity for rest. Frequent flurries of musket fire from pickets dueling with Confederate snipers kept men in a state of semi-consciousness most of the night. In an effort to halt the sniping Krzyżanowski ordered a company of skirmishers to take possession of a group of houses to the left of the Baltimore Pike. At 6:00 A.M. Lieutenant Carl Schwarz led a company from the Polish Legion into the outskirts of town to carry out the colonel's instructions. Confederate sharpshooters opened fire. Schwartz moved his men forward carefully, taking advantage of the cover available to them. In a few minutes they accomplished their goal without loss to themselves, although one bullet did find a target. Passing through a doorway, this errant shot killed twenty-year old Jenny Wade as she stood baking bread in her sister's kitchen.[74]

Throughout the morning Krzyżanowski moved about Cemetery Hill directing fire upon occasional snipers. Early that afternoon some 150 guns opened fire upon Cemetery Ridge. Confederate gunners directed their fire to the left of Krzyżanowski's position, but some rounds, fired upon the ridge from oblique angles, missed their target pouring shot and shell into Cemetery Hill. While the front lines escaped serious losses, the areas to the rear of Cemetery Ridge and on the southernmost portions of Cemetery Hill received considerable damage. Shells exploded caissons parked behind the lines, indiscriminately striking down both horses and men. Others fell upon the cemetery, shattering bodies and gravestones. One shell killed six horses, while another caused twenty-seven casualties in a single regiment.[75]

The lengthy bombardment was a trying experience because the men had no opportunity to retaliate for the punishment they received. Kriz moved about trying to ease the men's nerves with a few words of encouragement. To keep their minds off the holocaust about them, the troops resorted to cleaning their gunlocks, polishing their buttons and sewing their tattered clothing. No one doubted that General Lee would soon launch yet another attack upon their position. When it finally came, everyone was relieved to see the assault directed at another portion of the line. Throughout the climactic moments of "Pickett's Charge," Krzyżanowski stood upon Cemetery Hill prepared to defend it once again if the need arose. He listened anxiously to the alternating shouts and cheers to his left as the two contending armies once again met in a life-or-death struggle. He watched from atop the hill as the two forces fought for possession of a stone wall and a small clump of trees. He sighed with relief as the disorganized remnants of the once powerful rebel host recoiled back across the fire-swept fields.

Southern sharpshooters renewed their activities with a vengeance throughout the evening. Nevertheless, by morning a strange silence hung over the battlefield. With his curiosity aroused, Kriz detailed Lieutenant Schwarz, with ten men from the Polish Legion, to reconnoiter the town. Lieutenant Friedrich Lauber followed with an additional twenty soldiers. Gradually the two patrols inched their way along the streets of Gettysburg. No shots rang out. They looked into barns and outbuildings, behind rail fences and stone walls. They found nothing. As they passed by homes residents came forward to point out buildings used by rebel sharpshooters. Working quietly, the patrols entered the structures to find willing captives, many of whom were asleep after a long night of sniping at Cemetery Hill. Altogether Krzyżanowski's thirty-two men brought back 280 prisoners. More importantly, they brought the welcome news that Gettysburg lay devoid of hostile Southern troops.[76]

About 8:00 A.M. Kriz led the 119th New York and 26th Wisconsin across the wide, flat plains toward Seminary Ridge. He approached the rise with caution, trying to determine whether General Lee's forces might still be lurking about. Moving forward with his men spread out in skirmish order, Kriz ascended the low, sloping ridge to find the enemy gone. He made prisoners of forty-seven stragglers, then reported the welcome news to headquarters. The Battle of Gettysburg was over.[77]

ANALYSIS

Reflecting back on the past few days, Krzyżanowski's fatigued infantrymen could be justly proud of the achievements their sacrifices brought. Between July 1 and July 4 the brigade saw constant service in the forefront of the Union lines. On the first day the brigade endured the fire of several Confederate batteries aimed at it from front, flank and rear. Caught in a crossfire between two Southern brigades, Krzyżanowski lost over half of his men—considerably more than the famed "Light Brigade" lost at Balaclava—in just a few short minutes. Still the brigade maintained its discipline, retiring into town as the corps' rear guard. Then, together with the remainder of the Eleventh Corps, the brigade rallied on Cemetery Hill to face its pursuers. Seldom does a unit take such horrible losses and remain actively in the fight. Krzyżanowski's brigade did. Because it did, it helped preserve the strategic eminence upon which the Federal army anchored its line of battle during the next two days. "Krzyzanowski's brigade was placed in an untenable position when ordered to aid Barlow's Division on July 1," concluded historian Bradley M. Gottfried, author of *Brigades of Gettysburg*. "With both flanks 'in the air,' the brigade formed an inviting target for Doles's and Gordon's Confederate Brigades. No troops could have held their positions in this situation."[78]

More importantly, perhaps, were the comments of the men Krzyżanowski's brigade fought on those deadly fields north of Gettysburg on July 1, 1863. Although he would later glorify his brigade's efforts as if they swept the Yankees from the field with ease, in a letter to his wife dated July 7, 1863, less than a week after that fateful day, Confederate Gen. John B. Gordon wrote: "We charged the heavy lines of the Enemy & had a desperate fight. I consider the action of the Brigade as brilliant as any charge of the war—and it is so regarded by the officers of the army—I lost about 350 men." These sentiments were echoed by the men in the ranks who bore the brunt of the fighting against Krzyżanowski's brigade. Sidney Richardson Jackson, who served in the 21st Georgia, wrote about the contest on July 1 to his parents on July 8, 1863, calling it "a hard fight … our loss was very heavy on the right of us. I think they fight harder in their own Country, then they do in Virginia." Henry W. Thomas, historian of Doles' brigade, noted that Krzyżanowski's line "poured a volley into our line, killing and wounding many men." The Confederates attempted to cut the outflanked Union troops off from Gettysburg, he explained, but they could not do so and were instead forced to fight a "sharp engagement in the streets." In a letter home, Joseph Hilton of the 26th Georgia called the action "a stubborn fight." George W. O'Neal of the 31st Georgia recalled that the Yankees were "not well formed when we struck them," but nevertheless offered a "stubborn resistance." All of these eyewitness accounts of opposing soldiers point to the stubborn resistance offered by Krzyżanowski's brigade that day.[79]

Battered and bruised, the men never lost hope. Determination drove them on in spite of their losses. On July 2 Kriz personally let two of his decimated regiments in hand-to-hand combat to save Federal artillery emplacements on Cemetery Hill. The added weight of their assault helped tip the balance in favor of the North. Years later, Major Samuel McD. Tate of the 6th North Carolina, reflecting on the tarheels' assault on Cemetery Hill for the readers of *Confederate Veteran* magazine, stated: "The enemy stood with a tenacity never before displayed by them."[80]

The loss of the Cemetery Hill position on July 2 would have been a disaster. In Confederate hands, Cemetery Hill cut the Union line in two, placing both segments under direct fire from the captured guns near the cemetery. Commenting on the incident from the Southern point of view, noted historian Douglas Southall Freeman lamented that: "The whole of the three-days' battle produced no more tragic might-have-been than this twilight engagement on the Confederate left."[81]

Krzyżanowski's service did not go unnoticed. Gen. Alpheus Williams characterized Kriz as "a Pole but a good officer and [he] speaks English well." In his official report of the action, General Howard lauded Krzyżanowski for his "bravery, faithfulness and efficiency in the discharge of duty."[82] General Carl Schurz, in a special report on the battle sent to Gen. Howard, declared that Krzyżanowski "did not only his duty, but more than his duty; he exposed himself to the bullets of the enemy as freely as if he had been accustomed to see every one of them bring him honor."[83]

Forty-three Federal infantry brigades saw action at Gettysburg. Some of these were much larger than the depleted ranks that Kriz led north after Chancellorsville. Nevertheless, when historians tabulated the butcher's fill for Gettysburg Krzyżanowski's brigade ranked thirteenth in the number of casualties. The percentage of losses that it sustained, while remaining actively in the fight, was nearly three times above the average percentage that statistician Thomas L. Livermore calculated for the battle.[84]

The official records usually cited by historians list 669 casualties in Krzyżanowski's five regiments. Of this staggering total, seventy-five were killed, 388 wounded, and 206 captured or missing. But these figures are notoriously conservative. Compiled on July 4, they are also very inaccurate

The plaque north of Gettysburg commemorating the fighting by Krzyżanowski's Brigade on July 1, 1863.

---

in reflecting the true number of men killed and wounded. Many who later died, for example, were first reported as wounded, captured, or missing. Although later changed on the muster rolls, no one ever transferred these changes to the official records. Using the figures of independent researchers, it becomes evident that Krzyżanowski suffered not seventy-five killed, but at least 155![85]

Gettysburg was the largest battle ever fought on the North American continent. It marked, as later events unfolded, the geographic "high tide" of the Confederacy. It was the last serious offensive by the Army of Northern Virginia. Had it not been for Colonel Krzyżanowski and his maligned, but determined "foreign" infantry the results might have been quite different.

"The Most Distinguished Feats"

The Chattanooga and Knoxville Campaigns

The Battle of Gettysburg marked a milestone in the history of the Army of the Potomac. For the first time the Federal army in the East won an unmistakable victory over its old nemesis, Robert E. Lee's Army of Northern Virginia. Krzyżanowski exulted in the triumph. He placed much of the credit for the army's success on the shoulders of its new commanding officer, George G. Meade. Newspapers echoed these words of praise. For the first time, the exhilaration of success even produced uncharacteristically kind words for the Eleventh Corps. On July 4 the *New York Times*, previously a bastion of anti-foreign criticism, reported that the Eleventh Corps had redeemed the disgrace of Chancellorsville.[1]

Unfortunately, the good will engendered by the triumph did not long survive the echo of the guns. It was only a matter of time until the initial jubilation ceased. Subsequent stories in many newspapers completely neglected the crucial parts played by the Eleventh Corps at Gettysburg. Before long journalists completed their change of attitude by pointing accusing fingers at the despised "Dutchmen" for "running away" on the first day of the battle.

Disheartened and bewildered by these journalistic chameleons, Krzyżanowski's men shook their heads in disbelief. What more could possibly be expected of them? It is not surprising that the men took these stories as an offense to their honor, and to the memory of their departed comrades. For some, the journalistic aftermath of Gettysburg was the proverbial last straw. Very few enlisted men deserted, but many vowed never to re-enlist once their terms of service expired. Some officers, like General Schimmelfennig, requested immediate transfers to different theaters of operations where their talents might better be appreciated. Others requested immediate discharge. Major Henry Baetz of the 26th Wisconsin submitted a detailed letter of resignation in which he criticized the absence of any official denunciation of the fictitious accusations circulating in the "news" stories. In his case the fury that drove his pen must have been extreme for he had no immediate need to write the letter. He would receive a discharge anyway since he lost a leg at Gettysburg.[2]

The campaign did not end with Lee's retreat from that small Pennsylvania crossroads. The men of Krzyżanowski's brigade followed their colonel's commands when he led them south again on the evening of July 5. They left town via the street where four days earlier friends had greeted Henry Hauschildt. He was no longer with them. They headed back toward Emmitsburg along the road where Theodore A. Dodge felt his pulse beating quicker, his senses growing keener. He was no longer with them. They marched on hard dirt roads only recently soft with the mud that Bernhard Domschcke found so exhausting. He was no longer with them. They passed by the St. Joseph's College nunnery where Adam Muenzenberger received Communion. He, too, was no longer with them.

At Emmitsburg they headed across rough mountains toward Middletown. Intense, stifling July heat took its toll on the men. Drenched in their own perspiration, they pushed on when fatigue caused others to stop by the roadside to rest. The strenuous march limited the progress of many commands to less than anticipated. Krzyżanowski's brigade was one of the few that arrived in Middletown on schedule.[3]

Continuing on beyond the town, Kriz dispatched patrols to search for Confederate stragglers. Near Boonesboro on July 8 the Polish Legion fought a brief skirmish with marauding rebel cavalry. Before the raiders departed they captured Private N. M. Ahlers and wounded Private John Hoffenback.[4]

Marching with the remainder of the Eleventh Corps, Kriz continued on in pursuit of the enemy. At Hagerstown on July 11 his brigade marched through town to the cadence of enthusiastic "hurrahs" from the local emergency militia. Citizens lining the streets showered the men with an ovation of cheers that puffed them with pride. Beyond Hagerstown Krzyżanowski once again skirmished with Southern guerrillas, this time reporting no casualties.[5]

That night Krzyżanowski accompanied a group of Eleventh Corps officers into town for an evening of relaxation. Arriving at the Hagerstown Female Seminary, the small group of men affected their best manners. While Colonel von Gilsa played waltzes on the seminary's piano his fellow officers enjoyed the evening dancing with obliging young ladies, much to the disgust of the school's principal. As they danced, the corps commanders met in a council of war to decide upon the advisability of attacking Lee's army as it tried to re-cross the Potomac. The Eleventh Corps, along with two others, voted "yes." Five corps commanders voted "no," citing losses and the fatigue of their troops as excuses for not engaging the Confederates. As a result, Lee escaped into Virginia with his battered army intact.[6]

Following the council of war, Krzyżanowski led his men slowly toward the Potomac, watching for Confederate stragglers. His patrols skirmished briefly with bushwhackers at Funkstown, and at Donaldsville hidden assailants wounded a private in the 119th New York. Crossing the Potomac, Kriz cautiously advanced into the Old Dominion State. The constant threat of guerrillas made life hazardous, necessitating continuous vigilance. Confederate raiders attacked isolated patrols, captured supply wagons, and on one occasion came dangerously close to carrying off General Schurz.[7]

As the army continued on, pursuing Lee's forces at a respectable distance, its critical supply lines along the Orange and Alexandria Railroad came under repeated attacks. Clearly Meade could not ignore these attacks upon his vital supply line. Aware, as well, of the army prejudice directed toward the Eleventh Corps, Meade proposed to solve the situation by officially disbanding Howard's Corps. Under this plan, Howard would take a division with him when he assumed command of the Second Corps. Another division would be transferred to bolster the sagging manpower of the Twelfth Corps. Schurz's division, containing the bulk of the despised "foreigners," was to be dismembered to provide personnel for guard posts along the Orange and Alexandria Railroad. The War Department gave this proposal serious consideration, but in the end it vetoed the plan. The War Department felt that Schurz's division was not large enough for the task assigned to it, thus the Washington authorities decided to assign the entire Eleventh Corps to the project. Spread out in a large fan-shaped arc with its headquarters at Catlett's Station, the Eleventh Corps survived to fight another day.[8]

By the end of the Gettysburg Campaign Krzyżanowski's brigade was in bad shape. The 26th Wisconsin, which performed so brilliantly at Chancellorsville and Gettysburg, now formed a mere shell of a regiment. So few men answered the morning muster that Colonel Jacobs temporarily consolidated the regiment into five companies. Throughout the Eleventh Corps many regimental strengths shrank to less than 200 men. Those who remained were without adequate shoes, clothing and equipment. To strengthen the depleted corps, the War Department once again reshuffled its regiments. At the end of July new troops arrived to fill some of the gaps. Krzyżanowski received two additions to his brigade, the veteran 68th New York and the 141st New York. The 82nd Ohio left to be reassigned. Many of its men were not happy to be leaving the brigade. Lt. Col. David Thomson wrote to the wounded colonel, James S. Robinson, about the change, asserting "Krzyzanowski is the one we all desire to be under now."[9]

Following Gettysburg Krzyżanowski distributed generous amounts of praise upon his subordinates for their conduct during the recent operations. With new regiments constantly in the process of formation, many veterans left the ranks of his brigade to accept commissions or promotions in these newly recruited units. Within the brigade he recommended many men for promotion to fill vacancies resulting from combat losses. When no promotion proved forthcoming for his aide, Lieutenant E. Washington Brueninghausen of the 119th New York, he appealed to Governor Seymour of New York to appoint Brueninghausen to a vacancy in Krzyżanowski's own regiment, the 58th New York. The lieutenant merited the advancement, Kriz argued, because of his gallant behavior at Chancellorsville and faithful service at Gettysburg where he was wounded. Had it not been for his absence while acting as Krzyżanowski's aide, the colonel noted, Brueninghausen would long since have received this advancement. The governor replied that such a promotion could not be justified in view of the reduced strength of the 58th New York Infantry.[10]

Shortly, another letter arrived from New York Governor Horatio Seymour. This missive announced the appointment of Adolf C. Warburg to the rank of major in the 58th New York. Furious at this snub of his own deserving men, Krzyżanowski lost no time in rising to their defense. Tersely he informed Seymour that the new appointee, a man completely unknown to the colonel, could not be mustered into the regiment because the aggregate number of troops remaining after the Battle of Gettysburg was not sufficient to merit the appointment. By confronting the governor with his own rationale, Kriz left New York's chief executive with no adequate response. Adolf C. Warburg never appeared on the muster rolls of the 58th New York Volunteer Infantry.[11]

During this time of relative quiet, Carl Schurz once again took the opportunity to pen a request for Krzyżanowski's promotion. On August 31 he wrote to General O. O. Howard:

> Col. Krzyzanowski has been in command of his Brigade now for about 15 mos.., his conduct during that time never gave rise to the least complaint, it was exemplary in every respect. In every action in which his command had the honor to take part he distinguished himself by daring bravery, by strict obedience to orders and considerable skill in the handling of his troops. On every occasion he set a glorious example to his officers and men.
>
> Last winter he was recommended for a Brigadier Generalship and in consequence of charges against him, which since have been pronounced entirely groundless by the Judge Advocate General of the Army, his nomination was rejected by the Senate. With this stigma upon his honor, his services being rewarded with disgrace instead of an honorable recognition, with the consciousness of having been most unjustly sacrificed to false accusations, and with hardly any hope of seeing that injustice redressed, he went into the battles of Chancellorsville and Gettysburg. On both occasions he did not only his duty, but more than his duty; he exposed himself to the bullets of the enemy as freely, as if he had been accustomed to see every one of them bring him honor, reward and promotion.

> I would respectfully represent, General, that such conduct under such circumstances ought to be noticed by the Government. Treatment of so harsh a nature as he has experienced, is more frequently followed by clamorous complaint, sourness of feeling, negligence or resignation, than by increased alacrity in the performance of duty and intensified zeal for the cause. It is my humble opinion that such spirit ought to be cultivated, and I would respectfully request you, General, to have his claims properly laid before the Government.[12]

At Eleventh Corps headquarters, Howard endorsed the recommendation and forwarded it with the notation "Respectfully forwarded and cordially endorsed. It is recommended that Col. Krzyzanowski's case be reconsidered and justice done to him." Though approved, the nomination once again went no further. When it became apparent that the recommendations had been ignored, Gen. Howard once again wrote to Washington in December stating clearly: "I recommend a restoration of Col. W. Krzyzanowski to the rank to which the President appointed him and of which, I learn, he was deprived by false accusations. He has behaved with gallantry and marked promptitude, having commanded his brigade for a long time."[13] Unfortunately for the colonel, the recommendations on his behalf bore no fruit.

Due to his assignment along the railroad, Krzyżanowski enjoyed unusually bountiful times during the late summer of 1863. Unseasonably mild weather proved pleasant to the senses. With their camps now somewhat more permanent in nature, the men could use off-duty hours to write home, visit friends, engage in regimental contests, or join an occasional hunting party. Chaplains preached to large audiences, while German musicians found themselves much in demand throughout the army. With food supplies now plentiful, cooking became a favorite pastime. Chefs and self-proclaimed connoisseurs from many European ethnic groups prepared the delightful delicacies of their native lands. Their skill in the culinary arts gained such universal fame that officers from other corps, including General Meade himself, were known to find excuses for visiting their campfires around suppertime.[14]

Krzyżanowski attended one affair for which Captain Frederick Tiedemann donated several wild turkeys that he bagged on a safari into the surrounding countryside. Captain Otto von Fritsch of the 68th New York returned from leave that same day with a large barrel of lager beer to add to the festivities. Juicy helpings of fresh-roasted turkey, followed by bubbling cups of ever-popular lager succeeded in taking men's minds off the immediacy of the war. Many in the army poked fun at the Germans, stereotyping them due to their fondness for onions, sauerkraut and lager beer. Doctors later discovered that these ethnic staples proved to be excellent antidotes for dysentery, a disease which usually affected the Eleventh Corps less than the

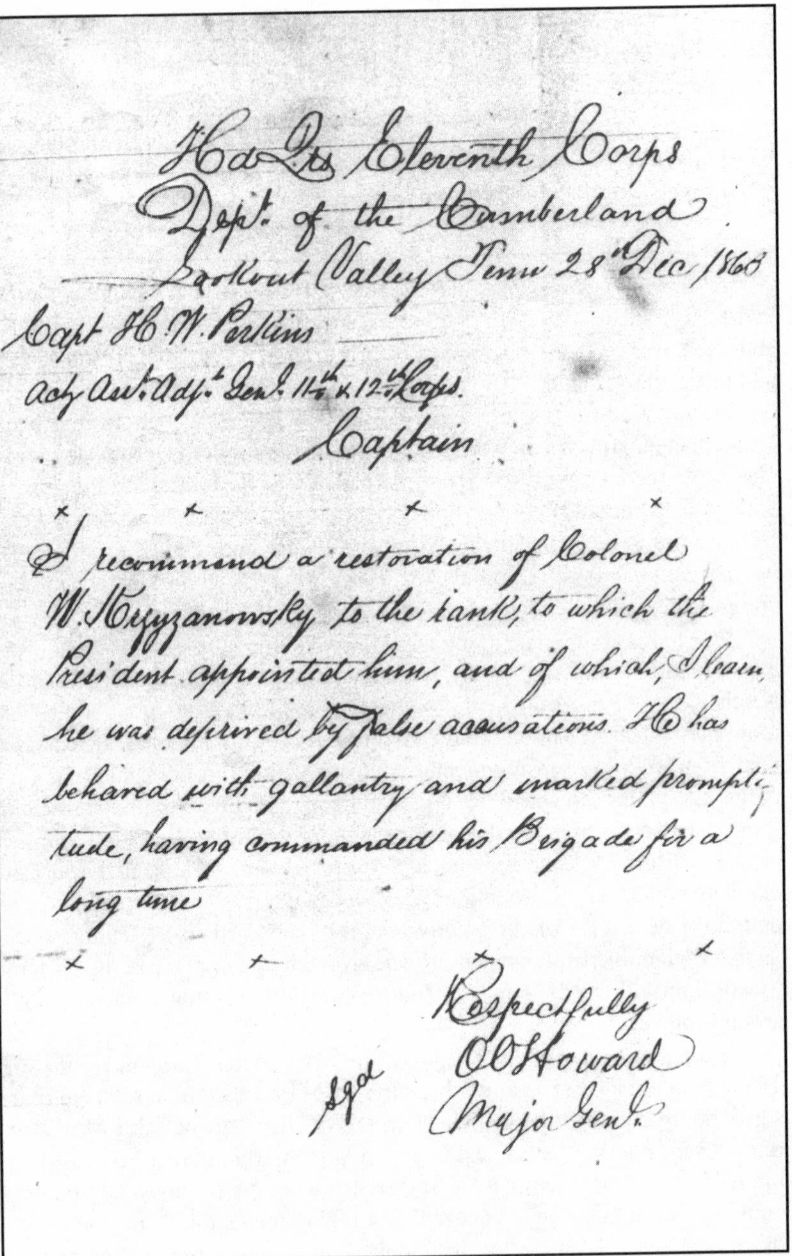

Hd Qrs Eleventh Corps
Dept. of the Cumberland
Lookout Valley Tenn 28th Dec 1863

Capt H. W. Perkins
Actg Asst. Adjt. Genl. 11th & 12th Corps.

Captain

I recommend a restoration of Colonel W. Krzyzanowsky to the rank, to which the President appointed him, and of which, I learn, he was deprived by false accusations. He has behaved with gallantry and marked promptitude, having commanded his Brigade for a long time

Respectfully
Sgd O. O. Howard
Major Genl.

A copy of Gen. Oliver O. Howard's endorsement of Krzyżanowski's nomination as brigadier general. This copy is taken from the letter books of the Eleventh Corps. *Courtesy of the National Archives and Record Service.*

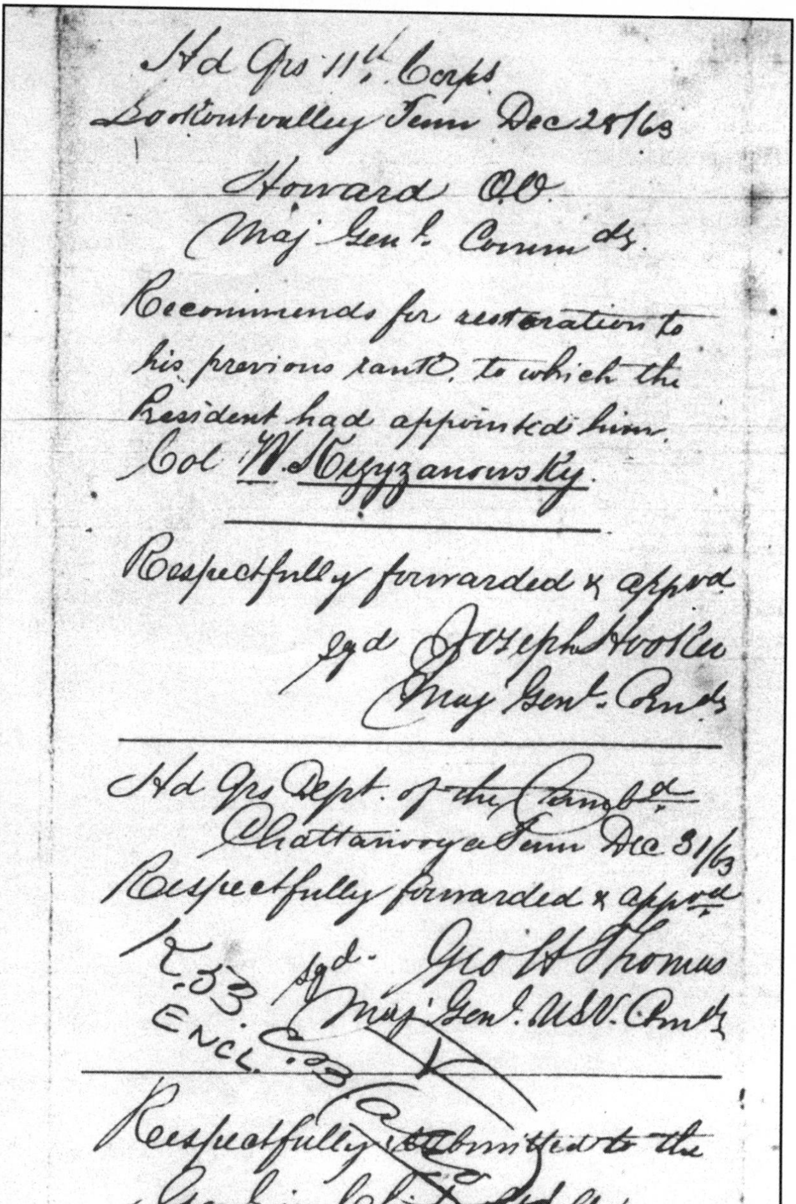
Hd Qrs 11th Corps
Lookout valley Tenn Dec 28/63
Howard O.O.
Maj Genl Commdg.
Recommends for restoration to
his previous rank, to which the
President had appointed him.
Col W. Krzyzanowsky.

Respectfully forwarded & appd
Sgd Joseph Hooker
Maj Genl Comdg

Hd Qrs Dept. of the Cumbd
Chattanooga Tenn Dec 31/63
Respectfully forwarded & approd
Sgd Geo H Thomas
Maj Genl USV Comdg
K.53
ENCL.

Respectfully submitted to the
Genl in Chief Halleck.

The jacket of Howard's letter of support for Krzyżanowski's promotion to brigadier general endorsed by Gens. Joseph Hooker and George H. Thomas for forwarding to General-in-Chief Henry Halleck. *Courtesy of the National Archives and Record Service.*

other army corps. In this case, the proverbial last laugh bore a distinctly "foreign" accent.[15]

Despite the abnormally mild weather, diseases flourished throughout August and September. A severe epidemic of typhoid fever swept through the camps disabling scores of men. Several fatalities occurred, including Private Alois Kötzdinger of the Sigel Regiment who drowned in the Rappahannock River. In early August, Kriz applied for a leave to attend to business in Washington. Although approved by the corps commander on August 11, Meade's headquarters disapproved the request noting that an order of the War Department prohibited officers from visiting the city and adding the comment that all able officers were needed and private business should be transacted by a power of attorney. Toward the end of August, however, Krzyżanowski contracted a serious case of bronchitis. His lungs filled, hampering his breathing. With little prospect for any further action that fall he decided that his presence could be spared until he recuperated. He applied for, and received, permission to take twenty days as sick leave on a "Surgeon's Certificate of Disability." On September 6 he boarded a train for Washington, leaving Colonel William Jacobs in command of the brigade. As the train chugged past guard posts and station houses, Kriz thought of his last visit to Washington so long ago. He dreamt longingly of the forthcoming reunion with his wife.[16]

A WESTWARD ODYSSEY

The train moved onward with Krzyżanowski staring into space, his mind lost on thoughts of his wife. Meanwhile, a thousand miles away, events began to unfold that would have a profound affect on the colonel and those under his command. For weeks Northern and Southern armies vied for position in an intricate series of maneuvers near Chattanooga, Tennessee. The campaign culminated on September 19-20 when General Braxton Bragg's Confederates defeated the Union forces in a bloody battle along Chickamauga Creek in Northwest Georgia. General William S. Rosecrans led his vanquished army back to Chattanooga where he determined to hold the city at all costs. While Bragg settled down to conduct a siege, Rosecrans telegraphed urgent appeals for help to the War Department in Washington.[17]

Responding to Rosecrans' appeals, Secretary of War Stanton, with the president's approval, ordered General Meade to dispatch two corps to proceed immediately to join forces gathering for the relief of Chattanooga. Meade regarded the order as an excellent opportunity to rid himself of two "problem" units. He chose the Eleventh Corps because of the army's prejudice toward it, and because it was under-strength. He chose the Twelfth Corps because it, too, was under-strength at this time, and its commander,

Henry Slocum, possessed a reputation as a military critic. Both of these corps traced their origins to Pope's Army of Virginia, yet, despite the recent campaigns, they were never accepted to full membership by the Army of the Potomac. The men in the Eleventh Corps felt just as happy to leave Virginia as the Army of the Potomac did to see them go. The relief expressed by Howard's men was tempered, however, by the War Department's decision to take Joseph Hooker off the shelf to lead the two corps. Few had any confidence in "Fighting Joe's" abilities after Chancellorsville, least of all the Eleventh Corps. Even General Howard had had enough of Hooker. The commander of the Eleventh Corps offered his resignation. Lincoln refused to accept it, and the mismatched command began its thousand mile Odyssey.[18]

While Krzyżanowski recuperated in Washington, marching orders arrived at Eleventh Corps headquarters on September 24. Colonel Jacobs led Krzyżanowski's brigade north from Rappahannock Station that same evening. After marching all night the tired command arrived at Manassas Junction early the next afternoon. There the men boarded waiting railroad cars for the trip to Alexandria, across the river from Washington. Kriz rejoined his brigade as it changed trains in Alexandria. He arrived to find that in his absence headquarters assigned Captain Frederick Otto von Fritsch to coordinate transportation for the brigade. The captain marveled at Krzyżanowski's cheerful attitude in accepting him as a member of his staff. He also complimented Kriz for the manner in which he volunteered his aid in making the move a successful one.[19]

At Alexandria the brigade cooked five days rations. Shortly, a long line of boxcars belonging to the Baltimore and Ohio Railroad appeared. The men clamored aboard, forty to sixty bodies shoving into each of the cramped cars. A pungent smell of manure greeted them, but speed was of the essence. No time could be wasted in cleaning out the wastes of the freight cars recent occupants. On the morning of September 26 the leading elements of the movement passed through Martinsburg, reaching Cumberland by mid-afternoon.[20]

At Benwood, on the Ohio River, the trains halted to deposit their load of human cargo. Grateful for the opportunity to get some fresh air, the men boarded ferries that carried them to Bellaire on the Ohio side of the river. Once again racing across the countryside, the air within the cars became hot and foul smelling. There was no opportunity to obtain food, water, or fresh air. Men found it impossible even to tend to the natural necessities of life. Sickened by the crowded conditions in the acrid cars, some soldiers chose to climb outside in search of relief. Perched precariously atop the boxcars, they enjoyed the fresh air and open scenery of southern Ohio. Unfortunately the urge to avoid the stifling atmosphere below placed the men in grave jeop-

Federal troops on a train passing through Harper's Ferry.
Courtesy of the United States Military Academy.

ardy when the speeding train passed under low bridges or entered darkened tunnels. Ernst Schaubhut, a drummer in the 58th New York, met his death by slipping from the roof of a boxcar as his train crossed a river near Zanesville.[21]

Enthusiastic crowds directed welcoming cheers toward the troops as their trains sped out of Ohio into Indiana. Wherever a momentary halt occurred the citizens offered refreshments to the huddled mass of humanity within the boxcars. Travel through the North proved quite different than marching along hostile Virginia roads. From Indianapolis the tracks turned south to Jeffersonville, a town on the Ohio River. Ferries carried men and equipment to Louisville, where they again boarded trains for Nashville. Miraculously, the bulk of the Eleventh and Twelfth Corps reached the Tennessee capital by October 1. "How we got the two Corps alive to Nashville in seven days it is difficult to explain," marveled Capt. von Fritsch, "as our men were so crowded, had so little chance to obtain water or food, and, locked up in the cars, had neither fresh air enough nor even the ordinary necessities of life."[22]

Krzyżanowski's brigade arrived at Bridgeport, Alabama, on October 2, 1863, only eight days after leaving Rappahannock Station. Within eleven and one-half days, two entire army corps numbering 17,500 men rested on the banks of the Tennessee River. In that short space of time ten batteries of artillery with forty-five guns, 717 wagons and ambulances, over 4,400 horses and mules, and all of the two corps' baggage traveled over some 1,192 miles of track. It was the largest, most successful rail movement in the entire history of warfare. This use of railroads opened a new dimension in military science heretofore explored on only a limited basis.[23]

A "HELLISH DANCE" IN TENNESSEE

Mud! If you had to describe Alabama that October you did not have to go beyond that simple word. Since early July the tri-state area surrounding Chattanooga sweltered under a scorching sun that cracked and hardened the ground like a kiln. Not a single drop of rain fell in the three months since then. Nature chose to remedy this oversight with a vengeance shortly after Krzyżanowski arrived in Bridgeport. Overnight a torrential downpour turned parched, blistered earth into clinging mucilage that entombed everything with wheels. Roads became impassable. Supplies grew scarce. When men opened barrels of crackers they were greeted by hundreds of glutted worms. Improperly packaged salt-pork rotted into contaminated refuse. For several days, until the deluge abated, the men subsisted on half-rations. Sutlers scalped food and other supplies at outrageous prices in blatant profiteering. Many soldiers followed the lead of Charles Wickesberg in the 26th Wisconsin by writing home for tea and new clothing.[24]

Despite the rain and mud, Krzyżanowski could not afford to waste time on inactivity. While the army prepared for its thrust toward Chattanooga, Kriz organized daily reconnaissance patrols to ascertain the strength and position of the enemy. It was a glamorless, fatiguing job, but one that was necessary if the coming campaign were to meet with success. On October 19, Carl Schurz reorganized his division into three brigades. This meant that Kriz lost the services of the veteran 75th Pennsylvania and 68th New York. Only four regiments remained under his command during the ensuing campaign: Colonel William Jacobs' 26th Wisconsin, Captain Michael Esembaux's 58th New York, Lt. Colonel John T. Lockman's 119th New York, and Lt. Colonel William T. Logie's 141st New York.[25]

In order to relieve the troops besieged in Chattanooga the Northern armies needed to secure possession of a rail and water route into the city. With this objective in mind the eastern infantrymen began their campaign on October 26. At Bridgeport Kriz led his men across the Tennessee River. With this great waterway safely behind him, he advanced northeast along the base of Raccoon Mountain. At Lookout Creek Confederate pickets burned a wooden bridge, but Krzyżanowski's skirmishers quickly put the rebels to

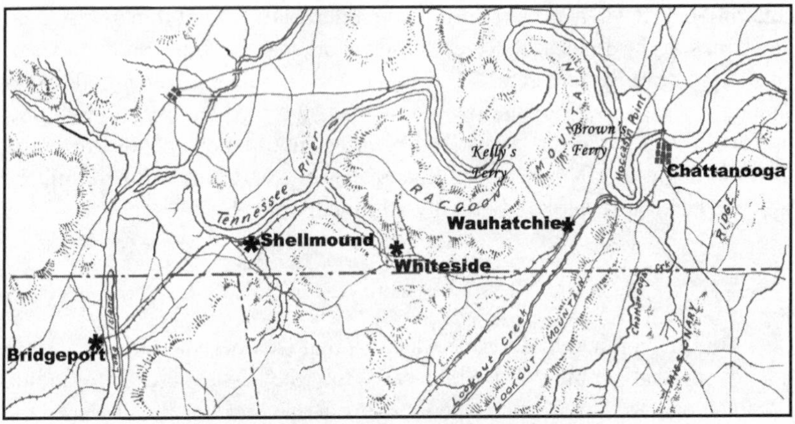

Map of the Chattanooga Campaign.
Adapted by the author from the Official Records.

flight. Kriz directed his men across the narrow stream with relative ease. Cautiously he advanced beyond it into Lookout Valley.[26]

Posted high above the narrow, rocky roads, on the steep, craggy slopes of Lookout Mountain, Confederate artillery lobbed shells upon the blue-clad infantry below. Krzyżanowski advanced with prudent caution, placing flankers to guard against any ambush. It was well that he did. The report of hostile muskets burst upon his skirmishers from a woods bordering the dirt road. Kriz quickly rushed reinforcements forward. Maneuvering his men diligently against the unseen sharpshooters, he soon outflanked the woods, turning its protective veil into a veritable trap for its occupants. With the proficiency of veterans who gained their experience the hard way—on the hard-fought fields of Virginia and Pennsylvania—Krzyżanowski's men methodically cleared the hostile area at a cost of one man dead and one wounded. Their marksmanship proved exceptional, killing four rebels and wounding at least eight more.[27]

By 3:00 P.M. Kriz reached Brown's Ferry on the Tennessee River, accomplishing the perilous transit of Lookout Valley. Smiling with success, General Hooker ordered a halt for the evening before all of his forces had arrived. Although most of the units lay around Brown's Ferry, General John W. Geary's division halted at Wauhatchie some three miles away. Observing this division of forces, Confederate General Bragg determined to destroy Geary's isolated force by means of a daring night assault by troops under the Eleventh Corps' opponent from the east, Gen. James Longstreet. He ordered General Micah Jenkins' division to attack Geary, taking care also to dispatch General Evander Law's command to prevent Hooker from sending relief to

Col. William K. Logie
141st New York Infantry
Courtesy of the U.S. Army Military History Institute.

the isolated Union division. Law placed his blocking force on a small hillock overlooking the Brown's Ferry-Wauhatchie Road.[28]

While Bragg maneuvered his forces for the attack, Hooker, repeating his earlier errors at Chancellorsville, congratulated himself upon the success of his movement while taking no additional precautions against a Confederate attack. In the twilight hours of October 28 he remained inactive, allowing his troops to cook supper, relax, and retire for the evening. As darkness enveloped Lookout Valley, firing occasionally broke out along the picket lines. Once again, as he had done nearly six months before, Hooker took but little notice of it.[29]

About midnight the familiar thunder of guns echoed down the valley from Wauhatchie. Roused by this unexpected alarm, Kriz rose in an instant. A quick series of orders brought his men into formation, ready to respond when needed. As the colonel formed his ranks, Hooker instructed Schurz to move his troops to Geary's aid. Kriz fell in line behind Hector Tyndale's brigade, which led a hasty rush into the darkness. Colonel Friedrich Hecker's brigade followed Krzyżanowski, with Orland Smith's brigade from Steinwehr's division bringing up the rear.[30]

Kriz marched back along the narrow road he advanced upon that afternoon. Though illuminated by a bright moon, the shadows of surrounding hills and woods produced an awesome, eerily ominous scene. Suddenly a blazing volley of musketry exploded out of the darkness to strike down several unsuspecting men in the lead brigade. Schurz ordered Tyndale to advance on the unseen enemy. Quickly he sent an aide to instruct Kriz to halt and await the outcome of the fight. It was a sound move. For all Schurz knew the murky shadows ahead might conceal a whole army.[31]

As soon as he received Schurz's order, Krzyżanowski stopped his advance. He moved his brigade off the roadway to make room for others, then formed his regiments in an open field facing the sound of the firing. Drawn up in double lines, the men stood prepared to either receive an assault or move forward as the situation might dictate. While Kriz deployed,

Colonel Hecker, receiving no order to halt, continued along the road until he passed Krzyżanowski's stationary brigade. At that point Hecker met one of General Howard's aides, who ordered him to halt as Kriz had done.[32]

By the time Orland Smith's brigade arrived, Tyndale's troops successfully uncovered the rebel positions. Side by side, Smith and Tyndale advanced up the small hillock against Law's Confederates. In minutes the Southerners began retreating. As they did, Hooker arrived upon the field in front of Krzyżanowski's brigade. Standing beside each other, the general and the Polish colonel peered into the night to catch a glimpse of the distant muzzle flashes.[33]

Throughout the fight confusion reigned among Northern generals. While Schurz effectively managed the assault upon Law, Hooker and Howard took it upon themselves to issue direct, and sometimes contradictory orders to the different brigade commanders. Missives arrived directing Krzyżanowski to move alternately to Wauhatchie and then to Chattanooga, a complete change of direction. Further orders called upon him to move to Geary, and then to hold his position. Finally, an order from Schurz obliged Kriz to move part of his brigade forward to close a gap between the brigades of Tyndale and Smith. The order specifically directed the colonel to lead his men in person because the position was one of great importance. In less than ten minutes Krzyżanowski led his two largest regiments into the breach, holding his ground until the conflict ended. He left behind him, at his original position, little more than color guards, his remaining two regiments being much depleted in strength after posting the division's pickets and detailing men to escort prisoners back to Chattanooga.[34]

When order finally replaced confusion among the generals directing the action, Hecker's brigade, reinforced by Krzyżanowski's 141st New York, received belated orders to advance to Geary's aid. Kriz spent a sleepless night holding the position assigned to him. At 6:00 A.M. he received orders to advance to Wauhatchie. The firing had long since ceased, but Kriz nevertheless carried out his directive with great alacrity. He covered the three miles in about an hour, arriving at Geary's headquarters in person at 7:15 A.M. Kriz placed his men on the far right of Geary's line where they extended the defensive line to include a vital railroad junction. According to Geary's report, Krzyżanowski's men carried out their task of constructing breastworks and traverses with a great deal of skill and cheerfulness.[35]

The Battle of Wauhatchie was a disorganized affair. In many respects it later defied explanation. Even the commanding officers involved produced conflicting, or at least differing, accounts of the action. Neither Confederate nor Union losses approached the terrible tolls exacted by Chancellorsville or Gettysburg, yet the result was impressive. The gateway to Chattanooga stood open and Rosecrans' forces received an early Christmas gift, a new lease on life.

The commanding generals were effusive in their praise of the Eastern soldiers. On November 1, Hooker transmitted to the troops his own compliments, along with those of Gen. George H. Thomas who commanded the troops besieged in Chattanooga. Howard wrote:

> It is with extreme pleasure that the Major General Commanding communicates to the troops comprising the 11th Corps and to the 2nd Division of the 12th Corps the subjoined letter from the Major General Commanding the Army of the Cumberland expressive of his appreciation of your distinguished services on the night of the 28th inst.
>
> It is a notable tribute to your good conduct from a brave and devoted soldier.
>
> The general hopes that it will inspire as much satisfaction in the breasts of his officers and men as it has in his own, and that we may all be stimulated by it to renewed efforts to secure the good opinion of our commander while we also emulate the courage and valor of our companions in arms.[36]

The attached letter from Thomas read:

> I most heartily congratulate you and the troops under your command at the brilliant success you gained over your old adversary (Longstreet) on the night of the 28th inst.
>
> The bayonet charge of Howard's troops, made up the sides of a steep and difficult hill over 200 feet high, completely routing and driving the enemy from his barricades on its top, and the repulse by Geary's Division of greatly superior numbers who attempted to surprise him will rank among the most distinguished feats of this war.[37]

Now that the vital supply line to Chattanooga was open it had to be protected. For the first three weeks in November the task of protecting this "Cracker Line" went to Krzyżanowski and his comrades in the Eleventh Corps. It was a glamorless assignment, but one which was essential to the success of the Chattanooga campaign.

Confederate artillery on the summit of Lookout Mountain, 1,464 feet above the valley below, dominated the landscape for miles around. Each day, with routine regularity, Southern gunners hurled explosive shells upon the Union lines. Though they did little actual damage, the shells did create some tense moments. The constant booming of rebel guns became so much a part of the soldiers' daily lives that they fashioned a game out of it. Eager eyes scanned Lookout Mountain for the puff of smoke that invariably identified the firing of a cannon. When one occurred the soldiers quickly placed bets on where the deadly projectile would hit.[38]

As the month progressed, rations became scarce. For a week, chilling rains fell almost daily. Intensified by the cool, damp climate, sickness spread throughout the ranks. When the brigade finally left Lookout Valley on November 22 it numbered only 979 men, less than a single regulation-size regiment.[39]

Krzyżanowski left Lookout Valley under orders to support General William T. Sherman's proposed assault on the Confederate lines east of Chattanooga. Crossing the Tennessee River on pontoon bridges at Brown's Ferry, Kriz led his troops north to Chattanooga. Marching past the city, he re-crossed the Tennessee River to the east, arriving on the far left of the Union position. The brigade moved into line in time to support Sherman's assault on Orchard Knob. Following this successful attack, the 26th Wisconsin fought a sharp skirmish at Citico Creek enabling Kriz to place his brigade so as to cover the otherwise exposed flank of the Northern army.[40]

For the next two days Krzyżanowski directed his men in silencing Southern sharpshooters so that guns could be moved up to support an assault on Missionary Ridge. As he stood watching the huge siege guns moved into position, his men brought in a number of recently captured Southern prisoners. One dejected officer from the group hailed Kriz as the band of captives trudged past.[41]

"General," the officer called, "please explain to me why you bring these large cannon."

"In order to drive you into the sea," came the reply, "so we can finish this hellish dance."

"Be careful, General," warned the rebel with the foreboding of a Shakespearean soothsayer, "that the fire from these cannon does not also touch you."

"How can this be possible?" asked Kriz, sensing an evil prediction of doom.

"Oh, very easily!" replied the disheartened Southerner. "The Confederacy is so tightly surrounded by your armies that if you fire into them it is apt to go right through them and into your own soldiers standing on the other side."

Not all of the Confederates were so despondent. Forty thousand defiant men rallied to their colors floating atop Missionary Ridge. On November 25 General Ulysses S. Grant, Federal commander-in-chief in the west, ordered an assault on the Confederate rifle pits at the base of Missionary Ridge. As the assault waves moved forward, Kriz pushed back the Southern skirmishers on the Union left, thus preventing the attackers from being caught in a deadly enfilading fire. Grant's men easily overpowered the rifle pits. Then, without orders, they surged up the steep slope. With Northern generals looking on in utter disbelief the Southern infantry on the crest of Missionary

Ridge broke, fleeing from the scene in absolute rout.[42]

Jubilant Union infantry followed the panic-stricken Confederates. Tons of abandoned supplies and equipment fell into the hands of Grant's victorious troops. Formal pursuit began on the following day, but had to be called off on November 28. Instead of continuing the pursuit of Bragg, Grant was obliged to answer the plea of Union forces under General Ambrose Burnside who were trapped in Knoxville by James Longstreet's corps from the Army of Northern Virginia.[43]

THE RELIEF OF KNOXVILLE

The most important factor in the relief of Knoxville was time. Burnside's army lay on the verge of starvation. A delay, even of a day or two, could spell doom for his troops. Krzyżanowski's men marched lightly, forsaking tents and supply wagons for the sake of speed. Weighted down with ammunition, the men were able to squeeze very little food into their blanket rolls or knapsacks.[44]

Marching steadily through damp, cool air, Krzyżanowski reached Riceville without incident at noon on December 1. That evening found him camped at Athens. More hard marching on the following day brought Kriz through Sweetwater and Philadelphia. On December 3 he led the division's advance upon Loudon, Tennessee, a major Confederate supply base. In battle array, his brigade pushed forward into the outskirts of the city, only to find it deserted of its defenders. Large quantities of supplies fell to Krzyżanowski's men, along with a hospital containing 300 sick and wounded enemy troops.[45]

After a brief halt to allow the rest of the scattered columns to consolidate, Kriz resumed the advance. East of Loudon the 141st New York fought a small skirmish with Southern guerrillas. Small, that is, for everyone except Henry Miller. It cost him his life.[46]

Continuing on in the face of sporadic sniping, Kriz made remarkable speed over the muddy roadways. By December 5 the Federal advance came within striking distance of Knoxville. This rapid movement of the Union troops foiled General Longstreet's plans for starving Burnside into submission. Convinced that he could not maintain his siege against the Northern reinforcements, Longstreet launched a disastrous frontal assault, then withdrew his troops back into Virginia. The Confederate siege of Knoxville failed because of the rapid marching and willing sacrifices of thousands of Union infantrymen. Not the least of these were the officers and men of Krzyżanowski's brigade.[47]

The end of the siege of Knoxville brought little rest for the rescuers. Krzyżanowski halted for one day, then, on December 7, began the arduous march back toward Chattanooga without ever having seen the city he helped save. With food supplies now exhausted, the nearby farms fell prey to Northern foragers struggling to survive off the countryside. Frequent rains covered the cold, rocky roads with thick, oozing mud. One man in four lacked shoes. Blankets were a luxury. Threadbare clothing proved inadequate against the icy December rains. Brutally cold winds brought sleet that produced a muddy bog by day, a frozen marsh at night. Perpetually damp clothing froze to men's bodies as they slept. Equipment parked overnight had to be pried free in the morning before it could be moved. Even the supply of coffee gave out, forcing the men to roast corn or wheat kernels as a substitute. It was, Krzyżanowski said simply, a "terrible ordeal."[48]

Lashed by freezing winds, pummeled by thunderstorms and sleet, intimidated by lightening, many of Krzyżanowski's weary men developed acute bronchitis. Tired, sore, cold and hungry, the ragged columns of scarecrows arrived back at their camps near Chattanooga on December 17. There were no supplies awaiting them. No one expected them back so soon. Rather than sustenance, the men found only words of censure from General Howard who chastised them for their foraging expeditions. Given the privations of the campaign, little else could realistically have been expected.

Analysis

Fortunately, the expedition commander displayed a better understanding of the circumstances surrounding the march. In a letter to Howard, General Sherman enthusiastically praised the conduct of the Eleventh Corps during the successful campaign, noting especially "a spirit of cheerfulness that was reflected in the conduct and behavior of your whole command. I beg you will convey to Genl. Schurz, Col. Buschbeck and all your officers the assurance of my personal and official respect.[49]

Freed from the prejudices of the Army of the Potomac and the eastern press, the Eleventh Corps performed well. Making an historic redeployment by railroad to Tennessee, it successfully relieved the Confederate sieges of Chattanooga and Knoxville in successive campaigns, in the process demonstrating its military capabilities not only against Braxton Bragg's army, but against the corps' old nemesis James Longstreet. For his part, Krzyżanowski also performed well, leading his men through grueling marches in severe weather, conducting scouting and patrol activities, and engaging the Confederates as part of the movement to save the trapped Union troops in Chattanooga. The plaudits of the western commanders were welcome words to the colonel and the other officers and men of the Eleventh Corps who found in the west both success and appreciation that had eluded them in the east.

— CHAPTER EIGHT —

"VETERAN VOLUNTEERS"

FURLOUGH AND FRAMEUP

By the end of 1863 the Federal government began to feel the pinch of reduced enlistments in Northern armies. Attempts to enforce mandatory conscription resulted in a series of draft riots throughout the North. In a further effort to attract recruits the Federal, state and local governments began to offer monetary bonuses to those who would sign up for three years of service. In an effort to reclaim the services of its trained, experienced personnel, the Northern government also attempted to induce men with two years experience into re-enlisting for an additional three years. In return for their continued services the government offered a $400 bounty plus thirty days leave with government transportation.[1]

This incentive appealed to many soldiers, but Krzyżanowski determined to leave nothing to chance. His own regiment was already beginning its third year of service. Thus, most of its members were eligible to re-enlist under this new system. The colonel held a profound belief in the cause for which he fought. Long months of hardship and sacrifice only served to strengthen the comradeship that bound him to the officers and men of his command. He hoped that the attachment he felt for his men was a mutual emotion through which he could appeal to them to continue the fight to its conclusion. Risking personal disappointment, Kriz announced that he would resign his command if his old regiment did not re-enlist.[2]

Word of this declaration quickly spread through the Eleventh Corps camps. On the same day he made his intention known a delegation from the Polish Legion informed him that they would re-enlist only on the assurance that their colonel remained in command. Responding to further inquiries, Krzyżanowski asked his old regiment to form ranks in the middle of a large field. Sitting astride his horse so that he might be seen by all, Kriz spoke to his comrades-in-arms as one soldier would to another. He commended them for their spirit and heroism. He emphasized his personal pride at the sacrifices they had made for their cause. Finally, he tenderly eulogized the dead and wounded no longer with them. The sincerity of his words was apparent, greatly touching his listeners. His oration complete, Kriz paused to look into the eyes of the faces ranged about him. Slowly, deliberately, he asked those who would serve with him until victory was achieved to take four steps forward. By ones and twos at first, then in a great surge, his adopted family responded to his plea. Surely this handful of men was not the decisive factor in the war, but that did not matter. For Kriz it was a day of immense personal satisfaction.[3]

The woodcut of Krzyżanowski that appeared in *Frank Leslie's Illustrated Newspaper*, March 12, 1864, announcing his reenlistment.

Krzyżanowski's men were the very first in the entire Army of the Cumberland to re-enlist as true "veterans." *Frank Leslie's Illustrated Newspaper* noted the occasion with a woodcut engraving of Kriz and the favorable comment that "All his regiments have re-enlisted asking but one question—whether he was to lead them."[4] Despite their past burdens and abuse, over seventy-five percent of the Eleventh Corps followed the lead of Krzyżanowski's men in re-enlisting as "Veteran Volunteers."[5]

January 8 was a day of great activity in Krzyżanowski's camp as men rushed about finalizing preparations for their thirty days leave. Captain Emil Koenig, whose Polish Legion numbered only 184 men, reorganized his regiment into four companies for the anticipated move. Company officers, he emphasized, would be held strictly accountable for the conduct of their men during the trip. Kriz left those who were not yet eligible for re-enlistment under the command of Colonel John T. Lockman from the 119th New York. The following day, January 9, 1864, the patchwork brigade of veteran regiments boarded trains for the journey north, then east. The 58th and 68th New York were bound for New York City. The 75th Pennsylvania accompanied them as far as Philadelphia, while the 82nd Ohio left the procession at Columbus to change trains for Kenton. The journey barely began when the 54th New York requested permission to join them. Kriz gladly consented, happy to once again share his accommodations with his old friends from the Schwarze Jäger.[6]

Arriving in Washington, D.C., Krzyżanowski's men found the capitol's streets lined with enthusiastic citizens voicing their greetings. As the veterans marched through the city, a newspaper correspondent reported that "their bronze features indicated the hardships they had passed through and the service they had performed. As they marched ... they won the admiration of all beholders for their manly and soldierly bearing. Although rough in appearance, they were the finest set of men that have yet returned from the seat of war. ... Their battle flags are literally torn to shreds, having been shot to pieces. So completely riddled are they that the names of the battles in which the regiment has been engaged could not be placed on them, and they are inscribed on a streamer of red, white and blue."[7]

At their rendezvous point, the men were presented floral wreaths by local ladies and a feast greeted them with delicacies they had not tasted in many months. "During the offering of the wreaths by the ladies," Krzyżanowski wrote, "and during the welcoming speeches which were made by the heads of the city, my heart, which had been hardened by the storms and thunders of war, accustomed to the sight of blood, death and conflagration, surrendered itself to the emotion of happiness, the signs of undeserved recognition bringing tears into my eyes."[8]

From Washington, Kriz led the remaining regiments to New York City, arriving about 10:00 A.M. on January 26, 1864. The reception the veterans received would have rivaled the Caesar's triumphs in Rome. Following a brief rest at the Erie Railroad depot, the men marched to the Atlantic Gardens. Thousands of people turned out to welcome them home. The 5th New York State Militia under Col. Christian Burger, outfitted in spanking new blue uniforms with immaculately polished buttons, presented quite a contrast to the faded, haphazardly stitched apparel worn by the veterans of so many bloody fields. Nevertheless, as the procession marched up Broadway to be personally reviewed by the mayor all eyes fell on the returning heroes. Ladies threw bouquets of garlands in their path, while men and boys cheered as loud as they could. At City Hall, the militia formed a guard of honor while the returning veterans marched past to present their torn and tattered colors to the mayor, returning them with honor to the city from whence they came forth to defend the Union. The banners of the 58th New York created a particularly poignant sight, being so severely torn by the rigors of campaigns and engagements.[9]

An eloquent speech by Mayor C. Godfrey Gunther led to an equally eloquent response by the Polish colonel. Following the review and attending ceremonies, the troops marched along Broadway to 14th Street, then down to the Bowery where the procession ended at the Atlantic Gardens. New York opened itself to these men, most of whom had not seen home in over two years. A saloon deep in the heart of the German Bowery offered free food and drink all that day and well into the night, a local newspaper reporting that "the soldiers 'fell to' in a vigorous manner, demolishing meats,

A *Carte de Visite* photograph of the presentation sword given to Krzyżanowski by the officers and men of the 2nd Brigade, 3rd Division, Eleventh Corps, Army of the Cumberland. *Courtesy of Steven Gunther.*

---

cakes, wines and lager in truly gigantic proportions." For Kriz, the personal highlight came at a banquet attended by some 3,000 people. Reunited with his beloved wife, he sat at the head table indulging himself in culinary delicacies he forgot even existed. He listened intently, trying to hold back the emotions which arose within him as the mayor delivered an eloquent welcoming speech. James T. Brady, who had handed the regiment its colors when it mustered into service in 1861, was on hand to receive the return of the tattered and torn remnants to the city whence they came. "Of the many receptions of returned volunteers," concluded the *New York Times*, the honors done yesterday to the Fifty-eighth and Sixty-eighth exceed them all, not possibly in splendor of 'turn-out,' but in a genuine hearty welcome."[10]

The New York press described another ceremony held at No. 99, First Avenue, in which Krzyżanowski received "a magnificent sword, sash and belt" following "a princely repast ... which the numerous guests partook with great and evident gusto, and which was heightened by the lively strains of a fine band." The presentation of the sword from a fraternal association included a gold scabbard and inscribed hilt with the Master Mason's Third Degree on one side and "From yours, S. Steinfeld" on the other. Mr. Steinfeld made the presentation, speaking eloquently

> of the gallant Colonel's ennobling qualities as a citizen, a patriot and a military commander. He said he had not failed to remember that when the tocsin of our country's danger was sounded, and the very seat of our federal government was threatened with pillage and desecration, the General, with

> martial energy, called around him a spartan band and threw himself into the breach beneath the eye of our President. He was well aware that he committed the sword into hands that would never suffer its blade to be sullied, or be sheathed until an honorable peace had been conquered.[11]

The citizens of New York treated Krzyżanowski's men like liberators. The men responded to their queries by ascribing to their commander, in their long-winded commentaries, far more than he ever really achieved. On February 4 the officers and men who served with Kriz met at Bang's Restaurant where the soldiers presented their commander with another sword. Dr. R. Dalon offered the presentation speech in German, while Kriz replied in English, noting that he was "proud of the gift and the gallant and noble men who presented it." He would, he concluded, draw it only "in defense of liberty." The sword's hilt had engraved upon it the Goddess of Liberty, the American eagle and a flag of stars. The silver scabbard had inscribed upon one side the battles in which the men fought, while the opposite side contained the inscription: "Presented by the officers and men of the Second Brigade, Third Division, Eleventh Corps as a token of their regard, December 25, 1863."[12]

For thirty days Kriz found himself in an Eden divorced from the trials and tribulations of army life. His most rewarding experience was certainly the opportunity to once again share his life with his loving wife Caroline. The restful atmosphere brought back memories of better times, of peaceful days and youthful abandon. Nevertheless, even now, while Krzyżanowski and his veterans enjoyed the rewards of their re-enlistments, forces were at work in the West to cast aspersion upon all they achieved.[13]

COURT OF INQUIRY

If General Hooker learned anything from the tangled web of deceit he weaved following Chancellorsville he certainly did not show it in his actions during the winter of 1863-64. Although most observers heaped praise upon the eastern infantrymen for their conduct at Wauhatchie, General Hooker refused to credit Schurz's division with its share in the fighting. Hooker claimed that Schurz arrived too late to aid Geary, and in his official report on the action he condemned Colonel Hecker for his failure to march to Geary's relief sooner.[14]

To Schurz, Hooker's actions meant but one thing—revenge for the disparaging comments that men of the Eleventh Corps made about Hooker's character and ability after Chancellorsville. What made Schurz even angrier was that Hooker did not observe the common courtesy of consulting him prior to making the statements public. Instead, Hooker released his accusations with no advance warning at all. Livid, Schurz demanded a formal Court of Inquiry.[15] Charles Howard summed up the salient points with exceptional clarity and foresight in a letter to his brother, General O.O. Howard:

> Schurz is going to have not so easy a victory with Hooker I think. Hecker will prove that I communicated an order for him to halt but Gen. Hooker will hold that he never authorized me to give any such order and moreover will affirm that he supposed Krzszanozki [*sic*] was marching on with his brigade. And I think Schurz cannot show that Krzysanowski [*sic*] had any order to halt.[16]

The sharp retort of a gavel brought the first session of the Court of Inquiry to order at 11:00 A.M. on January 29, 1864. The composition of the Court about to consider the testimony of the various witnesses was remarkable. Colonel Adolf Buschbeck, commanding the Second Division of the Eleventh Corps, served as presiding officer. Seated about him as colleagues were Colonel James Wood, commanding the Second Brigade, Second Division, Eleventh Corps; Colonel P. H. Jones of the 154th New York Infantry; and Captain W. H. Lambert of the 33rd New Jersey Infantry. General Schurz immediately noted the uniqueness of the arrangements. In a breach of usual procedures, not a single member of the tribunal ranked as a peer of the man upon whom the primary charges fell.[17]

When Captain Lambert, the recorder, read the terms under which Special Order No. 23 convened the Court, another discrepancy became apparent. General Schurz originally requested the Court of Inquiry in order to investigate the aspersions that General Hooker had cast upon himself and Colonel Hecker. The order authorizing the Court, however, empowered it to delve into the conduct of any portion of Schurz's command. A highly irregular procedure in the first place, Schurz further objected to broadening the scope of the inquiry because the principal witnesses from Krzyżanowski's brigade were not available for testimony. Schurz called upon General George H. Thomas, then commanding the Army of the Cumberland, for a ruling that would limit the Court's activities to the original complaint. Thomas refused.[18]

With these procedural questions settled, albeit in irregular fashion, the Court proceeded with the business of presenting the offending portion of the report in question. From the official commentary of General Joseph Hooker, the recorder read the following paragraph into the record.

> I regret my duty constrains me to except any portion of my command in my commendation of their courage and valor. The brigade dispatched to the relief of Geary by orders delivered in person to its division command-

> er, never reached him until long after the fight had ended. It is alleged that it lost its way, when it had a terrific infantry fire to guide it all the way, and also that it became involved in a swamp, where there was no swamp or other obstacle between it and Geary which should have delayed it a moment in marching to the relief of its imperiled companions.[19]

From this paragraph General Schurz inferred a damaging slur upon his conduct. Colonel Hecker, concluding that the brigade in question was his, deduced the same smear upon his reputation. Seeking to clarify the nature of the problem, the Court called to the witness stand the author of the offending remarks. "Fighting Joe" responded to several questions posed by the Court recorder.[20]

"What division," Lambert inquired, "is alluded to in the report?"

"The division of General Schurz," came the affirmative reply.

"Was General Schurz in command of the division?"

"He was," answered Hooker.

"What orders were given by you to the division commander?"

"To double-quick his division to the relief of General Geary," Hooker replied. "I gave the order to General Schurz direct, and sent word to General Howard, for the attack was a sudden one, and no time was to be lost."

"Were any other orders given to the commander of the division," Lambert asked, "or to the commanders of the brigades?"

"I had nothing to do with brigades," came Hooker's emphatic retort. "Orders were given for one brigade of that division to be sent to the hill now known as the Tyndale Hill."

The nature of the allegations thus became clear. Hooker ordered Schurz's division to Geary's aid. Hooker never countermanded or altered these orders, and never issued other orders to any of the brigades. The failure to relieve Geary, then, must rest on the shoulders of Carl Schurz.

Slowly, his eyes glaringly fixed on the witness, General Schurz rose to cross-examine his old nemesis.

"Do you consider all the statement in your report relative to the Third Division correct in every particular?"

"I do."

"You speak in your report of the brigade dispatched to the relief of General Geary," Schurz noted. "Which of General Schurz's brigades was that?"

Hooker would not be duped that easily.

"The whole division was under orders to go to General Geary," he replied. "Afterward one brigade was detached to go to attack the enemy on the Tyndale Hill; the remainder of the division was the brigade alluded to."

"You speak in your report of only two brigades," Schurz noted, referring to an obvious inconsistency in Hooker's story. "Was it known to you at the time that General Schurz had three brigades?"

"I am not positive," Hooker evaded, "but I think it must have been."

Schurz did not relent. He wanted a definite commitment on what Hooker professed to be his knowledge on the night in question.

"Did you see or hear anything of the Second Brigade [Krzyżanowski] of General Schurz's division being behind at the time you saw Colonel Hecker, or afterward?"

"I only saw," Hooker affirmed, "what I took to be Colonel Hecker's brigade of the division. If I had supposed there were two brigades behind I should have ordered them, irrespective of General Howard's orders, to the relief of General Geary."[21]

Several basic questions emerged from this testimony. Fundamental to the proceedings were the two original objections raised by Schurz and Hecker. Was (1) General Schurz or (2) Colonel Hecker guilty of misconduct during the Battle of Wauhatchie? Added to these queries were the statements that "Fighting Joe" offered as factual recollection during his testimony. Hooker positively asserted that: (3) he issued no orders directly to the brigade commanders, (4) he ordered Schurz's whole division to double-quick to Geary's aid, and (5) he did not know the whereabouts of the Second Brigade commanded by Col. Krzyżanowski.

In addition to these questions and assertions, two other points of interest arose on this, the first day of the inquest. Hooker stated that had he known there were two brigades of Schurz's division stopped, he would have ordered them forward "irrespective of General Howard's orders." This, of course, suggests that the two brigades were stopped under General Howard's orders. It is a point worth remembering. Secondly, it was apparent from comparing Hooker's initial report with his testimony that the commanding general was not aware of either the names of the officers leading Schurz's brigades, or even the number of brigades Schurz had at his disposal. This was certainly an inexcusable negligence, especially since the corps operated under Hooker's command for several months in the spring and summer of 1863 and again once the movement west commenced in September 1863. Surely this was but one example of the indifference the Army of the Potomac had held toward the "Dutchmen" of the Eleventh Corps.

In order to absolve Schurz and Hecker it was necessary to prove that: (1) Schurz had no available troops to effect the move, and (2) Hecker acted under orders in not advancing to Geary's aid. The Court proceeded with its task.

Regarding General Schurz, it was necessary to establish exactly what orders he received. For this purpose the Court swore in Captain Robert H. Hall, an aide-de-camp to General Hooker.[22]

"Did you carry any orders during the night of the engagement of

Wauhatchie?" Schurz inquired.

" I did," Hall replied.

"What orders did you carry, and to whom?" asked the bespectacled German-American.

"The order to General Schurz to move his nearest brigade, the brigade nearest to General Geary, to his assistance."

Thus it appears that the original order given to Schurz called for only one brigade to move to Geary's aid. Of course, it is very possible that Captain Hall delivered an erroneous order. Nevertheless, he stated clearly what order he did deliver, and that order called for but one single brigade. The order carried by Hall was followed by a similar order brought by Lieutenant Paul A. Oliver, who shed further light on the original directive as well as one that Schurz received instructing him to carry by assault what later became known as Tyndale Hill. General Schurz began the questioning.[23]

"What orders did you communicate to General Schurz?"

"I took the order to him to get his division or brigade—I am not certain which—under arms, and occupy the hill where we had the skirmish with one brigade."

The Court continued the questioning to clarify Hooker's order regarding the hill.

"At the time you carried General Hooker's order to General Schurz, what was the order?"

"It was," Lieutenant Oliver repeated, "to get his division or brigade under arms and occupy the hill, and put one brigade on the hill."

Later in the inquiry, in response to further questioning Oliver reiterated the same answer a third time. Captain Hall and Lieutenant Oliver were both members of General Hooker's staff, and thus had nothing to gain by aiding Schurz or Hecker. Under this circumstance, they would hardly be expected to give evidence that would contradict the word of their superior. Nevertheless, both indicated that Hooker's order probably called for only one brigade, Hall specifying "one brigade" in his orders and Oliver stating that either the division or a brigade were to occupy the hill with "one brigade" placed on the hill. Further evidence regarding these orders came when Schurz questioned a member of his own staff, Lieutenant Dominicus Klutsch of the 82nd Illinois.[24]

"State what you observed about the orders that were given," Schurz enjoined, "and the marching of the troops."

"General Schurz ordered me at night when he retired to call him whenever any alarm might be heard around the camp. It was about quarter to 1 o'clock when I heard the heavy firing and went down to the ambulance, after having called the other officers, to awaken General Schurz. When I was down at the ambulance, Lieutenant Oliver, of General Hooker's staff, in company with Lieutenant Colonel Otto, came down to the ambulance and reported to General Schurz that he immediately order his troops under arms and march one brigade to the front and have the others follow up the road. Major General Schurz gave orders to Captain O'Dell to go down to General Tyndale and tell him to have his brigade fall in right away and march toward the picket line toward Wauhatchie. It was five minutes past 1 o'clock when General Hooker himself passed our headquarters, and asked General Schurz if one brigade had been sent forward and the others ordered to follow up the road. General Schurz answered, that the first brigade lying right in front of division headquarters was marching accordingly. Lieutenant Colonel Otto was directed to communicate the orders given by General Schurz to the Second and Third Brigades."

The Court became curious about Klutsch's statement that Schurz ordered the Second and Third Brigades to "follow up the road." Did this order also originate with Hooker? The recorder, Captain Lambert, pursued the line of questioning.

"Do you remember the language of the orders given by Lieutenant Oliver to General Schurz?"

"You will have your men under arms, and the brigade which is first ready marched toward the firing."

"And," Lambert persisted, "do you remember what orders were given by General Hooker to General Schurz?"

"I remember," Klutsch recalled, "that General Hooker asked General Schurz if he had sent one brigade already, and General Schurz answered that the First Brigade was marching."

"Did not General Hooker say, 'Take the nearest brigade you have and throw it forward as fast as you can,' or words to that effect?"

"General Hooker repeated the order which Lieutenant Oliver brought, and said that the nearest brigade, or the first one that should be ready, should be sent forward immediately."

"Did General Hooker give any other orders relative to the other brigades?"

"Not to my knowledge."

"Do you know what orders were given by Lieutenant Colonel Otto to the Second and Third Brigades?"

"Not to the Third Brigade, but to the Second Brigade it was said to follow up the road toward the firing."

The inconsistency in Klutsch's testimony remained unresolved. He appeared to indicate that all of Schurz's division was alerted, but that Hooker had only ordered one brigade forward. In any case, Schurz moved forward with Tyndale's brigade while the other two brigades formed to follow in his wake. As Schurz moved toward Wauhatchie Lieutenant Oliver delivered the order to take what later became known as Tyndale Hill. As a witness to this event the Court questioned Schurz's aide-de-camp, Lieutenant Eugene Weigel.[25]

"Lieutenant Oliver brought the order to General Schurz to take the Tyndale Hill with that brigade," the Court noted. "What was the language used by Lieutenant Oliver in conveying that order to General Schurz?"

"I cannot give the exact words," Weigel admitted, "but the spirit of it was that he should take the hill with that brigade."

"Was the order communicated by Lieutenant Oliver a direct order purporting to come from General Hooker, or was it a suggestion of the lieutenant's own?"

"It was delivered as a direct order," Weigel asserted.

"Do you remember any remarks that General Schurz made when that order was brought to him?"

"General Schurz expressed surprise, as he had before received positive orders to march to General Geary with his brigade."

Thus, despite the confusion and faulty memories of some witnesses, a general outline appears. Schurz received an order to advance the first brigade he could to Wauhatchie. Schurz ordered the remaining two brigades to follow when ready. He reported these moves to Hooker, and then left at the head of Tyndale's brigade. In a few minutes Lieutenant Oliver arrived with an order for Schurz to take Tyndale Hill with the leading brigade. Schurz expressed surprise, but complied with what he believed was an order from Hooker. Soon he received news that his other two brigades were no longer following him. Captain Louis Orlemann reported that Krzyżanowski halted under Hooker's orders, while Major Charles Howard brought similar news from Hecker's brigade.[26] Schurz completed the capture of the hill, then, immersed in a deep mystification at Hooker's orders, rode back to find his commanding general. Upon finding Hooker, Schurz regained control of the Second and Third Brigades, which he then pushed through to Geary.

Although the testimony contained some inconsistencies, it was clear that Schurz acted under orders first in moving forward with one brigade, then in using that brigade to capture Tyndale Hill. From the testimony given by Schurz, Weigel and Oliver there remained no doubt that Schurz was ordered to take Tyndale Hill with the brigade that later gave the knoll its name. It was evident that Schurz instructed the Second and Third Brigades to follow him toward Wauhatchie, and just as obvious that he could not be held culpable in the event that these brigades failed to follow orders due to the later preemptory of orders from Gen. Hooker. The burden of proof shifted to Colonel Hecker.[27]

"Can you state," the recorder inquired of Colonel Hecker, "the conversation that occurred between General Hooker and yourself?"

Colonel Hecker replied with his narrative of the events at Wauhatchie.

"While marching on the main road from General Howard's headquarters, in the direction of Wauhatchie, Major Howard came up and asked, 'Where is Colonel Hecker?' I answered him, and he gave me an order to halt at the crossroads ahead of us, and bring my men into position, as there was firing from the hills on our left. I ordered two regiments, the Sixty-eighth New York and the Seventy-fifth Pennsylvania, to form line of battle toward the hill, and the Eightieth Illinois, in rear of the first line in column, doubled on the center. During the execution of this order Major General Hooker arrived, as I was halting. He asked me 'What troops are these?' I answered, 'Third Brigade, Third Division, Eleventh Corps, sir.' He asked me why I was halting there, or some words to that effect. I told him I had just received an order of that purport from Major Howard, and he then put to me the question about the other troops. As the head of his horse was directed toward Wauhatchie and the head of my horse square toward the hills, I leaned forward and pointed out to him the place where the Second Brigade was. He then ordered me to be ready to form, if necessary, front to the right; that is, front toward Wauhatchie. I gave orders accordingly. I thought he directed me so because he expected an attack, not only from the hill on the left, but from the valley also, as pretty nearly at the same time shots were fired down on the troops and the bullets whistled around us. I thought some of the shots came from the gap. Then General Hooker told me, and I remember the tone of his voice as if he had spoken but a quarter of an hours since, 'You stay here, colonel.' He then rode over to the Second Brigade."

Colonel Hecker's testimony narrowed the scope of the investigation to two of the major points of controversy. General Hooker maintained that he did not issue any orders to individual brigades. Hecker insisted that the general issued such an order, in person, to the colonel of the Third Brigade. Hooker further professed to be unaware of the existence of the Second Brigade. Hecker stated that he personally pointed out Krzyżanowski's position to the general. If Hecker's assertions could be proven, Hooker necessarily must be discredited. Furthermore, if Hecker could prove that Hooker ordered the Third Brigade to halt, or remain halted, he would absolve himself of any blame.

Quite naturally Hecker pursued the question of Hooker's orders to the Third Brigade. That was the question upon which his exoneration, and in a sense Schurz's, rested. He called Major Charles Howard, aide-de-camp to General Oliver Otis Howard, then commanding general of the Eleventh Corps.[28]

"Was not my column marching when you brought me [an] order," Hecker began, "and did I not stop in consequence of that order?"

"I believe that Colonel Hecker's column was marching each time on meeting it, and I believe that it is possible and even probable that I communicated the information that I received either from General Hooker in person or from some member of his staff, that Colonel Hecker was authorized by him to stop there. As to whether Colonel Hecker halted in consequence of anything that I communicated to him, I cannot decide."

"When with General Hooker," the colonel continued, "did you hear what orders were given?"

"As soon as I reached General Hooker I gave information that Colonel Hecker's brigade had arrived, and I understood, either from General Hooker himself, in person, or some of his staff, that Colonel Hecker's brigade was authorized by him to halt there. At this moment Colonel Hecker himself came up, and I remember that General Hooker recognized him, speaking somewhat familiarly, as though he knew him well. I remember afterward that either General Hooker or General Butterfield gave the order directing Colonel Hecker as to the formation, in order to face, if need be, either to the Smith Hill or to the front, as he had been marching."

Major Howard's testimony shook Hooker's story as a thunderbolt convulses a peaceful sky. Much as the distant clap of thunder heralds the coming of the atmospheric torrents, Howard's testimony proved to be the harbinger of a deluge yet to come. The Court called Lieutenant Rudolph Mueller, Hecker's aide-de-camp.[29]

"Did you hear Major Howard give the order to Colonel Hecker to go on to the cross-roads and halt there?"

"Yes, sir."

"Do you remember in what words these orders were given?"

"'March down to the cross-roads and halt there,' these words I heard distinctly," Mueller declared.

The Court called Lieutenant Albert Kramer, acting aide-de-camp to Colonel Hecker.[30]

"Do you remember how Colonel Hecker's column was stopped on its march to the front?" Schurz asked.

"Yes, sir; when we were marching in the direction of Wauhatchie, Major Howard came and gave us the order to stop at the cross-roads. At the same time General Hooker came up and had some conversation with Colonel Hecker."

"Did you hear," the recorder interrupted, "what orders Major Howard gave to Colonel Hecker?"

"Major Howard gave him the order to go to the cross-roads and stop there."

"Did you hear Major Howard give the order to Colonel Hecker?"

"Yes, Sir."

"What words did he use?"

"He said 'Go on to the cross-roads and stop there and form line of battle.'"

"Do you remember," Schurz continued, "the conversation between General Hooker and Colonel Hecker?"

"He asked, 'What troops are these?' Colonel Hecker said the Third Brigade, Third Division. He then asked where General Schurz was. Colonel Hecker said, 'He is in front, one of his aides is wounded.' He then asked, 'Where is the Second Brigade?' Colonel Hecker showed him the place in the field, and then, before he went away, he said, 'You stay here.' Colonel Hecker said, 'Certainly.' General Hooker rode away at the same time that a volley came from the hill. General Hooker gave us instructions so that we might change our front, if necessary, toward Wauhatchie."

The evidence mounted as the Court swore Captain Joseph B. Greenhut, acting assistant adjutant general of the Third Brigade.[31]

"State what you know of the movements of your brigade," Schurz directed.

"As we came up to the cross-roads Major General Hooker and staff were standing in the road. On seeing us approach General Hooker turned around and inquired what troops these were. Colonel Hecker replied that they were the Third Brigade, Third Division, Eleventh Corps. Upon which General Hooker inquired where General Schurz was. Colonel Hecker informed him that he must be somewhere in the front, as one of his aides who had been wounded had been carried to the rear a few minutes ago. He asked him what troops those were in the rear of him. Colonel Hecker replied they were the Second Brigade, Third Division. After standing on the road for about fifteen minutes there was a volley fired down from the hill. General Hooker ordered Colonel Hecker to form his brigade in such a manner as to be able to form a line of battle either to the right or to the front, concluding with the words 'stay here;' then rode off in the direction of the Second Brigade. We formed there as indicated by General Hooker, and remained somewhere in the neighborhood of an hour. During this time I saw General Hooker and staff standing in front of the Second Brigade. After we had been there very nearly and hour, I saw General Schurz and staff come from the front and proceed to where General Hooker was standing in front of the Second Brigade. In a short time General Schurz came back, and ordered Colonel Hecker to move forward. This was about 4 or 5 o'clock. It was long after Geary's firing had ceased."

Four eyewitnesses—Howard, Mueller, Kramer and Greenhut—corroborated Hecker's statements. None disputed the colonel's observations. The conclusions seemed inescapable. Hecker stopped due to an order delivered by Major Howard, an order subsequently confirmed in person by General

Hooker. Clearly, despite his earlier assertion, Joseph Hooker did issue orders to at least one brigade at Wauhatchie.

But what of the other discrepancy between the statements of Hecker and Hooker? Did Hooker really know where Krzyżanowski's Second Brigade was located? Colonel Hecker indicated that Hooker knew, and Hecker's story was confirmed by Captain Greenhut and Lieutenant Kramer. Under further examination they all repeated their assertions.

"Did any conversation occur between you and General Hooker," Schurz asked Hecker, "concerning Colonel Krzyzanowski's brigade?"[32]

"I am not positive whether he asked where the Second Brigade was, or where the other brigade was, or where the other troops of the division were, but my impression is that he asked for the Second Brigade, because I was leaning forward on my horse and pointing with my finger to troops on my left perpendicular to my line of battle. I told him that the Second Brigade, Colonel Krzyzanowski's, was halted there. After some further conversation with me he rode over in the direction of the Second Brigade, and I did not pay any further attention to him, for I was looking toward Wauhatchie, and toward the hills from which there was still firing."

"Where," Schurz asked Kramer, "did General Hooker ride to when he left you?"[33]

"He rode to the Second Brigade, Third Division."

"Did you see where the Second Brigade, Third Division was?"

"Yes, sir; about 100 or 150 yards from us on the left in front of the brigade."

"Did you see General Hooker near the Second Brigade, Third Division, after he had left you?" Schurz persisted.

"Yes," Kramer replied, "I saw him there. I believe he was dismounted there in front of the Second Brigade."

Turning his attention to Captain Greenhut, Schurz made sure that there would be no doubt left in the Court's collective mind.[34]

"Where did General Hooker go when he left you, after having given orders to the Third Brigade?"

"He went in front of the position that the Second Brigade occupied in the field, right in our front and our left."

"Did you see General Hooker remain with the Second Brigade any length of time?"

"Yes, sir; he was there the whole time that we occupied the position to which he ordered us."

General Schurz summoned a new witness, Lieutenant Colonel Theodore A. Meysenburg, assistant adjutant general of the Eleventh Corps. Triumphantly Schurz maneuvered for the *coup de grâce*.[35]

"Did you see General Hooker during the engagement; if so where?"

"When the firing commenced near our troops," Meysenburg replied, "I left headquarters to join General Howard. I did not find General Howard, but found General Hooker."

"Where?"

"In front of Colonel Krzyzanowski's brigade."

Once again the parade of witnesses pointed to the same conclusion as before—"Fighting Joe" Hooker lied. There was no doubt but that he knew the whereabouts of the Second Brigade. As Schurz later wrote in summation: "Even the name of its commander, Colonel Krzyzanowski, was pronounced, and that is a name which cannot well be mistaken for any other."[36]

Schurz was innocent. Hecker was innocent. What of Krzyżanowski? His case was not as clear as the others, nor could it be. Virtually all of the key witnesses—Krzyżanowski, Otto, Orlemann, staff officers, the regimental commanders—were away enjoying their veteran furloughs. Some of those present, such as Oliver Otis Howard, were never called to testify. Because the inquiry did not specifically cite Colonel Krzyżanowski there was practically no attempt to solicit information about the colonel from the witnesses that did appear. From the scraps of information presented, however, the puzzle of his actions can be pieced together. We know, for example, that when Schurz moved forward with Tyndale's brigade he sent Lt. Colonel Otto to order Krzyżanowski and Hecker forward.

"Did you see Lieutenant Colonel Otto?" Schurz asked Lieutenant Klutsch.[37]

"I saw him at the division headquarters speaking to Colonel Krzyzanowski, who was asking for instructions."

"Do you know what orders were given by Lieutenant Colonel Otto to the Second and Third Brigades?"

"Not to the Third Brigade," Klutsch replied, "but to the Second Brigade it was said to follow up the road toward the firing."

It is, then, significant that when Krzyżanowski began his march he was not under orders to move to the relief of Geary at Wauhatchie. His only instructions were "to follow up the road toward the firing." To follow what? To follow the First Brigade being led by Schurz.

When Captain Greenhut occupied the witness stand Schurz asked him to describe the movements of the Third Brigade.[38]

"After the column halted," Greenhut began, "Colonel Hecker sent me forward to inquire the cause. As I came to the head of the Second Brigade I inquired of Captain Orlemann where Major General Schurz was. He told me that he went forward with the First Brigade. I inquired of him if he had received orders that the Second Brigade was to halt there. He told me that he had. He did not inform me by whom he had received the orders."

Who issued these orders to halt? It was no secret. Lieutenant Weigel,

Schurz's aide-de-camp, told the Court all about the order.[39]

"After General Schurz had brought up the Second and Third Brigades," the recorder began, "who gave an order for the Second Brigade to halt?"

"It was an order from General Schurz." This statement is confirmed by Schurz's campaign report where he states: "I directed Colonel Krzyzanowski, commanding my Second Brigade, to occupy the gap north-east of the hill held by General Tyndale." He went on to say that at 6:00 A.M. he "ordered Colonel Krzyzanowski to leave a detachment in the position he then had, and to march with the remainder of his command to Wauhatchie. He reported there about 7 a.m." This is further confirmed by the Eleventh Corps log which notes that Krzyżanowski was ordered to march to Geary at 7:00 a.m.[40]

The statement provoked little notice when Weigel made it part of the Court's record. There was no reason it should have. When Schurz received the order from Lieutenant Oliver to assault Tyndale Hill he quite naturally ordered Kriz to stop and await the outcome of the fight. To have sent the Second Brigade rushing off into the darkness, exposed on the left to fire from a hostile hillock and in the front to the possibility of a major ambush, would have been foolhardy indeed. Schurz took a necessary precaution. Also, it is worth remembering here that Hooker earlier indicated that had he known of the existence of Krzyżanowski he would have ordered him forward "irrespective of General Howard's orders." Could it be that Krzyżanowski's halt was approved by Howard also?

The recorder continued.[41]

"How near each other were the Second and Third Brigades?"

"They were," Weigel maintained, "within 50 yards of each other, and drawn up, I think, in line of battle, and the Second Brigade was facing perpendicularly to the Third."

"How near to the Second Brigade was General Hooker?"

"Some 30 or 40 yards."

This was exactly the same position that Lieutenant Mueller described in his testimony.[42]

"Did you see the Second Brigade, Third Division, after you found them halted?"

"I saw a line of battle in the opening in front of us, fronting toward Geary's position, forming a right angle with us when we fronted toward the hill."

Thus Krzyżanowski marched out of camp, following Schurz toward Wauhatchie. Suddenly firing erupted to the left, ahead of the column. Lieutenant Oliver brought Hooker's order to take the hill. Schurz complied, ordering Krzyżanowski to await the outcome before moving forward any farther. Kriz formed line of battle, at which time General Hooker happened along. Hooker spoke with Hecker, who pointed out Krzyżanowski's position to the commanding general. Hooker ordered Hecker to "stay here," then moved over to a position in front of Krzyżanowski's brigade. At this point Captain Robert H. Hall, Hooker's own aide-de-camp, re-entered the picture. General Schurz asked Hall what orders he carried on the night of the engagement at Wauhatchie.[43]

"An order to the commanding officer of a brigade immediately in the rear of General Hooker's position to send some prisoners to Chattanooga. In reference to this order, I wish to explain that a number of prisoners came in and were questioned by General Butterfield. I was at some distance from the general. He turned to me and said: 'Tell the commanding officer of that brigade to send them to Chattanooga.' Believing he referred to the brigade itself, I gave the order to the commanding officer of the brigade to march to Chattanooga. Believing this to be an error, I reported what I had done to General Butterfield, and the mistake was corrected before the brigade had marched perhaps 50 yards."

"What brigade was it to the commander of which you gave the order to march to Chattanooga?"

"I did not know who was the commanding officer at that time. I did not know whose brigade it was. I have since heard it was Colonel Krzyzanowski's; indeed, I learned that fact the next day."

"From whom did you learn the next day that the brigade commander referred to was Colonel Krzyzanowski?"

"From some officer on General Butterfield's staff," Hall replied, "I have forgotten whom. It may have been General Butterfield; I am not certain."

"What order did you carry to the commander of the brigade after the mistake was corrected?"

"To bring his brigade back to its original position, and to send the prisoners to Chattanooga."

"In what position was the brigade when you delivered the order?" Schurz asked.

"It was in line perpendicular to the line of hills facing up the valley."

"Did General Hooker know that the brigade was there?"

"I presume he did; it was a very short distance from us, in General Hooker's rear."

"Did you see the commander of the brigade at any time in the presence of General Hooker or General Butterfield?"

"I do not remember that I did, and I should have remembered it if I had seen him."

"Did you see General Hooker ride or walk about [with] the commanding officer of the troops in position there?"

"Indeed, I do not remember."

"Were you with General Hooker when he came to that place: and did he then make any inquiry as to what troops those in position there were?"

"I was with him, and I heard no inquiry from him of that kind."

"Where did you find the commander of the brigade when you delivered the order?"

"He was with his brigade, I think, and was in front, close by his men."

"Were those troops the nearest to the place where General Hooker stood?"

"They were."

Captain Hall's testimony is of great interest. First of all, he did not remember seeing Krzyżanowski converse with Hooker, nor did he recall Hooker asking what troops the Second Brigade might be. These points are easily explained. He did not hear Hooker's inquiry because there may not have been one. Colonel Hecker had already told Hooker what troops they were. In addition, Hall admitted elsewhere that he was not with Hooker for the entire night, thus he may well have been absent when, and if, any such conversation or inquiries took place. Not remembering something that might have occurred in one's absence, of course, proves nothing.

Captain Hall claims that Krzyżanowski did not come over to talk with either Hooker or Butterfield. "I should have remembered it if I had seen him," he states. Why would he remember Krzyżanowski? He stated previously that he did not even know who Krzyżanowski was on that evening! The important point, which is easily overlooked, is that Hall admits that Butterfield gave him orders to deliver to "the commanding officer of that brigade." It is evident from this that Hooker's staff certainly did realize that the brigade standing near them, the closest one to them, was not a part of Hecker's brigade as they later claimed. They did realize that is was a separate brigade. If they did, and if they were thus willing to issue orders to its commander, they surely would have issued further orders if they were unhappy with the positioning or inactivity of the brigade.

The remainder of Captain Hall's sworn statement is similarly of great interest. Certainly his positive recollection shows that Hooker not only lied about not giving orders to the brigade commanders, but compounded this misstatement by issuing orders to at least two brigades. Through Captain Hall, Hooker's aide-de-camp, the mendacious general ordered Krzyżanowski to send a guard back to Chattanooga with some prisoners. The order was at first misunderstood by the staff officer delivering it, then corrected. In correcting the order Captain Hall instructed Krzyżanowski: "To bring his brigade back to its original position."

What did Hall say? What were his exact words to Krzyżanowski? Was it to resume his old position or to carry out his previous orders? Clearly it was to return to his original position. But what were the exact words; in what tone of voice were they delivered? Did he say, much as Hooker had to Hecker, go to your last position and "stay there"? The wording is important because in all probability it led Kriz to believe that he was still under the direct orders of General Hooker. Surely, had Hooker objected to the placement of Krzyżanowski's brigade after its abortive move he would have issued further orders to its commander.

Thus the puzzle nears completion; the picture begins to take its final shape. Colonel Hecker shows Hooker the position occupied by the Second Brigade. Hooker leaves, ordering Hecker to "stay here." Hooker takes a position in front of Krzyżanowski's brigade. He then orders Kriz to detach some men to escort prisoners back to Chattanooga. Captain Hall mistakenly orders the whole brigade to Chattanooga. At this point an incredulous Colonel Krzyżanowski dispatches Captain Orlemann to report the situation to General Schurz.

"Can you state about when and where Captain Orlemann reported to General Schurz that the Second Brigade was kept back?"

"I think," responded Lieutenant Weigel, "it was a little after this aide of General Hooker [Oliver] had brought the order to take Tyndale's Hill."

Note the wording of Schurz's question. He asks about Krzyżanowski's brigade being "kept back," thus indicating restraint. The brigade was being "kept back" by some outside force. This indicates that the brigade was no longer halted under Schurz's authority, but by order of some higher command. Krzyżanowski might easily be criticized for not later informing Schurz that he was not going to Chattanooga after all. This, of course, would be invalid because if he was still under Hooker's orders and had already so informed Schurz, there would be no reason to inform Schurz a second time. Then too, maybe he did send a second message to Schurz. We do not know. No one ever asked the question.

"Did you see Captain Orlemann of Colonel Krzyzanowski's staff?" Schurz persisted.[44]

"I saw him at the time that he brought the report to General Schurz that the Second Brigade had been stopped by orders from General Hooker, and had been ordered to Chattanooga."

Did you accompany General Schurz from Tyndale's Hill back, and where did you go with him?"

"I did; I accompanied him back to where we found General Hooker."

"Where did you find General Hooker?"

"We found General Hooker near the farm-house at the foot of Smith's Hill."

"Do you remember anything of the conversation that took place there?"

"I do," Weigel began. "General Hooker asked General Schurz why he had not pushed through with that brigade to General Geary, upon which

General Schurz told him that one of General Hooker's aides had given him the order to take the Tyndale Hill, and that he had no other troops with him. General Hooker told him he had given him the order in person to march through, and at the time did not seem to acknowledge this order of his aide's."

"Did you see Colonel Krzyzanowski at the time?"

"I did; Colonel Krzyzanowski was about 10 paces from General Hooker."

"State what happened then," Schurz commanded.

"General Schurz then asked General Hooker if he could now have his two brigades and then march the two brigades toward Tyndale's Hill."

"Do you remember what disposition was made of Colonel Krzyzanowski's brigade?"

"It was halted at the gap between Smith's and Tyndale's Hills, the whole of it with the exception of one or two regiments which accompanied the Third Brigade."

The puzzle is complete. All of the various nuances of the picture appear strikingly evident before our eyes. After sending Orlemann to inform Schurz of Hooker's orders directing him to Chattanooga, Krzyżanowski finds those orders countermanded by Captain Hall. Hall orders Kriz back to his previous position. Schurz arrives, confused by Hooker's orders to the Second and Third Brigades. By this time, the firing from Wauhatchie has long since ceased. Hooker has lost his opportunity to claim credit for rescuing Geary. The commanding general is mad. He hollers to Schurz to carry out his orders, mentioning once again the term "brigade." Hecker's brigade marches off to join Geary, reinforced by some of Krzyżanowski's troops. Kriz, who has been standing only "10 paces" from Hooker, is sent to fill the gap between Smith's and Tyndale's Hills. Later he is ordered to Wauhatchie to reinforce Geary. In fact, the Daily Log of the Eleventh Corps clearly recorded two entries that shed light on the issue at hand. At 4:30 A.M. the log contained the notation: "Col Hecker's Brig sent to support of Geary." Later, an entry recorded at 7:00 A.M. noted: "Kryzanowski's Brigade sent to Gen. Geary." Had this been entered into evidence, it clearly indicated the time at which Kriz was finally ordered to Geary's relief.[45]

Hooker first encountered problems through the prejudices that led him to neglect the Eleventh Corps to the point where he knew little about its organization or personnel. Secondly, he was no doubt betrayed by faulty staff work that led to many of the problems and misunderstandings that occurred. In the final analysis, however, Hooker, for whatever reasons, willfully and knowingly lied. Through his propensity for prevarication Hooker lost all credibility in the matter. It was obvious to everyone that those whom he accused—Schurz and Hecker—were vindicated.

Schurz and Hecker exulted in their victory, but for the Court of Inquiry it was a period of real angst. The members of the Court knew that when the inquest was completed they would have to return to the field under the command of the man whose accusations they refuted. Clearly they were faced with the dilemma of overwhelming evidence on one had, and discrediting their superior officer, a man of proven vindictiveness, on the other hand. In their final report they adopted a unique settlement that managed to vindicate Schurz and Hecker without dangerously detracting from Hooker's dubious reputation.

The Court concluded that because of darkness and distance it would, in any case, have been impossible for any of Schurz's elements to reach Geary before the firing at Wauhatchie stopped. As an attempt to avoid any real decision, this would suffice. But the Court did not stop there. Inexplicably, the Court declared "that the Second Brigade of the Third Division halted without authority and against the orders of the division commander. To the neglect, then, of Colonel Krzyzanowski to obey the order of his commanding officer may be ascribed the delay in sending re-enforcements to General Geary."[46]

The astounding conclusion that the Court reached regarding Colonel Krzyżanowski's conduct was more than absurd, it was criminal. Krzyżanowski was never previously accused. He had no way of knowing his conduct would be evaluated by the Court of Inquiry. He was not even present to defend himself. The Court never pursued his case during the inquiry, and the preponderant bulk of the testimony that was presented certainly pointed to no culpability on the part of the unsuspecting colonel.

The unwarranted and unsubstantiated verdict of the Court of Inquiry stands as a deliberate "whitewash" of the malicious machinations of Joseph Hooker. Faced with the dilemma of choosing between the weight of massive evidence and the potential wrath of a superior officer, the Court chose to avoid any real decision by placing the blame for a failure which it admitted did not exist on the one person who was not present to defend himself. The lamentable result is perpetuated to this very day—nearly a century and one-half after the event—as a tragic injustice that stains an otherwise exemplary record of courage, devotion, and ability.

— CHAPTER NINE —

"A MOST SPLENDID OFFICER"

THE FINAL MONTHS OF THE WAR

Krzyżanowski returned from his furlough to find conditions in the Army of the Cumberland quite different from when he left. Although he resumed command of his brigade, his days in the field were over. Headquartered at Whiteside, Tennessee, Kriz assumed the responsibility of guarding the vital Nashville and Chattanooga Railroad, the line that pumped life-sustaining supplies to the armies gathering for the invasion of Georgia. It was a responsibility that called for constant vigilance against spies, saboteurs and guerrillas who hoped to cripple the Union war effort by interrupting the strategic logistics system under Krzyżanowski's protection.[1]

Soon the assignment became permanent. During his tenure at the head of the Federal armies in the West, Ulysses S. Grant advocated the consolidation of the understrength Eleventh and Twelfth Corps. Under Grant's plan, Generals Hooker and Slocum would be shelved leaving Oliver Otis Howard to command the new hybrid. Following Grant's appointment as commander-in-chief of the Union forces, his replacement in the West, William Tecumseh Sherman, succeeded in effecting the desired consolidation. On April 4, 1864, Special Field Orders No. 105 created the new Twentieth Army Corps from the remains of the veterans of so many far-flung fields of conflict.[2]

For those detractors who lobbied so hard against the immigrant troops throughout the war, the liquidation of the Eleventh Corps brought victory. The veteran "foreign" regiments withered and died, their ranks depleted to the size of mere companies. Incredibly, but by now all too predictably, command of the Twentieth Corps went to the darling of the War Department, Joseph Hooker. Carl Schurz and Adolf von Steinwehr, who did not wish to serve under Hooker again, found themselves without commands, replaced as division leaders by Alpheus S. Williams, John Geary, and Daniel Butterfield. The brigades went to men named Knipe, Ruger, Tyndale, Candy, Ireland, Ward, Ross, Wood and Buschbeck. Of all these officers, only Buschbeck, the mastermind of the "Wauhatchie whitewash," retained command of his old brigade after the consolidation. Even the crescent, the badge of the Eleventh Corps, was abandoned in favor of the five-pointed star of the old Twelfth Corps. Nativists and Know-Nothings rejoiced. The Eleventh Corps was at last "Americanized."[3]

Concurrent with the upheavals that occasioned the formation of the Twentieth Corps, Krzyżanowski suffered through the dismemberment of his old brigade. He held back his emotions as he bade farewell to his officers and men, the surrogate family that he led through so many sanguinary conflicts in Virginia, Pennsylvania and Tennessee. After fighting in so many once-obscure places, this was their reward, to be splintered into four directions. The 141st New York went to the First Division, Twentieth Corps. The gallant 119th New York, heroes of the Dowdall tavern and Cemetery Hill, left for the Second Division. The battered and bruised Badgers who scorned their assailants at Chancellorsville and Gettysburg, headed to their new assignment with the Third Division. The Polish Legion reported, along with its colonel, to the Fourth Division. With heavy heart Kriz stood to watch his friends march off to new infernos of human conflict. He fought back the tears as he thought of those who would never return.[4]

To provide as effective a fighting force as possible in the new corps, the larger regiments were assigned to the first three divisions. To create the force necessary to guard the many small outposts along the essential railroads, the smaller regiments were detailed to the Fourth Division. Since Krzyżanowski had never been confirmed as brigadier general, but led his brigade as its senior colonel, when the brigade was dissolved he reverted to command of his regiment and was assigned, on April 21, along with the Polish Legion, to General Lovell H. Rousseau's Fourth Division.

Although no longer in command of a "combat" brigade, his seniority led to his appointment as commanding officer of the Federal troops protecting the railroad between Lookout Creek, Tennessee, and Bridgeport, Alabama, with his headquarters at Whiteside, Tennessee. Though his responsibility remained the same, its permanence proved a welcome metamorphosis in many ways. No longer living the life of a wanderer, Kriz became an administrative officer assigned to a permanent post where he could enjoy the comforts of civilization unknown in the field.[5]

At first a welcome relief from campaigning, guarding the railroad lines soon proved a drab, regimented existence that afforded little opportunity for distinction and a good chance of becoming the target for some Southern bushwhacker. Yet, as General Sherman said, the railroad was the "delicate point" of his whole campaign.[6] A half-dozen men could easily disrupt the single-line track in just a few minutes time. Sherman's relentless march on Atlanta would have been quite impossible without the successful maintenance of this artery of supply.

Following a few weeks of service at Whiteside, Krzyżanowski assumed command of Northeastern Alabama, with his headquarters at Bridgeport. Bridgeport contained huge storage facilities constructed when the small city served as the railhead for the relief of Rosecrans' besieged forces in Chattanooga. Now, with Sherman's armies preparing to deal a death blow to the Confederacy, the warehouses and cribs bulged with vast quantities of ordnance and provisions. An enormous railroad bridge spanned the Tennessee River at Bridgeport, providing the crucial link between that city and Chattanooga. To facilitate crossings, Federal engineers constructed a flat-bottomed pontoon bridge down river from the railroad span, lashing the pontoons to the railroad trestle for support. Strong fortifications protected the town and its environs. Several regiments of troops constantly garrisoned the area, while new recruits en route to Sherman's army drilled and maneuvered under the guiding eyes of a veteran drillmaster whom they called Colonel "Kriz."[7]

Northern Alabama contained substantial Unionist sentiment. The people were generally friendly, unlike most of the other areas Krzyżanowski traveled through below the Mason-Dixon line. An area of small farmers, the constant presence of warring armies took its toll on the economic fortunes of the populace. With the exception of the Federal supply base, Northeastern Alabama suffered from the effects of a widening depression. Many families were completely destitute, dependent for their sustenance upon government food subsidies arranged with the aid of Colonel Krzyżanowski. Subject, of course, to availability, about 300 local families received daily rations of flour and bacon. This generous treatment of the citizenry earned Kriz a reputation as a just, humane officer.[8]

In addition to his responsibility for rail traffic, Kriz was also accountable for the security of the Alabama towns of Stevenson, Decatur and Scottsboro, as well as the safety of that portion of the Tennessee River that flowed through his area of command. For the latter purpose Krzyżanowski received the services of Gunboat A. Under the command of Captain William A. Naylor, this small ship cruised the length of Krzyżanowski's area of command enforcing Federal directives, contacting Northern sympathizers, and soliciting intelligence regarding Confederate movements and arms caches.[9]

By the end of May, 1864, Kriz commanded a Bridgeport garrison that included thirty-four officers and 814 enlisted men. Augmenting this force were several "unattached" units including the 58th New York, 68th New York, 75th Pennsylvania, 133rd Indiana, 1st Michigan Engineers and Mechanics, and the 10th Battery, Indiana Light Artillery. Other units transited the area with regularity.[10]

Beginning in June, as Sherman's forces closed in on the beleaguered city of Atlanta, the Confederate command launched a desperate series of cavalry raids in an attempt to interdict the Nashville and Chattanooga Railroad. Bushwhackings and skirmishes occurred almost daily after June 10. In July Kriz received a report that his district was the target of 2,800 Southern cavalry and horse artillery. Determined to hold his position, he telegraphed for reinforcements. Although the crisis soon passed, the Federal authorities reorganized the area into the Department of the Defense of the Nashville and Chattanooga Railroad for better control and efficiency.[11]

Command of the new department went to Krzyżanowski's old friend from the Virginia campaigns, Major General Robert H. Milroy. Krzyżanowski's command was redesignated as the Third Brigade of Milroy's command. The colonel's forces at this time included his own 58th New York, the 68th New York, 106th Ohio, and the 9th Battery, Ohio Light Artillery. Recruits and returning convalescents increased the strength of the Polish Legion to 351 men, but the total force remained a small one. The strength of the brigade was dissipated still further by being strung out along the railroad right-of-way to garrison the various blockhouses and stations.[12]

Despite the wartime atmosphere, there were still occasions for levity during the fall of 1864. One day, while Krzyżanowski visited Stevenson, Alabama, a French fencing master appeared looking for General Schurz. When Kriz informed the visitor that Schurz no longer had a command in that area, the instructor inquired if perhaps the colonel would care to engage him for a few lessons. Sensing that the stranger was nothing but another camp follower who preyed upon the soldier's modest earnings, the colonel accepted his invitation to engage in a friendly crossing of the foils. After a few moments of thrusts easily side-stepped and slashes adeptly parried, the instructor found himself disarmed, at the mercy of his pupil. Indignantly, the Frenchman gathered up his equipment and rushed off in a huff, never to be seen about the camp again.[13]

Undoubtedly the happiest circumstance that Kriz enjoyed as a garrison commander was the opportunity to be reunited with his wife. At last in a position that offered some degree of permanence, Krzyżanowski sent for his family to join him. Though the life of a garrison commandant proved pleasantly different from life in the field, the seeming serenity only masked the more obvious manifestations of war.[14]

In August, on the eve of the fall of Atlanta, Confederate commander John Bell Hood ordered General Joseph Wheeler to lead 4,500 cavalry troopers in a last-ditch attempt to destroy the Northern supply system. Striking toward Tennessee, Wheeler captured Dalton, Resaca, and burned the railroad bridge at Etowah. The raiders destroyed some fifty miles of rail in eastern Tennessee, but Federal resistance proved so strong that Wheeler was unable to accomplish any significant reduction in traffic over the Nashville and Chattanooga.[15]

Following the frustration of Wheeler's cavalry, General Milroy went on an inspection tour of his widely dispersed units. Stopping first at Stevenson, Milroy and his staff encountered Colonel Wilson of the 135th Indiana, who accompanied them to Bridgeport. Kriz greeted Milroy warmly as a comrade from Pope's Army of Virginia. Although it was but a little over two years since the campaign of Second Bull Run it seemed at least that many decades. Milroy, too, was happy to be reunited with a man whom he remembered as "a noble fellow." Meticulously, the two officers rode about examining the fortifications in and around Bridgeport, all of which met the approval of the Department commander.[16]

With the successful completion of Milroy's inspection, the general invited Kriz to accompany him to Chattanooga so that he might point out to the general some of the positions of significance during the previous fall's siege. The colonel agreed, happy for the opportunity to continue reminiscing about their mutual friends and experiences. In Chattanooga they dined with the area commander, Major General James B. Steedman, following which the small gathering adjourned for a tour of nearby Lookout Mountain.[17]

Located near the bend in the Tennessee River opposite Chattanooga, Lookout Mountain offered a close aerial view of three states. The splendid sight of the countryside below impressed Milroy, as did Krzyżanowski's explanation of the layout of the recent battles fought in the area. Happily, the group posed for a picture atop the mountain. Then, following supper with the 13th Michigan Engineers, they returned to Chattanooga to catch the train for Bridgeport.[18]

On the following day Kriz provided Milroy with a small boat that the general used to visit the celebrated Nick-a-Jack and Cudjoes caves of novel fame. That evening, upon the general's return, he thanked Krzyżanowski for his hospitality before boarding the train for Tullahoma. There were few officers in the army more qualified to judge the services of Wladimir Krzyżanowski than the man who fought beside him in two major campaigns, the man who had known him as both a line officer and an administrator. In a letter to his wife that November, Milroy described the colonel as "a noble Pole and a most splendid officer. I think a great deal of him. He ought to be a Maj. Gen[eral]."[19]

By the end of 1864 Atlanta was in ruins. Savannah fell in December. Sherman's army reached the Atlantic, leaving behind it a swath of destruction that doomed the Confederacy to economic ruin. The success of Sherman's army, however, did little to relieve the pressure on the Nashville and Chattanooga. In January parts of Krzyżanowski's brigade skirmished at Elrod's Tan Yard, Roman's Landing, Ladd's House, and Hog Jaw Valley, Alabama, and at Johnson's Creek, Georgia.[20]

Krzyżanowski (standing on the right) with General Milroy (seated to right with white hair) on Lookout Mountain, July 13, 1864. The others are Col. Shannon of the 138th Indiana (2nd from left), Col. Wilson of the 135th Indiana (balding man to left of Milroy) and members of Milroy's staff.*Courtesy of Margaret B. Paulus.*

By March, 1865, Krzyżanowski lacked only one month of being in the Union Army four years. For three years and six months he ranked as a colonel, but for the past two years and ten months of that period he constantly carried out the functions of a brigadier general. While he led his troops from one sanguinary field to another, newer, less experienced officers received their promotions to brigadier. He did not complain, not even after the damaging blow to his reputation that the Court of Inquiry placed on record. He contented himself with the friendships he made and the knowledge that he was doing what he could to preserve the idealistic portrait of America which his mind embraced. Yet, it is evident that he also continued to maneuver for the cherished brigadiership. Throughout the summer and fall of 1864 various officers, prominent among them Carl Schurz, continued to lobby for Krzyżanowski's promotion. It is clear from various petitions and other correspondence that Kriz was not aloof from these attempts since some of them contained detailed personal information. One such letter from Maj. Gen. Robert H. Milroy, addressed directly to the president, read:

> Permit me to call your attention to the long standing, meritorious & much neglected claims of Col. W. Krzyzanowski of the 58th N. Y. V. V. I. for promotion. The Col is a noble Pole, who espoused our glorious cause

at the outbreak of the Rebellion, as a private, with all the zeal that actuates his unfortunate countrymen in their love of Liberty & Free Government. He served with distinction in Comd of his gallant Regt in the 11th A. C. in Va. & after that Corps was transferred to the army of the Cumberland he bore a conspicuous part in Comd of a Bgd up to & including that of Mission Ridge. He has been complemented for gallant conduct &, I believe, recommended for promotion by every Genl. under whom he has served. For over two years he has Commanded a Brigade & part of the time a Division. He was Educated at a Military Institution of high reputation in Europe. Was one of the leaders in the Polish Revolution of '48. Has a splendid military experience. Has a high order of intellect. Is brave, energetic. A stern disciplinarian. In short he possesses all those qualifications, both physical & mental, that make him every inch a soldier and qualify him for an able and accomplished General. Were he a West Pointer, with one fourth of his merits and qualifications, he would have long since been a Maj. Gen. Both justice & Merit demand his promotion, and no higher tribute could be paid to genuine, deserving military worth, than by granting it.[21]

Another letter from John S. Tarkington of Indianapolis, dated November 14, 1864, likewise contains too much specific information not to have been personally influenced by the Pole. It read:

> You asked me to write what I wanted to say. 1st, Col. W. Krzyzanowski 58th N.Y. was appointed Brig. Genl. in 1862-3 but after confirmation by Senate the vote of confirmation was reconsidered as he left a Col. Why? He went at the first call for 75,000, as a private, was made Captain of his company from District of Columbia, then raised a regiment in the city of N.Y. for 3 years, was in the Potomac army through all its varied fortunes acting a Brigade Commander for 3 years, came with Sherman's advance when Potomac army came west: belongs now in 20th Corps, was in 11th Corps, was at Chancellorsville held one half of his brigade firm against Jackson's onslaught, was on Cemetery Hill with his brigade at Gettysburg. He is a Pole with an entire German brigade until July last when 75 Pa. went from Bridgeport to Nashville. He has had the 68th & 58th N.Y. 75 Pa. & 106 Ohio as his brigade, though at Bridgeport other troops 135th Ind, 133rd Mo were under him. I was much pleased with the man during my stay of two months at Bridgeport, his men are proud of him, and I know he must be a good fighter. He was for Father Abraham from the first, though he had served under Fremont and knew him. He is radical as German Republicans are generally. He was a Republican in Washington city, & President of a club when to be so to a German was treason to his nativity as well as political rights for Know-Nothings and that party, with the mass of foreigners, were synonymous: and I know he did good service to prevent disaffection on account of Fremont among his command. His family reside in Washington, also his father-in-law. His three years term must be about out. He caused his

> brigade to reenlist. If he cannot be made Brig. Gen. I would as a matter of justice to myself like to know why, because I must be very much mistaken if he does not deserve it. He is a ruling man, as tender hearted as a child as strong as a horse as brave as—his services attest. I have written more than I intended, and will not engage your attention about this matter I desired to write of.[22]

His wishes finally appeared to be granted when, on March 2, he received an official nomination to the rank of brevet brigadier general. In a letter to his wife after receiving news of the nomination, Gen. Milroy wrote: "Read the gratifying intelligence today that my old friend and fellow soldier Col. Krzyzanowski is breveted a Brig. Gen. He amply merits a Maj. Generalship and had he been a West Pointer would long since have received it."[23]

Krzyżanowski was, of course, appreciative of his nomination, but as the war wound to its inexorable conclusion the jubilance of victory cast into the background any personal satisfaction that he might have felt. His spirits soared at the news of General Lee's surrender, the culminating event that he equated with the triumph of the Union—of reunion and liberty.[24]

On the heels of this exhilarating news came the horrible trauma of Lincoln's assassination. Krzyżanowski held a deep admiration and respect for Lincoln, whom he considered to be the greatest man America ever produced. Kriz thought of Lincoln the man in terms of Lincoln the ideal. To his mind, as to many others, the Illinois rail-splitter had long ago become the personification of the ideals for which he fought. Lincoln was a symbol. His essence assumed proportions larger than life. His death brought corresponding grief and bewilderment that sought escape through bitterness and revenge.[25]

The news of Lincoln's death brought celebrations to a standstill throughout the North. Grief replaced joy in the hearts of soldiers and civilians alike. "Why had it happened?" some asked incredulously. But for Krzyżanowski the answer was all too plain. For four long years the bloody, fratricidal conflict raged through the land. In the end the Southern armies proved less than invincible. With the defeat of Lee, Krzyżanowski noted, a generous North merely disarmed the rebels and allowed them to go home. But, Kriz wrote, "All of these losses and sacrifices were still not enough for the Southerners. They still had to resort to conspiracy, treason and murder."[26] To Krzyżanowski there was no question. Unable to achieve their aims on the battlefield, the Southern leaders plotted the assassination of the heart and soul of the Northern war effort. The South was guilty of Lincoln's murder.

Perhaps, in retrospect, this was an unwarranted assumption based on the emotions of the moment. The circumstantial evidence, however, certainly proved conclusive to Kriz and thousands of others who lived through four bitter years only to find their leader taken from them in their hour of triumph. Was it a conspiracy? Krzyżanowski certainly thought so. He pointed to the fact that there were abortive plans to kill several other government officials on the same night that Lincoln attended his last performance at Ford's Theater. The conspirators, of course, were all Southern sympathizers. Some had even served in the Confederate Army. There was, too, sufficient motive for the South could well assume that the death of Lincoln would be of benefit to the former Confederate states. Lincoln's successor, Vice President Andrew Johnson, was all that Lincoln was not—a Democrat, a Southerner from Tennessee, and, until 1862, a slaveholder!

Johnson's actions on assuming the Presidency only served to convince Krzyżanowski that the supposed plot was indeed very real. In attempting to implement Lincoln's plan for a moderate Reconstruction, Johnson granted liberal terms for the restoration of Southern political representation, and systematically pardoned all but the very highest placed of the Confederate officials. Krzyżanowski interpreted this as confirmation of all his gravest suspicions. "From the tone of Johnson's speeches," the Pole lamented, "it became clear that he believed the South was victorious."[27] As the number of pardons increased to over 100 per day by September, so too did Krzyżanowski's bitter thirst for revenge. He became incensed at the appointment of former Confederates to positions of political influence. An outspoken supporter of Lincoln's politics during the martyred president's lifetime, Kriz unconsciously gravitated further from Lincoln's policy of magnanimity with each passing day. Soon he became a vocal supporter of the Radical Republicans who voiced his own shrill cry of revenge.

The revival of Southern politics immediately following Appomattox appeared to Krzyżanowski to represent a rejuvenated secessionist movement seeking to revive the dormant Confederacy. He condemned Johnson for welcoming Southern representatives back to Washington despite their flagrant disregard for even the minimal conditions that Johnson himself placed upon their reentry into the political arena. He viewed these actions as a betrayal of the sacrifices he and his comrades made during the war, thus he became even more emotionally linked to the emerging wave of radicalism in the Republican Party.[28]

Krzyżanowski reserved his most caustic criticism for Johnson's failure to pursue the conspiracy surrounding Lincoln's assassination. While Kriz acknowledged that the government offered a reward for the capture of Jefferson Davis and other Confederate leaders, he felt that their efforts were a farce because the former president of the Confederacy was already in Federal hands. "This was a comedy," he declared, "no-one believed it—the government hunting down the Southerners was in the hands of a

Southerner."[29] And what of Davis' confinement? "It was a strange imprisonment. He was treated more like a prince than a prisoner."[30]

Throughout the summer of 1865 the Federal government functioned under the permissive directives of Andrew Johnson. Congress did not convene until December. During this long period of grace the Southern states, convinced that they would have to accept the end of black servitude, conspired to pass laws known as the Black Codes. These "codes" were in reality legislative attempts to limit the participation of blacks in the political, economic and social life of the South. The Black Codes attempted to circumvent Federal laws by enforcing local statutes that would restrict blacks from exercising their new Constitutional rights.

Simultaneous with these events many ex-Confederates, emboldened by Johnson's failure to enforce even his own rules for Reconstruction, began a systematic persecution of loyalists and blacks throughout the South. A high incidence of bushwhackings and violence toward freedmen supported this conclusion. In four Alabama counties alone, for example, there were twenty-one known murders of freedmen in a period of just two months! Amid this violence and uncertainty following the demise of the Confederacy, the responsibility for maintaining order fell on the local military governors.[31]

Determined to put an end to the flagrant disregard for Federal law by diehard slavery advocates, and in so doing to reverse the trend of pro-slavery political resurgence in the South, Krzyżanowski waged an all-out campaign against these acts of violence. In one instance Sheriff Benjamin Snodgrass of Scottsboro, Alabama, arrested fifteen Northern sympathizers on a series of obviously fictitious charges. It was a form of intimidation commonly practiced by unrepentant rebels during 1865. Kriz ordered the proceedings halted as a violation of the loyalists' rights. Snodgrass, a self-proclaimed anti-Unionist who employed Confederate guerrillas as his guards, ignored the order. The local court, likewise consisting of ex-Confederates, continued with the sham trial. Krzyżanowski, acting under the authority vested in him as the military commander in an area under martial law, dispatched a detachment of black troops to Scottsboro to enforce his edict. The soldiers closed the court, released the prisoners, and sent the sheriff off under Federal arrest to a Nashville prison.[32]

Certainly this action may appear highhanded, but it was within the authority of the military commander to assume control when there was evidence that loyalists or freedmen were being intimidated. It was not an isolated incident, it occurred in virtually every state in the South. Kriz, of course, never doubted either the legitimacy of his authority or the justice of his cause. He saw it as his responsibility to protect the lives and property of all citizens against the few who sought to overturn the will of Congress and the Constitution. President Johnson might well pardon the murders of

Lincoln, but Krzyżanowski was determined that these die-hard rebels would not deprive others of their rights within his sphere of authority.

As the political events unfolded, Kriz had a job to do. Although Lee had surrendered in early April, other Confederate armies remained in the field requiring continued vigilance, both of the enemy and sometimes his own command. In June, for example, he arrested a lieutenant in the 106th Ohio and three privates, charging the officer with making out false discharge papers to enable three privates from the 58th New York to desert. In August, when a train passed through Stevenson a soldier in the 4th Kentucky, without provocation, threw a stone at a black railroad employee fracturing the man's skull. "I would ask to have the Officer in Command arrested," Kriz wrote to Col. John G. Parkhurst, the Provost Marshal General in Nashville, "who is responsible for the conduct of his men till the perpetrator of this foul deed in discovered." In September he wrote to Capt. J. F. Blickensdoerfer, Acting Assistant Inspector General in Huntsville, Alabama, returning some of the captain's reports due to their incompleteness and "informality." Kriz cautioning him to observe the regulations in General Orders No. 6 of the Military Division of Tennessee when writing his reports, detailing in his letter some of the information required. "You will carefully instruct yourself," he concluded, "and furnish the necessary reports correct and with promptness."[33]

Yet while he continued to perform his role as an officer, his nomination as brigadier general continued to languish. Recommendations from Gens. Franz Sigel, Oliver Otis Howard, Carl Schurz and Edward Canby arrived in Washington to support the nomination, as did the following letter to President Andrew Johnson signed by 34 officers of the 135th Indiana Regiment:

> We the undersigned Officers of the 135th Regt. Ind. Vols. organized from the Eighth Congressional District of Indiana and at present at Bridgeport, Ala, do voluntarily and cheerfully recommend Your Excellency the appointment of W. Krzyzanowski Colonel of the 58th Regt. New York Vols. and commander of this post as Brigadier General U.S.V.
>
> We make this recommendation in consideration of his past gallant services in the field and also from the ability diligence and courtesy which he has manifested toward us while under his command. Believing that by his appointment the interest of the army and government would be materially advanced we honestly hope that speedy action may be taken in the premise.[34]

Even as this letter wound its way to Washington, the long-sought, long-deserved, long-awaited promotion materialized. Krzyżanowski signed his oath of office as a brigadier general in Nashville on July 1, 1865.[35] The promotion came none too soon because even as he signed, the Union Army was already being dismantled. One of the last units to be deactivated, the 58th New York Infantry mustered out of the Federal service at Nashville, Tennessee, on October 1, 1865. For Krzyżanowski the day brought sadness. Parting with those he grew so attached to was no easy task. No doubt he recalled that day long ago when he first enlisted as a private in the District of Columbia Militia. But that was a different era, the country had changed since then and so had he. The long years of hardship since that fateful day left his health impaired. He no longer moved with his old alacrity. He had become tired with the weight of the travails and privations of his service.[36]

Slowly the train began to pull away from the station. It was a long way to his home in Washington. The general had ample opportunity to reflect upon his career. Surely he thought back on his four years in the military with pride, yet the pride lay tempered by memories of friends who never enjoyed the laurels of triumph their lives helped to ensure. Perhaps he thought of Henry Bohlen, the paternal Philadelphian who died at Freeman's Ford. No doubt he thought of the fury and disappointment of Second Bull Run. He remembered Chancellorsville where Charles Pizzala, Frederick Braun and scholarly Elias Peissner met their fate. And then there was Gettysburg! How could he forget the field where he lost half of his command? He languished over the fate of friends and comrades: Franz Mahler, Louis Dietrich and Edward Antoniewski. He thought of these and more. Then too, there were Henry Baetz and Theodore Dodge, each with but one leg. Bernhard Domschcke returning emaciated from a Confederate prison. As the train jolted along there were others who could no longer enjoy the view of nature that Kriz studied from the coach. Charles Wickesberg escaped the savagery of Gettysburg with a wounded wrist. The following year he fell at Resaca. In Wisconsin, Barbara Muenzenberger mourned for her husband Adam who lay beneath the anonymous turf of a Richmond prison. There were many who would not forget the hell that war really was.

"THOSE WHO WERE FAITHFUL"

THE RECONSTRUCTION ERA

The postwar months were a time of apprehension and uncertainty in Krzyżanowski's life. The sudden cessation of formal hostilities, followed closely by the dismemberment of the vast Union Army, left him not only jobless but for the first time in years without the close companionship of his former comrades-in-arms. In May of 1866, in the company of Louis Seldner, he took a two week trip through Virginia. Although the purpose of the trip is uncertain, Seldner later recalled that Krzyżanowski was "suffering with shortness of breath & frequent shooting pains in his ribs." He attributed this to the injuries Kriz received at Gettysburg. Seldner later boarded with Kriz in New York City from 1867 through May 1869, noting that the Pole frequently had to stop speaking and take deep breaths, often "bringing his hands over the side of his chest as if in pain." To a greater or lesser extent, these afflictions would remain with Kriz for the rest of his life.[1]

Returning to his home at 351 8th Street West in Washington, D.C., Krzyżanowski was soon drawn to what he thought would be greater prospects for the future in New York City. Sustained by the loving attentions of his wife, he settled into an apartment at 213 East 48th Street in New York to begin a new life. It soon became apparent, however, that his search for a civilian position in an economy glutted by the postwar manpower abundance would not be easy. Week after week he sought out satisfactory employment, only to meet with continuous rebuff. Steadily his meager resources dwindled to the point where necessity forced him to swallow his pride and seek advances from more fortunate friends.[2]

During this period of stress the Masons once again approached Kriz in an attempt to revive his interest in their organization. Their efforts proved fruitless due to Krzyżanowski's financial status and the fact that he sought camaraderie through affiliation with a group of men with whom he shared much closer bonds. On February 12, 1868, the Secretary of Eureka Lodge No. 243 finally struck Krzyżanowski's name from the Masonic records, citing nonpayment of dues as the reason for the action. By this time the lure of Krzyżanowski's old comrades brought him into the nucleus of activists who sought to form lasting bonds between the men whom fate united in the recent struggle to preserve the Union. Soon after his arrival in New York, despite his economic problems, Kriz assisted in the formation of Koltes Post No. 35, Grand Army of the Republic, which developed into the largest veterans post in New York State. The founders appropriately named the organization after Colonel John Koltes, a comrade who fell on the sanguinary field at Second Bull Run, with Kriz officially mustered into the post on June 7, 1867. Largely for his organizational efforts, Kriz was elected Junior Vice Department Commander of the State of New York, the third person to hold the office since its inception in 1866. Later, when employment took him to Georgia, he was elected to the GAR's National Council of Administration from that state, serving also as Assistant Inspector General based at Macon, while still later, encouraged by several close friends, Kriz took the lead in organizing Von Steinwehr Post No. 192 of which he mustered in as the very first charter member and first post commander on January 10, 1883. This association, which enabled him to maintain ties to his former companions-in-arms, provided some therapeutic relief from the problems that beset him in everyday life. Perhaps it also encouraged him further to solidify his allegiance to his adopted country by becoming a United States citizen. On March 18, 1868, he appeared before Chief Justice D. Cartter in the Supreme Court in Washington, D.C., to swear that he was a native of "Poland," that "having enlisted in the Army of the United States and having been honorably discharged therefrom," he renounced any allegiance to any other power, "and particularly to the Kingdom of Prussia of which country he has hitherto been a subject." Krzyżanowski was officially tied to the adoptive nation he had served through four long years of bloodshed and hardship.[3]

The G.A.R. posts served as a sounding board for the programs and pronouncements of amateur politicians unsettled by the turn of events following Appomattox. As the Confederate surrender faded beneath the cloak of historical romanticism, Krzyżanowski lamented the continued hegemony of Andrew Johnson whose administration distributed myriads of pardons and appeasements. It was a time, he wrote, when "those who wanted to divide the Union seemed to become the government leaders, while we, who protected the nation with our best, were forced to bow to them and to become the servants of traitors."[4] Doggedly determined to pursue his own concept of American union, Kriz maintained close ties with Radical Republicans who sought to win the peace that followed the successful conclusion of the war.

To Krzyżanowski, alliance with the Radicals appeared the only answer to the abyss he saw the nation heading for during the long months of 1866 and 1867. He found in the Republicanism of Abraham Lincoln the unswerving principle of liberty under a firm national government that reflected the ideal he had relished since the patriotic childhood stories of his native land. The alternative to this nationalism was Andrew Johnson's moderation, a policy that signaled the return to power of those who so recently attempted disunion by force. This was brought home clearly to Krzyżanowski when Congress finally reconvened in Washington during December 1865. Waiting to take their seats in the forthcoming Thirty-ninth Congress were the men Johnson agreed to accept as the legitimate legislators of the unrepentant South. They included not only the vice president of the former Confederacy, but four Confederate generals, five Confederate colonels, six Confederate cabinet officers, and fifty-eight former Confederate legislators. Predictably, these relics of the Old South steadfastly refused to accept even President Johnson's limited terms for repatriation of their states.[5]

Krzyżanowski also saw in the Radical Republicanism of Thaddeus Stevens the American complement of the principle of universal democratic freedom that Kriz inherited from the Polish liberalism of 1846. The humanitarian reforms attempted on behalf of the freedmen by the Radicals stood in conspicuous opposition to Johnson's veto of the Civil Rights Act of 1866. This proposal attempted to repudiate the anachronistic Dred Scott decision through legislation guaranteeing the civil rights of all Americans. Johnson's veto of this bill was but one incident in an ever-increasing chain that further alarmed Northerners and Republicans. In the summer of 1866, a summer tainted by cruel, deadly riots against blacks in Memphis and New Orleans, Johnson vetoed a bill to extend the Freedman's Bureau. As a compromise measure to assuage the South and reconstitute the Federal Union, the moderates in Congress then proposed the Fourteenth Amendment, a virtual restatement of Johnson's own original criteria for the reestablishment of normalcy. Under its terms the South could return to the Union without being forced to accept black suffrage. Johnson advised his Southern friends to reject the measure and hold out for even better terms after the Radical defeat in the 1866 Congressional elections. Flushed with the sudden success of renewed defiance, States' Rights Southerners rejected the Fourteenth Amendment, and with it any chance for support from moderate Northerners.[6] Their attitudes astounded Krzyżanowski. "The death of Lincoln and the transfer of authority in a different direction," he wrote, "changed things so much that when one awoke and read the morning paper one wondered whether this was a dream, or if one had slept several years before awakening."[7] The Johnson Administration, he feared, was "filling government posts with their own underlings, and removing those who were faithful to the Union. They seemed to be waiting for an opportune moment to again form a new Confederacy."[8]

Krzyżanowski was not the only one upset by the uncompromising attitude of Southern diehards. The nation's electorate overwhelmingly reaffirmed their faith in Republican leadership that fall by giving undisputed control of both the Senate and the House of Representatives to the anti-Johnson forces. In the former, forty-two Republicans won seats as opposed to only eleven Democrats. In the latter, 143 Republicans easily outvoted 49 Democrats. The supporters of union and freedom won an overwhelming victory, far in excess of the two-thirds needed to override presidential vetoes. Krzyżanowski felt vastly relieved. "The Republicans," he commented, "were able ... to regain command of the government, thus defeating the South as they had upon the field of battle. The Southerners could not help themselves. As they lost control over the slaves, so did their control over the North end."[9]

The elections of 1866 were only a hint of what was to come. The Radicals, once in office, quickly moved to offset Southern influence in the government. In March 1867, they divided the South into five military districts to enforce the provisions of their own strict Reconstruction policy. In the following year the struggle between the executive and legislative branches of government culminated in the impeachment of the chief executive. In a dramatic vote, Johnson escaped conviction when the Radicals failed by a single vote to get the required two-thirds majority.

In 1868, Krzyżanowski enthusiastically supported the "bloody shirt" campaign of Ulysses S. Grant, being active in several political organizations in New York City including the Loyal Veterans' Grant Club, as well as organizing and serving as president of the German Veterans' Republican Grant and Colfax Club.[10] Grant's election as president proved to be the final triumph of the Radical Republicans. With Grant in office Krzyżanowski believed that the ideals of nationalism and freedom were once again in safe hands.

The passage of time mollified, to some extent, the overwhelming drive for revenge that initially drew Kriz into the camp of the Radicals. This was replaced by a sincere belief that the reactionary elements who glorified the "Old South" and the "Lost Cause" must be decisively defeated in the field of politics as they had been on the field of battle. Consumed by his dread of Southern resurgence, Krzyżanowski wanted a United States that was truly indivisible. With these principles firmly imbedded in his psyche, the former general once again sought entry into political life. It was a natural choice, for it mirrored the ancient ideal of the Polish nobility that held public service, whether in the military or in government, as the highest form of patriotism. If nothing else, Wladimir Krzyżanowski was a man tied to his past.

REVENUE SERVICE IN GEORGIA

Ulysses S. Grant took office as the eighteenth president of the United States on March 4, 1869. With the aid of several key endorsements, including that of the new Secretary of War, William W. Belknap, Krzyżanowski obtained an appointment to the Internal Revenue Service on May 8 of that same year. Under the terms of the First Reconstruction Act passed by the Radicals in March 1867, the South was divided into five military districts. On May 26, 1869, he took the oath of office as the Supervisor of Internal Revenue for the District of Georgia and Florida. For a salary of $2,500 per year, Kriz took on the responsibility of overseeing Treasury Department operations that included offices at Jacksonville and Fernandina in Florida, and Atlanta, Augusta, Macon and Savannah, Georgia.[11]

Krzyżanowski established his own headquarters at Macon, an overtly hostile area known to be a crossroads for smugglers dealing in cotton, tobacco, and alcohol. The rampant anti-Union sentiments made it doubly difficult to enforce Federal directives in an area containing a thin, widely dispersed population. Nevertheless, cheered by the recent Republican political victories, Krzyżanowski immersed himself in his work, hoping to help reestablish law and judicial government in the South.[12]

Much to his disappointment, Kriz found that the political victory of Ulysses S. Grant in 1868 only served to increase the vigor of reactionary forces in the South. "The Southerners were beside themselves with rage," he noted. "They could not stand to see the reins of government slipping out of their hands."[13] Unable to win victory on the battlefield or at the polls, the South resorted to a secret quasi-military organization determined to rectify the situation through the use of fear, intimidation and violence. This Ku Klux Klan, Krzyżanowski stressed, "was maintained along military lines, the express purpose being to keep blacks from voting by means of intimidation, flogging, or murder."[14]

Kriz detested the Klan and all of the un-American principles that it embraced. "This organization," he explained, "sought the cover of darkness for its activities. They fell upon Republican homes doing terrible things. These unknown knights, these stranglers of liberty, these tools of tyranny, rode clothed in long white robes with their faces covered by a dark mask. ... Their horses were decorated in the same manner with sheets and robes. This clothing served not only to frighten their victims, but also to mask their own identity."[15] To Kriz there was no worse threat to American liberty than this bigoted, self-proclaimed guardian of inequity. "It became so powerful," he said, "that its tentacles reached into the highest echelons of government. It must be stopped."[16]

At a loss to explain this behavior, Krzyżanowski asked the residents of

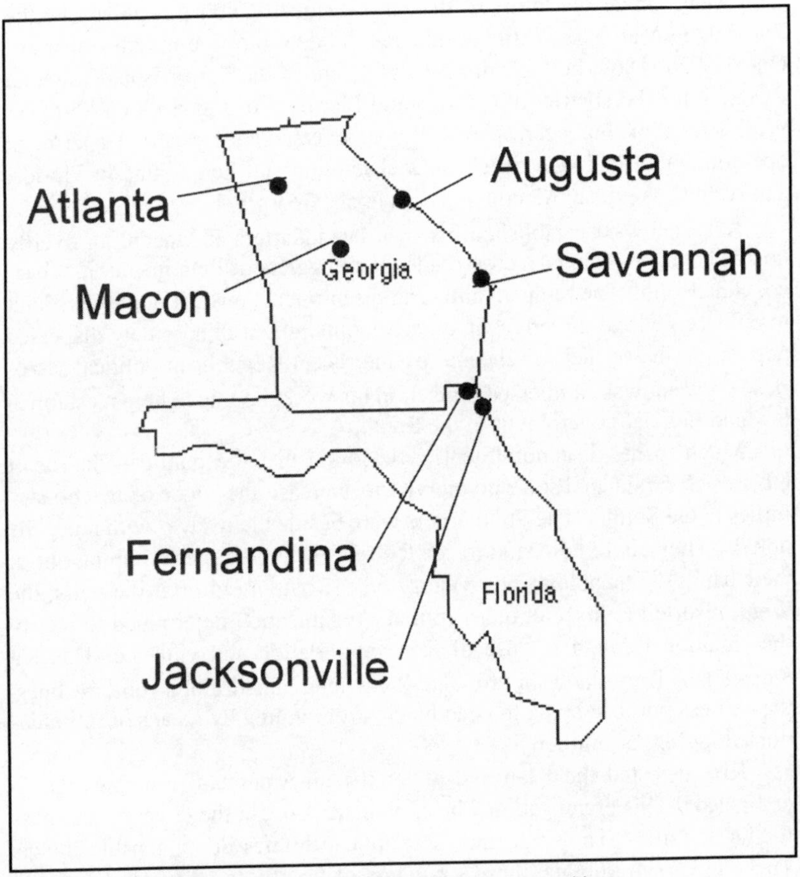

Map of the area covered by Krzyżanowski as
Supervisor of Internal Revenue for the District of Georgia and Florida.

his district why they held such an attitude of superiority over Northerners attempting to rebuild the South. The Southerners were, the they indignantly replied, aristocrats. Yet, they had difficulty explaining how this could be true.

"What makes you think you are an aristocrat?" Krzyżanowski queried.

"We are the descendants of noble Huguenots," one young man replied, "whereas the Northerners are descendants of the scum of the European continent. Our forefathers came to this country to escape religious persecution, while their forefathers came to escape prison."[17]

It was a strange statement coming from a resident of Georgia, a state originally founded as a colonial refuge for imprisoned debtors. Kriz argued with the man, stressing the common heritage of the early English settlers and the similar motivations of subsequent immigrants. He noted the contributions to American liberty made by such men as his countryman Tadeusz Kościuszko, but to no avail. The emotional mentality of the Klansman and the secessionist, the bigot and the bully, allowed no room for facts or rational arguments.[18]

Because of his position as Supervisor of Internal Revenue, Krzyżanowski had to spend much of his time attending social functions for the benefit of politicians, financiers and other visiting dignitaries. "Feast followed feast," he wrote, "banquet followed banquet; in place of the firing of cannon we enjoyed the popping of champagne corks."[19] Time and time again people who overindulged in the seeming pleasures of alcoholic escape exhibited their provincial xenophobia in praise of their own sections or states. It was not the type of talk Krzyżanowski liked to hear. To him, the important consideration was that they were all Americans. It was wrong, he believed, for people to place petty parochialism above the essence of American unity.

On one particular occasion the long-winded banquet oratory dragged on most of the night with each succeeding speaker attempting to outdo the former in praise of his own native state. Finally Governor Harrison Reed of Florida rose to introduce Kriz. The governor launched into a lengthy commendation of Krzyżanowski's services during the war, following which he called upon the former general to propose a toast. Rising slowly, his face revealing obvious embarrassment at the prolonged encomium, Kriz thanked the governor for his kind words and proceeded with the toast. He apologized for not being able to sing the praises of his city, his section, or his state as the other gentlemen had. Nevertheless, he continued, "I am very proud to be a citizen of all the United States."[20]

The brief toast made a dramatic impression upon the gathering. Newspaper editors printed and reprinted the remarks, but Kriz felt that all of this attention and praise were certainly undeserved. He only spoke from his heart about what he believed. His only thought was to make people aware of the fact that they were all Americans; citizens of the United States, not merely citizens of Georgia, Florida, Tennessee, or New York. Throughout his dealings with officials and residents in the South he stressed this concept of commonality. Friendship, he said, was the medicine that would heal the nation's wounds. The North must certainly enforce the Constitutional laws, but to obtain lasting harmony both North and South must pursue a reciprocal friendship.[21]

Unfortunately this policy did not always work. The virulent Ku Klux spirit rampant in Krzyżanowski's Supervisory District forced the Federal agents to be continually on guard against persistent attempts to defraud the government. The most widespread attempts at deception involved nonpayment of the Federal tax on alcoholic beverages. Agents constantly searched to uncover clues leading to the illegal distillers. Kriz often led his men into the field in person to end the illicit activities. His effectiveness can be judged through his successes. Between November 14, 1870, when Krzyżanowski conducted his first raid, and April 25, 1871, a period of just over five months, units under his command uncovered eighty operating distilleries and eighty-five completed stills. The raiders seized or destroyed 122,260 gallons of beer and mash, 1,794 gallons of wine, 700 gallons of peach and apple brandy, 390 gallons of corn whiskey, 595 bushels of corn meal, seventy-nine bushels of malt, five mules, three wagons, two oxen and one horse.[22]

Despite these successes, Krzyżanowski found his office inundated with new cases. During the first three months of 1871 the situation grew to the point where Krzyżanowski requested the services of one or two companies of United States cavalry to halt the proliferation of illegal alcohol and tobacco throughout his district. In addition to this, he requested that the Commissioner of Internal Revenue—former Union General Alfred Pleasonton—appoint several assistant assessors to handle the backlog of cases brought to his attention. If implemented, Kriz maintained, these recommendations would greatly increase federal revenues from spirits and tobacco.[23]

Though vigorous in his pursuit of illicit activities, Krzyżanowski's very diligence placed him in the midst of a struggle between two federal administrative departments. When he submitted a bill to the Office of the Quartermaster General for $1,914 for expenses incurred in hiring and feeding horses used by U.S. troops in breaking distilleries in Georgia, the Quartermaster General wrote to Secretary of War Belknap to protest payment of the expense. "As the Military appropriations pay the troops detailed to aid in this duty," he explained, "and Regulations provide for the food and clothing, and all necessities of the troops, the Quartermaster general doubts the propriety of putting upon the appropriations of the Army, the extra expenses of hire of horses and feed of horses, hired by the Internal Revenue Department, to carry those detailed, to assist them in their civil duty." There was no question about the legitimacy of the bill itself, for the Quartermaster General also noted that the expense appeared justified but should be funded from the Treasury Department because the purpose of the expenditure was to enforce the revenue laws. Belknap returned the bill to Krzyżanowski with the following explanation: "As stated in the accompanying letter of the Quartermaster General on the subject, the account seems justly chargeable to appropriations for collecting the revenue or to that for civil expenses of the Treasury Department."[24] Although Kriz had done nothing wrong, the delay in paying these bills because of the dispute between the two government agencies reflected poorly against him with the local population and made it more difficult for him to obtain support on credit in the future.

Aside from his continuing duties, Kriz also faced the hostility of local ex-Confederates. At some point, a story appeared in the *New York Herald* in which Krzyżanowski was said to have declared on a trip to Washington, D.C., that he had been notified by the mayor of Savannah that his life was in danger if he remained in the city. Whether a true rendition of actual events or not is difficult to say after nearly a century and a half. Regardless, the story became known in Savannah and provoked an angry reply from its mayor. On January 16, 1871, the *Savannah Morning News* published an article stating that

> Mayor Screven, deeming it but just that prompt contradiction should be given the Krzyzanowski slander, alleged by the Washington correspondent of the New York Herald to have been circulated in Washington, has transmitted the following official communication to the editor of the Herald:
>
>> I observe in your journal of the 10th inst. the following extract; Colonel Krzyzanowski, Supervisor of Internal Revenue for the States of Georgia and Florida, who has just arrived here from Savannah, reports that he was notified by the mayor of that city that his life was unsafe while he remained in Savannah. It appears that this officer had rendered himself obnoxious to the enemies of the administration, on account of his efficient manner in prosecuting parties guilty of violations of the revenue laws, and in breaking up illicit distilleries throughout the state.
>
> As the foregoing conveys to the world a report not founded on facts, I desire to state, through the medium of publication, that Colonel Krzyzanowski is wholly unknown to me, either personally or officially, and that I have never had any communication or relations with him whatsoever.[25]

When he became aware of the controversy, Kriz wrote to Mayor Screven, in the words of the *Savannah Morning News*, "in which he repudiates the statement made by the correspondent of the *New York Herald*."[26] Further contradiction came from a Colonel Robb who supposedly had accompanied Kriz on a visit to the White House during which the offending comments had been made. The *Savannah Morning News* soon reported: "The Agents of the Associated Press are requested by Colonel Robb, collector of customs in Savannah, to state, in connection with certain publications copied from a Washington dispatch to a Northern paper that he has not had an interview with the President, has not visited the Executive Mansion in company with Col. Krzyzanowski, and has made no allusion to anyone about outrage in Savannah."[27] Regardless of the veracity of the allegation, this was but one small episode in the ongoing battle between ex-rebels and the federal officials assigned to duty in the South. The situation was exacerbated by the numerous scandals of the Grant administration.

Working under a presidential administration that was, at that time, the most corrupt in American history, it is significant to note the efficiency with which Krzyżanowski operated, a fact alluded to in the first quotation from the *Savannah Morning News* cited above. While revenue agents in some areas took bribes from distillers, arrangements which later became public as the "Whiskey Ring" scandal, Krzyżanowski's investigations led to the arrest of twenty-four persons in the ninety days between January and the end of March, 1871. During that same period Kriz expended $3,607 in carrying out his duties, while bringing in confiscated goods whose estimated value enriched the federal coffers by $18,285. The government's profit margin on the illegal alcohol crackdown, when judiciously administered, was thus quite lucrative.[28]

During the period following the Civil War, when Krzyżanowski remained unemployed, he accumulated several outstanding debts to friends who lent him aid until his appointment to the post in Georgia. In an attempt to repay these obligations promptly, Kriz decided to invest in a private enterprise. In early August 1870, he established W.B. Krzyzanowski & Co., a retail and wholesale furniture business located at 188 Broughton Street in Savannah, Georgia. To purchase the business Kriz obtained a loan of $2,200 in cash from John H. Gould, Collector of Customs at Savannah, and agreed to assume liability for between $5,000 and $6,000 in debit notes. Krzyżanowski also secured a partner, Theodore B. Marshall, who contributed between $7,000 and $8,000 to finance the enterprise.[29]

Krzyżanowski's association with the firm lasted less than one year. In the face of mounting scandals in the South, the Commissioner of Internal Revenue made it known that he frowned on the possible conflict of interest which might arise from a public official engaging in private business. Not

An advertisement for "W. Krzyzanowski & Co." appearing in the *Savannah Morning News*.

---

wishing to compromise himself, Krzyżanowski repaid Gould's loan, with interest, and sold his share of the business to J.C. McNulty on March 17, 1871. Later that year, the Blackstone National Bank filed suit against "Krzyzanowsky & Co." for unpaid loans. In December, the bank obtained a judgment against Theodore B. Marshall for \$811.11 plus interest, keeping the affair before the public long after Kriz had severed his relationship with the firm.[30]

Short though this business venture was, it proved disastrous. During the spring or summer of 1871, Joseph A. Roberts, a Savannah businessman, made a trip to New York City. While at the Astor House he overheard a conversation between John Gould and Theodore B. Marshall, Krzyżanowski's two financial associates. During the dialogue, Roberts said, Gould openly proclaimed his affiliation with W.B. Krzyzanowski & Co., stating that the capital he poured into the business came, in fact, from the revenue office under his jurisdiction. Roberts reported these comments directly to the Treasury Department, which hurriedly dispatched an investigator to look into the situation.[31]

The first thing that the investigator discovered in Savannah was that the district's books were in shambles. As it turned out, A.S. Alden, the bookkeeper, utilized an unorthodox system of entries for recording payments.

When a citizen paid his tax to Alden's office, the bookkeeper simply marked a check after the individual's name to indicate that he had paid his assessment. Since Alden indicated no dollar amount, it was impossible to determine how much money the Savannah office collected. In this way the monthly statements could easily be made to appear in order, and if a close examination were conducted it could not possibly prove definite evidence of fraud. While the taxpayers received a receipt stating that they met their obligations, the only thing that the government retained to indicate the amounts of revenue collected was the word of A.S. Alden and John H. Gould.[32]

Investigator Yaryan further uncovered damaging evidence that as early as the spring of 1870 Alvin B. Clark, Acting Assessor for the First Georgia District, informed Krzyżanowski that something irregular was taking place in Savannah. Krzyżanowski, it appeared, failed to act upon this report. In his defense, Krzyżanowski argued that he *had* investigated. He maintained that Clark's report indicated something was wrong with the stubs and receipts of Gould's bookkeeper. Kriz personally brought the matter to Gould's attention. Gould, in turn, called Alden on the carpet for the discrepancies and later explained to Krzyżanowski that the problem resulted from an $8,000 entry being debited twice. When Alden corrected this error, Gould maintained, the books would balance. Mr. Clark, Krzyżanowski noted, was present at the meeting and did press the issue after the explanation, nor did Clark indicate that Gould might be involved in the irregularity. Krzyżanowski thus assumed that the problem was satisfactorily resolved.[33]

In support of Krzyżanowski, Clark asserted that the Supervisor's story was correct. Clark indicated that he did not press the issue further because he lacked any evidence that would call for a further investigation of the case by Krzyżanowski. In addition to this support, Deputy Commissioner Williams testified that when he indicated to Krzyżanowski, in late March, 1871, that irregularities might indeed exist, Kriz immediately "used all possible means to secure his [Alden's] arrest."[34]

Further damaging allegations came from R.R. Brawley, the bookkeeper for W.B. Krzyzanowski & Co. from its inception until February 6, 1871. Brawley indicated that at Gould's order he recorded substantial credits to the personal accounts of Krzyżanowski, Marshall and a blind entry marked "Bank Account." Gould's involvement is explained very simply because Theodore Marshall hired him as business manager for the firm. Gould certainly acted within the power of attorney granted to him by Marshall. Krzyżanowski, immersed in his duties at Macon, left the actual management of the company to Marshall, thus Kriz may have had no knowledge of Gould's appointment. Indeed, Kriz testified to the effect that he was unaware of Gould's connection with the furniture business other than through the loan he provided for Krzyżanowski earlier. A survey of the business ledger of the company shows that between October 19, 1870, and February 25, 1871, Krzyżanowski's account increased by a total of $43.75.[35] This certainly does not indicate what one might expect to find in a case of embezzlement or other misuse of funds.

Continuing his investigation, Inspector Yaryan found evidence corroborating Krzyżanowski's explanation of his business dealings with Gould. Yaryan noted, for example, that Krzyżanowski paid Gould amounts of $1,500, $500, and $700 to retire the original debt owed to the latter. In addition, Yaryan uncovered evidence indicating that Gould was involved in a whole series of frauds, of which his apparent dealings in the furniture business formed only a small part. It became obvious to Yaryan that Gould and Alden were working in collaboration to defraud the government by submitting false financial statements.[36] "I consider Alden," Yaryan wrote, "the most hardened, impudent, and bold faced rogue that it has ever been my duty to have intercourse with."[37]

While Yaryan criticized Krzyżanowski for not uncovering the irregular bookkeeping practices earlier, he generally absolved Kriz of any implication in the embezzlement conspiracy. "It is certain," Yaryan reported, "that he realized no pecuniary benefit from the whole transaction, but on the contrary lost what money he put in."[38]

As soon as solid information was presented implicating his employees, Kriz attempted to arrest them. On April 8 the *Savannah Morning News* reported that "The government really is taking steps to arrest Major Gould. The Palatka, Fla. *Herald* says W. Krzyzanowski, the general Supervisor of the Revenue Department arrived in that place recently and chartered a steamer and went in pursuit of Gould, who recently decamped from Savannah with $53,000." There followed a lengthy series of articles on government corruption including an investigation of Deputy Collector Wellman of Savannah charged with embezzling $11,000.[39] All of these kept alive the prevailing atmosphere of suspicion and mistrust.

Despite Krzyżanowski's acquittal by the Treasury Department, the conservative elements in Savannah leaped at the chance to rid themselves of this man who made his living by imposing upon them the hated statutes of the Federal government. Georgia gained re-admission to the Union in 1870, and by the fall of 1871 political power in the state rested firmly in the hands of the conservative upper classes that ruled the Peach State prior to the war. In October 1871, the same month during which Yaryan exonerated Krzyżanowski, the Grand Jury in Savannah indicted the Supervisor on charges of fraud. On October 30, the *Savannah Morning News* carried a brief item notifying its readers: "Deputy United States Marshal Freeman, on Friday, arrested Gen. W. Krzyzanowski, supervisor of Internal Revenue, on a charge of embezzlement." Once arrested, Kriz found that Georgia was no place for a Federal official to expect sympathy. Humiliated, he remained confined to his cell until his wife managed to contact some friends who posted the required bond.[40]

Despite his innocence, the Grand Jury indictment achieved the results that its Southern backers hoped for. On November 1, 1871, Commissioner of Internal Revenue J.W. Douglas dispatched the following note to Secretary of the Treasury George S. Boutwell.

> Sir,
>
> W. Krzyzanowski Supervisor for Georgia and Florida, having been indicted by the Grand Jury at Savannah, Georgia, I deem it required for the good of the Service that he be removed from his position as Supervisor, and would so respectfully recommend.[41]

Douglas was, of course, correct. With all of the scandals involved in the Reconstruction, and in the Grant Administration, the Treasury Department could ill-afford to chance bringing upon itself additional censure. Boutwell personally presented the matter to President Grant, whereupon the two decided to appoint a new Supervisor in Krzyżanowski's place.[42] The final blow came in the form of a letter from Boutwell to Krzyżanowski dated November 2, 1871. "Sir, Your services as a Supervisor in Internal Revenue under this Department [for Georgia and Florida] are hereby discontinued to take effect from this date."[43]

— Chapter Eleven —

"I Feel That I Have Done My Duty"

Special Agent, United States Treasury

Dismissal from the revenue service was an onerous burden for Krzyżanowski to bear. Throughout his term of office his monthly statements of expenses and receipts were never once questioned. He conducted his official duties with diligence, as seen from his success in disclosing illicit dealings. Nevertheless, he found himself ousted from his position due to a scandal in which he, himself, stood exonerated. The disappointment bore doubly hard upon this man whose training and socialization in Poland left him with a deep respect for public service.

Sadly, Krzyżanowski led his family north to Washington. Having lost what money he put into his furniture business, he once again had to bear the degrading necessity of securing loans from his friends. Fortunately, there were others who sympathized with his plight. On November 11, 1872, he received an appointment as Special Agent for the Treasury Department. His commission instructed him to report for assignment to Special Agent G.J. Kinsella in New Orleans.[1]

Service in New Orleans

Krzyżanowski glowed with exuberance. For him, it was a new lease on life. He took the oath of office the very same day. On the morning of November 17 he helped his family aboard the train for New Orleans, arriving there on the evening of the 22nd. When he arrived in New Orleans, Kinsella informed him that to earn his five dollars per day, plus expenses, Kriz would be responsible for investigating cases of smuggling and for overseeing the general operations of the customs officials in the New Orleans area.[2]

Kriz spent the remainder of November acquainting himself with not only his duties, but also with the localities under his jurisdiction. At the docks, for example, he observed the procedure that the officials used in inspecting the steamships *Liberty* and *Margaret*. Later he took an active part

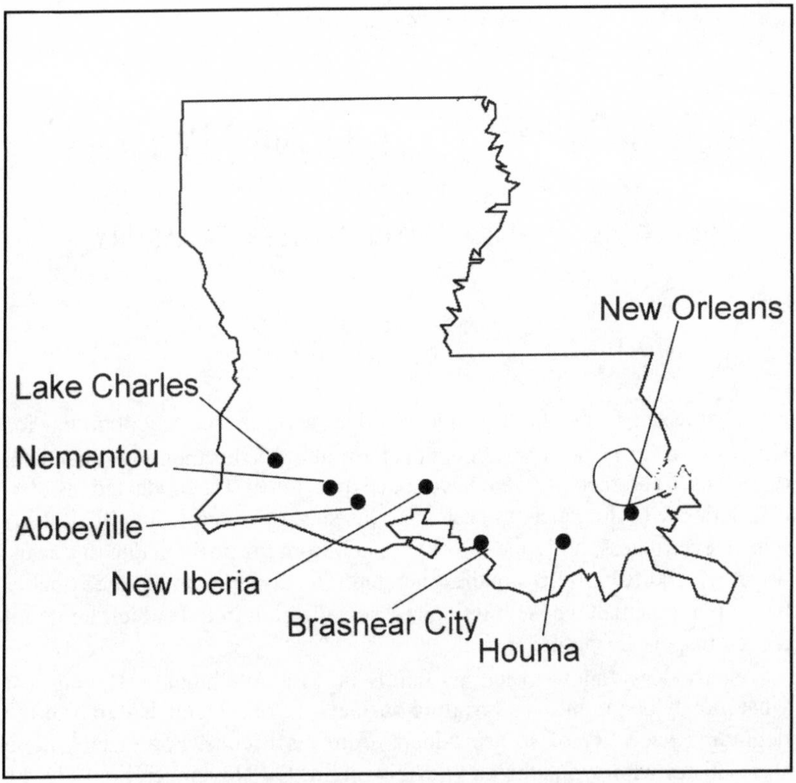

Map of the area covered by Krzyżanowski as
Special Agent for the Treasury Department in New Orleans.

in searching for contraband aboard the brig *Charlotte Bock* and the steamship *Juniata*. Always quick to recognize the efforts of his subordinates, Kriz noted in his first monthly report that Inspectors D.J. Hutchinson, F. Hutchins, and A.C. Stuart "have shown vigilance and they deserve credit for their energies."[3]

By December Krzyżanowski found himself working long hours to catch up on a constantly rising volume of reports and inspections. Throughout that month, and the first half of January, 1873, he conducted rigorous investigations of the bonded warehouses throughout the district. His duties also called for frequent visits to the levee where he supervised the inspection of both the ships' cargo and the passengers' baggage. On January 13 he left New Orleans to inspect the outlying areas of his district where he encountered many problems and irregularities.[4]

Krzyżanowski's first action involved reports that Captain E. Collins of the steamer *Gettysburg* was unloading freight which the captain then smuggled up Bayou Terrebonne to Houma. Detecting smugglers was a difficult, sometimes dangerous task. Kriz diligently surveyed the Houma area trying not to arouse suspicions, a difficult task for someone who was obviously an "outsider" to the natives. He found no illicit goods. Further investigations into the activities of J. Wolf, another suspect, similarly turned up nothing to indicate wrong-doing. Finally, a thorough search of Wolf's store failed to turn up any suspicious goods.[5]

After a short visit to Brashear City, Kriz moved on to Abbeville, traveling via water to acquaint himself with the coastline between Bayou Teche and Bayou Vermillion. He found the area honeycombed with rivers, ponds, and mysterious passages. Surely, he thought, it was a smuggler's dream. What better landscape could anyone ask for if they wanted to cover their trial? It would certainly be difficult for anyone, even a small army, to uncover smuggling routes in this maze of waterways. Nor did the position of the customs station help any. Kriz found that the local inspectors operated from a station located some sixteen miles up Bayou Vermillion. They were, Krzyżanowski noted in his report, "unable to guard anything except what comes up Bayou Vermillion and the whole coast between the mouth of the Teche and Vermillion Bayou is totally unguarded."[6]

In addition to the awkward placement of the customs station, Krzyżanowski's eyes also observed that the yawl provided for the agents' use was totally unfit to operate beyond the tranquil confines of the bayou. In his official report Kriz correctly surmised that for the revenue service to be effective there should be at least two minimal changes. First, the customs station should be located at Hackerberry Point which offered a commanding position on the coastal approaches. Second, an adequate yawl should be provided for the agents' use because much of their effectiveness was necessarily curtailed under current conditions that limited their activities to the placid bayous and solid lands.[7]

Having once discovered these shortcomings, Krzyżanowski continued his investigation further. His examination of the revenue station itself revealed the startling fact that Inspectors Brookshear and Hanchett kept no receipt books at all! A few days later, at Galveston, Krzyżanowski found a similar situation where no records were kept. He readily recognized, of course, that this practice encouraged many different forms of misappropriation. He remembered all too well the villainous machinations of A. S. Alden that led to Krzyżanowski's recent dismissal as Supervisor of Internal Revenue. Kriz certainly wanted no repetition of that calamity; consequently, he quickly dispatched a written report directly to the Treasury Department in Washington. In the report he not only pointed to the dubious practices of the local officials, but also indicated that the Galveston office was overstaffed. He suggested the removal of the Inspector at Galveston, following that with a recommendation as to who might be appointed in his place.[8]

At Galveston Kriz also uncovered a lead to Captain Collins, the man suspected of smuggling cargo from the *Gettysburg* onto Timbaker Island. Through assiduous questioning Krzyżanowski discovered that Collins paid a visit to Brashear about January 1. Kriz determined to follow this lead to see if anything might come of it. Traveling overland, he searched the areas surrounding Nementou, Calcaieu, and Lake Charles. His persistence paid off. On the east bank of the Nementou river he found a store run by a Mr. Victoran which stocked large amounts of English ale and porter. Although there appeared to be no direct evidence of smuggling, Kriz found it suspicious that such extensive quantities of these items were kept in such a remote place.[9]

From Victoran's store Krzyżanowski continued on to New Iberia where he found further confirmation of Collins' visits to Victoran's establishment. Krzyżanowski's prudent queries also yielded the theory that some of the smuggled goods were hauled overland to be sold in Opelousas and Washington, Louisiana. Kriz thought it apparent that his first suspicions regarding Captain Collins were correct. He recommended that a careful watch should be kept on Collins, and that the system of revenue stations should be revamped to provide more efficiency. In line with the latter recommendation, he suggested that the New Iberia station would be more productive if it were moved to Lake Arthur. In addition, he pointed out the need for a revenue station on the Nementou River, a major artery for smuggling that remained open to illegal traffic.[10]

Krzyżanowski continued his inspection tour through February and March, 1873, concentrating his activities in the areas surrounding Lake Pontchartrain and Lake Manchae. Though he found no evidence of smuggling in these areas, he did take note of several deficiencies in the local revenue offices. Constantly on the move, Kriz explored several bayous, as well as the towns of Mandeville, Lewisburg and Covington. With the Georgia debâcle still fresh in his mind, he left no stone unturned in his search for evidence of illegitimate activities. His monthly reports arrived in Washington promptly, containing sound recommendations for the increased efficiency of operations in his district.[11]

Not all of Krzyżanowski's time was spent in the outlying areas. In New Orleans he frequently visited both warehouses and dockyards. Here he also exposed practices that called for revision. At the New Orleans customs house, for example, he observed that female passengers suspected of smuggling were examined in private by a stewardess. Kriz reasoned that since the stewardesses were in no way responsible to the government they could not be counted upon as reliable investigators. To solve the problem he recommended that a female examiner be appointed in New Orleans to close this potential gap in surveillance.[12]

Throughout the spring, into April and May, Krzyżanowski carried out his duties with diligence and precision. He completed his investigations with such thoroughness that on June 9, 1873, through the recommendation of Carl Schurz, Kriz received an appointment as Special Agent for Customs District 15 in the Washington Territory. Kriz was eager to accept the appointment immediately, but it came at an inopportune moment. Caroline was in the midst of a serious illness which the physicians felt would require her to stay in bed two to three weeks. Kriz certainly entertained no thought of leaving his wife, despite the new appointment. He wrote to the Treasury Department acknowledging receipt of the new nomination, but indicating that he could not possibly leave his wife at that time. He requested leave to care for her before his departure for Port Townsend and was relieved to obtain the Department's approval.[13]

SERVICE IN THE WASHINGTON TERRITORY

With Caroline at last able to travel, the family boarded the *City of Richmond* on July 12, 1873, for a trip up the Mississippi to St. Louis. From there, the journey would continue by rail. Once on board the steamboat, Krzyżanowski decided to pass some of his idle hours in the gambling casino. During his years in the army Kriz became quite adept at card games. Early in the war he even played with General Robert Schenck who later wrote a celebrated treatise on draw poker. Kriz was no longer the innocent novice who lost his family's savings while waiting for a ship in Hamburg. It did not take him long to detect the dubious methods by which one riverboat gambler fleeced a likeable young chap out of $200. No doubt remembering his own painful initiation into the world of chance, Kriz sympathized with the young man. Determined to rectify the matter, he entered a game with the professional gambler and deftly exposed him as a cheat. Enraged at the gambler's dishonesty, the captain of the boat forced the swindler ashore at the earliest opportunity. The much relieved young man received as a stake for the future all of the money that the gambler was forced to leave behind—over $600.[14]

From St. Louis the Krzyżanowski family traveled by rail to San Francisco. There, on August 2, they boarded a steamship for the last leg of their journey to Port Townsend, the primary port of entry and headquarters for the Puget Sound Customs District in the Washington Territory. After settling his family into a house and enrolling his son Joseph in school, Kriz reported for duty to Special Agent Rufus Leighton in Port Townsend on

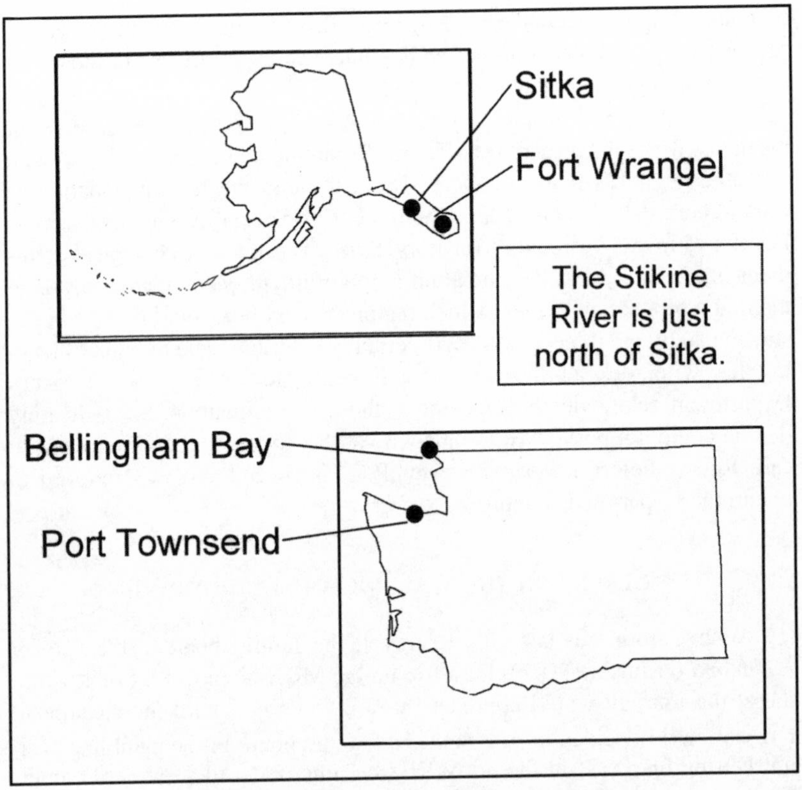

Map of the area covered by Krzyżanowski as
Special Agent for Customs District 15 in the Washington Territory.

August 11, 1873.[15]

As his first duty in his new post Krzyżanowski familiarized himself with the area under his jurisdiction. To accomplish this he spent several days cruising the picturesque waterways around Port Townsend. He capped his tour of the area with a visit to nearby Victoria, British Columbia, where his inquiries and observations convinced him that there was little incentive to smuggle anything beyond the small scale attempts of legitimate passengers.[16]

Kriz completed the remaining days of August by visiting several coastal towns, but noted in his first report from the Washington Territory that he was unable to complete his tour of the islands in Puget Sound for lack of a safe boat. The craft assigned to the revenue service, he commented, had even been pronounced unseaworthy by the local ship builders. In view of the numerous water approaches to Port Townsend, and the unacceptable condition of the revenue boat, Krzyżanowski's first recommendation was the hiring of a sloop capable of operating in all of the various passages.[17]

In September Krzyżanowski received an assignment to investigate affairs at the customs houses in Portland and Astoria. After a lengthy analysis of the procedures and records at these two stations, Kriz concluded that all was in order. This left him free to cruise the length and breadth of Puget Sound, ranging as far as Bellingham Bay in the north and Scathet Head in the South. The search paid off for Kriz soon spotted a ship whose name sounded familiar. Checking his record books he found that the sloop *Foam* cleared Port Townsend for Victoria on May 29. She had not been heard from since. The long absence of her name on the customs records struck Krzyżanowski as suspicious because the vessel normally spent its time plying between two or three local ports. Kriz overtook the *Foam*, boarder her, and began his investigation.[18]

The ship's master explained that his vessel changed owners after departing from Port Townsend. Paperwork and other delays prevented her return. The answer did not convince Krzyżanowski. He brought the ship into Port Townsend where, after informing the collector on duty, he turned the vessel over to Inspector A.B. Young for further investigation.[19]

At the end of September Krzyżanowski received orders to investigate reports of illegal activities in Alaska, the frozen northland purchased from Russia in 1867. His first stop was the customs house in Sitka. There he alertly noted that the Federal customs collector was actively engaged in storing smuggled alcoholic beverages in the Federal warehouse. These illegal spirits were then sold to the local saloons at a handsome profit. Further inquiries proved that the former collector embezzled fines that he collected and knowingly signed payroll vouchers for periods of time when he was not on duty. Such investigations were naturally fraught with danger for the evidence Krzyżanowski amassed could well lead to a long stretch in a Federal penitentiary for the guilty parties. It stands as a measure of Krzyżanowski's honesty to note that one and one-half years before the *St. Louis Democrat* exposé on the infamous "Whiskey Ring," Kriz busily uncovered similar cases of fraud in the remote Alaskan wilderness.[20]

Before he left Sitka, Kriz also investigated a complaint filed by the owner of the schooner *Nellie Edes* which had been impounded by Collector Chapman. Arena Phillipson, owner of the vessel, charged that the collector illegally impounded the ship's registry during a dispute with her husband. Krzyżanowski collected affidavits from the owner, her husband, and the builder of the ship, a man named Nicoli Chechenoff. All three stated that Chechenoff constructed the ship for Arena Phillipson who remained the sole legal owner of the vessel. Further confirmation of this came from a former revenue official and from Captain J.A. Webster of the United States revenue cutter *Reliance*. Kriz forwarded these documents to the Secretary of the Treasury along with his own conclusion that the action of Collector Chapman was a complete "misrepresentation ... actuated by personal feelings against Mr. Phillipson."[21]

Before returning to Port Townsend one other problem demanded Krzyżanowski's attention. Reports of rich gold discoveries along the upper Stickine River in Canada appeared to be creating a potentially volatile situation in the American territories that surrounded the mouth of that waterway. Cursory inquiries convinced Krzyżanowski that the stories of a substantial gold discovery were true. Upon his arrival in Ft. Wrangel, a few miles from the mouth of the Stickine, Krzyżanowski found his worst fears justified.[22]

With the discovery of gold upriver, Ft. Wrangel was sure to become the center of commerce in that area. Already miners and traders were gathering at the port. Some five tons of foreign goods stood stacked upon her docks. Hurriedly, Kriz sketched out his report to the Secretary of the Treasury, indicating that time was of the essence. Only the severity of the weather, he explained, prevented the Stickine country from being overrun by prospectors and businessmen. Kriz cautioned that unemployed miners arriving in Ft. Wrangel were already busily devising ways to accumulate profits before leaving for the gold fields. In double violation of the law, many of these men openly imported liquor from Victoria and sold it to the Indians. Illicit stills proliferated, compounding the problem.[23] The only government official in the area, Krzyżanowski explained, was a deputy collector, and "he is powerless, the physical strength being against him, so he is unable to enforce the law."[24]

Krzyżanowski reported that the situation in Ft. Wrangel might well become critical once the mining season opened. Already, he noted, a merchant from Portland planned to open a trading post at the mouth of the river. By late February or early March, Kriz explained, the weather would begin mitigating, thus inaugurating the full frenzy of the gold rush. He urged the Treasury Department to move the revenue cutter *Reliance* off the mouth of the Stickine to contest the illegal activities rampant in that area. In addition, he recommended that the Department make plans to establish a permanent customs house at the mouth of the Stickine because Ft. Wrangel lay some eight miles distant along the coast. Without these precautions, Kriz felt, it would be impossible to enforce the revenue laws and the country might erupt into violence once the inevitable crush of gold fever took hold.[25]

En route home from his investigative tour of Alaska, Krzyżanowski decided to stop off in Victoria. The discovery of gold along the upper Stickine, he reasoned, would certainly have an impact on the residents in British Columbia. This impact would no doubt have repercussions in the American-controlled areas of Alaska; thus, Kriz wanted to examine in person the prevailing Canadian attitudes. It was well that he did. He found the Victoria merchants engaged in intensive preparations to begin shipping all conceivable types of merchandise to the gold fields at the earliest possible hour. While that, in itself, presented only a problem of volume, Krzyżanowski's adroit queries uncovered a far greater problem.[26]

In order for the merchants in Victoria to ship goods up the Stickine River to the gold fields they had to land their merchandise in American territory, thus becoming liable to United States import duties. The Canadian merchants correctly feared that the imposition of these customs duties would impair their ability to compete with American merchants from San Francisco and Portland. American businessmen could land their goods at Ft. Wrangel without having to pay these tariffs. Thus, the Americans would be able to undercut Canadian prices on goods that would eventually end up in Canada anyway. The chance geographical location of the gold discovery fostered a difficult problem indeed.[27]

Seeking to regain a competitive status, the merchants in Victoria called upon their government to impose a rule whereby "all vessels carrying goods from any of the U. S. ports for the mines, should come in to Victoria and pay the duties there, regardless if such vessel had cleared from one port of the U.S. to another, and from the latter Port the goods are to be shipped into B.C."[28] Clearly this type of law would inflame the emotions of American merchants. Krzyżanowski realized this, discerning also the possibility of violence if the two hostile forces did not come to some agreement. He cautioned the Secretary of the Treasury about the situation, forwarding at the same time a detailed report on his observations and recommendations to ease the tension of the situation. It was the first such warning that the Secretary received concerning the possibility of trouble between Americans and British Columbians. Using Krzyżanowski's report as a guideline, the Secretary took effective action to defuse the potentially explosive situation, while at the same time ensuring that the government received its proper revenues.[29]

Despite his conscientious efforts on behalf of the government, in addition to his impeccable reports, Krzyżanowski returned to Port Townsend on December 4, 1873, to find himself again the center of controversy. Once more he found his career in Georgia coming back to haunt him. From Monticello, Florida, three men wrote to the Treasury Department demanding payment of bills incurred by Krzyżanowski during his tenure in Macon. The debts stemmed from an investigation into illegal alcohol and tobacco traffic in Florida during which Kriz signed vouchers of $27.50 for the rental of a horse, $55.00 rental on a wagon and two-horse team, and $17.00 worth of forage. A search of the records indicated that these bills, amounting to $99.50, indeed remained outstanding.[30]

In response to these claims William A. Richardson, the Secretary of the Treasury, requested that Krzyżanowski provide some explanation of the debts and why they were never paid. Kriz replied immediately, explaining that upon his dismissal from the post in Georgia he left all of his books and accounts in the hands of his clerk in Macon. Once Krzyżanowski arrived in Washington, D. C., he personally sent in vouchers for all of the various debts the clerk in Macon reported as being due. It was apparent, Kriz wrote, that through some oversight these bills were never brought to his attention. Following his service in Georgia, Krzyżanowski noted, he was without employment, thus precluding him from repaying the debts himself. While in New Orleans, Caroline became very ill necessitating a further outlay of money in medical expenses. Currently, the general explained, he was engaged in repaying obligations incurred while out of work in Washington. During all of this time, he maintained, he kept his creditors well-informed of his problems. The Treasury Department, he pointed out, was well aware of his financial problems from the beginning. I hope, he concluded, that "leniency will be extended to me under these circumstances."[31]

Why the Treasury Department refused to reimburse Kriz for these bills, obviously incurred in the line of duty, remains a mystery. Of all the periods in his life, the time he spent in Georgia proved the most lasting nemesis. For years the problems he encountered there followed him wherever he went causing continual mental and financial drain. It is to his credit that despite these difficult financial circumstances Krzyżanowski never stooped to using his public office for self-aggrandizement as others did. Throughout his long years in public office, despite constant need, he was never once guilty of financial misconduct.

In spite of his problems, Kriz could not pause to rest or reflect. His position as Special Agent kept him constantly occupied. From Port Townsend he journeyed to Seattle to examine the customs house. Unlike so many occasions in the past, he found this office in perfect order. By the end of the month he once again returned to Port Townsend. At last, in January, he found some time to rest. The revenue sloop leaked so badly that repairs took most of the month. When it again set sail in February, new leaks once more forced it into port.[32]

Around the beginning of March, 1874, Krzyżanowski read two important newspaper articles. The first reported that the British government decided to require all vessels carrying goods for sale in the Stickine mining areas to pay duties in British Columbia before unloading their cargoes. This was the exact situation that Krzyżanowski had foreseen three months previously. Because of his earlier report the Treasury Department had the time necessary to devise a specific strategy for implementation in just such an eventuality. Kriz could well indulge in a smile of success.[33]

The second newspaper story indicated that Selucius Garfielde, the revenue officer in Olympia, had become addicted to gambling. The report stated that the official regularly lost substantial amounts of money at the tables of a local saloon. Although this was not strictly within the bounds of Krzyżanowski's jurisdiction, the situation bothered him. He felt that some investigation should be made as the problem could have grave consequences if the situation was as bad as the newspapers described it. Kriz mailed the clipping to the Supervising Special Agent in Washington, D.C., along with a request for instructions on whether an investigation should be launched. The reply came in the affirmative, sending Kriz off to Olympia.[34]

When he arrived, Krzyżanowski found Garfielde's office empty. He finally located the official in one of the town's gambling establishments. Through inquiries addressed to several different individuals regularly doing business with the customs house, Krzyżanowski found that Garfielde spent most of his off-duty hours, as well as many of his office hours, in the local saloons and gambling houses. Further investigations turned up the interesting intelligence that Garfielde sent messages to Special Agent Leighton at Port Townsend imploring the latter to order a halt to Krzyżanowski's visits and investigations. "The unanimity of opinion about the character of Mr. Garfielde," Krzyżanowski concluded in his report, "is remarkable and appalling."[35] The evidence he uncovered, supported by seven corroborating affidavits, was conclusive enough for the Treasury Department to relieve Garfielde of his commission.

Kriz spent the better part of April cruising about Puget Sound and the Straits of Juan de Fuca in search of smugglers. He logged 310 miles in April, boarding several suspicious vessels to examine their papers and cargo manifests. During May he covered 285 miles, as well as investigating the best means by which wool smuggling might be curtailed once the shearing season began.[36]

Returning to Port Townsend near the end of May, Krzyżanowski found a letter from the Secretary of the Treasury awaiting his attention. He opened it and began reading. Dumfounded, his eyes stumbled over words informing him that his "services as Special Agent will terminate the thirty first of May."[37] No reason was given. One hypothesis maintains that Kriz retired from public life to settle down to the privacy of his family. This is doubtful. On his commission, issued November 11, 1872, there is a handwritten comment that reads: "Cancelled by letter of removal to take effect May 31, 1874."[38] Clearly this implies removal from office. We are left to ponder why. Perhaps it was a result of the political patronage system at work. Regardless, once again Kriz worked diligently, unsparingly, honestly, only to find his life again in ruins about him. In despair, he wrote to Senator George Boutwell from Port Townsend on May 19, 1874:

I must beg you to pardon me for trespassing on your valuable time; but the kindness I have received from your hands encourages me to appeal to you again, in my hour of trouble.

Few days ago during my absence from here, on official duties, a dispatch came to my address signed by the Hon. Wm. A. Richardson Secretary of the Treasury, informing me, that my "services as Special Agent will terminate the thirty-first instant." A severer blow I would not have received, here I am a stranger in a strange country, without friends, and without means even, to provide for my little family, over four thousand miles from those who know me best.

I do not know the cause of my removal and must therefore infer that I am again the victim of some malicious combination, as my conscience is as clear as the sun is pure. I am at a loss to know why I am thus persecuted. I have been true to the party from its infancy and when I held no position under the Government. When the National Capital was threatened by traitors, I grasped my musket and went in to the ranks to protect the same. When the Rebels threatened to break up this Government and were tearing down the National Flag, I renewed my pledge and reentered the Union Army, serving to the end of the war.

It is therefore, that I feel more severely the way I am treated by my Government. True my services have been but insignificant in comparison to others; but I feel that I have done my duty; I sacrificed all that I possessed, I carried my life to the altar of my adopted Country, and has there any one done more than this? My life has been spared by the protecting hand on High; but my business was sacrificed; and I had to ask the Government for a position. In my state of life it is not easy to find employment, as I would in former days, neither have I means to go in any business. I must beg you, for your protection again and I hope you will intercede for me so that I may receive some position out here. Any thing by which I can provide honourably for my family.

I will feel grateful to you and I pledge myself that I will bring no discredit upon your recommendation.

Hoping you will favor me with few lines.[39]

Where would he go? What would he do? In his distress he gravitated south to friendlier areas where he might find consolation and friendship. His mind thought of San Francisco with its influential G.A.R. posts and its large, active Polish community. Yes, he thought, San Francisco!

— CHAPTER TWELVE —

"WITHOUT INJURY TO HIS DIGNITY"

LIFE IN SAN FRANCISCO

Krzyżanowski arrived in San Francisco at a fortuitous time. While the eastern United States began to decline into the depression caused by the Panic of 1873, California remained isolated from this economic disaster. Good harvests and promising business ventures drove California's economy upward after 1869. The wide fluctuations of the mining industry made the San Francisco stock market an attractive lure for speculators. In the spring of 1873, near San Francisco, a mining syndicate headed by James Fair unearthed a massive vein of silver some fifty feet wide with an estimated value in excess of $500 million. Speculation reached epidemic proportions. Money flowed readily from hand to hand.[1]

Arriving in the midst of plenty, Krzyżanowski encountered little difficulty lining up backers for his own business venture. Through contacts in the local G.A.R. and the Polish community, Kriz was able to obtain loans from C.L. Luniewski, Rudolph Korwin Piotrowski, and Edward S. Salomon. With this capital Kriz purchased the New York Casino, located at 236 Montgomery Street, on October 1. Intent upon settling down to a permanent home after so many years of wandering, Kriz joined the infant Polish Society of California and enrolled his son Joseph at St. Ignatius College, later to become the University of San Francisco.[2]

Active involvement in community affairs brought Kriz a great deal of popularity, especially within the local Polish community where he assumed a leadership position in the Towarzystwo Polskie w Kalifornji [Polish Society of California] formed on January 23, 1873. Active in the Society's efforts to raise money for the newly-founded Polish National Museum and Treasury in Rapperswyl, Switzerland, he also participated as a member of the committee formed to educate Americans on the abuses of the Russian authorities and send petitions to the president of the United States asking protection for American citizens of Polish descent living in Turkey during the Russo-Turkish War in 1877-78.[3]

His business became a rendezvous for G.A.R. veterans and immigrant groups alike. Indeed, his association with the latter group of individuals led him to an acquaintance with two individuals whose later fame in the United States was surpassed only by their notoriety in their native Poland. In both cases—Helena Modjeska and Henryk Sienkiewicz—Kriz lent a helping hand as they began their careers.

Shortly after his arrival in San Francisco, Krzyżanowski joined a group of prominent Poles who met at the docks along San Francisco Bay to welcome a group of fellow exiles. Standing on the pier waiting for the expected vessel to dock, Krzyżanowski had time to reflect on those who stood near him. His gaze fell upon the elite of California's Polish-American community. Close by Kriz stood Captain Rudolph Korwin Piotrowski, the general's business associate. Holder of the coveted Polish *Virtuti Militari* decoration for service during the 1830 revolt, Piotrowski was a founding member of the Polish Society of California. His unique character formed the prototype of the captain in "After Dark," a short story written by Newton Booth.[4]

Captain Casimir Bielawski paced anxiously about the dock. A surveyor by profession, he chaired the Polish Committee in San Francisco during the crisis of 1863, and was the current chairman of the Polish Society of California. He enjoyed the lasting distinction of having Mt. Bielawski in Santa Clara County as his namesake. Next to Bielawski stood Dr. Ladislas Pawlicki who declared California his home after deserting from the Russian corvette *Rynda* in San Francisco Bay during November 1863. He preferred exile to serving against his countrymen during the Polish uprising that year.[5]

Journalist Julian Horain stood on the docks next to Edmond Brodowski, one-time United States consul at Breslau. In the midst of the growing crowd stood Alexander Bednawski, a noted civil engineer, Wincenty Ludnicki, a veteran of the 1830 revolt who owned a jewelry store near the famous Sutter's Creek, and Captain Franciszek Wojciechowski, another veteran, who owned a stable of horses on the outskirts of the city. It was a prestigious gathering, indeed, but one well suited to the expected guest—Helena Modrzejewski.[6]

Born in Kraków in 1840, Helena was the daughter of Prince Władysław Sanguszko, the brother of novelist Joseph Conrad's tragic Prince Roman. At an early age Helena developed a keen interest in the theater, progressing rapidly until her talents won her lead roles throughout Poland as Camille, Adrienne, and Lady Macbeth. In 1868 she married Count Karol Chłapowski and settled down to a career on the Warsaw stage. There the Chłapowskis helped form a discussion group composed of democratic patriots whose interest in the arts paralleled their own. Intellectuals in the circle debated the issues of the day, continually hoping for new means to accomplish their goal of Polish independence. They eagerly read political news from abroad, but nothing made quite the impression upon them as did the beautiful pastoral scenes of America painted by travelers, ship owners, and land speculators.

Particularly appealing were the letters of Julian Horain, the San Francisco journalist, who was once a member of the Chłapowski circle.[7]

The lure of freedom and open lands drew many in the circle to dream of settling in the New World. In preparation for their journey they sent Juliusz Sypniewski and a Podlasie journalist named Henryk Sienkiewicz to explore possible areas for settlement in the United States. These two Poles warmly recommended the San Francisco area because of its apparent opportunities and the large colony of ex-European revolutionaries residing there.[8]

Before leaving Poland the Chłapowski group formed a company in Kraków with assets of $48,000. Leaving Poland by separate routes, the travelers rendezvoused in Berlin. From there they journeyed overland to Bremen where the group of thirty-three actors, painters, editors, orators and litterateurs embarked for America. Now, their long journey nearing completion, they hove into sight of the crowded pier where their fellow exiles awaited them.[9]

The joyous greeting completed, Kriz and his fellow Poles took their new friends to examine several likely locations for their proposed colony. The new group decided on a 150 acre plot in the Santa Ana Valley near the old German settlement of Anaheim. Here, with the help of their neighbors, the Poles prepared to cultivate the soil while pursuing their own artistic endeavors. Although most such Utopian communities based their existence on some social, religious or political ideal, the Poles came solely to enjoy the serenity of California's rustic beauty and the freedoms offered by the Constitution of the United States. As a colony of intellectuals they dwarfed even the fabled Brook Farm of Thoreau, Dana, Hawthorne and Fuller.[10] "They had no problem in life to settle," noted one author, "no theory to prove, no cause to wage for downtrodden humanity, no degeneracy to regenerate."[11] In the end, it was this very intellectual ambiance that proved their undoing.

Unfortunately for the colonists, their flesh proved much weaker than their collective spirit. They formed a symphony club, a debating society, and other intellectual forums, but they were almost totally unable to cope with the complexities of agrarian life. While the intellectuals tended to their respective avocations, hired hands tended to the basic work of preparing fields and planting crops. Though eager, the idealists did not know the first thing about farming. Soon animals began to die. While the Poles staged elaborate dramatic performances, the irrigation ditches dried and the alfalfa withered in the fields. One day, as the symphony club entertained the group with selections from Bach, the barn burned to the ground.[12]

Visitors marveled at how the Poles could retain their cheerful "Bohemian-like" nature in the face of disasters that "would have driven crazy any colony of ordinary farmers."[13] Lyman Busby, their neighbor, put

Madame Helena Modjeska.
Courtesy of the Bowers Museum.

it thusly:

> Never had finer folks about. Talk about good nature, you ought to have seen how jolly they used to be when everything on the farm was drying up in the sun and the animals were all sick and dying. They never wore long faces. When they all saw that farming was a mighty hard, dirty job, totally unfit for educated gentlemen like them, they fiddled, painted and scribbled and cracked jokes. If ever there was a set of happy, smart men anywhere it was that colony of Poles. They lost every dollar they put into their co-operative farming scheme. They were no more cut out for plowing, harvesting, and doing the round of chores of a farm than a Hottentot can figure in Algebra.[14]

Count Karol Chłapowski.
Courtesy of the Bowers Museum.

Henryk Sienkiewicz.
Courtesy of the Polish Museum of America in Chicago.

Disaster piled upon disaster. Slowly, by ones and twos, the impractical romantics began to depart the crumbling colony for Paris or for their native land. Almost as soon as she arrived in America, Helena thought of returning to the stage. Now, with financial problems setting in, she determined to cast her lot on the American stage. She and her husband discussed the idea with their San Francisco friends, from whom they received enthusiastic encouragement. San Francisco's Polish community relished the thought of seeing the darling of the Warsaw stage playing before American audiences. Most enthusiastic of all was General Krzyżanowski, his mind leaping back in time to the memories of his beloved homeland.[15] Krzyżanowski's advice, Karol Chłapowski wrote, was "the most practical of all. He will be of great help in our theatrical negotiations." Modjeska commented in a letter to Poland only that Krzyżanowski "runs a tavern, but keeps his air of a nobleman."[16]

The first major stumbling block that Helena had to overcome was her lack of fluency in the English language. As a tutor she hired Johanna Tucholsky, the eighteen-year-old daughter of a prosperous Polish attorney. While Helena labored to master the words and phrases of her adopted tongue, Krzyżanowski explored his contacts in San Francisco to obtain an audition for the Polish actress. Because of her heavy accent, Helena was reluctant to travel to San Francisco. Using the utmost tact, Krzyżanowski manipulated Helena's own fondness for the theater to break through the psychological barrier created by these fears. Kriz knew that the actress held a high regard for the genius of Edwin Booth. One day he casually mentioned to her that the celebrated actor was appearing in San Francisco, knowing full well that she could not resist the opportunity to see Booth perform. Once settled in a hotel room in the city, it was much easier for Kriz to convince her to attend meetings with several of the city's theater managers.[17]

Captain Kazimierz Bielawski
Courtesy of the Polish Museum of America in Chicago.

To arrange for the interviews, Krzyżanowski enlisted the support of Edward S. Salomon. The two men became close friends during the Civil War when Salomon led the 82nd Illinois Infantry in the Eleventh Corps. After the war Salomon went on to serve as Governor of the Washington Territory, residing in Port Townsend at the time that Kriz arrived to take on his duties as Special Agent for the Treasury Department. Retiring into private life, Salomon became a successful San Francisco attorney. When Krzyżanowski chose to settle in the same city, Salomon lent his friend some $2,500 to aid him in establishing his saloon business.[18]

The two friends spent seemingly endless hours knocking on theater doors. They found that foreigners were not particularly in vogue on the San Francisco stage at that time; thus, Helena's rich accent became a dual liability. Much laborious effort finally bore results. The men obtained for Helena an audition at the Grand Opera House, one of the most prestigious theaters in the city.[19]

All of Helena's Polish friends attended the audition. Their minds and hearts were thankful for the great opportunity to see her first successful step toward stardom on the American stage. The individual movements of these fervent spectators echoed through an otherwise barren theater. No special lighting lit the stage, no elaborate scenery graced the background. Yet when Helena moved gracefully onto the stage the seats gently creaked as their occupants leaned expectantly forward. As the actress began to speak, her audience hung on each heavily accented phrase. Suddenly, after only a few short lines, the theater manager rose from his chair.[20]

"She is no good!" he exclaimed.[21]

Edward S. Salomon.
Courtesy of the U.S. Army Military History Institute.

"Gentlemen," cried the startled actress, her eyes riveted on the small gathering of supporters, "what have you exposed me to!"

"Oh, the rascal," muttered Captain Piotrowski under his breath.

Shock gripped the small audience as Helena ran sobbing from the stage. The silent, interminable seconds which followed suddenly ceased, broken by the commanding voice of General Krzyżanowski.

"He is an ass, Madam, it is not for this blockhead to pass judgment on an artist like you."[22]

While this outburst probably put the theater manager in his place, it gave little solace to either audience or actress. Both lamented over the humiliation. Krzyżanowski felt especially disappointed due to his long exertions and the inescapable feeling that he was somehow responsible for the debâcle. Most disconsolate of all was the actress. She remained so disheartened that she rejected an offer for a new audition that Krzyżanowski and Salomon feverishly worked to arrange for her. Nothing that her friends could say would convince her to set foot on another American stage. No amount of pleading, no measure of cajoling succeeded in moving her. In the end, with everyone else on the verge of conceding that their pleas were a lost cause, Captain Piotrowski hit upon the key that unlocked the barrier of despondency.[23]

"Well," he began calmly, "if one such knave was able to frighten you, certainly you are not a Polish woman."[24]

Helena's eyes opened wide. Her jaw clenched with determination.

"Do with me then what you want, my friends."

Elated, Krzyżanowski and Salomon arranged for an audition before John McCullough, a seventy-year-old actor of great renown. In fairness to the actress, McCullough insisted that she do the scene of her choice in her native Polish. She selected the immortal balcony scene from Romeo and Juliet. Again attended by her faithful followers, Helena entered upon the stage, in the words of the local press, "every inch a queen." Slowly her lips began to move, emitting long streams of melodic Polish syllables. The audience sat transfixed as if controlled by some magical spell. Finally Captain

Piotrowski could contain himself no longer. Emotion welled within him, forcing the old soldier to clear his throat. Sienkiewicz leaned gently toward him to whisper in his ear. The sweet musical tones of his native language wrought a profoundly sentimental feeling that penetrated to the very marrow of Krzyżanowski's being. He had forgotten how beautiful his mother tongue could be. His mind flashed back to Poland, to his youth, to his long disrupted family. Faintly he heard someone whisper into his ear. He pretended that something had fallen into his eye.[25]

McCullough, his silver hair streaming down upon his shoulders, rushed onto the stage.

"You are the greatest artist I have ever seen and I foretell you unusual triumphs on our stage!"[26]

He insisted that Helena sign a contract to appear in one of his productions. Once she polished her English the only problem that remained was to choose what name she would appear under: Opid, her family name, Modrzejewska, the name of her first husband, or her current married name of Chłapowska. Helena favored the second as it was her stage name in Warsaw where she enjoyed such good fortune. McCullough remained skeptical. No one would be able to pronounce it. Finally the two reached a compromise by shortening Modrzejewska to Modjeska. Thus Helena Modjeska received her first billing on the American stage.[27]

Krzyżanowski and Salomon handled the publicity for her opening, set for August 13, 1877. Dutifully they went about the city encouraging friends to purchase tickets to the performance. It was an off week at the California Theater, most of the preparations were for the upcoming production of Cleopatra starring popular Rose Eytinge. On Helena's opening night Krzyżanowski, Salomon, Sienkiewicz, and all of the actress' Polish compatriots crowded into the theater. "Our Lady," as the Poles referred to Modjeska, made her appearance in the second act of *Adrienne Lecouvreur*, playing the title role. A large burst of applause rose spontaneously from the Polish section as Helena came on stage. The Americans in the audience remained largely indifferent. Then Modjeska began to speak. The fluid, professional presence of the actress began to captivate the theatergoers. Intrigued by the quaint accent, heads began to lean forward, faces began to lose the impassive countenance of the bored. Cold curiosity turned into an emotional bond between actress and audience. As the final curtain descended the listeners were wild with applause.[28] Sienkiewicz wrote to friends in Warsaw: "The theater audience roared, shouted, clapped, stamped their feet." A reviewer for the newspaper *Alta California* wrote: "A week ago her name was little known to us and rarely read about. In a year's time it will be more famous than that of the French celebrity, Sarah Bernhardt."[29]

In the weeks that followed Modjeska's triumphal entry into the

American theatrical world, her Polish friends went about with inflated egos. The success of *Adrienne Lecouvreur* launched Modjeska on a long series of successes that included triumphal tours of the United States and Europe. Her name became a familiar word. Her long career marked the final stages of the great era of nineteenth century Romanticism. Years later, as she prepared her memoirs, she thought back on her acquaintance with Krzyżanowski. "The General," she wrote, "took a more lively interest than any other of my Polish friends in my future dramatic career in this country."[30]

The successful beginning of Modjeska's American career formed the topic of discussion for quite some time at Krzyżanowski's tavern. There the San Francisco Poles met to socialize and discuss their native land. The New York Casino was a small business employing a cook, a waiter, and two bar-keepers, but its informal atmosphere attracted many steady customers. In addition to various beers and liquors, Krzyżanowski stocked for his customers a wide variety of meat, fish, poultry, sausage, vegetables, and baked goods. For their further enjoyment, his patrons could select from several leading brands of cigars as they engaged in card games, chess, and other recreations.[31]

Governor Salomon, who gave so unstintingly of his time on behalf of Modjeska, was particularly fond of the Poles. He came to the tavern almost every evening to see Krzyżanowski. The two often joined Julian Horain and Henryk Sienkiewicz in playing cards. Horain spoke no English other than the oddly pronounced phrase "I lofe you" with which he constantly teased all of the young ladies to whom he was introduced. Salomon spoke no Polish. To remedy the problem Salomon learned enough Polish phrases so that by combining them with an energetic sign language he could make his bids understood.[32]

One of the things Sienkiewicz marveled about in the United States was the respect for labor that appeared so universal. To him, the epitome of this ideal was Krzyżanowski. He observed that the general frequently tended bar or otherwise catered to the desires of his guests without any injury whatever to his dignity or social position. The specter of a one-time general and important government official serving drinks in a saloon was more than he could readily comprehend. It would certainly never occur in Europe. Yet, it appeared perfectly acceptable in the United States.[33] In his letters home, Sienkiewicz wrote, with obvious reference to Krzyżanowski:

> The respect for labor which I mentioned earlier permits an individual to engage in any kind of work without injury to his dignity and social position. Many high public officials are engaged in commerce, industry, or a craft—only to the extent, of course, that time permits. After leaving public office, they enter some type of

> business, unperturbed by the fact that they had previously been important government officials. I am myself acquainted with a former brigadier-general and wartime government official in Georgia who at present is the owner of a huge saloon and who himself frequently serves beer and whiskey to his guests. Of course, according to European standards, this is something incredible. But the only thing that would arouse curiosity here would be a European's surprise at things so simple and natural.[34]

Nor was this the only observation that Sienkiewicz made in the generals' casino. A professional writer, Sienkiewicz spent much of his time studying American customs and mannerisms. The New York Casino, in fact, provided him with a miniature test tube in which he could observe the varied personality traits of the people who frequented the general's saloon. Later, when he returned to Poland, Sienkiewicz took with him the nucleus for several of his characters and short stories. Even before his departure he wrote such illuminating pieces as "Charcoal Sketches," "In the Gold Country," and "Letters From My Travels in America." His real fame, however, came in Poland. There he penned his immortal Trilogy—*With Fire and Sword*, *The Deluge*, and *Pan Wołodyjowski*—followed by *The Knights of the Cross* and *Quo Vadis?* In 1905 he received for his efforts the Nobel Prize for literature. In forming the realistic characters that won him this coveted recognition, he drew extensively upon the acquaintances he cultivated in Krzyżanowski's tavern. Captain Piotrowski became the famous Polish Fallstaff, Zagłoba. Captain Wojciechowski became Longinus, the knight of the Podbipieta family in *With Fire and Sword*. Others served as models for Ursus and Lygia. There can be little doubt that buried beneath the exterior of one or more of Sienkiewicz's many characters there lies the inspiration of Włodzimierz Krzyżanowski.[35]

Krzyżanowski, of course, was unaware of the effect that his establishment might have on the young writer with whom he conversed and played cards. Nevertheless he must have delighted in his position as a tavern-keeper for it allowed him time to enjoy the camaraderie of his old G.A.R. companions. There were certainly many occasions when they talked long into the night about their memories of the war. Most of all, he cherished the company of his Polish friends whose voices brought back to him the familiar phrases of his youth. Throughout this period he forged close bonds with his fellow Poles, joining them in patriotic celebrations and taking an active part in forming a Polish committee in San Francisco in 1878.[36] Tragically, this life which offered him so much in the way of psychological satisfaction was doomed to disaster. As he gloried in the companionship his subconscious had pursued since the disruption of his childhood world, forces over which he had no possible control fused to cause his downfall.

The economic boom during which Krzyżanowski established his business soon fell before the advancing waves of recession. The Panic of 1873 that led to a widespread depression in the east finally reached the west coast during the winter of 1874-1875, about the same time that the silver bonanzas began to taper off. A state-wide business stagnation set in. On August 26, 1875, the prestigious Bank of California collapsed. Its owner, unable to face his bank's demise, committed suicide. Nearly all of the banks in San Francisco suspended operations. A severe drought during the winter of 1876-1877 further aggravated the deteriorating economy. By the end of 1876 the annual harvests fell fifty percent. Hundreds of unemployed miners wandered about the city. In January 1877, the Consolidated Virginia Mine ran out of ore. Its stock crashed, causing California investors a loss of $100 million. Unemployment reached well over 30,000 in San Francisco alone.[37]

In the face of mounting economic ruin Krzyżanowski appears to have maintained a remarkable degree of sangfroid. Although his business was not directly affected, the continued deterioration of the economy could not help but reach him eventually. As times became economically tight his business had to suffer. People stayed home, no longer able to afford the nightly excursions to his tavern. Nevertheless, Kriz devoted much of his time to his own pet project—the career of Helena Modjeska. As business fell he kept up his spirits by means of his nightly gatherings with the Poles who continued to frequent his saloon, if only for a chat or a friendly game of cards. For months he fought to break even, increasingly less able to match his costs with his rapidly diminishing income. Finally, creditors hounded him until he could put them off no longer. Broken, as his father was so many years before, he finally filed a petition for bankruptcy at 11:20 A.M. on December 8, 1877.[38]

The petitions that Krzyżanowski filed revealed some $17,238.91 in debts, including $191.50 owed to five employees. Chief among the creditors were those from whom he obtained his original loans: C.L. Luniewski, $500; Rudolph Korwin Piotrowski, $1,000; and Edward S. Salomon, $2,500. At the same time he listed as his assets the tavern, including its stock and furnishings, valued at some $9,500. His only other asset was a life insurance policy held with Pacific Mutual.[39]

On December 12 attorney Paul Neumann filed Krzyżanowski's abstract. A month later, on January 16, 1878, T.G. Cockrell was designated as the assignee during a meeting of the creditors. Cockrell filed his report on January 31 as the case moved ever closer to its conclusion. April 11 saw the beginning of the final act. On that date the assignee filed his petition for the sale of Krzyżanowski's personal property under the Federal bankruptcy laws. The tragedy was complete. His life once again destroyed, he escaped with only his family's personal apparel that, under the law, remained exempt from confiscation. Worse still, his failure left a lasting residue of disaffection among many who supported his endeavors. Loss of their friendship must certainly have been his bitterest disappointment.[40] Life in California, which began with such promise of happiness and success, ended in such utter destitution that later he could only remember it as the "dark period in my life in the United States."[41]

— CHAPTER THIRTEEN —

"WOUNDS WHICH DO NOT HEAL"

A RETURN TO FEDERAL SERVICE

The failure of Krzyżanowski's casino left him destitute. It was nearly impossible to find employment in San Francisco. Without capital, all hope of establishing a new business was relegated to the realm of fantasy. Once again, taking pen in hand, he swallowed his pride to ask Carl Schurz and his other friends to help him obtain a government appointment. Schurz did his best, but the economy remained tight and new civil service laws reduced the number of political appointments available. On January 17, 1878, as his bankruptcy proceedings neared completion, Kriz appealed to Congressmen A. L. Eickhoff and Benjamin A. Willis, suggesting a possible position, reviewing his service to the nation, and asking their intercession on his behalf. To the former he wrote:

No 838 Market Street
San Francisco, Cal
Jan 17th 1878

My Dear Sir:

Henry has probably, in his letters to you, mentioned about my misfortunes.

I have lost all! And am now out of business entirely, and therefore, I have to appeal to my friends, and request them to help me to some position.

Permit me to suggest to you how you can assist me, and I know, Mr. Eickhoff, that you will not shrink from it.

About a month ago I wrote to Secretary Schurz, and explained to him my situation. If you would be so kind, and see the Secretary, I know that something can be found for me, and should it require some more endorsements from members of Congress, I think that friend Willis, will not refuse me, and I suppose that Hon. H. Davis from here will also endorse me. The position, regarding which, I have written to the Secretary, is the Treasury Agency, for the Seal Islands, in Alaska. The position is held today by John

Morton, who, however, is very sick on the Island, and would have returned last Fall and resigned had the weather permitted it: now, he cannot return until the beginning of June but there seems to be the opinion that the Department will send some one to the Islands by the first vessel which will sail from here, and that will be about March.

Please do not think hard of me, Mr. Eickhoff, for troubling you, only necessity could compel me, to ask for a position, as I do not know what to do with myself.

The Seal Islands would suit me, as it is not expensive to live there, and I would be able to save a little.

Having served the country faithfully in the hour of its perils, I think that in my old days, I am entitled to a little consideration.

Hoping that you will take the interest of a friend in this matter, and that I will soon have cheerful news from you, that you have accomplished the object and that I will be provided for."[1]

Eickhoff did not refuse him. After consulting with Secretary of the Treasury John Sherman, he addressed the following letter to Sherman on January, 30, 1878.

Dear Sir,

In accordance with your suggestion, I herewith transmit a letter of General Krzyzanowski.

Although it is a private letter, addressed to me, I do not hesitate to lay it before you, as it states in a simple way, his case, appealing to the Government of his country, which he bravely defended in the days of its peril, for aid and support.

I second this appeal and take the liberty to express the hope that it may not be in vain.

I am, dear sir, with highest esteem,

Your obedient servant,
L. Eickhoff[2]

On the back of Eickhoff's letter Congressman Benjamin A. Willis wrote his own endorsement. An old friend of the general's, Willis served as an officer in the 119th New York Infantry of Krzyżanowski's brigade. He wrote:

I desire to unite with my colleague Hon. Mr. Eickhoff in his commendation of Gen'l. Krzyzanowski. I can certify from personal knowledge of his gallant services in defense of his adopted country, also as to his fine administrative qualities. I sincerely hope that the Hon. Sec'y. of the Treasury will comply with the request.

Benjamin A. Willis[3]

Secretary Sherman responded on January 31, 1878.

> Sir,
>
> I have the honor to acknowledge the receipt of your note ... in which you enclose one from Gen. Krzyzanowski in which he makes application for an appointment as Treasury Agent at the Seal Islands, Alaska.
>
> The law now in force authorizes the employment at the Seal Islands of only one Special Agent and one Asst. Agent and both of these places are now filled by persons who have been somewhat recently appointed and I consider it quite improbable that any vacancy will soon occur in either of these offices.
>
> I have no authority to send anyone to the Seal Islands and grant them compensation therefore except the regularly authorized Special Agents. You will therefore see that at present it is not within my power to make Gen'l. Krzyzanowski's appointment.[4]

Rejection piled upon rejection as Krzyżanowski's situation became progressively more destitute, forcing him to obtain loans from friends in San Francisco to support his family while he continued to call upon his friends in the East to intervene on his behalf. Typical of the support he received was this letter from attorney Simon Wolf in Washington, D.C., to Secretary Sherman:

> I have the honor most respectfully to urge the appointment of General W. Krzyzanowski, now of San Francisco Cal, as inspector at Panama. The General who is an active and zealous Republican, served faithfully and gallantly in the late war, for a long time under the personal observation of the Secretary of the Interior, who knows him well, for some years he acted as Supervisor of Int Rev in the State of Georgia, it was at a time when the agents of the Govt also did Considerable business in setting up Conventions. The General active and zealous no doubt did his share, the Consequence was that he incurred the Enmity of some other politicians, who did not rest until they had him removed, and indeed indicted. Very shortly after this, Secy Boutwell, after having thoroughly satisfied himself of the injustice done the general, appointed him as Revenue Agt at Alaska, in which Capacity he served successfully, and was recalled simply to make room for some one else, and not for any Cause. Since this the General has been residing in San Francisco trying to Earn a livelihood, he stands well in that City, is universally respected, and has done yeoman service in behalf of Truth and Hard money. He is deserving of recognition, and I hope he may get it.
>
> P.S. You are well aware that he was recently appointed by your Department as Revenue Agt for Alaska, and before his Commission was sent, it was revoked, owing to the fact, that it was believed his Record as an official in your Dept was not good, upon investigation it was discovered that he was

> not removed from his last position for any Cause, but it was too late to make good the action had, therefore this is a fitting opportunity to do him Justice, for it is a fact that it has worked him great wrong wherever he is Known, the Press having noticed his appointment and favorably.[5]

Wolf mailed his recommendation to Secretary Schurz who forwarded it to Sherman with the following notation:

> I fully endorse the within. Genl. Krzyzanowski served under me during the war. He was a meritorious officer and had the confidence of his superiors in every respect. I warmly commend this application to the favorable consideration of the Secretary of the Treasury.[6]

Through the efforts of Secretary Schurz and his other friends in Washington, Krzyżanowski also obtained the offer of a position in Panama at $2,500 per year. On October 23, Kriz took the oath of office as Special Inspector to reside in Aspinwall, Panama.[7]

Krzyżanowski embarked for Panama aboard the steamer *Granada* on November 20, 1878. Behind him he left his impact on history—the rising career of Helena Modjeska. Behind him, too, he left the young writer Henryk Sienkiewicz who used the general's tavern to further his own literary career. He left his son, Joseph, in the care of Thomas F. Ryan, under whom the young man was to study law. Finally, he left the shattered dreams of a secure life.[8]

Arriving in Panama, Krzyżanowski completed a grand circuit in which his wandering took him to virtually every area of American control. He could now boast that "no boundary of the United States was unknown to me. In fact, I have lived several years on each of the four boundaries."[9] Reflecting back upon his experiences in war and peace, in government and private life, Kriz at last became aware of the vast complexities that formed the American nation. Recalling an earlier analogy, he commented: "I now stopped being a fly and became aware of all its [the United States'] wheels, cogs, and everything that made it function."[10]

Krzyżanowski's duty in Panama required him to supervise the landing and trans-shipping of merchandise crossing the Isthmus. Should any evidence of fraud or smuggling be uncovered he was to report his findings directly to the Special Agent at either San Francisco or New York. In addition to this investigative role, he had to prepare and submit monthly reports to the Treasury Department on all of his transactions. To carry out these directives, Kriz had to inspect the baggage of passengers, as well as verify that the cargo of each vessel was correctly listed on the ship's manifest. That he carried out these tasks assiduously can be seen in his report for May, 1879, where he systematically listed every item a ship carried, including "1 corpse."[11]

Krzyżanowski found Panama to be a beautiful new land, rich in exotic fruits and picturesque beaches. Despite its natural beauty, however, it was also a very unhealthy land harboring dangerous fevers and other tropical diseases. Within a few months Caroline became very ill. Sadly, Kriz had to send his wife to Washington, D.C., where she could hope for some recovery under the tender care of her family. Torn from all of those whom he relied upon for the friendship that nurtured his soul, Krzyżanowski now suffered the ultimate trial of separation from the one person whose emotions were most closely linked to his own. In June he directed the Secretary of the Treasury to forward $100 of his salary for May to his sister-in-law, L.A. Burnett, for the care of his wife. Later, he sent his entire pay for September and November. It was all that he could do. Though he longed to be with Caroline, to once again reunite his family, all his efforts appeared doomed to failure.[12]

Distraught over the illness of his wife, Kriz found himself confronted with another, more immediate problem, when a revolt broke out in Aspinwall on the evening of June 7, 1879. The revolutionaries attempted to install a provisional president, but were frustrated by government troops who pursued them into the jungles. Transit across the Isthmus ceased from June 8-15. Unable to load, ships delayed their departures. Tons of merchandise piled up on the docks in each of Panama's coastal ports. Though brief, the revolution proved damaging to American commerce and left Krzyżanowski working long hours to unclog the overburdened port areas.[13]

In November a violent storm caused considerable damage to shipping and shore installations as well. Rains inundated the Panama Railroad for seventeen miles. Communications across the Isthmus were cut for over a month, causing freight and passengers to pile up in the port cities much more than they had during the brief summer revolt. The burden of normalizing this trade once again fell upon Kriz. The importance of his task can be seen in the fact that from July through November, the Aspinwall and Panama City customs houses logged 959 passengers and $2,830,376.30 in freight.[14]

Due to the storm in late November, the trans-shipment of cargo remained paralyzed until January 4, 1880 when the railway finally reopened. In the flurry of activity that followed the resumption of trade, the chief engineer attempted to smuggle bay oil aboard the *Acapulco*. He did not succeed. Krzyżanowski alertly uncovered not only the contraband, but also the New York connections of a larger smuggling ring. With the evidence that Krzyżanowski uncovered, the authorities in New York successfully arrested the conspirators and seized the illicit goods as the smugglers began off-loading it.[15]

Working long hours, Kriz soon became susceptible to the diseases that abounded in Panama's tropical climate. On April 7, 1880, R.H. Carterm,

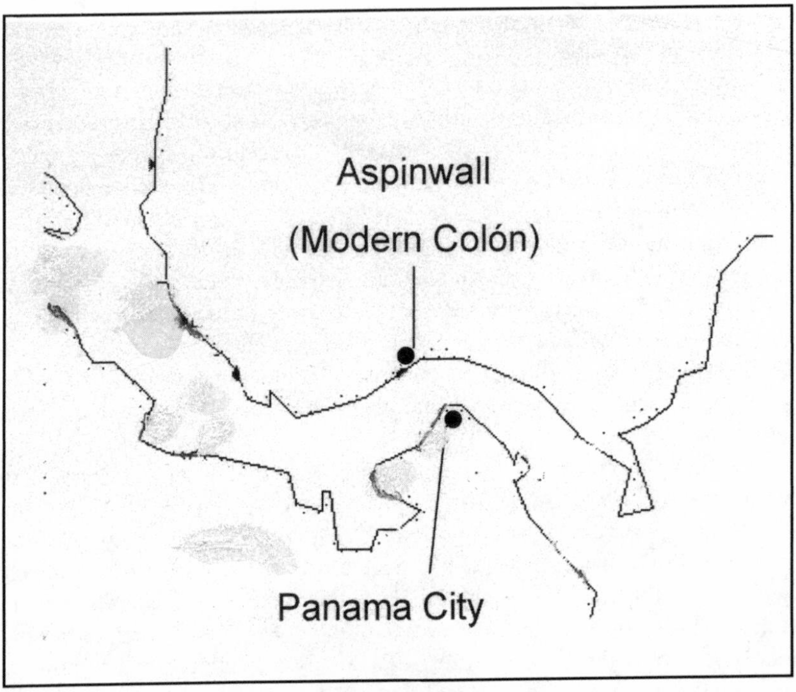

Map of Panama.

Special Inspector for the Port of Panama, died of fever. Soon the United States Consul was down with the disease, and Krzyżanowski began to exhibit symptoms as well. Consumed by the desire to be with his wife, Kriz found his own illness provided him with the opportunity to once again be reunited with her. On the advise of his physician, Kriz requested a sixty-day leave of absence. He left Aspinwall June 7, 1880, arriving in New York on the 15th.[16]

In New York Harbor, Kriz had to sit patiently aboard ship for three days due to a yellow fever scare. Once ashore he rushed to Washington to be with Caroline. He found her gravely ill. Instead of recuperating, her condition had deteriorated to the point where paralysis left her nervous and unable to speak. Heartbroken, Kriz spent every minute trying to encourage her, to revive her spirits. Though she remained unable to converse, she slowly appeared to regain some of her strength until she was at least able to go out briefly under the care of her husband.[17]

Happy, at least, to be with his wife after their long months of enforced separation, Kriz found yet another joy awaiting him in Washington. In his accumulated mail at 715 K Street, Northwest, was a letter from Poland. Nervously, but expectantly, his hands trembled as he opened the envelope.

Once inside, his eyes eagerly scanned the phrases of his youth. To his great joy he found that it was a letter from Emily Metzig, the niece with whom he spent his childhood in Poznań. He smiled as she explained that she was married. He studied the photographs she enclosed of herself and her children. Again and again he read the letter, recalling those moments of his youth that delighted him.[18]

On July 22 Kriz replied to the unexpected letter that reunited him, at least in spirit, with his lost family. "Only those who do not know their family or relatives," he began, "those who do not know their fatherland, those who spent their youth in foreign places and the greatest part of their lives in exile, would be able to feel this tremendous happiness when after 40 years, thinking that I have been forgotten in my native land, I have felt such happiness, such comfort, upon receiving your letter with photographs enclosed. I cannot describe the happiness that is in my heart."[19]

Kriz went on to narrate the problems his wife had and to describe in glowing terms the wonders of the American capital city. It "is without doubt the most beautiful city on earth," he said. "Its streets are broad, its buildings beautiful. Many of the homes have fountains in their gardens, from which crystal-clear water falls. The city has many parks and many flower gardens. Great care is provided by the government to keep these neat and orderly. Europeans arriving here are amazed. Paris, London, Vienna and Berlin are large and beautiful cities, but Washington is a veritable Garden of Eden."[20]

Finally, Kriz closed with the hope that he might continue to hear from his niece. "My happiness is ending for in a few days I will be forced to return to Aspinwall, Panama, for another two years. ... Now, from myself and my wife, we embrace you and kiss you. Please remember that I am alive and your letters bring me great happiness."[21]

As the summer drew on Krzyżanowski indeed became somber with the knowledge that he would once again have to journey to Aspinwall. Still, his wife's sickness and his impending return to Panama were not the only problems that beset him that summer. On June 17 Captain Francis Lessen of San Francisco wrote to Secretary of the Treasury John Sherman to complain that Krzyżanowski had failed to make good on a debt to the captain which now stood overdue by thirteen months. Lessen enclosed a copy of the debit note for $150 plus ten percent interest, commenting that Krzyżanowski continually put him off in his attempts to collect the obligation. Lessen asked if Secretary Sherman might intervene on the creditor's behalf. Once again the omnipresent chain of financial reverses resurfaced to haunt Krzyżanowski, magnifying the anguish he felt for his wife and family.[22]

In response to Sherman's inquiry, Kriz replied that he incurred the debt in 1875, long before his employment by the Treasury Department. The debt, in fact, was but one of many that drove Krzyżanowski into eventual bank-

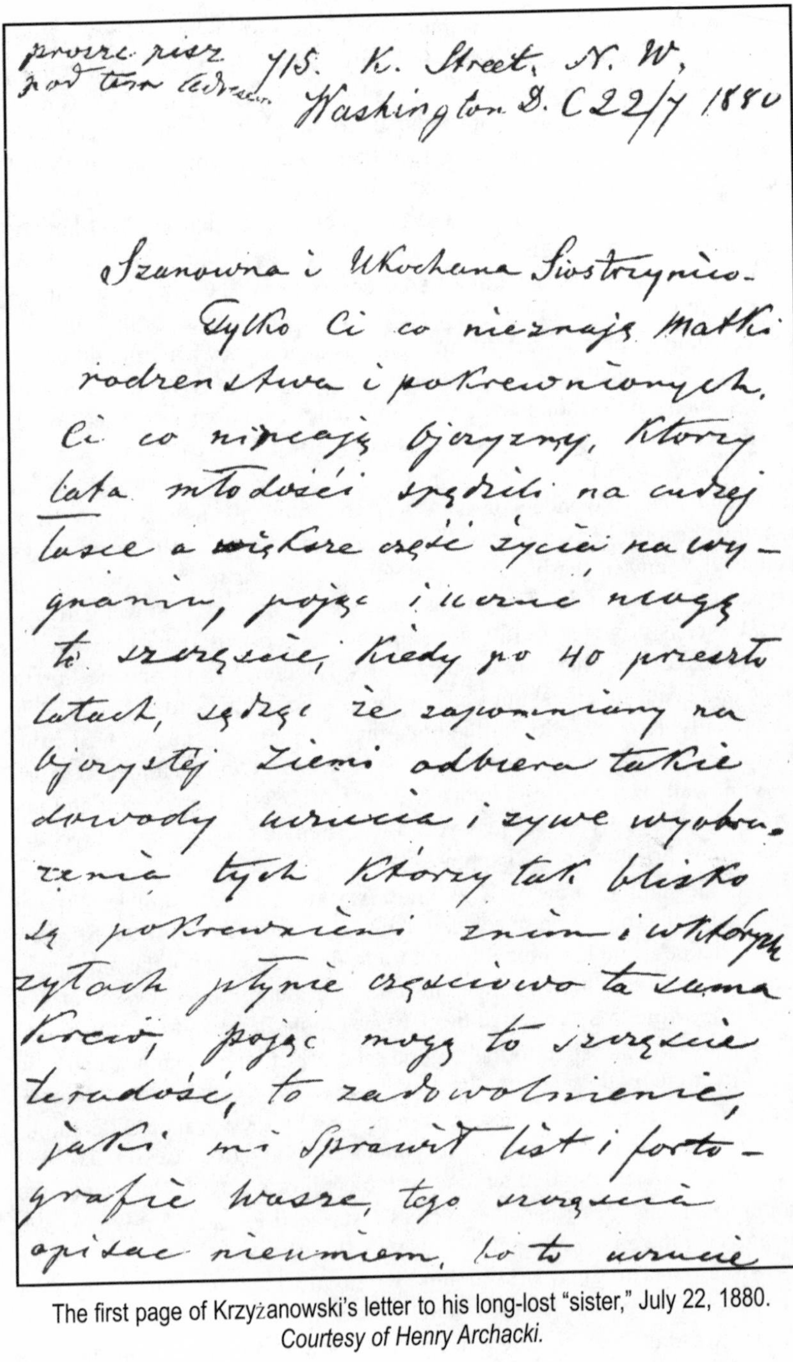
prosze pisz pod tym adresem
715. K. Street. N. W.
Washington D. C 22/7 1880

Szanowna i Ukochana Siostrzynico.
Tylko Ci co nieznają Matki rodzeństwa i pokrewnionych. Ci co nimają Ojczyzny, Którzy lata młodości spędzili na cudzej łasce a większe części życia na wygnaniu, pojąć i uczuć mogą to szczęście, kiedy po 40 przeszło latach, sądząc że zapomniany na ojczystej Ziemi odbiera takie dowody uczucia i żywe wyobrażenia tych Którzy tak blisko są pokrewnieni z nim i w których żyłach płynie częściowo ta sama krew, pojąć mogą to szczęście te radość, to zadowolnienie, jakie mi sprawił list i fotografie wasze, tego szczęścia opisać nieumiem, bo to uczucie

The first page of Krzyżanowski's letter to his long-lost "sister," July 22, 1880.
Courtesy of Henry Archacki.

ruptcy in San Francisco. Under the bankruptcy laws, Kriz was free from legal obligation for these debts. Nevertheless, he determined to repay them in full as he still felt a binding moral obligation for their refund. Kriz had, in fact, already made several payments to California creditors, but could not retire the debts as rapidly as he would have liked due to his limited income and the demands made upon his resources by his wife's illness. Lessen refused to accept the ruling of the bankruptcy court. Despite Krzyżanowski's good intentions, the captain badgered him incessantly about the past debt. To Secretary Sherman, Kriz wrote:

> Being unfortunate in business in San Francisco, I have turned over on the 24 of December 1877 all my property to my creditors and been obliged to take the insolvency act. When I received the present appointment from the Hon. Secretary, I hoped to be able to save enough to pay my creditors in full and be exonerated from debts, regardless that I have been released by law; I have paid some; Unfortunately about one year ago, my wife took sick in Panama and I have been obliged to send her here, for medical treatment, and she has been in Drs hands all that time; Only the expenses of the sickness have prevented me for the present, from paying off as fast as I hoped to do under ordinary circumstances. This I have written to Mr. Lessen but he seems to have no regard for it.[23]

Fortunately Secretary Sherman realized that Krzyżanowski was acting not only within the law, but going beyond the requirements of the law to try and settle obligations that the legal system did not recognize. Sherman accepted Krzyżanowski's explanation, and the general left after a few days to resume his investigations of the bay oil trade in Panama. The parting in Washington was emotional, but Kriz held out the hope that he might receive a transfer closer to Washington once his term in Panama expired.

Throughout the fall, and into the summer of 1881, Krzyżanowski applied himself to the investigation of illegal trade. Frequently he personally rode the train between Aspinwall and Panama City to keep a close watch on the possibility of subterfuge. During all of these long months he sent the bulk of his salary to Washington to care for his wife and retire his debts. By August he lay prostrate with fever. But still he could not rest. The letters he received from his wife's family brought the tortuous news that Caroline was no better.[24] In his torment he sought solace in news from Poland. "The heart's nourishment is the love of the family," he wrote to his niece Emily, "the tie that binds the heart of the children to their parents, the brothers to the sisters, and to the near relative, without this the heart weakens and dies and loses all its noble feeling. Oh how beautiful was the adage or proverb of our forefathers who said 'let us love each other.'"[25]

Receiving word that his wife's condition was deteriorating, Kriz applied for leave to be at her side. In great haste he boarded a ship heading north, racing to console Caroline in her hour of need. As the ship plodded along at what must have seemed a snail's pace, Kriz reflected on his life, his problems, and how they all seemed small compared to the apprehension he felt for his wife's health. He wished the ship had wings to ensure his arrival before it was too late. Yet even this wish went unfulfilled. Caroline died of hemiplegia on January 11, 1882.[26] The news of her death threw him into the depths of despair. Broken in spirit, he could not escape the haunting memories of his love. Even after the passage of more than two years his mind stood obsessed with this despondency. In April, 1884, he confided to Emily that "there is no happiness for me. I lost that which was dearest. There are wounds which do not heal rapidly such as my wound."[27]

As his loneliness increased Kriz became progressively more dependent upon the letters he received from Poland. "I wish you knew how I long for that time when I can enter your circle and embrace you in the old Polish style," he told Emily. "Torn away from everything which tied me to your hemisphere I wish I were where my heart is."[28] His overriding fear during those long months of grief was that he would lose the reassuring phrases from across the sea. "Please do not abandon me," he pleaded, "nor deprive me of the happiness with which your letters fill me. Do not untie the ties that bind me to your mother and my beloved sister [Emily]. Remember, even though I were a stranger, even as a fellow Pole do not deny me what happiness these letters give me."[29]

Weakened by the emotional stress that afflicted him after Caroline's demise, Krzyżanowski once more contracted "Panama fever." Recovery proved difficult as his heart no longer retained the will to resist the ravishes of that tropical disease. On June 13, 1882, he received a one month leave of absence effective June 15, after which he would terminate his service in Panama. Heartbroken and dispirited, he hobbled up the gangplank of the ship that would carry him, for the last time, back to New York.[30]

"THE LIGHTHOUSE-KEEPER"

In 1881 Henryk Sienkiewicz published "Latarnik" [The Lighthouse-Keeper],[31] a short story that he claimed was based on "a real occurrence" described to him in a letter from San Francisco resident Julian Horain. The story line involves a Polish immigrant selected as a successor to a lighthouse keeper who has mysteriously disappeared. The position is one of responsibility that requires someone of trust, for any failure could mean doom for passing ships and those aboard. The Pole performs well until one day a package arrives for him. Opening it, his gaze falls upon a book written in the beloved language of his childhood. Closer examination reveals a collection of poetry by Adam Mickiewicz whose patriotic verses brought the lonely lighthouse keeper back to his formative years, to his beloved homeland. But as he savored the rhythmic stanzas, his mind lost to the reality about him, the sun began to set. Soon it was dark, yet he read on. While he wept tears of happiness at the phrases of his youth, out on the ocean a passing ship wrecked on a reef. Wrapped in visions of his homeland, he had forgotten to light his lamp. He would be dismissed from his job, cast away for his inattention to duty.

It has long been known that Sienkiewicz used the characteristics of people he met in Krzyżanowski's New York Casino in San Francisco as the basis for some of the characters in his fiction, but there has to date been no suggestion that Kriz himself appears in Sienkiewicz's writings. Perhaps in the tale of human emotion and weakness that is "The Lighthouse-Keeper" we can detect the familiar countenance of the aging Pole. Although literary license allowed Sienkiewicz to elaborate his story for effect, the essentials of Krzyżanowski's life emerge quite clearly as the original building blocks for the character of the "Lighthouse Keeper." The setting for the story is Aspinwall, the very place where Kriz served as a customs official. The lighthouse keeper is described as a wanderer who led "a roving life" not unlike the tavern keeper's sojourns to New York, the Midwest, Virginia, the District of Columbia, his frequent moves during the Civil War, and then his federal service in Alabama, Georgia, South Carolina, Louisiana, the Washington Territory, Alaska, and San Francisco before Aspinwall. The lighthouse keeper—Skawiński by name—is described as possessing the "bearing of a soldier" with white hair, blue eyes and a complexion "as sunburnt as a creole's." By the time of his appointment in Aspinwall, Kriz's dark hair had turned white, his grey-blue eyes recalled the color Sienkiewicz remembered from San Francisco, and his skin certainly remained "sunburnt" from his service in the field with the army and his outdoor activities as a customs agent over many years. Skawiński had led a bayonet charge, just as Kriz had at Cross Keys. The fictional Pole had crossed the Great Plains and served aboard ship, as had Kriz, and he had suffered recurring dashed hopes much as had the real-life tavern-keeper in San Francisco.

But aside from the general personal characteristics of the lighthouse keeper, Sienkiewicz's portrait of the fictional protagonist's personality is most interesting when compared with Krzyżanowski.

"You've tried different occupations?" asks the person interviewing Skawiński for the lighthouse job.

"It's because I never could find peace anywhere," replies Skawiński.

"Why?"

"Fate," the aging Poles explained as he "shrugged his shoulders."

Clearly this dialogue could easily have replaced Skrawiński with Krzyżanowski, a man who moved about frequently, held various positions, but could never find the peace and stability for which he longed.

"Hardworking and honest," Sienkiewicz says of Skrawiński, "he had often made a little money, and in spite of all his precautions and the greatest prudence had always lost it." Could any description better fit the travails of Włodzimierz Krzyżanowski? He lost the money he invested in his furniture business during the Reconstruction, lost his tavern in San Francisco, and lost his Treasury Department positions in Georgia and the Washington Territory. Whenever he began to feel himself secure, able to settle down, his life was again subject to disappointment and upheaval. Yet, there is more. Skrawiński was "robbed by his partner" in business, much as Kriz had been betrayed by associates in Savannah. Skrawiński was "gripped by a terrible homesickness, which the most trifling circumstance would rouse; the sight of swallows, of grey birds resembling sparrows, snow on the mountains, or some tune like he had once heard." From his letters to relatives in Poland we know of Krzyżanowski's great homesickness during the period in his life that corresponded with his meeting Sienkiewicz, and of the nostalgic meetings of Poles and Civil War veterans in the New York Casino which Sienkiewicz observed on many occasions during his stay in San Francisco. All were occasions for melancholy reminiscence and expressions of homesickness, as was the general's close affiliation with San Francisco's Polish community and the career of Helena Modjeska.

"There was also this curious thing about him," Sienkiewicz explained, "that after so many disillusions he was always full of confidence, and never lost hope that all would still be well." This description fit Kriz well, as we see in his writings not only his longing for his homeland, but also the recurring theme that a new beginning would yield the peace and security he sought. Sienkiewicz's description of Skrawiński could easily substitute the name of Krzyżanowski for the author's fictional character: "[H]e never gave in under his troubles. He crawled upwards as laboriously as an ant. Thrust down a hundred times, for the hundred and first time he would calmly begin his journey over again. In this way he was something quite extraordinary."

With the wreck of the ship, Skrawiński lost his job. Sienkiewicz's description of his departure—to New York just as Krzyżanowski had done—could well have been written by an observer of Kriz's similar departure.

> A few days later Skawiński might have been seen on the deck of a vessel going from Aspinwall to New York. The poor old man had lost his post. New ways of a wanderer's existence had opened again before him. Again the wind had blown the leaf away to cast it forth by land and sea, to make sport of it at its will. During those few days the old man had grown very shrunken and bent: only his eyes shone.

"GHOST-LIKE MEMORIES"

Krzyżanowski arrived in New York Harbor in late July, 1882. This was where his adventurous exile began some thirty-six years before. The changes wrought by those eventful years were less evident than one might think. Kriz was older now, to be sure. A portly stature replaced the thin countenance of the youth who once glimpsed his first sight of America in this same harbor. His brown hair had long since turned grey. In place of the robust exuberance of youth there was the slow, measured movement of a man aged beyond his years by asthma, fevers, and mental distress. Yet there were many similarities between the two men who viewed New York so many years apart. Both came to escape—one from prison and the other from the inhospitable atmosphere of the tropics. Both came amid the anguish of losing their families. Both came with nothing in their pockets, hoping to establish new lives in America's most populous metropolis. Both had to begin life anew from the shattered remnants of the past.

Once in New York, Krzyżanowski reestablished his old acquaintances in an effort to recover from his tragic loss. Through active participation in veterans' affairs he began to break free of the depression that grasped tightly about his soul. A charter member of Von Steinwehr Post No. 192, G.A.R., on January 10, 1883, he was listed as the first entry on the membership list and post commander, residing at 213 East 48th Street. Though he never overcame his grief, the support of his former comrades-in-arms helped him to reconcile himself to life without Caroline.[32]

Seeking further strength he naturally gravitated to New York's Polish community, for it represented to him the closest contact he could hope for with his fatherland. With little to bind him to the United States but the memory of his departed wife, he began to dream of a return to what he remembered as the friendly confines of his native soil. "You write, dear niece, about your modest home," he wrote to Emily, "to me the most modest home in my native land would look better than the greatest palace here. In the former burns the heart of the family, in the latter just the emptiness. I have gone through many changes of fortune during my life, sometimes through brilliance, sometimes through darkness. The greatest brilliance which lights our heart is that which is mirrored in the hearts of those whom we love. Without this light, the heart is always in mourning."[33]

On September 12, 1883, Krzyżanowski participated in the New York bicentennial celebration of King Jan III Sobieski's decisive victory over the immense armies of the Ottoman Empire at the Battle of Vienna. Dr. Henryk Kałussowski, a close associate of leading European revolutionaries from Mierosławski to Mazzini and Kossuth, came from Washington, D. C., to act as chairman of the event. Correspondents from as far away as Vienna's *Neue Freie Press* and the French *Journal de Paris* sat in the audience as General

Krzyżanowski rose to the podium to deliver the keynote address in both Polish and English to the assembled dignitaries.[34]

Such activities kept Krzyżanowski's mind busy, offering him relief from the pangs of the past. Similarly, he enjoyed the opportunity to prepare the memoirs of his American experience. Working through the winter of 1882 into the spring of 1883, Kriz, at the behest of the Polish magazine *Kłosy*, committed to paper his impressions of the United States and his analysis of the Civil War. Edited somewhat by the magazine's staff, these reminiscences appeared in print in 1883.

Writing for a Polish audience, Krzyżanowski employed the traditional romantic prose of Polish literature. He made no pretense of being a good writer, but indicated that he hoped only to record his reactions and observations during his movements throughout the United States. In his thoughts one can see the deep longing for the lost homeland of his youth submerged beneath a passionate love for his adopted country. His opening paragraph is so revealing of his state of mind at the time that it bears repetition.

> Stirring the ashes of years gone by should not be allowed. I, however, wandering back in my mind through years gone by, notice ghost-like memories surrounded by gravestones, standing white and sad as if to surround me in an embrace, and tears begin to flow. Tears are unworthy of a soldier. Only to women are they permitted. Yet, who can remain cold when surrounded by gravestones and memories of bygone youth? How often jealousy arose within me as I watched those who were surrounded by landscapes of their native land rock to their native songs, satiated with clear tones of their native language. These people were able to prolong their youth by living in familiar surroundings. However, not all of us are able to do this. Despite my wanderings, I have no regrets.[35]

As he thought back over his experiences in America, seeking to reconcile them with his undying idealism, he developed a philosophy of the American character and conscience. The idealistic nature of the expectant immigrant, tempered by the realities through which he lived, gave birth to a patriotic panorama embracing two separate lands and cultures. "My thirty year stay in America" he wrote,

> has filled me with a deep gratitude for its hospitality. Occasionally tears of gratitude fill my eyes regarding this nation of liberty and equality for embracing me and providing me with a home. But the battles I have fought, the men I have seen killed, prove once again that the Yankees are not as naive as they seem. These memoirs of my adventures and career are meant to be just that, I do not wish to hurt anyone, especially this nation, this land of freedom, that accepted a fugitive from Prussian absolutism and rewarded him so well for his meager services.[36]

"There never was another nation," Krzyżanowski asserted, "whose future looked as promising"[37] as that of the United States. "It has existed for just under one hundred years ... but it has performed miracles of advancement."[38] He attributed this to a staggering amount of natural resources, a willingness to extend the freedoms of citizenship to immigrants, and the successful blending of the entire spectrum of society into "a powerful nation that knows how to hold its standard of liberty without class oppression, revolution, or communism."[39]

Reflecting on his experiences, Krzyżanowski marvelled at the inventiveness of the Americans. Likewise he took the opportunity to condemn those European journalists who stereotyped Americans as collectively illiterate. No European, Kriz cautioned, could ever completely understand the puzzling contradictions that form the American character. The American is, at the same time, "scrupulous, honest, quiet yet talkative, quixotic, a firm believer in God at times and yet at times an unbeliever. He is a man chasing after the almighty dollar, yet he will not sell himself out. He has a deep-rooted patriotism, is bright, intelligent, loves comfort, is hospitable, and very practical."[40]

In his memoirs Krzyżanowski displayed a keen awareness of history, as well as an accurate knowledge of that which he described. Only on rare occasion can one find fault with his information, and those exceptions may well result from the editing of his original manuscript prior to publication. The one major, recurring misconception which appears to result from Krzyżanowski's recollections is the belief that he occupied a position as the first governor of Alaska. This interpretation of the memoirs was accepted by virtually all of the early Polish-American historians, including the frequently cited works of Mieczysław Haiman. As they were originally published, the memoirs also state that Kriz was "asked to govern the state of Alabama" after the Civil War, and that he later became "governor" of Florida and Georgia. From these passages it is clear that what Krzyżanowski meant was that he served as a governor in the administrative sense—an administrator. He only meant that he was a government employee charged with administering government policies, not that he occupied the specific executive position of "governor" of the various states he named. It is possible that Krzyżanowski's original statement, and the phraseology that appeared in *Kłosy* were not the same. Perhaps the misconception arose from an unwitting assumption on the part of the magazine's editors. It is interesting to note, however, that the Nobel Prize-winning author Henryk Sienkiewicz used the same terminology when he spoke of Krzyżanowski in his own letters.[41]

John H. Kinkead, the first official governor of Alaska, received his appointment in 1884. It was therefore impossible that Krzyżanowski could have held that position. From 1867 to 1877 the United States Army governed Alaska. From 1877 until 1884 it came under the jurisdiction of the Treasury Department. During all of this time, Krzyżanowski's only contact with Alaska came as a result of his activities as a Special Agent in the Washington Territory during 1873-74. In later years Joseph Krzyżanowski, the general's son, confirmed the fact that he had no recollection of his father ever being governor of Alaska. All he remembered was what actually occurred, his father's trips on behalf of the Treasury Department.[42]

Although Kriz never served as governor of Alaska, his brief connection with that area did play an important part in its early history. His activities as Special Agent led to a more effective administration of Alaska that enabled people residing there to live in greater safety and prosperity. It is for this that he should be remembered.[43]

Krzyżanowski titled his work *Wspomnienia z Pobytu w Ameryce Podczas Wojny 1861-1864* [Memoirs of My Sojourn in America During the War 1861-1864]; thus, it is only logical that his major contribution to the world's body of historical knowledge rests with his observations on the causes, conduct and results of the Civil War. To Kriz there was no doubt as to the primary cause of that vast fratricidal conflict. "The seeds of the Civil War were sown by the magnates who owned vast estates, whose aristocratic way of life was supported by slavery."[44] In contrasting the two antebellum societies, Kriz noted that in the North "each man was equal and each man used his own sweat and blood to carve out of life whatever he could."[45] In the South, however, the plantation owners and their families were maintained "by the blood, sweat, and tears of the blacks."[46] The most important cause of the Civil War therefore, stemmed from the single overriding wrong that the abolitionists sought to eradicate. "The institution of slavery," Krzyżanowski insisted,

> holding millions in chains, could not exist in a country dedicated to personal liberty. This blot had to be removed and its roots torn out. Every American of good faith felt the same way. The Southerners in their greed for material gains, and in their eagerness to maintain their aristocratic way of life, were indeed responsible for the beginning of the war. It is strange, indeed, that these Southerners, these descendants of people who fled Europe to gain freedom, were the first to start the institution of slavery that denied that freedom to the blacks. The plight of four million enslaved blacks stirred the Americans to the core, as it did the Europeans. This was a battle between the Renaissance and the Dark Ages, between peace and anarchy, a battle for the life or death of the United States. No civil war was ever fought for so noble a cause.[47]

But Krzyżanowski was not naive enough to suppose that this complex event grew out of a single cause. He noted too, for example, the differences in the Northern and Southern economic systems.

> Before the war cotton was picked and exported to foreign countries for processing, and then imported in the form of finished goods. After the war cotton mills sprang up all over the South; thus, instead of hurting the South, the war brought new riches. The South was not only able to provide for its own needs, but was able to export its finished goods to foreign countries as well.
>
> Unfortunately, before the war the Southerners were not able to comprehend this. They felt that slavery was absolutely essential to their existence. The stronger the Southerners grew politically, the more their members became key figures in the government, and the stronger grew the anti-slavery movement in the rest of the country. The terrible trade in human flesh—plus the Compromise of 1850 which enabled the Southerners to reclaim any runaway slaves, created a reaction in the hearts of the people of the free states. In vain the South threatened secession, in vain they tried to convince the country that its very existence depended upon the exportation of cotton. The idealists of the nineteenth century would not, and could not, become blind to the plight of four million people.[48]

Krzyżanowski attributed Southern successes in the antebellum years to the South's ability to maintain a political dominance despite its numerically smaller population. Seventy-three years before the publication of Kenneth M. Stampp's celebrated book on the subject, *The Peculiar Institution*, Kriz noted that the reins of power in the South rested in the hands of only 15,000 people who comprised the class of plantation owners employing ten or more slaves. These Southern states, he noted, were able to exert more than their share of influence in Congress because they could elect Representatives on the basis of a black population that was unable to express its will at the polls. Through this means, he said, a Southern district of 150,000 people might in reality comprise only 25,000 eligible voters. Because whites were the only people able to vote in the South, they returned the same Senators and Representatives to office year after year. The seniority these men established enabled the South to virtually steal the power to govern from the more numerous Northern population.[49]

As a result of these political successes, Kriz reasoned, the Southerners began to feel that their section was invincible. "The Southerners were blinded by their successes," he wrote, "they failed to realize that the greatness of a country is dependent upon the liberty and the well-being of its individual citizens. ... The Southerners believed blindly in their cause, and in their invincibility."[50]

Imbued with a deep sense of Polish history, Kriz did not overlook the obvious parallels between the theory of States' Rights and Poland's own cancerous *liberum veto*. "The Civil War did not ruin the country," he asserted, "but formed a cornerstone for building the colossus known as the United States of America."[51] He explained his position thusly:

> The Civil War really united the country into one powerful nation. Until the Civil War all the Southern states maintained that the Union was a loose confederation of sovereign and independent states, united only when voting for one common president. This difference seems minute, but it spells the difference between a really united nation and a loosely connected confederation of sovereign states. Such a loose confederation would never have withstood its external enemies.
>
> The Southerners hoped to divide and weaken the states. Under their conditions any state would be able to withdraw from the Union at any time it wished. The Civil War put an end to this, it really united the states and made them a powerful nation. ...
>
> The propaganda by the Southern states concerning the sovereignty of each state was so strong that a citizen of Kentucky would feel himself superior socially to a citizen of Philadelphia. In turn, the citizen of Philadelphia would not consider a citizen of Cincinnati his social equal. This truly tended to separate instead of uniting the states. People tended to introduce themselves with words such as "I am a Virginian," or "I am a Marylander." A patriotic American should have realized that he was a citizen of the United States, and should have ignored any boundaries existing between the states. The Civil War killed this strong feeling of sectionalism.[52]

A lifelong advocate of the powers of a good education, Krzyżanowski placed much faith in the public school system of the North. "No one is getting rich on education," he noted, "because the son of a millionaire studies side by side with the son of a beggar in the public schools from the elementary levels through college."[53] Though not as idealistic as Krzyżanowski made the system out to be, he did draw a valid comparison with the South. He maintained that the lack of such a system of universal education in the South was one of the major differences between the two sections of the country. But Kriz did not stop there, he felt much more strongly about this fundamental difference. Had the Northern system of education been present in the South, he argued, "the Civil War might have been avoided."[54] "I am proud to say," he concluded, "that the first man to recognize this, and to try to do something about it, was my countryman Tadeusz Kościuszko. In 1800, when the Congress of the United States, recognizing his services to this country, voted him $15,000 and a land grant, Kościuszko refused to accept the money or the land. Instead, he attempted to donate it toward building schools for the education of Negroes."[55]

Continuing his comments on American society, no doubt with consciously sentimental thoughts of his wife, Krzyżanowski set about to explain to his countrymen in Europe the position of women in the mosaic of American life.

> Higher institutions of learning are also open to women. Women, upon graduation, usually accept positions for which they were educated. I state sincerely that it is wonderful to have a wife who is able to shoulder some of the burdens and responsibilities of raising a family or helping a husband in his business. If the husband's financial status is such that a wife's help is unnecessary it is still nice to have someone who can converse intelligently on current subjects. Education does not necessarily make a woman less feminine.
>
> The American woman has more liberty than any other woman in the world. She rides alone, visits alone, is able to have visitors, and is very much esteemed by her husband. ... There are many women in America who are holding professorships in colleges. There are countless numbers who are teachers in the elementary system. ... Unlike the title "lady" in Europe, the American lady is any woman of good breeding and intelligence.[56]

While some of Krzyżanowski's statements regarding the role of women may appear naive or antiquated when viewed in the light of later standards, it is important to remember that he wrote his memoirs for a Polish audience in order to point out to them the differences between the two societies. By mid-nineteenth century standards, his views were quite liberal.

Though he attempted to eliminate from his memoirs any personal reminiscences of his own private life, Kriz could divorce neither himself nor his ideals from his writing. His every description shows him to be a sincere, sensitive man who avoided offending or speaking ill of people whenever possible. In only a few cases, such as when talking of the Southern slaveholders, did he vent unyielding obloquy without some word of optimism. His memoirs reveal him to have been an enlightened liberal who accepted the opinions and attitudes of others, even if he did not share them.

Written during a truly traumatic period in his life, Krzyżanowski's memoirs helped to remind him of other, brighter days. He thought of his youth, of his friends, and certainly of his many wartime comrades. Thinking back upon his military career his heart lightened as he thought of the changes he helped to bring about in America, the lasting friendships he made. "The passage of time," he wrote, "stirs in my heart continuous memories of joy, of sorrow, this was the life! It is true they were difficult times; however, they were times to stir the blood. Twenty years have gone by since I unbuckled my sword, I have become old and gray, but even today I would, with youthful energy, stand at the head of my legions."[57]

Cheered by these thoughts of happier times. Krzyżanowski reconciled himself to the fact that life must go on. A ray of hope once more kindled within him. He sought once more a return to public life.

— CHAPTER FOURTEEN —

A "GENIAL AND LOYAL SPIRIT"

TWILIGHT YEARS AND BEYOND

On October 16, 1883, Krzyżanowski again assumed the role of Special Agent for the United States Treasury Department. His assignment this time was sure to keep him busy for he found himself detailed to Customs District No. 2 at New York City, the largest revenue operation in the country. The magnitude of Krzyżanowski's responsibility increased greatly over his previous assignments as a Special Agent. His commission, which defined his obligations in general terms to include "the prevention and detection of frauds upon the customs revenue," sent him probing about the city's warehouses and on board the harbor's incoming vessels.[1]

Once again Krzyżanowski carried out his duties faithfully. He found, however, that the fevers he contracted in Panama robbed his body of its normal resiliency. Asthma attacks, which he began to experience after his injury at Gettysburg, increased in severity as well as frequency. The recurring illnesses forced him to curtail his activities to the point where he had to take several days sick leave.[2]

Upon the election of Grover Cleveland, a Democrat, to the presidency in 1884, Krzyżanowski's continued service in the New York customs house became doubtful. Personal appeals by Carl Schurz and L.Q. Lamar finally convinced the new Secretary of the Treasury, Daniel Manning, to conduct a special review of Krzyżanowski's case. Manning found a record of service that did not fail to impress him. The *New York Times* explained to its readers: "In politics he is a staunch Republican. President Cleveland appointed him on his war record, although there were about 20 Democratic applicants."[3] Kriz remained as one of the few Republican appointees to continue in their positions after the Democratic victory.

Krzyżanowski made a determined effort to live up to the confidence that the new administration placed in him, but deteriorating health began to plague him with increasing frequency. On April 8, 1884, Kriz filed a petition for a veteran's invalid pension, claiming that during the Battle of Gettysburg he "was thrown from his horse and his horse then fell on him and injured his lower limbs and depriving him of the use of them to a great extent." On May

Krzyżanowski around 1883.
Courtesy of the National Archives and Records Administration.

Erazm Jerzmanowski.
Courtesy of the Polish Museum of America in Chicago.

26 of the following year, E. Washington Brueninghausen, who had been a member of Krzyżanowski's staff at Gettysburg, filed an affidavit in support of his comrade's claim, verifying that he was personally present at the time of the event and that the general "was thrown from his horse, and the horse falling on him injured his lower limbs."[4]

During 1885, while illness made his daily life more difficult, Kriz carried out significant investigations that exonerated several people suspected of smuggling goods into the country. In addition to this, he handled the difficult, argumentative task of deciding cases involving the application of customs rules to marginal products that did not fit precisely into the neat categories outlined in the Treasury Department's guidelines. Although his health appeared to improve during the summer, new respiratory attacks confined him to his bed for long periods in August and December.[5]

Although his job occupied most of his time, Kriz nevertheless remained involved in Polish affairs. In the fall of 1885 he was active in the formation of a Central Welfare Committee in New York City funded largely through the generosity of Polish America's first millionaire, Erazm Jerzmanowski, vice president of the Equitable Gas Light Company. Among the Committee's officers in addition to Jerzmanowski were Dr. Wincenty Żółnowski, Krzyżanowski's long-time physician, Ignatius Pawłowski, and Rev. Hieronymus Klimecki. Although his involvement in the Polish community provided an opportunity to maintain friendships, he could not escape the burden of sorrow and loneliness bequeathed to him by the death of his wife. His letters to Emily became increasingly despondent, expressing a firm desire to return to Poland. "How wonderful it would be were I to be suddenly transplanted to your home," he wrote. "I wonder if you would recognize me. I am fond of these dreams for they make my life bearable. In my imagination I have broken the Christmas wafer with you and my family, wishing that in the coming year I may actually join with you in this holy and ancient Polish ceremony."[6]

As the months passed, Krzyżanowski's loneliness grew. Nothing seemed to help—not the G.A.R. nor even the local Poles. His friends suggested he find another companion to ease his depression, but he preferred to keep the memory of Caroline alive. "It is difficult to find new happiness in one's advanced years," he wrote, "especially for one who was once so fortunate, but now has lost his happiness." More than two years of loneliness apparently changed his mind when he met Pelagia Borkowska, described as a Polish countess of "medium years" who impressed those about her as "a woman of great charm and personal appeal whose accomplishments and superior character were apparent to everyone. She was a lady of culture, very musical, [who] spoke eight languages." Whether through true affection, or perhaps an attempt to relieve himself of this deep sense of loss, Krzyżanowski married Pelagia Maria Borkowska on November 1, 1885. Whatever the reason, it is doubtful that he ever regained the peace of mind that deserted him with the death of Caroline. In fact, the marriage did not last long and the two parted ways, Kriz to remain in New York City while Pelagia took up residence in San Francisco with Joseph Krzyżanowski where she lived until her death in 1905.[7]

Hoping to improve his health, Krzyżanowski requested a transfer to the drier climate of the American southwest. On January 20, 1886, the Treasury Department ordered him to report to Special Agent Lovell Jerome in Tucson, Arizona. Before he received this latest directive, however, a severe asthma attack left him bedridden under the constant care of Dr. Zółnowski. Unable to leave his bed, Kriz wrote to ask permission to delay his departure until his health improved. The Department agreed.[8]

The long winter of 1885-86 was especially difficult for Krzyżanowski as his health deteriorated steadily. With the return of warmer weather in mid-March, 1886, Kriz began to regain some of his strength. He felt well enough to write Emily of his planned trip west and his hope that he might soon return to his native land. Although still too weak to resume his duties as Special Agent, Krzyżanowski forced himself to pursue some of his less strenuous activities involving the social societies to which he belonged. With the beginning of a new, massive wave of Eastern European immigration into the United States during the 1880s, a philanthropic spirit became

Krzyżanowski's residence in New York City.
Courtesy of the Polish Museum of America in Chicago.

popular among the Polish communities residing in New York. Though lacking the resources to contribute financially, Krzyżanowski cooperated in the establishment of an immigrant aid society of which he became president. A long-time advocate of Polish-American solidarity, Kriz often lamented the sad condition of disorganization among the Poles residing in the United States.[9] When he returned to New York from Panama, he expressed these frustrations succinctly in a letter to Count Ludwik Plater, a leader in the movement to organize Polish immigrants in the nations where they resided. "I agree with the esteemed count's opinion concerning the union of all Poles in America," Krzyżanowski began,

> I have for many years remonstrated and demonstrated what could be gained by doing so and also what great gains our brothers in the Old Country would acquire. But I have come to the conclusion that it will be difficult with our people. We might have accomplished something if we had ... leaders who were honest and patriotic. They could have led our people. What has happened among us here is very shameful. We have lost the faith or confidence of the Americans. There is also a class here that on the political road will [do] whatever they can in seeking Polish votes, and if anyone speaks up or points out their faults he is immediately defamed and slandered by the press. This is sad but true.[10]

Regrettably, Krzyżanowski was correct. His own disappointing attempts to raise funds for the January Insurrection in 1863 proved the truth of his words. Yet even in his declining years Krzyżanowski was not one to cast about idle lamentations. He remained an activist to the end, pursuing that which he viewed as just and desirable.

In May, 1886, delegates from some twenty-five Polish-American societies, representing cities across the nation, met in New York to celebrate the anniversary of the Constitution of the Third of May. Thousands of people jammed into New York's Irving Hall to participate in the festivities. For Kriz the occasion offered two greatly appealing lures: the opportunities to renew old friendships and to once again speak out in support of Polish unity. As he mingled among the participants he found many familiar faces; men like Karol Chłapowski, the Honorable Benjamin A. Willis, and Franz Sigel.[11]

The long parade of speakers touched on many subjects, not the least of which was a sentiment favoring a federation of all Polish societies in the country. Erazm Jerzmanowski, who first voiced the proposal, had already been elected president of the Polish National Alliance. Krzyżanowski rejoiced at the prospect that his dream of a united Polish America might be accomplished. In his brief speech he wholeheartedly endorsed the project. Unfortunately for his aspirations, as well as those of future generations of

Polish-Americans, the physical work of molding a united organization did not progress as easily as the election of an executive officer. In the west, as Krzyżanowski had foreseen, Reverend Father Dominik Majer arose to lead a Roman Catholic faction in a struggle for control against the eastern wing under Jerzmanowski. These divisive influences led to the formation of new societies that substantially decentralized and reduced the power and influence of the Polish population in the United States.[12]

At the age of sixty-two, weakened by his long battle with a multitude of illnesses, Krzyżanowski could not afford to expend the energy he put into his attempt to promote Polish-American unity. By the end of 1886 his asthma returned, accompanied by pleurisy, uremia and chronic Bright's disease. Confined to his bed in the home of Mrs. Maier, an adopted daughter, Krzyżanowski suffered increasingly painful headaches, respiratory discomfort and diarrhea. His blood pressure rose. Sharp pains pierced a chest wracked with frequent convulsions.[13] His deteriorating condition led Krzyżanowski, early in 1886, to seek an increase in his veteran's pension due to his increased disability. In this effort, he once again enlisted the support of his wartime comrades and his friends in the Polish community. In May, Carl Schurz signed an affidavit attesting to the injuries Krzyżanowski received at Gettysburg, and the fact that he complained of the lingering effects of these wounds during the remaining months of the war when he was under Schurz's direct observation. Dr. Żółnowski also provided an affidavit certifying that he first treated Krzyżanowski for asthma in 1868 and had been involved in his treatment thereafter. In response to the latter affidavit, John C. Black, Commissioner of Pensions, asked Żółnowski whether he had documents to verify the condition and treatment. The doctor responded: "I would respectfully state, that I have had the general under my care continuously since 1868 that the General has never been situated pecuniarily to meet the expense of medical attendance and for this reason and being an intimate friend of the General and of the same nationality as myself, I never have made any charges against the General for my professional services hence my testimony is from memory."[14]

In 1884, Kriz received a pension of $15 per month, but his rapidly deteriorating medical condition caused him to seek a further increase in his invalid's pension to $22.50 to cover the increased cost of his medical bills. In support, Carl Schurz brought his considerable political influence to bear in an attempt to speed consideration of the application. On September 28 the German politician wrote to L.Q.C. Lamar to thank him for his intercession on behalf of Kriz: "Your kind letter of the 24th reached me yesterday. I thank you very much for having made General Krzyzanowski's case 'special.' His physicians apprehend that he will not survive the coming winter."[15]

With the examination of Krzyżanowski's claim proceeding, a medical examination took place on November 2. The examining physician reported the general was 68 years old, weighed 273 pounds, had a sallow, yellowish skin, and suffered from kidney disease, asthma, pleuritis and dilatation of the heart. The report continued: "When walking he takes very short steps and has the gait of a feeble old man. … He is not able to perform any manual labor owing to his great feebleness. … He requires regular aid and attention by another person."[16] As a result of the report, the government increased Krzyżanowski's pension from $15 to $22.50 per month on November 28, citing his asthmatic condition. Yet, Kriz quickly renewed his petition for a further increase, noting that the recent increase ignored his chronic pleuritis, palpitation of the heart and Brights disease of the kidneys. His circumstance, he argued, required that he have the constant assistance of an attendant, a condition that should qualify him for the $50 per month payment made to those requiring such assistance.[17] Carl Schurz once again wrote in support.

> General Krzyzanowski received an increase of pension but only a very small one, from $15.00 to $22.00. I cannot but think that in making that award the circumstance was left out of view that in his present condition, he needs an attendant to watch with him day and night, and, if I remember rightly, that would entitle him to an increase of $50. If that is granted it will only serve to lighten the burden on his last days a little, for as the attending physician informs me, he will, in all probability, die before the end of the winter, and may go off at any moment. I am so well acquainted with the circumstance—I visited him two or three times a week—that I might add an affidavit to strengthen his claim.
>
> I send you the enclosed papers with the request that you see them transmitted to the Commissioner of Pensions in such a manner as to secure prompt action on the case.[18]

Given the fragile nature of the general's health, together with the usually lengthy bureaucratic process, Schurz wrote again in early January 1887 to prompt officials to an early decision.

> Pardon me for troubling you again about the Krzyzanowski case. The poor man had very severe spasms yesterday, and the Doctor says that this is a sure sign in this case of the approaching end although the patient may still linger for a few weeks. In the meantime he will require more care and more medicine etc. than ever before. As you are aware when his pension was increased, but only a trifle he applied for a re-rating. This was some five weeks ago, and I hoped the decision of the matter would be had long ere this. If that decision is favorable, the increase will be of importance to the patient just now more than ever. If it is unfavorable, it would be well for the general's friends here to know it, for then other arrangements to provide for his needs would have to be made. I mean arrangements of a somewhat regular and reliable nature.

> We should, therefore, be very glad to know, *as soon as possible*, by return mail if it can be done, how the matter stands, and it is under these circumstances that I venture to tax your good nature once more. Will you be kind enough to have the necessary inquiry made at the Pension office at your earliest convenience?
>
> Accept my cordial wishes for the new year, and I shall be obliged to you for expressing my good wishes to the Secretary too, as well as to my old friends in the Department.[19]

Throughout December and January, Krzyżanowski fought the increasing pain in an attempt to overcome this latest onslaught of maladies. He felt encouraged that the Treasury Department kept him on its payroll despite his prolonged absence.[20] On January 26, Dr. Alfred Meyer was called to the general's bedside. He reported "the general had a severe pulmonary hemorrhage today probably consequent upon the circulatory disturbance of a contracting chronic pleurisy."[21] On the morning of January 31, 1887, Isaac Wilson and C.A. Mainz arrived at 130 St. Mark Place to obtain Krzyżanowski's signature on the monthly payroll voucher. The general was so weak he could barely scribble a rough "X" on the appropriate line. The two men witnessed the mark, then returned the voucher to Special Agent James A. Jewell.[22] On the back of the paper Jewell wrote a short, cryptic notation: "Since the receipt of these papers of Gen'l Krzyzanowski I have learned that he died today."[23]

EPILOGUE

On the morning of February 3, 1887, a priest celebrated a Mass for the salvation of General Krzyżanowski's soul. From St. Stanislaus, Bishop and Martyr Church a long procession of mourners filed its way toward Greenwood Cemetery where scores of Poles and Civil War veterans gathered in solemn silence. Slowly the general's coffin approached, guarded, as he would have wanted, by his old comrades of Post 192, Grand Army of the Republic. Next to the grave a tall, thin figure stood with bowed head to deliver a touching eulogy. "He has made many friends," Carl Schurz concluded, "by his genial and loyal spirit." As he spoke his voice quivered with emotion. Then, to the ceremonial rituals of full military honors, dressed in his beloved green uniform of the Von Steinwehr Post, the mortal remains of Włodzimierz Krzyżanowski were consigned to the earth next to those of his cherished wife Caroline—united once again in death.[24]

For fifty years the general and his wife slept beneath the sod of Lot 5499, Grave 737, Greenwood Cemetery. It was not, however, to be their final resting place. On the fiftieth anniversary of his death a later generation of Polish-Americans formed a committee to honor and perpetuate the memory of his accomplishments. As a contribution to the ceremonies, George Sudnik, a noted artist, executed a portrait of the general. Meticulously, Benjamin T. Anuskiewicz, chairman of the General Krzyżanowski Memorial Committee, sought to prepare a suitable recognition for the general. Aided by the Committee's historian, Joseph F. Czechlewski, he arranged for elaborate ceremonies. Though unable to locate the general's survivors, the two men secured legal permission for the reburial of the Krzyżanowskis. When, near the completion of the arrangements, the general's son Joseph was finally located, he interposed no objection to the committee's plans.[25]

To begin the commemoration of the fiftieth anniversary of Krzyżanowski's death, the committee held a memorial program in New York City on January 31, 1937. Beginning with a solemn Mass at St. Stanislaus, Bishop and Martyr Church, the program continued with a luncheon at the Polish National Home followed by services and the placing of a wreath at the general's gravesite in Greenwood Cemetery. The day concluded with a lengthy program of speeches and music at the Washington Irving High School Auditorium. For the occasion, a memorial booklet outlined the life and contributions of the honoree. The publication included a message from Count Jerzy Potocki, Ambassador of Poland:

> Polish Embassy
> Washington
>
> January 19, 1937
>
> Dear Sir,
>
> The memory of Brigadier General Wlodzimierz B. Krzyzanowski is another living link in the history of the two great Republics.
>
> Descendant of those heroic warriors who fought for the cause of freedom and democracy, General Krzyzanowski had brought here his great ideals.
>
> Cherishing in his heart the dreams of the greatness of his father's land and the spirit of sacrifice for the right cause, the brave General had served with courage and faith his adopted country, attaining here the highest distinction and thus setting a noble example for millions of his brothers living in this country.
>
> Today's commemoration of this great hero will strengthen again the friendship between our two nations.
>
> Yours sincerely,
> Jerzy Potocki
> Ambassador of Poland[26]

Sullen, rain-swept skies looked down upon some 200 people who stood ankle-deep in the mud of Greenwood Cemetery to honor General Krzyżanowski on October 9, 1937. The Reverend Felix F. Burant offered a

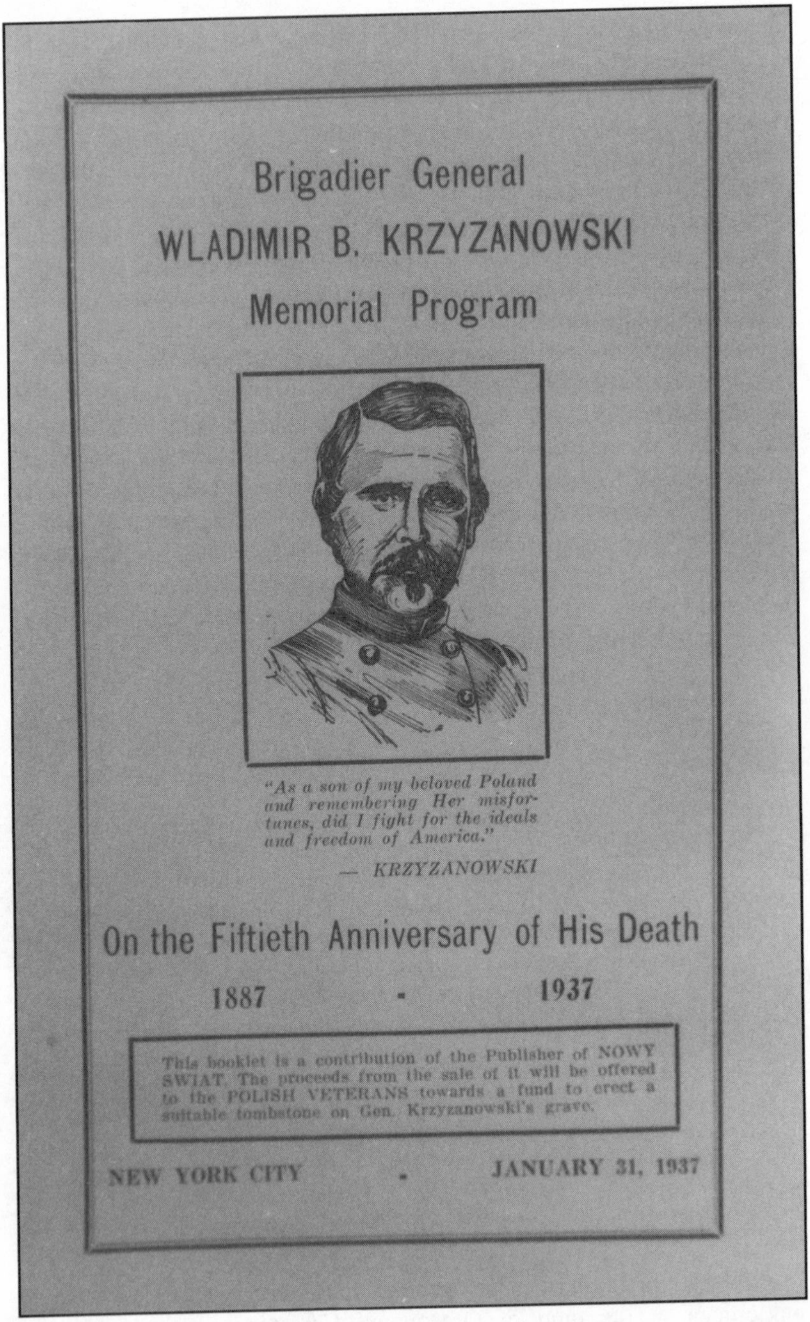

Brigadier General
WLADIMIR B. KRZYZANOWSKI
Memorial Program

"As a son of my beloved Poland and remembering Her misfortunes, did I fight for the ideals and freedom of America."

— KRZYZANOWSKI

On the Fiftieth Anniversary of His Death

1887 - 1937

This booklet is a contribution of the Publisher of NOWY SWIAT. The proceeds from the sale of it will be offered to the POLISH VETERANS towards a fund to erect a suitable tombstone on Gen. Krzyzanowski's grave.

NEW YORK CITY - JANUARY 31, 1937

Krzyżanowski's Memorial Program from 1937.
Courtesy of Henry Archacki.

brief prayer. Placing a wreath on the grave, Dr. Sylwester Gruszka, Consul General of the Republic of Poland, offered the respects of his country. Further wreaths appeared, donated by veterans' associations and several Polish clubs. As the ceremonies drew to their conclusion a unit of the 18th United States Infantry fired volleys above the gravesite. Tears mingled with the rain as the trumpeter sounded the haunting, melancholy notes of Taps.[27]

At 11:45 that morning, President Franklin D. Roosevelt spoke over the radio to eulogize the services of General Krzyżanowski. Throughout the day groups of people gathered to pay their respects to the general at ceremonies held in the Church of Our Lady of Częstochowa, the 69th Regimental Armory, St. Patrick's Cathedral and St. Stanislaus Church. At 7:30 that evening the Memorial Committee held its observance in the auditorium of Washington Irving High School. The 18th Infantry band played, speeches were read, but the highlight of the evening was a tearful rendition by the local Polish singing societies of the Battle Hymn of the Republic.[28]

October 11, 1937, dawned bright and clear in Washington, D.C. At 7:15 A.M. a delegation from New York arrived by train with the remains of General Krzyżanowski and his wife. At 10:00 A.M. a military detachment provided by Colonel Jonathan Wainwright, commanding officer at Ft. Myers, escorted the remains through the gate of Arlington National Cemetery. As the melody of Roman Dzikowski's *General Krzyżanowski Memorial March* floated gently across the slopes, echoing in the trees, the honorary pall bearers approached the freshly prepared grave. Four Polish-American recipients of the American Distinguished Service Cross stood to one side. Opposite them were four men possessing Poland's *Virtuti Militari*. Count Jerzy Potocki, Ambassador of the Republic of Poland, briefly addressed the assemblage of dignitaries. Several Polish-Americans made brief remarks while dozens of wreaths and bouquets were placed to adorn the grave.[29]

Once again, Taps signaled an end to the proceedings. Slowly the crowd broke up, adjourning to place wreaths at the Tomb of the Unknown Soldier, and the monuments to Pułaski and Kościuszko in the city of Washington. The Polish Embassy hosted a reception beginning at 4:00 P.M., followed by a dinner at the Wardman Park Hotel. As the guests sat eating and discussing the events of the day, quiet descended on the freshly turned earth in Arlington National Cemetery's Western Division, Section 1, Lot 832.[30]

In his memoirs General Krzyżanowski expressed what he felt was a need for someone with a "Homeric nature" to pen the world's greatest epoch, the history of the United States. "The acts and their results," he said, "are like an endless chain."[31] He was right. To change even one small, seemingly insignificant event in the long chain that is history would be to alter the direction of that sequential chain. The effects of the lives of millions of

Krzyżanowski's disinterment from Greenwood Cemetery in 1937. Seated in the center is the general's son Joseph and his wife. Seated to the right is his granddaughter Caroline Potter. *Courtesy of Henry Archacki.*

Members of the 18th United States Infantry place a flag over Krzyżanowski's casket while the Rev. Felix F. Burant offers a prayer. *Courtesy of Henry Archacki.*

Count Jerzy Potocki, Ambassador of the Republic of Poland, delivered an address before the reinterment in Arlington National Cemetery, along with other special events to mark the occasion on October 11, 1937. *Courtesy of Henry Archacki.*

Krzyżanowski's tombstone in Arlington National Cemetery.
Author's photograph.

The General Krzyżanowski Memorial Committee arrayed behind the portrait painted by George Sudnik. Henry Archacki is seated, second from the right. *Courtesy of Henry Archacki.*

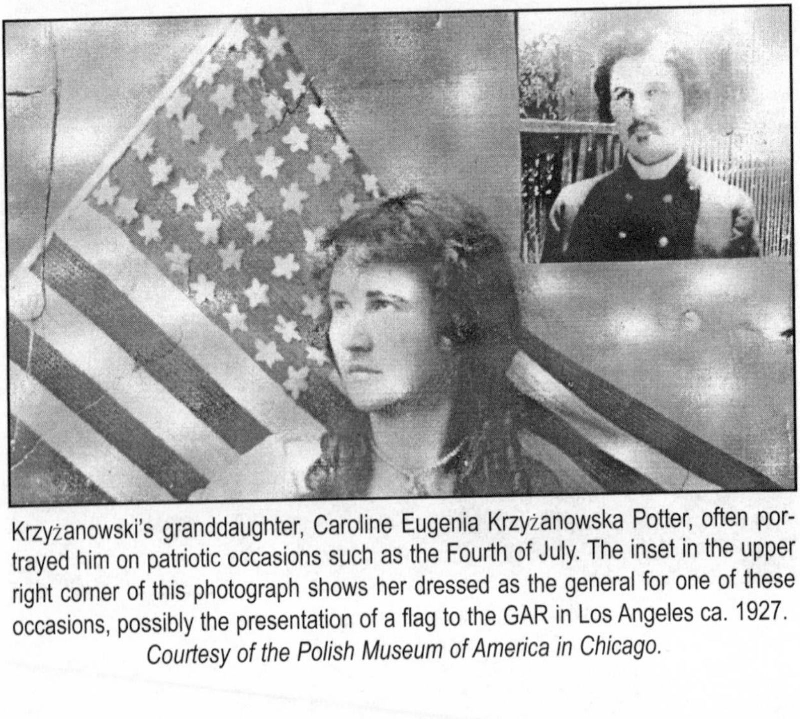

Krzyżanowski's granddaughter, Caroline Eugenia Krzyżanowska Potter, often portrayed him on patriotic occasions such as the Fourth of July. The inset in the upper right corner of this photograph shows her dressed as the general for one of these occasions, possibly the presentation of a flag to the GAR in Los Angeles ca. 1927. *Courtesy of the Polish Museum of America in Chicago.*

men and women are still being felt today—not the least of whom was Włodzimierz Bonawentura Krzyżanowski.

Who was General Krzyżanowski? What legacy did he leave to history? In Poland he aided in the organization of the Mierosławski Insurrection of 1846, a movement that provided an example for other oppressed peoples who followed the lead of their Polish neighbors in 1848. Fleeing the wrath of a vengeful despot in Europe, Krzyżanowski sought asylum in the United States. There he helped to create, in its formative stages, the vast network of railroads that grew to become the very arteries of American economic life.

In 1861 Włodzimierz Krzyżanowski left a happy, secure home to help extend to other oppressed people the freedoms he was unable to restore to his native land. Wherever duty took him, his service elicited comments such as "distinguished" and "faithful." At Cross Keys, as colonel of the Polish Legion, he personally led an assault that stemmed the advance of triumphant Confederate infantry. Had his troops faltered, General Frémont's army may well have been encircled.

Near Groveton, Krzyżanowski's under-strength brigade successfully engaged Stonewall Jackson's vaunted veterans, inflicting more casualties than it received. On the following day, at Second Bull Run, Kriz held a crucial position on the Federal left flank against superior Confederate forces. Had they broken, Confederate infantry could have seized the bridges over Bull Run, thus cutting off the escape routes of the Northern troops.

Though much maligned following the disaster at Chancellorsville, units of Krzyżanowski's brigade made the first effective stand against the Southern onslaught. This heroic effort won the time necessary for the evacuation of the vital baggage trains and artillery pieces. Smarting under the stigma of Chancellorsville, the brigade fought with renewed determination at Gettysburg where over half of the men on the firing lines on July 1 became casualties. Their blood preserved for the Army of the Potomac the crucial high ground of Cemetery Hill. On the following evening, when Confederate infantry stood within easy reach of victory atop those dominating heights, Krzyżanowski personally led two of his skeleton regiments in a counterattack which helped to clear the hill of enemy invaders.

Moving west, hard marching and iron endurance by the general and his troops helped to break the Confederate sieges of Chattanooga and Knoxville. The *Official Records*, a generally conservative source, indicates that Krzyżanowski's brigade lost some 1,369 men during its service. The brigade, like any other, certainly had its compliment of unprincipled deserters and "skedaddlers," but it also had its share of heroes. During every major battle in which it actively engaged, it rendered distinguished service while occupying a crucial part of the line. Throughout the discouraging series of defeats in the east, the general and his men displayed one of their main

This memorial card from October 1937 commemorates Kazimierz Pułaski and Krzyżanowski. *Courtesy of Henry Archacki.*

---

strengths, the ability to remain steadfast in the face of adversity. Furthermore, the services of General Krzyżanowski and his troops helped to dispel the virulent anti-foreign sentiments rampant during the decade of the 1850s, and to prove, in the words of Bruce Catton, "that Krzyżanowski is as good an American name as Cabot."[32]

In reflecting on the general's services to his adopted country, noted Civil War historian James I. Robertson commented:

> Men of widely diverse origins marched onto the fields of battle to stake their lives on principles each considered just. Therefore, their accomplishments, as well as our remembrance of their deeds, transcends all nationalities, races and creeds. If General Krzyzanowski was born a Pole, he died an American. Likewise should we all, whether Northerners, Southerners, or Americans by adoption, take heed from his example and take increased pride in being Americans, one of another, united forever.[33]

Bruce Catton, the Pulitzer Prize-winning author of the seminal trilogy on the Army of the Potomac, commented at the New-York Historical Society in a speech commemorating the one hundredth anniversary of the departure of Krzyżanowski's 58th New York Volunteer Infantry for the war:

> Serving the country of their adoption with heroism, with endurance and with unshaken loyalty, these men served us who live a century later in

A commemoration of Krzyżanowski's military service drawn by Henry Archacki. *Courtesy of Henry Archacki.*

> a way that is profoundly important. They broadened the whole concept of American citizenship. They helped America become in fact what it had always been in theory—the eternal homeland of men who love liberty for themselves and for others.[34]

Undoubtedly Krzyżanowski will be remembered most for his services during the perilous days of the Civil War. Yet, to say that his star reached its zenith in 1863, and fell into decline thereafter, is to simplify the story beyond the point of distortion. Soon after the war he entered public service, through which he hoped to promote American unity and protect his adopted land from fraud and corruption. Throughout a period of massive public scandals he remained aloof from the lure of personal gain, intent upon carrying out his duties to the best of his ability. In doing so, he worked toward the increased efficiency of the Federal revenue service and thus the protections of honest citizens against those who wished to profit at the expense of justice.

In his private life Krzyżanowski became a prime mover behind the beginning of Helena Modjeska's successful dramatic career in the United States. The general's casino provided a relaxed, informal atmosphere where the young author Henryk Sienkiewicz obtained much of the material he later used in the development of characters and plots for the literary works that brought him the Nobel Prize.

Finally, Krzyżanowski's memoirs stand as an excellent source reference for the thirty-five year period in American history between 1847 and 1882. His descriptions of the United States and its people provide us with an insight through which we might better understand those crucial formative years of the nineteenth century. His espousal of the abolitionist, pro-Lincoln, and at times Radical Republican ideals make his comments on the decisive Civil War era especially revealing to historians and laymen alike.

Włodzimierz Krzyżanowski was a living, breathing human being who moved through space and time. He encountered other human beings, affected them, and, in turn, was affected by them. He was reflective, eloquent, honest, sentimental and popular. He was a leader. Raised in the tradition of nineteenth century Polish democratic and patriotic idealism, he constantly pursued their fulfillment in Poland and the United States. He loved his native land, yet he was awed by the potential power of his adopted nation. He recognized with gratitude the debt that he owed to the United States for accepting him as a refugee from European absolutism and allowing him to share in the fruits of American democracy. he would rest content with the knowledge that his efforts helped make the United States a better place for people to live, and a leader in his own fight for liberty and justice.

Appendix A

Honors Received by Krzyżanowski

The following is a list of gifts of honor received by Krzyżanowski as recorded by Ksieniewicz from interviews with the general's son Joseph.[1]

1861 — A cup from the Republican Party of New York City.

1861 — A horse with full equipment and field glasses by from the ladies of Washington.

1862 — A whip decorated with gold from the Swiss volunteers in his regiment.

1862 — Gold spurs presented by his officers.

1862 — A silver cup presented by French soldiers fighting in America.

1862 — A gold chain from his staff officers.

1864 — A diamond ring from the citizens of Cincinnati.

1864 — An artistic pipe from the citizens of Bridgeport, Alabama.

1864 — Two diamond start, twin insignias of a brigadier general, from the ladies of New York.

Date Unknown — Beautiful silver service presented by the citizens of Washington.

Joseph Krzyżanowski reported, as indicated by Ksieniewicz, that all of these valuable gifts were in the possession of Pelagia Krzyżanowska, his second wife, and were lost in the San Francisco earthquake and fire of 1906.

APPENDIX B

REPORT OF COL. KRZYŻANOWSKI ON THE BATTLE OF CROSS KEYS

HDQRS. FIFTY-EIGHTH REGT. NEW YORK VOLS.,
Mount Jackson, June 12, 1862.

I have the honor to submit to you the following report in regard to the engagement of June 8:

After the arrival of my regiment near the field of battle to the left of the battery of the First Brigade, I received your orders to move to the right, when Brigadier-General Stahel asked me to come up to his assistance. I at once formed my regiment into line, being in column by division, and advanced to the place indicated by General Stahel. I was at that time in the middle of a large rye field, skirted by woods immediately on the right of the battery and in front of my regiment, into which direction I moved in line up to and just beyond a fence at the outskirts of these woods, looking for the troops I was to assist and for the enemy. On the right of my position was another open field, on the opposite side of which I saw a column move by the flank toward the left of our lines, and upon a hill I perceived a battery opening fire toward our right. In order to find out whether I was on the left I sent one company out as skirmishers to keep up the connection on that side and by throwing them a little forward to give information of the enemy's advance.

Directly after this Captain Schirmer came up, and seeing the battery he told me if I would protect him with my regiment he would bring up a couple of guns and open fire upon the enemy's battery. He did so, and soon silenced the latter, when the enemy engaged my skirmishers, who slowly retired toward the regiment for the purpose of giving my men a chance to fire. Captain Schirmer now withdrew his guns and soon the whole regiment was engaged. Keeping up a constant fire, which told greatly among the enemy's lines, I now gave the command to charge bayonets, and succeeded in driving him back about a hundred yards.

To my greatest dismay I noticed at this instant two regiments coming out of the woods on the right of the enemy's battery, and having no reserve to fall back on I thought it imprudent to remain any longer, and consequently gave the command orders to retire while a heavy musketry fire was poured upon my men. I retired behind the battery of Captain Wiedrich, who now opened a heavy fire upon the enemy.[2]

APPENDIX C

REPORT OF COL. KRZYŻANOWSKI ON THE SECOND BATTLE OF BULL RUN

HDQRS. SECOND BRIGADE, THIRD DIVISION,
Near Arlington Heights, September 3, 1862.

At about 5.30 o'clock a.m. on the 29th of August I received orders from General Schurz to advance with my brigade. It was done in the following order: Two regiments in company column, left in front, and one regiment, the Fifty-fourth New York Volunteers, as reserve. On the right of me was Colonel Schimmelfennig with his brigade and on the left General Milroy's brigade. A line of skirmishers having been established, we advanced toward the woods through which the Manassas Gap Railroad runs. As soon as we entered the woods I dispatched my adjutant to ascertain whether the line of skirmishers was kept up on both wings, and finding such was not the case, and that I had advanced s little faster than General Milroy's and Colonel Schimmelfennig's column, I halted my skirmishers to wait until the line was re-established. However, being informed that General Milroy was advancing, I sent the Fifty-fourth Regiment to take position on my right wing and to try and find the lines of Colonel Schimmelfennig's skirmishers, and then I advanced, together with the former.

Scarcely had the skirmishers passed over 200 yards when they became engaged with the enemy. For some time the firing was kept up, but our skirmishers had to yield at last to the enemy's advancing column. At this time I ordered my regiments up, and a general engagement ensued. However, I soon noticed that the Fifty-fourth and Fifty-eighth Regiments had to fall back, owing to the furious fire of the enemy, who had evidently thrown his forces exclusively upon those two regiments. The Seventy-fifth Regiment Pennsylvania Volunteers, which up to this time had not taken part in this engagement, was (at the time the Fifty-eighth and Fifty-fourth retired) now nobly led on y Lieutenant-Colonel Mahler upon the right flank of the enemy, and kept him busy until I had brought the Fifty-eighth at a doublequick up to its previous position, when those two regiments successfully drove the enemy before them, thereby gaining the position of the Manassas Gap Railroad. The Fifty-fourth had meanwhile been ordered by General Schurz to take position with the Twenty-ninth Regiment New York State Volunteers in the interval of my brigade and that of Colonel Schimmelfennig.

At this time I observed on my right the brigade of General Roberts to whom I explained my position, after which we advanced together a short distance, but he soon withdrew his forces, ascertaining that he got his brigade in between the column of our division. We had occupied the above-named position only a short time when the enemy again tried to force us back, but the noble conduct of my troops did not allow him to carry-out his design, and he did not gain one inch of ground. We were thus enabled to secure our wounded and some of our dead, and also some of the enemy's wounded, belonging to the Tenth South Carolina Regiment. We held this position until 2 p.m., when we were relieved by a brigade of General Kearny's division, and retired about one-fourth of a mile toward our rear, where we also encamped for the night.

Most nobly did the troops behave. Amongst the officers I must mention the names of Lieutenant-Colonel Mahler, Seventy-fifth Regiment Pennsylvania Volunteers; Lieutenant Gerke, of the same regiment, who was in command of the skirmishers, and Lieut. W. Bowen, who was on that day acting adjutant of that regiment. Of the officers of the Fifty-eighth Regiment New York State Volunteers I have to make particular mention of the gallant conduct of Maj. William Henkel, who was wounded, but who remained for three hours longer on the battlefield, until his pains became too violent; also of the adjutant, Lieutenant Stoldt, of that regiment, who did valuable service with the skirmishers. Of the Fifty-fourth Regiment New York State Volunteers Lieutenant-Colonel Ashby and Adjutant Brandt deserve great credit. The different members of my staff executed my orders promptly—Captain Theune being severely wounded while performing his duty, and Lieutenant Schmidt most gallantly cheered the men and conducted the line of skirmishers to my greatest satisfaction. Captain Maluski and Captain Weide did valuable service on that day.

On the succeeding day, August 30, at about 8 a.m., I received orders to form my regiments company column left in front. This being done, a new order directed me more toward the left, where I took position in line with the brigade of General Stahel. Here we remained until afternoon, when we were ordered up toward the stone house, where my battery took position.

I received orders to move my infantry to the right of Colonel Koltes' brigade and then to advance, which had scarcely been done when we became engaged with the enemy and kept up a brisk fire until, after the lapse of about half an hour, one of the enemy's batteries compelled us to retire toward a deep ravine just in the rear of our lines. Seeing, however, that the enemy moved toward our left I again ordered my men up, changing my front a little toward the left, our left wing resting upon the right wing of a brigade, the name of which I was unable to ascertain. After some fifteen minutes of constant firing of our two brigades I gave orders to my regiments to cease firing, still holding the same position, while the enemy withdrew. I then consulted with the brigade commander on my left, asking him to advance farther in company with me, which he, however, refused to do.

My forces being too weak to advance alone I remained inactive for a few minutes until General Schurz sent orders to retire across the run and remain in reserve. I did so until 8 p.m., when a new order arrived for me to retire about one-fourth of a mile farther, where nearly the whole corps was collecting. Having no special orders I rested my men, who after their day's work were only glad enough to do so, until 2 a.m. 31st, at which time I was informed by a cavalry scouting party that all the troops had fallen back. I at once mounted my horse and went toward the hospital, at which place I had seen General Sigel and General Schulz at about 9 p.m. on the evening of the battle. Finding nobody besides the physicians and the wounded men there I returned to my men and ordered them to fall in for the purpose of marching to Centreville, whither our forces were said to have gone. I must insert here that I only had the Fifty-eighth New York State Volunteers and Seventy-fifth Pennsylvania Volunteers with me at that time,. the Fifty-fourth having been detailed by General Sigel late on the evening before. Arriving with my troops at the stone bridge across Bull Run, the same was in a blaze of fire and not fit to be crossed, which circumstance compelled me to ford the river with great difficulty, as the banks are very steep. I arrived at Centreville at 6 o'clock a.m., after finding the Fifty-fourth Regiment encamped alongside of the road, and joined my division.

In the engagement of the 30th of August the troops under my command behaved very well in general. The Seventy-fifth deserves again to be especially mentioned for its bravery. Lieutenant-Colonel Mahler, of the same, was wounded; also Lieutenant Ledig. Lieut. W. Bowen, the acting adjutant, was killed, and Lieutenant Froelich. The Fifty-fourth Regiment suffered severely, a number of officers and men being wounded.

The gallant conduct of First Lieutenant Wertheimer, of this regiment, deserves to be noticed, who, while the enemy's batteries were pouring a perfect hail of lead into our lines, nobly grasped a guide flag and cheered the men to follow him. Lieutenant-Colonel Ashby, of this regiment, Captain Wahle, Captain Ernewein, and Adjutant Brandt, on this day again behaved bravely. The Fifty-eighth Regiment was more fortunate in regard to the loss of officers, but suffered intensely in the ranks. All the officers deserve credit for their behavior on that day. As to my staff I was as unfortunate as I was on the previous day—losing one of my aides-decamp, Lieutenant Schmidt, who was severely wounded in the thigh. He showed great coolness and courage. The balance of my staff most promptly executed my orders. I have also to mention the gallant conduct of First Lieutenant Chesebrough, of General Schenck's staff, whom I met on the battle-field, and who assisted me for some time. I was unfortunate enough on that day to lose my horse, which was shot under me.[3]

APPENDIX D

REPORT OF COL. KRZYŻANOWSKI ON THE BATTLE OF CHANCELLORSVILLE

NEAR BROOKE'S STATION, VA.,
May 15, 1863.

SIR: I have the honor to submit to you the following report about the engagement of May 2, near Wilderness Run, Va.:

About 11 a.m., May 2, I received your orders to withdraw two regiments from the position my brigade had occupied since the previous day, they being at that time placed in reserve fronting to the south. The position which was assigned to the two regiments was a reserve for the First Division, and, fronting to the west, partly formed the extreme right wing of the whole army. The Twenty-sixth Wisconsin and the Seventy-fifth Pennsylvania Volunteers were ordered to take this position.

About 11 p.m. I received orders to detail one regiment of my brigade for picket duty, to relieve the Eighty-second Illinois Volunteers, for which duty I ordered the Seventy-fifth Pennsylvania Volunteers, with the exception of about 60 men, which were in excess of the number required for picket duty. Of these, 45 men were detailed to form part of the skirmishing line. To replace the regiment thus detailed, I ordered the Fifty-eighth New York Volunteers, which still occupied the place assigned to it the day before. The disposition of my troops before the engagement was, consequently, as follows (see annexed sketch):(*) The Seventy-fifth Pennsylvania Volunteers on picket, except 60 men; One hundred and nineteenth New York Volunteers on the left wing of the First Brigade, Third Division, deployed in line along the Orange Court-House Plank road, fronting south, and the Twenty-sixth Wisconsin and Fifty-eighth New York Volunteers in the position above indicated, fronting west. I remained with my staff with the two last-named regiments. About 400 paces in front of the latter two regiments, the skirmish line of 80 men of the Twenty- sixth Wisconsin Volunteers and 45 men from the Seventy-fifth Pennsylvania Volunteers; the Twenty-sixth regiment Wisconsin Volunteers in close column to the center on the extreme right, and the Fifty-eighth New York Volunteers on the left, with deploying distance between them.

About 6 p.m. firing was heard in front toward the left of my line, and but a short time afterward I discovered a part of the First Division coming down upon the left of my troops in the greatest disorder. Meanwhile the firing drew nearer. I inquired into the cause of the disorder, and was informed by officers and men of that division that the enemy came in such force and was pushing so rapidly that they were obliged to fall back. My skirmishers retained their position, and were not engaged until some minutes afterward, when, after some resistance, the enemy's force obliged them to fall back upon the regiments, which was done in good order, as also the deploying into line of the latter.

It appeared, however, that the enemy came upon our lines in an oblique direction, completely outflanking my forces on the right, and messing in front of them, in consequence of which it became necessary to withdraw; but, not desiring to take the responsibility, I sent one of my staff officers, Lieutenant [Louis H.] Orleman, to you, with a request for re-enforcements, but I received orders from you to fall back to the border of the woods on the right of the intrenchments, which woods, being very thick, caused the wing companies of the regiments to be detached. When the intrenchments were abandoned, my troops fell back upon the line occupied by General Berry's division. Here I was joined by the Eighty-second Ohio Volunteers, Colonel Robinson, part of the Eighty-second Illinois Volunteers, and the One hundred and fifty-seventh New York Volunteers, Colonel Brown. We occupied this position for upward of one hour. The firing having by that time been somewhat discontinued, and my forces being separated from the rest of the corps, I concluded to make proper efforts to join the rest of the corps near a large farm house north of Chancellorsville, in which I succeeded. Nearly one hour later I received orders to proceed to Chancellorsville, and there join the remainder of the troops.

As to the behavior of the troops under my command, I must confess that they behaved well and to my satisfaction. The Twenty-sixth Regiment Wisconsin Volunteers, as well as the Fifty-eighth New York Volunteers, stood their ground until it became untenable. The officers exerted themselves to cheer their men.

Of the One hundred and nineteenth New York Volunteers I cannot mention much, from the fact that this regiment was detached from the rest of the brigade. I have ascertained that it fought well.

Of the Seventy- fifth Pennsylvania Volunteers, the skirmishers reflect credit on their regiment.

It would be doing injustice to many if I should particularly mention the name of any line officer. I therefore leave such to the respective regimental commanders. I cannot, however, refrain from mentioning the names of Col. W. H. Jacobs, Lieutenant-Colonel Boebel, Major Baetz, and Adjutant Schlosser, all of the Twenty-sixth Wisconsin Volunteers, who led their men to the best of their abilities and with coolness; also Capt. E. Koenig, of the

Fifty-eighth New York Volunteers, who, after Captain Braun, its commander, had been killed, took command of the regiment.

Of Col. E. Peissner, One hundred and nineteenth New York Volunteers, I can speak only with admiration, he having cheered his men at the moment he fell, as I am told by many of his officers.

Lieutenant-Colonel Lockman, of the same regiment, is said to have acted bravely and with coolness.

Respecting the officers on my staff, I have reason to express my entire satisfaction, they having executed my orders with the greatest promptness, and every one of them has received marks which prove that they have been in the midst of the shower of lead.

The total loss of the brigade is, as near as can be ascertained, as follows:

Officers and men	Killed	Wounded	Missing	Total
Officers.	6	5	10	21
Enlisted men	55	189	169	413
Total	61	194	179	434

I have the honor to be, general, your most obedient servant,

W. KRZYZANOWSKI,
Col., Comdg. 2d Brig., 3d Div., 11th Army Corps.

Maj. Gen. CARL SCHURZ,
Commanding Third Division.[4]

APPENDIX E

ITINERARY OF THE SECOND BRIGADE, COL. KRZYŻANOWSKI COMMANDING, DURING THE REOPENING OF THE TENNESSEE RIVER

October 1, the brigade arrived at Nashville, and established camp near Bridgeport, Ala., October 2.

October 19, the Seventy-fifth Pennsylvania Volunteers and Sixty-eighth New York Volunteers were transferred to the Third Brigade, Third Division, Eleventh Corps, Colonel Hecker commanding, in pursuance with Special Orders, No. 209, headquarters Eleventh Corps, dated October 19.

October 27, the brigade left Bridgeport, Ala., and reached Lookout Valley, opposite Lookout Point, October 28.

October 28 and 29, in the night an engagement took place with Longstreet's corps, which, however, the Second Brigade took little share in. A patrol of 150 men, under the command of Major Clan-batty, of the One hundred and Forty-first New York Volunteers, discovered first the movements of the enemy, and much contributed to the favorable results.[5]

APPENDIX F

KRZYŻANOWSKI'S STAFF OFFICERS

UNDER GENERAL SIGEL[6]

Capt. Roderick Theune – Acting Assistant Adjutant General
Capt. Charles Worms – Acting Assistant Quartermaster
Capt. Alexander Małuski – Acting Aide-de-Camp
Lt. Max Schmidt – Acting Commissary of Subsistance
Lt. Gustav Stoldt – Provost Marshall
Lt. Louis H. Orlemann – Topogrphical Engineer
Lt. E. Washington Brueninghausen – Ordnance Officer.

NOVEMBER 1863[7]

Surgeon Louis Schulter, 68th NY – Surgeon in Chief
Capt. Frederick Winter, 75th PA, – Acting Assistant Inspector General
Capt. Max Schmidt, 58th NY – Acting Copmmissary of Subsistance
Capt. Louis H. Orlemann, 119th NY – Acting Topographical Engineer
Capt. Otto Fritsch, 68th NY – Acting Aide-de-Camp
Capt. Louis Galecki, 58th NY – Acting Aide-de-Camp
Lt. F. W. Hundhausen, 26th WI – Acting Assistant Quartermaster
Lt. E. Washington Brueninghausen, 119th NY – Acting Provost Marshall
Lt. F. Ehrlich, 75th PA, – Assistant Adjutant General

ENDNOTES

CHAPTER ONE
"THE SON OF A FOREIGN LAND"

[1]From President Franklin D. Roosevelt's address on the occasion of the reinterment of Włodzimierz Krzyżanowski in Arlington National Cemetery in 1937. A copy of this address appears in Appendix A through the courtesy of Mr. Henry Archacki.

[2]In the first edition to this book Krzyżanowski's date of birth is given as June 9, 1824, based on a faulty translation of an original document. Since that time, various sources in Poland, including the *Polski Słownik Biograficzny* (Vol. XV, 624), have given his birth date as July 8, 1824. This date is also substantiated by documents contained in his pension files and in the National Archives and documents in the genealogical databases of the Church of Jesus Christ of Latter-Day Saints, Batch No. 8814611, Source Call No. 1553210 (accessed at the Web site www.familysearch.com, August 3, 2000). See also, Bogdan Grzeloński, ed., *Ameryka w pamiętnikach Polaków: Antologia* (Warsaw: Wydawnictwo Interpress, 1988), 110; Zdzisław Grot, "Generał Włodzimierz Krzyżanowski w świetle własnych wspomnień oraz listów pisanych do rodziny," *Kronika Miasta Poznінia*, Vol. XV, No. 1 (March 31, 1937), 87. Stanisław Krzyżanowski first settled in Śląsk, then moved to land at Rożnowo that he purchased from Jan Gliszczyński. Stanisław married Elżbieta Pągowska in 1804. Their four children were Marianna (b. 1805), Teodożja (b. 1808), Józef (b. 1809) and Nemezy (b. 1811). Elżbieta died in 1819, after which Stanisław married her younger sister, Ludwika, in 1821. Their children were Stanisława Ludwika (b. 1822), Ludwik Wincenty (b. 1823; died in infancy), Włodzimierz Bonawentura (b. 1824) and Edmund. This information comes from page 2 of an untitled, undated (probably ca. 1937) manuscript biography of Gen Krzyżanowski by Casimir Ksieniewicz in the Benjamin T. Anuskiewicz Collection, archives of the Polish Studies Program at Central Connecticut State University (hereafter cited as "Ksieniewicz"), which was most likely derived from Grot, 87. Krzyżanowski's family were members of St. Catherine's Parish (Św. Katarzyny) in Rożnowo as confirmed by parish records. See the parish web site at: http://www.roznowo-lukowo.archpoznan.org.pl/r_img.php?img=mapka.

[3]Ksieniewicz, 3-4; Grzeloński, 110.

[4]Ksieniewicz, 3-4; Grzeloński, 110.

[5]Grot, 88; Grzeloński, 110; Archiwum Państwowe w Poznaniu, II, *passim*; Anuszkiewicz manuscript, 3.

[6]Ksieniewicz, 4-5.

[7]Grot, 88-89.

[8]Grot, 88; letter, Krzyżanowski to Emily Metzig, September 29, 1885.

[9]Włodzimierz B. Krzyżanowski, *Wspomnienia z Pobytu w Ameryce Podczas Wojny 1861-1864* (Chicago: Polish Museum of America, 1963), 43. Krzyżanowski's

memoirs were originally published as a series of articles in the Polish magazine *Kłosy* in 1883. They were translated into English for the author by Stanley J. Pula in 1969. Hereafter cited as *Wspomnienia.*

[10] *Polish Encyclopaedia* (Geneva, Switzerland: Polish National Committee of America, 1926), I, 516-517.

[11] Krzyżanowski, *Wspomnienia*, 11; *Demokrata Polski* (London), Jan. 13, 1862.

[12] Stanisław Arnold and Marian Żychowski, *Outline History of Poland* (Warsaw: Polonia Publishing House, 1962), 107, 111, 116-117; Grzeloński, 110; *Polish Encyclopedia*, I, 517.

[13] *Polish Encyclopedia*, I, 517; Oscar Halecki, *A History of Poland* (New York: Roy Publishers, 1966), 235-36.

[14] Arnold and Żychowski, 116.

[15] Letter, Royal magistrate of Samter [Szamotuly] to the Hon. Ritter und Elder von Beurmann, Royal Chief Magistrate of the Province of Posen [Poznań], Sept. 11, 1846.

[16] Krzyżanowski, *Wspomnienia*, 11-13.

[17] Krzyżanowski, *Wspomnienia*, 11-12; Ksieniewicz, 14-15.

[18] Krzyżanowski, *Wspomnienia*, 11-12; Ksieniewicz, 14-15.

[19] Krzyżanowski, *Wspomnienia*, 13.

[20] Krzyżanowski, *Wspomnienia*, 13-14.

[21] Krzyżanowski, *Wspomnienia*, 13-14.

[22] The initial quote is from Krzyżanowski, *Wspomnienia*, 13-14; the indented quote of the 1881 letter is quoted from Ksieniewicz, 12. Ship manifests for the port of New York list a "W. Krysawoski," age 23, arriving from Hamburg on January 25, 1847.

[23] Krzyżanowski, *Wspomnienia*, 15.

[24] Krzyżanowski, *Wspomnienia*, 15; Grot, 90.

[25] Letter, Krzyżanowski to Emily Metzig, Sept. 29, 1885.

[26] Krzyżanowski, *Wspomnienia*, 15.

[27] Rev. Francis Bolek, *Who's Who in Polish America* (New York: Harbinger House, 1943), 188.

[28] United States Census for 1850, Cabell County, Virginia, 10th District, Tract 16. He is listed as "Waldimir Kryszanowski."

[29] Letter, Krzyżanowski, to Henryk Kałussowski, "From the Woods," Jan. 1, 1852. Although "Bielaski" is only identified by last name, Aleksander Bielaski was a government employee in Washington, D.C., during this same time period and would no doubt have been in almost daily contact with Kałussowski and his circles of Poles. There can be little doubt that it is this Bielaski to whom the letters refer.

[30] Letter, Krzyżanowski, to Kałussowski, "From the Woods," Feb. 16, 1852.

[31] Letter, Krzyżanowski, to Kałussowski, from Guyandotte, March 8, 1852.

[32] *Ibid.*

[33] Krzyżanowski, *Wspomnienia*, 28-36.

[34] Krzyżanowski, *Wspomnienia*, 17, 32.

[35] Ksieniewicz, 28; letter, Krzyżanowski to Emily Metzig, Sept. 29, 1885.

[36] Letter, Krzyżanowski to Emily Metzig, Sept. 29, 1885.

[37] Andrew H. Boyd, complr., *Boyd's Washington and Georgetown Directory*

(Washington, DC: Taylor & Maury, 1860), 99, 185; United States District Court for the District of Columbia, Marriage Records/Marriage Licenses, 1853-1862, National Archives, RG 21, Box 1, contains Krzyżanowski's marriage license to Caroline dated Dec. 27, 1853; marriage information is in International Genealogical Index, File No. 1985312, The Church of Jesus Christ of Latter-Day Saints, accessed at www.familysearch.com, Aug. 3, 2000; documentation on the birth of Joseph Krzyżanowski is in International Genealogical Index, File No. 2034610, The Church of Jesus Christ of Latter-Day Saints, accessed at www.familysearch.com, Aug. 3, 2000; Grzeloński, 111, claims that Caroline Burnett brought "a considerable dowry" to the marriage.

[38]Krzyżanowski, *Wspomnienia*, 42.

[39]Krzyżanowski, *Wspomnienia*, 20-22, 29, 42.

[40]Michael J. Duszak, "Colonel Kriz of Washington," *Polish American Studies*, XXIII, No. 2 (Autumn, 1966), 108.

[41]Ksieniewicz, 28; Duszak, 108; *Daily National Intelligencer*, April 5, 1861; Roy P. Bassler, *The Collected Works of Abraham Lincoln* (New Brunswick: Rutgers University Press, 1955), IV, 319.

[42]Krzyżanowski, *Wspomnienia*, 53.

[43]Krzyżanowski, *Wspomnienia*, 20.

[44]Krzyżanowski, *Wspomnienia*, 49.

CHAPTER TWO
"FREE MEN ARE BROTHERS"

[1]"Gli Uomini Liberi Sono Fratelli" was the motto of General Jan Henryk Dąbrowski's "Polish Legion" that fought under Napoleon I in Italy. The unit's marching song would later become the Polish national anthem.

[2]Krzyżanowski, *Wspomnienia*, 66; *Daily National Republican*, April 11, 1861 and April 12, 1861; Metzner, 19; New York State Archives, Grand Army of the Republic, Department of New York Records, Box 60, Post 192; Henryk Dmochowski to Kałussowski, April 18, 1861, in the Kałussowski Papers; General Index Cards, Krzyżanowski File, Civil War Soldier Records, National Archives.

[3]Ksieniewicz, 36; Sr. Mary Patricia Jurczyńska, "A Study of the Participation of the Poles in the American Civil War," M.A. thesis, Saint John College, Cleveland, Ohio, 1949, 31.

[4]Krzyżanowski, *Wspomnienia*, 66-67.

[5]Jurczyńska, 31; Ksieniewicz, 36; Krzyżanowski, *Wspomnienia*, 69; *Daily National Republican*, April 22, 1861, and April 23, 1861; Krzyżanowski, Declaration for Invalid's Pension, courtesy of Mr. Joseph Piekarczyk, Sr.; Company B, District of Columbia Militia documents, National Archives, M538, Roll 2; National Archives online documents accessed at www.itd.nps.gov/cwss on July 4, 2003.

[6]Krzyżanowski, *Wspomnienia*, 69.

[7]*Ibid.* The newspaper quotation is from an undated clipping in the 58th New York Volunteer Infantry file, New York State Military Museum, Saratoga, NY.

[8]Ksieniewicz, 37; Grot, 95; Joseph A. Wytrwal, *Poles in American History and Tradition* (Detroit: Endurance Press, 1969), 149.

[9]*Daily National Republican*, April 24 and 26, 1861, May 10, 14 and 27, 1861, and June 18, 1861.

[10]Ksieniewicz, 36, 38; *Daily National Republican*, July 9, 11, 25 and 29, 1861; Company B, District of Columbia Militia, National Archives, M538, Roll 2; National Archives online documents accessed at www.itd.nps.gov/cwss on July 4, 2003; Krzyżanowski, Declaration for Invalid's Pension; Frederick H. Dyer, *A Compendium of the War of the Rebellion* (New York: Thomas Yoseloff, 1959), *passim*.

[11]Krzyżanowski, *Wspomnienia*, 71; Ksieniewicz, 25.

[12]Letter, Ward H. Lamon to Governor Edwin D. Morgan, Sept. 10, 1861; Ksieniewicz, 26.

[13]Wytrwal, 152; *The New York Times*, Oct. 11, 1861, 1.

[14]*The New York Times*, Oct. 11, 1861, 1.

[15]Minutes, Eureka Lodge 243, Free and Accepted Masons, 1854-1866, 265, 267 (courtesy of Mr. Henry Archacki); Henry Archacki, *Historical Sketch of Kościuszko Lodge: Number 1085 F. and A. M. 1928-1953* (New York, m. p., 1953), 39.

[16]*Demokrata Polski* (London), Jan. 13, 1862.

[17]Letter, Kałussowski to "Dear Lady," Dec. 21, 1862, Kałussowski Papers. Florian Stasik notes the controversy over the competition of Germans and Poles, and accusations that Krzyżanowski did not assist Poles, in his history of the Polish antebellum political emigration. He concludes that "there was no justification for this thinking" because Kriz "had a reputation as a good Pole and was highly esteemed among the Polish political émigrés." See Stasik, *Polish Political Emigrés*, 178.

[18]Letter, Kałussowski to "Dear Romuald," May 21, 1869, Kałussowski Papers.

[19]Letter, Krzyżanowski to Kałussowski, Sept. 4, 1861, Kałussowski Papers.

[20]Letter, Krzyżanowski to Kałussowski, Sept. 6, 1861, Kałussowski Papers.

[21]Letter, Krzyżanowski to Kałussowski, Sept. 7, 1861, Kałussowski Papers.

[22]Letter, Krzyżanowski to Kałussowski, Sept. 9, 1861, Kałussowski Papers.

[23]Letter, Krzyżanowski to Kałussowski, Sept. 12, 1861, Kałussowski Papers.

[24]Letter, Krzyżanowski to New York Gov. E. D. Morgan, Sept. 16, 1861.

[25]Col. Eugene A. Kozlay diary, Nov. ?, 1861.

[26]Letter, Krzyżanowski to Kałussowski, Sept. 21, 1861, Kałussowski Papers.

[27]Letter, Krzyżanowski to Kałussowski, Oct. 3, 1861, Kałussowski Papers.

[28]Frederick Phisterer, *New York in the War of the Rebellion, 1861-1865* (Albany: 1890), 2502, 2510, 2513; Regimental Papers, 58th New York Infantry, National Archives, Microfilm M551, Roll 79; Ksieniewicz, 27.

[29]Regimental Descriptive Books, 58th New York Infantry, on file in the National Archives. Krzyżanowski's enrollment information is contained on microfilm in the National Archives, M551, Roll 79.

[30]"The Polish Legion in the Civil War," *Naród Polski*, LXXVII (March 7, 1963), 8; English-language press as quoted in Ksieniewicz. 28-29.

[31]See Appendix B for a muster roll of company officers as they appeared in 1861. Henry Archacki Papers, press release of the American Polish Civil War Centennial Committee, 100th anniversary of the marching out of the 58th New York; Phisterer, 2507.

[32]Phisterer, 87, 2502; letter, Frederick P. Todd, Director of the West Point Museum, to Brigadier General Charles Stevenson, September 4, 1963; *The New York*

Times, November 6, 1861, 1, and November 9, 1861, 3; *War of the Rebellion: A Compilation of the Official Records of the Union and Confederate Armies* (Washington, DC: U.S. Government Printing Office, 1882-1902, hereafter cited as *O.R.*), III, 1, 623 and III, III, 748; Thomas Hillhouse to Simon Cameron, October 30, 1861; Thomas Hillhouse to Brig. Gen. L. Thomas, Oct. 18, 1861.

[33]*The New York Times*, Nov. 6, 1861, 1, and Nov. 9, 1861, 3. The newspaper quotation is from a *New York Express* clipping dated Nov. 8, 1861, in the 58th New York Volunteer Infantry file, New York State Military Museum, Saratoga, NY.

[34]Wilhelm Kaufmann, *Die Deutschen in Amerikanischen bürgerkriege* (Munich and Berlin: R. Oldenbourg, 1911), 484-485; Carl Wittke, *Refugees of Revolution: The German Forty-Eighters in America* (Ann Arbor: University Microfilms, Inc., 1952), 229; Samuel Bates, *Martial Deeds of Philadelphia* (Philadelphia: 1875), 643; J.G. Rosengarten, *The German Soldier in the Wars of the United States* (Philadelphia: 1886), 214; Ella Lonn, *Foreigners in the Union Army and Navy* (Baton Rouge: Louisiana State University Press, 1951), 199-200; Frank Taylor, *Philadelphia in the Civil War, 1861-1865* (Philadelphia: The City, 1913), 99.

[35]Krzyżanowski, *Wspomnienia*, 70.

[36]Phisterer, 2508, 2518; *O.R.*, I, V, 716.

[37]Alfred Emory Lee, "Campaigning in the Mountain Department," *Magazine of American History*, XV (1885), 391; Carl Schurz, *Reminiscences of Carl Schurz* (New York: McClure Co., 1907-1908), II, 345; George B. McClellan, *McClellan's Own Story* (New York: Charles L. Webster & Co., 1887), 138, 165.

[38]McClellan, 138; Henry Steele Commager, *The Blue and the Grey* (Indianapolis: Bobbs-Merrill Co., 1950), 318; Krzyżanowski, *Wspomnienia*, 104.

[39]Bates, *Martial Deeds*, 479; McClellan, 266; Phisterer, 1210, 1234; Krzyżanowski, *Wspomnienia*, 104; Samuel Bates, *History of Pennsylvania Volunteers, 1861-1865* (Harrisburg: B. Singerly, 1869-1871), II, 915; Schurz, *Reminiscences*, II, 345.

[40]Diary, Leonard Schlumpf, 45th New York Infantry, Civil War Times Illustrated Collection, U.S. Army Military History Institute, Carlisle Barracks.

[41]Schurz, *Reminiscences*, II, 345; Bates, *History*, II, 915; Lee, "Mountain Department," 392.

[42]Taylor, Philadelphia, 100; Phisterer, 2516; Schurz, *Reminiscences*, II, 346; Lee, "Mountain Department," 392; Bates, *History*, II, 916; National Archives, Report of Gen. Rosecrans to the War Department, April 19, 1862.

[43]Bates, *History*, II, 916; Schurz, *Reminiscences*, II, 346.

[44]Lee, "Mountain Department," 385-388; Phisterer, 158; Bates, *History*, II, 916; Dyer, 901.

[45]Henry Bohlen, report on the Battle of Cross Keys, *O.R.*, I, XII, I, 669; E.P. Alexander, *Military Memoirs of a Confederate* (Bloomington: Indiana University Press, 1962), 104; Vincent J. Esposito, *The West Point Atlas of American Wars* (New York: Frederick A. Praeger, 1959), 53.

[46]Esposito, 53.

[47]Bohlen, report on Cross Keys, 669; Wladimir Krzyżanowski, report of the 58th New York at the Battle of Cross Keys, *O.R.*, I, XII, I, 672-673.

[48]Bohlen, report on Cross Keys, 669; Krzyżanowski, report on Cross Keys,

672-673.

[49]*Ibid.*

[50]Darrell L. Collins, *The Battles of Cross Keys and Port Republic* (Lynchburg, VA: H. E. Howard, Inc., 1993), 61.

[51]Bohlen, report on Cross Keys, 669; Krzyżanowski, report on Cross Keys, 672-673.

[52]Bohlen, report on Cross Keys, 669; Krzyżanowski, report on Cross Keys, 672-673.; Collins, 61.

[53]Bohlen, report on Cross Keys, 669; Lonn, 505; Kaufmann, 307; William F. Fox, *Regimental Losses in the American Civil War* (Albany: Albany Publishing Company, 1889), 562; Margaret B. Paulus, "Papers of Robert Huston Milroy," unpublished manuscript copy in the Purdue University Library.

[54]Krzyżanowski, *Wspomnienia*, 72-73; "Milroy Papers," letter to wife, June 15, 1862, I, 47-49; *The Rebellion Record* (New York: G. P. Putnam, hereafter cited as *R.R.*], VI, 29.

[55]Robert K. Krick, *Conquering the Valley: Stonewall Jackson at Port Republic* (Baton Rouge: Louisiana State University Press, 1996), 197.

[56]*O.R.*, Series I, XII, Part 1, pp. 672-673.

[57]Krick, *Conquering the Valley,* 207.

[58]Krzyżanowski, *Wspomnienia*, 72-73.

[59]Krick, *Conquering the Valley,* 204.

[60]*O.R.*, Series I, XV, 669-70.

[61]Krick, *Conquering the Valley,* 202.

CHAPTER THREE
"I FIGHTS MIT SIGEL"

[1]Milroy Papers, letter to wife, June 15, 1862; Carl Schurz, letter to parents, June 12, 1862; William Houghton, letters to father, June 12, 1862 and June 23, 1862.

[2]Lonn, pp. 175-177; Schurz, *Reminiscences*, II, 348.

[3]Schurz, *Reminiscences*, II, p. 347; Ezra J. Warner, *Generals in Blue* (Baton Rouge: Louisiana State University Press, 1964), 376-377.

[4]Wittke, 234; *Supplemental Report of the Joint Committee on the Conduct of the War* (Washington: U.S. Government Printing Office, 1866), II, 177.

[5]Rosengarten, 225; Lonn, 108-181, 340; Warner, 427; Robert L. Reynolds, "A Man of Conscience," *American Heritage*, XIV, No. 2, 21; Adolf E. Zucker, "Carl Schurz," *Amerika und Deutschland* (New York: Appleton-Century-Crofts, Inc., 1953), 167-170.

[6]Dyer, 349-350; quotation from Kozlay's diary, July 5, 1862.

[7]Alfred E. Lee, "Cedar Mountain," *Magazine of American History*, XVI (1886), 82-86; *O.R.*, I, XII, III, 453.

[8]Lee, "Cedar Mountain," 86; Schurz, *Reminiscences*, II, 351; John Pope, "The Second Battle of Bull Run," *Battles and Leaders*, II, 460.

[9]Schurz, *Reminiscences*, II, 353; Lee, "Cedar Mountain," 160-161; *O.R.*, I, XII,

III, 353.

[10]Schurz, *Reminiscences*, II, 353.

[11]*Ibid.*

[12]Frederick Braun, Report of the 58th New York during Pope's Campaign at Groveton and Second Bull Run, *O.R.*, I, XII, II, 314-315; Schurz, *Reminiscences*, II, 355; Jacob Roemer, *Reminiscences of the War of the Rebellion* (Flushing: Estate of Jacob Roemer, 1897), 53-54.

[13]Braun, Pope's Campaign, 315.

[14]Milroy Papers, I, 71; Braun, Pope's Campaign, 315; Schurz, *Reminiscences*, II, 356; James S. Lyon, *War Sketches: From Cedar Mountain to Bull Run* (Buffalo: Young, Lockwood & Co., 1882), 14.

[15]Roemer, 59; Alfred C. Raphelson, "Alexander Schimmelfennig," *Pennsylvania Magazine of History and Biography*, LXXXVII, No. 2 (1963), 162; Braun, Pope's Campaign, 315.

[16]*Ibid.*

[17]*Ibid.*

[18]Roemer, 59-60, 63; Regimental Descriptive Book, 58th New York Infantry; Annual Reports of Casualties, 58th New York Infantry.

[19]Roemer, 59-60, 63; Alfred E. Lee, "From Cedar Mountain to Chantilly," *Magazine of American History*, XVI (1886), 274.

[20]Roemer, 59-60, 63; Regimental Descriptive Book, 58th New York Infantry; Annual Reports of Casualties, 58th New York Infantry.

[21]Roemer, 59-60, 63.

[22]Lee, "to Chantilly," 274; Fitzhugh Lee, *General Lee* (Greenwich: Fawcett Publications, 1961), 185; Lyon, 17.

[23]Schurz, *Reminiscences*, II, 360; Lee, "to Chantilly," 373-376, 378-380; Braun, Pope's Campaign, 315; Roemer, 63.

[24]Schurz, *Reminiscences*, II, 361; Pope, "Second Bull Run," 471-472; *O.R.*, I, XII, III, 958 (letter, Pope to Sigel, August 29, 1862).

[25]*Ibid.*

[26]Edward J. Stackpole, *From Cedar Mountain to Antietam* (Harrisburg: The Stackpole Co., 1959), 173; Lee, "to Chantilly," 468.

[27]Lee, "to Chantilly," 467; Schurz, *Reminiscences*, II, 362.

[28]Włodzimierz Krzyżanowski, Report on Groveton and Second Bull Run, *O.R.*, I, XII, II, 311-312; Schurz, *Reminiscences*, II, 362; Kaufmann, 550; Carl Schurz, Report on the Battles of Groveton and Second Bull Run, *O.R.*, I, XII, II, 296.

[29]Krzyżanowski, Second Bull Run, 311-312.

[30]Edward J. McCrady, *Gregg's Brigade of South Carolina in the Second Battle of Manassas* (Richmond: n.p., 1885), 15, 17; J.F.J. Caldwell, *The History of a Brigade of South Carolinians Known First as "Gregg's," and Subsequently as "McGowan's" Brigade* (Philadelphia: King and Baird, 1886), 34; John J. Hennessy, *Return to Bull Run* (New York: Simon & Schuster, 1993), 205; Krzyżanowski, Second Bull Run, 311-312; Kaufmann, 550.

[31]McCrady, 16-17; Kaufman, 550; Samuel McGowan, Report on Gregg's Brigade from August 16-September 2, 1862, *O.R.*, I, XII, II, 680; Krzyżanowski,

Second Bull Run, 311; Schurz, *Reminiscences*, II, 363-364; Hennessy, 205.

[32]Krzyżanowski, Second Bull Run, 311; Hennessy, 205-06.

[33]Roemer, *passim*.

[34]Roemer, 18-19, 29, 32; McCrady, 20.

[35]McCrady, 20; Caldwell, 34; Krzyżanowski, Second Bull Run, 311; Roemer, 18-19, 29, 32, 67-68.

[36]McCrady, 20; Caldwell, 34; Krzyżanowski, Second Bull Run, 311; Roemer, 18-19, 29, 32, 67-68; Hennessy, 206.

[37]McCrady, 20; Hennessy, 206.

[38]McCrady, 20; Caldwell, 30-31; Krzyżanowski, Second Bull Run, 311; Hennessy, 215.

[39]Schurz, *Reminiscences*, II, 363-364.

[40]*Ibid.*

[41]Roemer, 70.

[42]Schurz, Second Bull Run, 299; letter, Josiah C. Williams to Parents, July 27, 1862; Lee, "to Chantilly," 470.

[43]Lonn, 506; Schurz, Second Bull Run, 297; Schurz, *Reminiscences*, II, 367; Frederick F. Schrader, *1683-1920* (New York: Concord Publishing Co., 1920), 119; Adolf E. Zucker, *The Forty-Eighters: Political Refugees of the German Revolution of 1848* (New York: Columbia University Press, 1950), 196.

[44]*Medical and Surgical History of the War of the Rebellion* (Washington: Surgeon General's Office, 1870-1888), Surgical, II, 703; Stephen Kovacs, Report of the 54th New York at Groveton and Second Bull Run, *O.R.*, I, XII, II, 314.

[45]Krzyżanowski, Second Bull Run, 312; Regimental descriptive Book, Cos. A-D, 58th New York Infantry; Kaufmann, 511.

[46]Krzyżanowski, Second Bull Run, 312; Regimental Descriptive Book, Cos. A-D, 58th New York Infantry; Kaufmann, 511; *The New York Times*, September 1, 1862, 1; *Medical and Surgical History*, Surgical, III, 321 and Surgical, II, 973; Mieczysław Haiman, *Historja udziału polaków w amerykańskiej wojnie domowej* (Chicago: Drukiem Dziennik Zjednoczenia, n. d.), 240.

[47]Schurz, Second Bull Run, 299; Lee, "to Chantilly," 470.

[48]*Ibid.*

[49]Schurz, *Reminiscences*, II, 371.

[50]Lee, "to Chantilly," 471; Krzyżanowski, Second Bull Run, 312; Schurz, *Reminiscences*, II, 368-369.

[51]Schurz, *Reminiscences*, II, 368-369.

[52]*Medical and Surgical*, Surgical, II, 973 and III, 321.

[53]Lee, "to Chantilly," 473-474; McGowan, Groveton, 681; Warren W. Hassler, *Commanders of the Army of the Potomac* (Baton Rouge: Louisiana State University Press, 1962), 69-72; McCrady, 7, 25; Schurz, *Reminiscences*, II, 371; Dyer, 294-297, 313-315, 349-352.

[54]John C. Ropes, *The Army Under Pope* (New York: n.p., 1881), 104, 107, 213; McCrady, 22-24, 33; Caldwell, 37-38; McGowan, 681-682; Alexander, 205.

[55]McCrady, 18, 20.

[56]Lee, "to Chantilly," 576; Hassler, 73.

[57]Hassler, 73; Lee, "to Chantilly," 576-577; Schurz, *Reminiscences*, II, 371.

[58]Lee, "to Chantilly," 574-578; Schurz, Groveton and Second Bull Run, 301; James H. Stine, *History of the Army of the Potomac* (Washington: Gibson Brothers, 1893), 149.

[59]*Ibid.*; David G. Martin, *The Second Bull Run Campaign* (Conshohocken, PA: Combined Books, 1997), 234.

[60]Krzyżanowski, Second Bull Run, 312; Stine, 150; Phisterer, *New York*, 2685; Joseph Tyler Butts, *A Gallant Captain of the Civil War* (New York: F. Tennyson Neely, 1902), 22.

[61]Krzyżanowski, Second Bull Run, 312-313; Harry Simonhoff, *Jewish Participants in the Civil War* (New York: Arco Publishing, 1963), 135; Thomas S. Townsend, *Honors of the Empire State in the War of the Rebellion* (New York: A. Lovell & Co., 1889), 374, 380; *Official Army Register of the Volunteer Force of the U. S. Army for the Years 1861, '62, '63, '64, '65* (Washington: Adjutant General's Office, 1865), II, 504; Phisterer, *New York*, 480; Bates, *History*, II, 917; Lee, "Chantilly," 579; Kovacs, Groveton and Second Bull Run, 314; Hennessy, 405; Lonn, 506-507.

[62]Bates, *History*, II, 917; Horace H. Cunningham, *Field Medical Services at the Battles of Manassas* (Athens: University of Georgia Press, 1968), 53; Taylor, 284.

[63]Annual Reports of Casualties, 58th New York Infantry; Regimental Descriptive Book, Cos. A-D, 58th New York Infantry; Krzyżanowski, Second Bull Run, 312; *The New York Times*, September 2, 1862, 1; Ksieniewicz; Lonn, 328; Zucker, *Forty-Eighters*, 322.

[64]Zucker, *Forty-Eighters*, 322; Ksieniewicz; Phisterer, *New York*, 2514; Krzyżanowski, Second Bull Run, 312; Max Schmidt Pension File, National Archives.

[65]Schurz, Second Bull Run, 301; Kovacs, Second Bull Run, 313-314; Krzyżanowski, Second Bull Run, 312-313; Phisterer, *New York*, 2515-2516.

[66]Schurz, Second Bull Run, 301; Bates, *History*, II, 918; Krzyżanowski, Second Bull Run, 312-313; *Union Army*, I, 412.

[67]Krzyżanowski, Second Bull Run, 312.

[68]*The New York Times*, September 1, 1862, 1; Schurz, *Reminiscences*, II, 373-374; Lyon, 32; Lonn, 506-507; Schurz, Second Bull Run, 301; Milroy Papers, I, 73.

[69]Roemer, 82, 311, 316.

[70]Edward T. Downer, "Ohio Troops in the Field," *Civil War History*, II (1957), No. 3, 8; Lee, "Chantilly," 578-580; Schurz, Second Bull Run, 301; Hennessy, 405.

[71]Braun, 315.

[72]Schurz, *Reminiscences*, II, 476-477; Lee, "to Chantilly," 580; Lyon, 32; Schurz, Second Bull Run, 303.

[73]Krzyżanowski, Second Bull Run, 313; Braun, 315.

[74]Braun, 315.

[75]Hennessy, 405.

[76]Schurz, Pope's Campaign, 296-303; Krzyżanowski, Second Bull Run, 312; Townsend, 131, 183; Roemer, 82.

[77]Carl Sandburg, *Abraham Lincoln: The War Years* (New York: Harcourt, Brace and World, Inc.), II, 536, 544, 552; Milroy Papers, letter to wife, September 4, 1862, 73-74; Krzyżanowski, *Wspomnienia*, 72-73.

CHAPTER FOUR
"FOR LIBERTY AND JUSTICE"

[1]Regimental Descriptive Book, Cos. A-D, 58th New York Infantry.

[2]Braun, 314-315; Krzyżanowski, *Wspomnienia*, 73.

[3]Ksieniewicz, 48.

[4]Krzyżanowski, *Wspomnienia*, 72-73.

[5]*Ibid.*

[6]Lincoln Papers, Returns for Defenses of Washington, Sept. 30, 1862; Lincoln Papers, Sigel to Henry Halleck, Sept. 14, 1862 and Sigel to Lincoln, Sept. 26, 1862; Richard B. Irwin, "Washington Under Banks," *Battles and Leaders*, II, 542.

[7]Raphelson, 156-161, 180; Zucker, *Forty-Eighters*, 336-337.

[8]Krzyżanowski, *Wspomnienia*, 73, 75.

[9]Dyer, 320.

[10]Wittke, 213; Zucker, *Forty-Eighters*, 324-325; Schurz, *Reminiscences*, II, 406; Lincoln Papers, George S. Koontz to Lincoln, Sept. 10, 1862; Lincoln Papers, Lincoln to Stanton, Sept. 10, 1862.

[11]Charles Doerflinger, "Familiar History of the Twenty-Sixth Regiment Wisconsin Volunteer Infantry," 5; Adam Muenzenberger to wife, Nov. 25, 1862; Regimental Descriptive Book, 26th Wisconsin Infantry.

[12]*Dictionary of Wisconsin Biography* (Madison: The State Historical Society of Wisconsin, 1960), 105; Regimental Descriptive Book, 26th Wisconsin; Wittke, 163-164, 229; Zucker, *Forty-Eighters*, 54, 111, 280; J. J. Schlicher, "Bernhard Domschke," *Wisconsin Magazine of History*, XXIX (1945-1946), 322; Bernhard Domschke, biographical papers, State Historical Society of Wisconsin.

[13]Doerflinger, 1, 6; Sigel to Samuel P. Heintzelman, Oct. 3, 1862, *O.R.*, I, XIX, II, 380.

[14]Regimental Descriptive Book, Cos. A-D, 58th New York Infantry; Muenzenberger to wife, Nov. 12, 1862.

[15]Edwin B. Quiner, *The Military History of Wisconsin* (Chicago: Clarke & Co., 1866), 747; Bates, *History*, II, 918; Muenzenberger to wife, Nov. 12, 1862 and Nov. 29, 1862.

[16]Muenzenberger to wife, Nov. 19, 1862, Nov. 25, 1862, and Nov.29, 1862.

[17]Muenzenberger to wife, Nov. 25, 1862.

[18]Quiner, 747; *O.R.*, I, XXI, 936; Dyer, 1426; Muenzenberger to wife, Dec. 16, 1862.

[19]Muenzenberger to wife, Dec. 21, 1862, Dec. 28, 1862, and Jan. 1, 1863.

[20]*Union Army*, II, 93; Muenzenberger to wife, Jan. 1, 1863.

[21]Muenzenberger to wife, Jan. 1, 1863.

[22]*Ibid.*

[23]*Ibid.*

[24]Theodore A. Dodge diary, Library of Congress microfilm, Jan. 1, 1863.

[25]Dyer, 1426; Schurz, *Reminiscences*, II, 401; Robert Leckie, *The Wars of*

America (New York: Harper & Row, 1968), 454.

[26]Dodge diary, Jan. 23, 1863.

[27]Muenzenberger to brother-in-law, Jan. 1, 1863, and letters to wife, Jan. 9, 1863 and Jan. 29, 1863.

[28]Dodge diary, Feb. 22, 1863.

[29]Dodge diary, Feb. 23, 1863.

[30]Dodge diary, March 3, 1863.

[31]Krzyżanowski, *Wspomnienia*, 71; Józef Chodkiewicz, *Album Jubileuszowy* (New York: Druk "Tygodnika Polskiego," 1916), 127.

[32]Salvatore Mondello, "America's Polish Heritage as Viewed by Miecislaus Haiman and the Periodical Press," *The Polish Review*, IV, Nos. 1-2 (Winter-Spring, 1959), 110; Mieczysław Haiman, *Polish Past in America, 1608-1865* (Chicago: Polish Roman Catholic Union, 1939), 156; Joseph W. Wieczerzak, *A Polish Chapter in Civil War America* (New York: Twayne Publishers, 1967), 127; Chodkiewicz, 126-127, 134; Joseph M. Piekarczyk, Sr., "Polish Contribution in the Civil War," unpublished paper dated September 23, 1968; Joseph M. Piekarczyk, Sr., "Polish Patriotism and Contribution in the American Civil War," unpublished paper dated Oct. 4, 1960; Polish Museum (Chicago), Ms 424 (March 14, 1863, meeting at Steuben Hall), 1 and Ms 423, 2-3. The officers of the newly elected committee were Dr. W. Mackiewicz as president, Romuald I. Jaworowski as vice president, and Józef Gacka as secretary. The members of the committee were the following: Henryk Kałussowski, Gen. Włodzimierz Krzyżanowski, Major Aleksander Raszewski, Col. Józef Kargé, Ksawery Karczewski, Capt. Aleksander Małuski, Jan Pychowski, J. Markson, W. Piotrowski, Cichocki, Wincenty Kochanowski, I. Biskupski, Mieczysław Hlasko and the cashier, J. Wiśniowski. The Polish population in the United States at the time of the Civil War is usually given as about 30,000. The U.S. Census recorded 7,298 in 1860, but this may have been an undercount since some there was no legal entity named Poland and some Poles may have been counted as Germans, Austrians or Russians. The true figure is probably somewhere between the census number and 30,000, most likely closer to the former.

[33]Wieczerzak, *Polish Chapter*, 134, 215.

[34]Haiman, *Polish Past*, 147; Wieczerzak, *Polish Chapter*, 134, 215; Mieczysław Haiman, *Polish Pioneers of California* (Chicago: Polish Roman Catholic Union, 1940), 74; *Echo z Polski*, Oct. 10, 1863; *Głos Wolny* (1863), 62.

[35]Letter, S. Wrotnowski to R. J. Jaworowski, May 20, 1864, Polish Museum (Chicago), Ms 424.

[36]Mieczysław Haiman, "The Debt to Men of Polish Blood," *The Polish Review*, V, No. 22 (July 4, 1945), 7; *New-Yorker Staats-Zeitung*, July 4, 1863 (editorials by Oswald Ottendorfer and Henryk Kałussowski); *The Irish-American*, Dec. 1, 1863 (account of November Insurrection).

[37]Letter, Carl Schurz, Oct. 28, 1862, National Archives, Officers Papers.

[38]Schurz, *Reminiscences*, II, 60.

[39]Lincoln Papers, Carl Schurz to Lincoln, Dec. 3, 1862.

[40]Bruno S. Figura, "What's in a Name," *Polish American*, March 12, 1966, 9; Raphelson, 165; Schurz, *Reminiscences*, II, 60, 407.

[41]Officers' Papers, National Archives.

[42]Conversation from Raphelson, 165.

[43]Krzyżanowski, *Wspomnienia*, 53.

[44]Dodge diary, March 11, 1863.

[45]Dodge diary, March 16, 1863.

[46]Letter, officers of Krzyżanowski's brigade to Abraham Lincoln, President of the United States, from Stafford Court House, March 16, 1863.

[47]Dodge diary, March 16, 1863.

[48]Letter, Carl Schurz to Edwin M. Stanton, June 27, 1863.

[49]Regimental Papers, 58th New York Infantry, National Archives.

Chapter Five
"A Hell of a Fix"

[1]Oliver Otis Howard, *Autobiography of Oliver Otis Howard* (New York: Baker & Taylor, 1907), 349-350; Noah Brooks, *Washington in Lincoln's Time* (New York: Rinehart & Co., 1958), 54.

[2]Hassler, 127; Joseph G. E. Hopkins, *et al.*, *Concise Dictionary of American Biography* (New York: Charles Scribner's Sons, 1964), 451; Warner, 233-234; Walter H. Hebert, *Fighting Joe Hooker* (Indianapolis: Bobbs-Merrill Co., 1944), 21.

[3]Hassler, 132-134; John Bigelow, Jr., *The Campaign of Chancellorsville* (New Haven: Yale University Press, 1910), 47-48; Howard, *Autobiography*, 348.

[4]Hartwell Osborn, "On the Right at Chancellorsville," MOLLUS-Illinois, IV, 176; Howard, *Autobiography*, 348; Warner, 237, 239; Hopkins, 485.

[5]Doerflinger, *passim*; Carl Schurz to parents, March 26, 1863; Bruce Catton, *Glory Road* (Garden City, NY: Doubleday & Co., 1952), 175; Warner, 237-238.

[6]Butts, 32.

[7]Howard, *Autobiography*, 349-350; Brooks, 54, 56; David S. Sparks, Inside Lincoln's Army (New York: Thomas Yoseloff, 1964), 232; Schurz, *Reminiscences*, II, 88.

[8]Kenneth A. Bernard, *Lincoln and the Music of the Civil War* (Caldwell, OH: The Claxton Printers, 1966).

[9]Brooks, 45, 56.

[10]Muenzenberger to wife, April 12, 1863.

[11]Schurz, *Reminiscences*, II, 409; Bates, *History*, II, 919; Van Dyke Papers, letter to father, April 27, 1863; Howard, *Autobiography*, 353; Muenzenberger to wife, May 7, 1863; Bigelow, 174, 187.

[12]Howard, *Autobiography*, 355; Bigelow, 187, 197; Theodore A. Dodge, *Addresses and Reviews* (Boston: Henry S. Dunn, 1898), 93.

[13]Schurz, *Reminiscences*, II, 409; Muenzenberger to wife, May 7, 1863; Doerflinger, 8; Schurz, Report on the Chancellorsville Campaign, *O.R.*, I, XXV, I, 647.

[14]General Order No. 47 quoted from Bigelow, 223.

[15]Schurz, Chancellorsville Report, 650; Muenzenberger, letter to wife, May 7, 1863.

[16]Matthew F. Steele, *American Campaigns* (Washington: The Telegraph Press, 1909), 335-336; Schurz, Chancellorsville Report, 650; quotation from Bigelow, 258.

[17]Dodge, *Addresses*, 96; Howard, *Autobiography*, 361.

[18]John A. Carpenter, "O. O. Howard: General at Chancellorsville," *Civil War History*, III, No. 1 (March 1957), 50; Bigelow, 278; Augustus C. Hamlin, *The Battle of Chancellorsville* (Bangor, ME: n.p., 1896), 55; Catton, *Glory Road*, 182; Hassler, 142.

[19]Dodge Diary, May 2, 1863.

[20]Carpenter, 51-52; Darius N. Couch, "The Chancellorsville Campaign," *Battles and Leaders*, III, 163; Hamlin, 75-76; Bigelow, 285; Hassler, 143.

[21]Carpenter, 50; Bigelow, 278; Hamlin, 55; Catton, *Glory Road*, 182.

[22]Nathaniel McLean, Report on the Chancellorsville Campaign, May, 1863, *O.R.*, I, XXV, I, 637; Raphelson, 169; Samuel H. Hurst, *Journal-History of the Seventy-Third Ohio Volunteer Infantry* (Chillicothe, OH: n.p., 1886), 56.

[23]Bigelow, 285; Quiner, 748.

[24]Bigelow, 133, 290; Catton, *Glory Road*, 182; Hamlin, 55-57, 65; Alexander, 333.

[25]Steele, 340; Howard, *Autobiography*, 371; Raphelson, 167-168; Fitzhugh Lee, 238.

[26]Raphelson, 167-168.

[27]Oliver Otis Howard, "The Eleventh Corps at Chancellorsville," *Battles and Leaders*, III, 197; Adolf von Gilsa, Chancellorsville Report, *O.R.*, I, XXV, I, 636; letter, J. F. Freauff to Samuel Yohe, May 16, 1863, *Rebellion Record*, III, 590; Bigelow, 296; Hamlin, 37, 65-66.

[28]Schurz, *Reminiscences*, II, 423; Dodge, *Addresses*, 23, 25; Hamlin, 39-40; Phisterer, *New York*, 497; *Medical and Surgical History*, Surgical, I, 177; Dodge Diary, 1862-1863; Theodore Ayrault Dodge, *The Campaign of Chancellorsville* (New York: Da Capo Press, 1999 [reprint of 1886 edition]), 96.

[29]Dodge Diary, Mary 5, 1863.

[30]Doerflinger, 2-3; Muenzenberger to wife, May 19, 1863.

[31]Doerflinger, 2-3.

[32]*Ibid.*

[33]Schurz, Chancellorsville Report, 655; Regimental Descriptive Book, Cos. A-D, 58th New York.

[34]Schurz, Chancellorsville Report, 655; Schurz, *Reminiscences*, II, 424; Regimental Descriptive Book, Cos. A-D, 58th New York; Phisterer, *New York*, 191, 2508, 2515; Townsend, 374; *Medical and Surgical History*, Surgical, I, xxxvii.

[35]Schurz, Chancellorsville Report, 655; Regimental Papers, 58th New York.

[36]Krzyżanowski, Chancellorsville Report, 667; Doerflinger, 8; Muenzenberger to wife, May 7, 1863.

[37]Krzyżanowski, Chancellorsville Report, 667.

[38]Regimental Descriptive Book, 26th Wisconsin; Doerflinger, 8; Muenzenberger to wife, May 7, 1863.

[39]*Medical and Surgical History*, Surgical, II, 639; Regimental Descriptive Book, 26th Wisconsin; Doerflinger, 8.

[40]Doerflinger, 8.

[41]Krzyżanowski, Chancellorsville Report, 666-667; Schurz, Chancellorsville Report, 667.

[42]Doerflinger, 3, 8; Krzyżanowski, Chancellorsville Report, 667.

[43]Doerflinger, 3.

[44]Doerflinger, 1-2, 4; Schurz, Chancellorsville Report, 656; Schurz, *Reminiscences*, II, 424; Henry I. Kurtz, "'Those Damned Dutchmen' from Ohio," *Civil War Times Illustrated*, I, No. 7 (1962), 40.

[45]Hamlin, 100-101, 126, 148-149; Schurz, *Reminiscences*, II, 426; Alexander, 337.

[46]Krzyżanowski, Chancellorsville Report, 667; Krzyżanowski quote from Ksieniewicz, 52-53.

[47]Muenzenberger to wife, May 7, 1863; Schurz, Chancellorsville Report, 657; Schurz, *Reminiscences*, II, 431-432; William Houghton, letter to father, May 8, 1863.

[48]*New York Times*, May 5, 1863, 1, 8; *Morning Telegraph* (Harrisburg, PA), May, 1863; *Pittsburgh Post*, May 6 and May 8, 1863; *Indianapolis Daily Journal*, May 1863; *Frank Leslie's Illustrated Newspaper*, May 23, 1863, 130; *Daily National Intelligencer*, May 6, 1863.

[49]Schurz, *Reminiscences*, II, 433 (contains letter from Schimmelfennig); Schurz, Chancellorsville Report, 658; *New York Times*, May 28, 1863.

[50]Krzyżanowski, *Wspomnienia*, 77.

[51]Schurz, *Reminiscences*, II, 433; Abner Doubleday, *Chancellorsville and Gettysburg* (New York: Charles Scribner's Sons, 1882), 27, 53, 150.

[52]Dodge diary, May 7, 1863.

[53]Dodge diary, May 10, 1863.

[54]Dodge, *Addresses*, 96; G.W. Nichols, *A Soldier's Story of His Regiment* (Kennesaw, GA: Continental Book Co., 1961), includes quotes from a report by Dodge, 88-89, 99, 102-04, 106, 108.

[55]Muenzenberger to wife, May 19, 1863.

[56]Charles Wickesberg, letter to family, May 21, 1863.

[57]Letter, Howard to Hooker, May 25, 1863, National Archives, RG 393; *O.R.*, I, XXV, Pt. 1, 629.

[58]Fox, *Regimental Losses*, 34; Regimental Descriptive Books, 26th Wisconsin, 58th New York, 75th Pennsylvania, and 119th New York.

Chapter Six
"A Portrait of Hell"

[1]Krzyżanowski, *Wspomnienia*, 77; Oliver Otis Howard, list of German troops in the Eleventh Corps, May 21, 1863, *O.R.*, I, XXV, I, 660.

[2]Dyer, 320; *Annual Report of the Adjutant General of Ohio, 1863* (Columbus: The State, 1864), 342; *Union Army*, II, 408.

[3]Esposito, 93.

[4]Catton, *Glory Road*, 172; Stine, 430.

[5]Dodge diary, June 12, 1863 and June 13, 1863.

[6]Emil Koenig, Report of the 58th New York at Gettysburg, *O. R.*, I, XXVII, I, 739; Howard, *Autobiography*, 386, 390; Muenzenberger to wife, June 22, 1863.

[7]Catton, *Glory Road*, 172; Dodge diary, June 22, 1863.

[8]Dodge diary, June 23, 1863.

[9]Howard, *Autobiography*, 386, 390; Catton, *Glory Road*, 172.

[10]Koenig, Gettysburg Report, 739; Muenzenberger to wife, June 22, 1863; Dodge diary, June 17, 1863.

[12]Dodge diary, June 18, 1863.

[13]Muenzenberger to wife, June 24, 1863.

[14]*Ibid.*

[15]Dodge diary, June 25, 1863.

[16]Howard, *Autobiography*, 386; Charles Wickesberg to family, July 6, 1863; Dodge diary, June 26, 1863.

[17]Hassler, 156, 159, 160, 163; Comte de Paris, *History of the Civil War in America* (Philadelphia: Porter and Coates, 1883), III, 914; Schurz, *Reminiscences*, III, 4.

[18]Koenig, Gettysburg Report, 739; Schurz, *Reminiscences*, III, 3; Muenzenberger to wife, June 30, 1863.

[19]Koenig, Gettysburg Report, 739; Taylor, 101; Phisterer, *New York*, 1091; Alfred E. Lee, "Reminiscences of the Gettysburg Battle," *Lippincott's Magazine* (Philadelphia: J.B. Lippincot & Co., July, 1883), 54; R.K. Beecham, *Gettysburg: The Pivotal Battle of the Civil War* (Chicago: A.C. McClurg, 1911), 34.

[20]Lee, "Reminiscences of the Gettysburg Battle," 54.

[21]Muenzenberger to wife, June 30, 1863. The translation of *Morgenrot* is by Francis Owen and is not a literal translation, but conveys to meaning of the original. It is taken from www.geocities.com/Athens/Atlantis/2816/germans/morgen.html (retrieved June 30, 2000).

[22]Koenig, Gettysburg Report, 739-740; Howard, *Autobiography*, 408.

[23]William F. Fox, *New York at Gettysburg* (Albany: J. B. Lyon, 1900), 15; Schlicher, 452; Schurz, *Reminiscences*, III, 4; Schurz, Report on the Battle of Gettysburg, *O.R.*, I, XXVII, I, 727; Theodore A. Dodge, "Left Wounded on the Field," *Putnam's Magazine*, IV (1869), 318; Dodge diary, July 1, 1863; Lee, "Reminiscences of the Gettysburg Battle," 55; Col. James S. Robinson, "Address at the Dedication of the Gettysburg Monument," Gettysburg National Military Park Archives.

[24]Robinson, "Address."

[25]Schlicher, Domschke quotation from 452; Dodge, "Left Wounded," 318; Schurz, Gettysburg report, 727.

[26]Lee, "Reminiscences of the Gettysburg Battle," 55-56.

[27]Oliver Otis Howard, Report on the Battle of Gettysburg, *O.R.*, I, XXVII, I, 702; Lee, "Reminiscences of the Gettysburg Battle," 56.

[28]Dodge, "Left Wounded," 318; Charles Wickesberg to family, July 6, 1863.

[29]*Ibid.*

[30]*Pennsylvania at Gettysburg* (Harrisburg: William Stanley Ray, 1919), I, 438;

Schurz, *Reminiscences*, III, 7; Schurz, Gettysburg Report, 727; Richard A. Baumgartner, *Buckeye Blood. Ohio at Gettysburg* (Huntington, WV: Blue Acorn Press, 2003), 41.

[31]Doubleday, 138; Comte de Paris, 559, 570; Frederick C. Winkler, "Winkler's Reminiscences of Frank Haskell," unpublished manuscript in the University of Wisconsin-Milwaukee Library, n.d., 4-5, 7.

[32]Benjamin A. Willis, Report of 119th New York at Gettysburg, *O.R.*, I, XXVII, I, 742; Harry W. Pfanz, *Gettysburg: The First Day* (Chapel Hill, NC: Univ. of North Carolina Press, 2001), 220; David G. Martin, *Gettysburg July 1* (Conshohocken, PA: Combined Books, 1995), 265; Dodge, "Left Wounded," 317, 319; Fox, *New York*, 15; Baumgartner, 41-42, 54; Chapman Biddle, *The First Day of the Battle of Gettysburg* (Philadelphia: J. B. Lippincott & Co., 1880), 118, says that Kriz formed his brigade "in a field farther to the right, near to and east of the Carlisle Road."

[33]Fairfax Downey, *The Guns at Gettysburg* (New York: David McKay Co., 1958), 48; John M. Vanderslice, *Gettysburg* (Philadelphia: 1897), 66; Dodge diary, July 28, 1863; letter, Joseph Gillis to sister, July 22, 1863; Baumgartner, 54.

[34]*Pennsylvania at Gettysburg*, I, 438; Downey, 48; Vanderslice, 66; Dodge diary, July 28, 1863; Joseph Gillis to sister, July 22, 1863.

[35]Dodge diary, July 1, 1863.

[36]Hubert Dilger, Report on Gettysburg, *O.R.*, I, XXVII, I, p. 754; Thomas W. Osborn, Report on the Eleventh Corps Artillery at Gettysburg, *O.R.*, I, XXVII, I, 745; Schurz, *Reminiscences*, III, 8; Bates, *Martial Deeds*, 225.

[37]August Ledig, Report of the 75th Pennsylvania at Gettysburg, *O.R.*, I, XXVII, I, 745; Taylor, 101; Chapman Biddle, *The First Day of the Battle of Gettysburg* (Philadelphia: J.B. Lippincott, 1880), 39; Pfanz, *Gettysburg: The First Day*, 220.

[38]Hunt, "Gettysburg," 281; Cecil W. Battine, *The Crisis of the Confederacy* (New York: Longmans, Green & Co., 1905), 193.

[39]John B. Gordon, *Reminiscences of the Civil War* (New York: Scribner's Sons, 1904), 151; Jubal A. Early, *Autobiographical Sketch and Narrative of the War Between the States* (Philadelphia: J. B. Lippincott, 1912), 267-268.

[40]Gordon, 151; Early, 267-268; Gary Kross, "The XI Corps at Gettysburg July 1, 1863," *Blue & Gray Magazine*, XIX, No. 2 (Dec. 2001), 22.

[41]Charles K. Fox, *Gettysburg* (New York: A. S. Barner & Co., 1969), 16; Downey, 49-50.

[42]Nichols, 116.

[43]Pfanz, 237; Lee, 57; Stine, 479; A. Wilson Green, "From Chancellorsville to Cemetery Hill: O. O. Howard and Eleventh Corps Leadership," in Gary W. Gallagher, ed., *The First Day at Gettysburg* (Kent, OH: Kent State University Press, 1993), 80.

[44]Pfanz, 237; Baumgartner, 54.

[45]Krzyżanowski, *Wspomnienia*, 79; Baumgartner, 54.

[46]Krzyżanowski's Declaration for Invalid's Pension; Pension file, Examining Surgeon Certificate, application No. 510381, medical exam of June 11, 1884 and medical exam of pension increase, Nov. 2, 1886; Ksieniewicz, n.p.; *Frank Leslie's Illustrated Newspaper*, March 12, 1864, 391; Ksieniewicz, n.p.; Surgeon Stein's affidavit of Jan. 16, 1885, in Krzyżanowski's invalid pension file says: "I saw general

Krzyzanowski fall from his horse. I treated the General who had sustained concussion of the Lungs. He had hemmorhage and would complain of severe pain about the Chest." Carl Schurz's affidavit dated May 3, 1886, in the invalid pension file affirmed that "on the first day of the battle of Gettysburg … Col. W. Krzyzanowski's horse was shot under him in action, that according to the best of his knowledge and recollection, he fell under his horse, that when he (Schurz) saw him (K) immediately afterwards, he (K) breathed with difficulty, that when that day's engagement was over, he (Schurz) asked him the said W. Krzyzanowski to retire and put himself under treatment, which however he declined to do. That Col W. Krzyzanowski remained under his orders until Jan. 1864 and that during that period he frequently heard him complain of difficulty…." A medical exam for an application for pension increase dated Nov. 2, 1886, found that his symptoms persisted and had led to various ailments in his more advanced years that made him unfit for even less strenuous forms of manual labor. Speaking of the injuries sustained at Gettysburg, the examiner reported: "He says that he began to have pains immediately after the accident and that these pains have continued to increase until he is in his present condition. He thinks he is rated for low as he is not able to perform any manual labor." "When walking he takes very short steps and has the gait of a feeble old man. There seems to be no cause for this except old age." Kidney disease. "He is not able to perform any manual labor owing to his great feebleness." Skin sallow. Conjunction yellowish. "He requires regular aid and attention by another person."

[47]Taylor, 101; *O.R.*, I, XXVII, Pt. 1, 745; *Annual Report of the Adjutant General of the Commonwealth of Pennsylvania for the Year 1866* (Harrisburg: Singerly & Myers, 1867), 395-397; Bates, *History*, II, 920, 922; *Medical and Surgical History*, Surgical, I, 84, and Surgical, II, 986; Schurz, *Reminiscences*, III, n.p.; John P. Nicholson, *Pennsylvania at Gettysburg* (Harrisburg: n.p., 1893), I, 31; *Pennsylvania at Gettysburg. Ceremonies at the Dedication of the Monuments Erected by the Commonwealth of Pennsylvania,* Vol. I (1904), 434; Hermann Nachtigall, *History of the 75th Regiment, Pa. Vols.* (North Riverside, IL: 1987, transl. by Heinz D. Schwinge and Karl E. Sundstrom), 22.

[48]*Medical and Surgical History*, Surgical, III, 206, 428; David Thomson, Report of the 82nd Ohio at Gettysburg, *O.R.*, I, XXVII, 744; Reid, 475; letter, David Thomson to "My dear Little Mary," August 5, 1863 and to "My dear Mary," July 16, 1863; Baumgartner, 41, 63; Lee, 56.

[49]*Medical and Surgical History*, Surgical, II, 80-81, 625, 893, and Surgical, III, 281; Phisterer, *New York*, 497, 3404-3404, 3407-3409; *Union Army*, II, 136; Lonn, 524; Dodge, "Left Wounded," 3221, 325; Regimental Descriptive Book, 119th New York; Dodge diary, July 28, 1863; *National Tribune*, August 19, 1897; *Ceremonies and Addresses at the Dedication of a Monument by the 119th Regiment, N. Y. State Vols. at Gettysburg, July 3, 1888* (Boston: Wright & Potter Printing, 1889), 13.

[50]Schurz, *Reminiscences*, III, *passim*; *Medical and Surgical History*, Surgical, III, 82, 293, 314; Scott, 267-268; Kaufmann, 480; Regimental Descriptive Book, 26th Wisconsin.

[51]Koenig, Report on Gettysburg, 739-740; Phisterer, *New York*, 2506, 2526; monument plaque of the 58th New York at Gettysburg; Regimental Descriptive Book, 58th New York.

52Howard, *Autobiography*, 417; W. Fox, *Gettysburg*, 22; Charles H. Howard, "The First Day at Gettysburg," *MOLLUS-Illinois*, IV, 258; Schurz, *Reminiscences*, III, 10-11; Oliver O. Howard, Gettysburg report, 703-704.

53Zucker, *Forty-Eighters*, 54, 111; Lonn, 327; Kaufmann, 514; Baumgartner, 41; Lee, 56; Robinson, "Address"; *O.R.*, I, XXVII, Pt. 1, 744; letter, David Thomson to "My dear boy," July 5, 1863 and to "My dear Mary," July 16, 1863; Alfred Lee Pension File, National Archives.

54Surgeon Stein's affidavit of Jan. 16, 1885, Krzyżanowski's pension file; Carl Schurz's affidavit dated May 3, 1886, Krzyżanowski's pension file.

55Alexander Małuski, manuscript memoirs, Paris, Feb. 1, 1881 (translated for the author by Ludwik Ziarnik); Alexander Małuski Pension File, National Archives.

56Letter, Krzyżanowski to Gov. Horatio Seymour, New-York Historical Society; Edward Washington Brueninghausen, Pension File, National Archives.

57*Annual Report of the Adjutant General of Ohio, 1865* (Columbus: n.p., 1866), 79; Thomson, 744; Kaufmann, 514; Zucker, *Forty-Eighters*, 54, 111; Bradley M. Gottfried, *Brigades of Gettysburg* (Cambridge, MA: Da Capo Press, 2002), 318, 344.

58James Longstreet, *From Manassas to Appomattox* (Bloomington: Indiana Univ. Press, 1960), 356; Simonhoff, 77; W. Fox, *New York*, 25; Butts, 78, 80; Phisterer, *New York*, 3405, 3409; Schlicher, 435; William H. Jacobs, Report of the 26th Wisconsin at Gettysburg, *O.R.*, I, XXVII, 746; Schurz, *Reminiscences*, III, 35-36; Gordon, *Reminiscences*, 151; Muenzenberger to wife, August 30, 1863; Wickesberg to family, July 9, 1863.

59Schurz, *Reminiscences*, III, 35-36; Schlicher, *passim*.

60Howard, *Autobiography*, 419.

61Koenig, Gettysburg report, 740; Schurz, *Reminiscences*, III, 20.

62George A. Thayer, "Gettysburg, as We Men on the Right Saw It," *Sketches of War History*, II, 34; Schurz, Gettysburg report, 730; Steele, 388; Butts, 82.

63Simonhoff, 77-78; Butts, 83.

64Downey, 87, 97-99; Schurz, *Reminiscences*, III, 22; Simonhoff, 78; Koenig, Gettysburg report, 741; *Medical and Surgical History*, Surgical, III, 302; Regimental Descriptive Book, 58th New York; Edward Antoniewski, Widow's Pension File, National Archives.

65Beecham, 198; Alexander, 411; Henry J. Hunt, "The Second Day at Gettysburg," *Battles and Leaders*, III, 312.

66Alison Moore, *The Louisiana Tigers* (Baton Rouge: Ortlieb Press, 1961), 120; Howard, Gettysburg report, 706; Young, 432; Vanderslice, 93; Kaufmann, 563.

67Quotations from Schurz, *Reminiscences*, I, 25.

68Samuel Tate, Report of the 6th North Carolina at Gettysburg, *O.R.*, I, XXVII, II, 486; Vanderslice, 94; Young, 275; Downey, 103; Beecham, 199.

69Schurz, *Reminiscences*, III, 24-25; Howard, *Autobiography*, 429; Schurz, Gettysburg report, 731.

70*Ibid.*

71Regimental Descriptive Book, 58th New York; Schurz, *Reminiscences*, 24-25; Ksieniewicz, 60; Willis, Gettysburg report, *O.R.*, I, XXVII, I, 742-43.

72Stine, 518; Howard, *Autobiography*, 430; Vanderslice, 95; Doubleday, 183;

Alexander, 411; Schurz, *Reminiscences*, III, 25; Butts, 83; Winkler, 12.

[73]Earl Schenck Miers and Richard A. Brown, *Gettysburg* (New Brunswick: Rutgers Univ. Press, 1948), 183.

[74]Koenig, Gettysburg report, 741; Frederick Ray, *Gettysburg Sketches* (Gettysburg: Times & News Publishing Company, 1963), n.p.; *O.R.*, I, XXVII, Pt. 1, 739.

[75]Schurz, *Reminiscences*, III, 28, 30; Butts, 87; Jacob Hoke, *The Great Invasion* (New York: Thomas Yoseloff, 1959), 363.

[76]Koenig, Gettysburg report, 741; Schurz, *Reminiscences*, III, 34; Willis, 743; Schurz, Gettysburg report, 731; Bates, *Martial Deeds*, 144.

[77]*Ibid.*

[78]Gottfried, 345.

[79]The observations of participants in this paragraph are based on archival materials in the collections of the Gettysburg National Military Park. These include the John B. Gordon Papers, Vertical File 5; 21st Georgia File; 26th Georgia File; 31st Georgia File; Henry W. Thomas' History of the Doles-Cook Brigade.

[80]*Confederate Veteran*, XXI, 456.

[81]Richard Harwell, *Lee* (New York: Charles Scribner's Sons, 1961), quotes Freeman on 333.

[82]Haiman, *Polish Past*, quotes from Howard's official report on 120.

[83]Letter, Carl Schurz to Oliver O. Howard, Aug. 21, 1863 [National Archives, Officers Papers]; Pfanz, *The First Day*, 236.

[84]*O.R.*, I, XXVII, I, 183; Thomas L. Livermore, *Numbers and Losses in the Civil War in America, 1861-1865* (Boston: Houghton Mifflin Co., 1901), 102-03; Stine, 550-52.

[85]*O.R.*, I, XXVII, I, 183; Robert W. Wells, *Wisconsin in the Civil War* (Milwaukee: Milwaukee Journal, 1964), 58; Fox, *Regimental Losses*, 32-33; W. Fox, *New York*, 217, 226.

CHAPTER SEVEN
"THE MOST DISTINGUISHED FEATS"

[1]*The New York Times*, July 4, 1863, 1; Schurz, *Reminiscences*, III, 53; Krzyżanowski, *Wspomnienia*, 78.

[2]Schurz, *Reminiscences*, III, 53.

[3]Thomson, Gettysburg report, 744; Howard, Gettysburg report, 708.

[4]Regimental Descriptive Book, Cos. A-D, 58th New York; Annual Report of Casualties, 58th New York.

[5]Koenig, Gettysburg report, 741; Butts, 90; *New York Times*, July 23, 1863, 8.

[6]Howard, Gettysburg Campaign, 708-709; Miers, 285; Butts, 90.

[7]Butts, 90; Howard, Gettysburg Campaign, 709-710.

[8]Winkler Papers; Howard, Gettysburg Campaign, 710; George G. Meade to Henry Halleck, July 29, 1863, *O. R.*, I, XXVII, I, 105; Howard, *Autobiography*, 448.

[9]Winkler Papers; Quiner, 75; *O. R.*, I, XXVII, III, 803; Letter, David Thomson

to James S. Robinson, August 23, 1863, James S. Robinson Papers, Ohio Historical Society, MSS 29, Box 1.

[10]Letter, Krzyżanowski to Governor Seymour, July 16, 1863.

[11]*Ibid.*

[12]Schurz to O. O. Howard, Aug. 21, 1863, Officers Papers, National Archives; Schurz to Headquarters, Sept. 3, 1863, RG 393, National Archives.

[13]O. O. Howard to Capt. H. W. Perkins, Dec. 28, 1863, Generals Papers, National Archives.

[14]Butts, 91; Howard, *Autobiography*, 448-449; Bell I. Wiley, *The Life of Billy Yank* (New York: Grosset & Dunlap, 1952), 312.

[15]Butts, 91; Howard, *Autobiography*, 448-449; Wiley, 312.

[16]Krzyżanowski's pension form, Adjutant General's Office, War Department; Regimental Descriptive Book, 26th Wisconsin; Winkler Papers; Special Orders No. 177, RG 393, Pt. 2, 5322, National Archives; RG 393, Pt. 2, Vol. 18, National Archives.

[17]John Atkinson, *The Story of Lookout Mountain and Missionary Ridge* (Detroit: Winn and Hammond, Printers, 1893), 4; Hebert, 250.

[18]Hartwell Osborn, "The Eleventh Corps in East Tennessee," *MOLLUS-Illinois*, IV, 348; Bruce Catton, *Never Call Retreat* (Garden City: Doubleday & Co., Inc., 1965), 255.

[19]*Union Army*, II, 93; Winkler Papers; Osborn, "East Tennessee," 349-350; Bates, *History*, II, 920.

[20]Butts, 96; Osborn, "East Tennessee," 350; Remington, 113.

[21]Howard, *Autobiography*, 435; Regimental Descriptive Book, Cos. A-D, 58th New York.

[22]Howard, *Autobiography*, 453, 455; Turner, 292; Remington, 113; Butts, 96.

[23]Krzyżanowski, Itinerary of Krzyzanowski's Brigade in the Knoxville Campaign, *O. R.*, I, XXXI, I, 111; Winkler Papers; Osborn, "East Tennessee," 350; Brooks, 64; *Evening Post* [N.Y.], Sept. 26, 1863; Schurz, *Reminiscences,* III, 56.

[24]Joseph S. Fullerton, "The Army of the Cumberland at Chattanooga," *Battles and Leaders*, III, 719; Winkler Papers; Howard, *Autobiography*, 457; Butts, 96; Wickesberg, letter to family, Oct. 17, 1863.

[25]Krzyżanowski, Knoxville campaign, 111; Dyer, 456; *O. R.*, I, XXXI, I, 804.

[26]Adolph von Steinwehr, Report on the Battle of Wauhatchie, *Rebellion Record*, III, 587; Joseph Hooker, Report on the Battle of Wauhatchie, *Rebellion Record*, VII, 583; Krzyżanowski, Knoxville campaign, 112; Schurz, *Reminiscences*, III, 59; Ulysses S. Grant, "Chattanooga," *Battles and Leaders*, III, 687; Butts, 98.

[27]Schurz, *Reminiscences*, III, 59-60; Winkler Papers; Butts, 98.

[28]Schurz, *Reminiscences*, III, 59-60; Hooker, Wauhatchie report, 584; Grant, "Chattanooga," 687; Butts, 98; Howard, *Autobiography*, 463-464.

[29]Mark Mayo Boatner, *The Civil War Dictionary* (New York: David McKay Co., 1961), 895-896.

[30]Osborn, "East Tennessee," 359; Howard, *Autobiography*, 467; Schurz, *Reminiscences*, III, 60-65.

[31]Schurz, *Reminiscences*, III, 61, 65; Winkler Papers; Osborn, "East

Tennessee," 360.

32 *Ibid.*

33 Proceedings of the Court of Inquiry, 151, 165-166, 170, 183; Butts, 98-99.

34 Proceedings of the Court of Inquiry, 151, 165-166, 170, 183; Butts, 98-99; Osborn, "East Tennessee," 361; Howard, *Autobiography*, 467; Hooker, Wauhatchie report, 584; Schurz, *Reminiscences*, III, 62-64; Steinwehr, Wauhatchie report, 587.

35 Schurz, Wauhatchie report, 110-111; Proceedings of the Court of Inquiry, 160, 189-190; Howard, *Autobiography*, 470; John W. Geary, Report on Wauhatchie, *O.R.*, I, XXXI, I, 118. The Daily Log of 11th Corps in the Clements Library at the University of Michigan notes that Col. Hecker's brigade was ordered to Geary's relief at 4:30 A.M. and Krzyżanowski's brigade was ordered to Geary at 7:00 A.M.

36 General Orders No. 5, Headquarters of 11th and 12 Corps, Nov. 1, 1863.

37 Gen. George H. Thomas to Gen. Joseph Hooker, Oct. 30, 1863.

38 *O.R.*, I, XXXI, III, 4; Schurz, *Reminiscences*, III, 69, 71; Howard, *Autobiography*, 472.

39 New York State Monument on Lookout Mountain; Phisterer, *New York*, 2518; *O.R.*, I, XXXI, II, 17; Howard, *Autobiography*, 479; Schurz, *Reminiscences*, III, 72.

40 Carl Schurz, Report on the Knoxville Relief, *O.R.*, I, XXXI, II, 382; Schurz, *Reminiscences*, III, 72; Winkler Papers.

41 Schurz, Knoxville relief, 382; Krzyżanowski, *Wspomnienia*, 88 (includes following quotations).

42 Boatner, 145-147; *Union Army*, 136; Schurz, *Reminiscences*, III, 74.

43 Schurz, *Reminiscences*, III, 78; Oliver Otis Howard, Report on Knoxville, *O.R.*, I, XXXI, II, 350.

44 Schurz, Knoxville relief, 382-383; Schurz, *Reminiscences*, III, 78; Winkler Papers; Wickesberg, letter to family, Dec. 19, 1863.

45 Winkler Papers; Schurz, Knoxville relief, 382-383; Quiner, 752.

46 Schurz, Knoxville, 382-383; Regimental Descriptive Book, 141st New York.

47 Winkler Papers.

48 Quiner, 752; Winkler Papers; Schurz, *Reminiscences*, III, 80-83; Colonel Aden C. Cavins, letter to wife, Dec. 19, 1863; Krzyżanowski, *Wspomnienia*, 80.

49 Schurz, *Reminiscences*, III, 82-85; Butts, 102; Oliver Otis Howard to Officers of Eleventh Corps, Dec. 8, 1863, *O.R.*, I, XXXI, III, 358; William T. Sherman, letter to O.O. Howard, Dec. 16, 1863, O.O. Howard Papers, Bowdoin College.

CHAPTER EIGHT
"VETERAN VOLUNTEERS"

1 Krzyżanowski, *Wspomnienia*, 82; Ksieniewicz, p. 97; Grot, 102.

2 *Ibid.*

3 Krzyżanowski, *Wspomnienia*, 81-82; *Frank Leslie's Illustrated Newspaper*, March 12, 1864, 391.

4 *Frank Leslie's Illustrated Newspaper*, March 12, 1864, 391.

5 Osborn, "East Tennessee," 378.

[6]Krzyżanowski, *Wspomnienia*, 82; Order Book, Cos. F-K, 58th New York; Regimental Papers, 58th New York; Daily Log of 11th Corps, University of Michigan; *O. R.*, I, XXXIII, I, 25; Krzyżanowski to Carl Schurz, Jan. 6, 1864.

[7]Newspaper quotation from an undated clipping in the 58th New York file, New York State Military Museum, Saratoga, NY.

[8]Ksieniewicz, 68-69.

[9]Krzyżanowski, *Wspomnienia*, 83-84; Butts, 105-105; Ksieniewicz, 69-70.

[10]Krzyżanowski, *Wspomnienia*, 83-84; Butts, 105-105; Ksieniewicz, 70-71; undated newspaper clipping, 58th New York file, New York State Military Museum.

[11]Ksieniewicz, 72; undated newspaper clipping, 58th New York file, New York State Military Museum.

[12]Ksieniewicz, 73.

[13]Krzyżanowski, *Wspomnienia*, 83-84.

[14]Hooker, Wauhatchie Report, 584.

[15]Herbert, 260; Schurz to parents, Feb. 20, 1864; Proceedings of the Court of Inquiry at the XI and XII Headquarters in regard to the Wauhatchie Affair, *O. R.*, I, XXXI, I, 137-216 [this source contains the testimony of the principals involved in the case and will be cited hereafter as Proceedings], 137.

[16]Charles Howard to "My dear brother," Jan. 24, 1864, O. O. Howard Papers, Bowdoin College, Brunswick, Maine.

[17]Proceedings, 137.

[18]Proceedings, 139, 214-215.

[19]Proceedings, 138.

[20]The testimony reproduced in the following conversations is extracted as it was given at the original inquest. In some cases the order of the testimony has been altered so that it may be organized more effectively under the appropriate questions. Nevertheless, the words spoken were those of the participants. General Hooker's testimony came from Proceedings, 140.

[21]Proceedings, 141, includes Geary's testimony.

[22]Hall's testimony is from Proceedings, 160.

[23]Oliver's testimony is from Proceedings, 149-151.

[24]Klutsch's testimony is from Proceedings, 163-164.

[25]Weigel's testimony is from Proceedings, 167-168.

[26]Proceedings, 146, 165.

[27]Hecker's testimony is from Proceedings, 171.

[28]Major Howard's testimony is from Proceedings, 147.

[29]Mueller's testimony is from Proceedings, 153.

[30]Kramer's testimony is from Proceedings, 155-156.

[31]Greenhut's testimony is from Proceedings, 142-143.

[32]Hecker's testimony is from Proceedings, 170.

[33]Kramer's testimony is from Proceedings, 155.

[34]Greenhut's testimony is from Proceedings, 143.

[35]Meysenburg's testimony is from Proceedings, 169.

[36]Proceedings, 195.

[37]Klutsch's testimony is from Proceedings, 163-164.

[38]Greenhut's testimony is from Proceedings, 143.

[39]Weigel's testimony is from Proceedings, 166.

[40]*O.R.*, I, XXXI, Pt. 1, 110-11; Eleventh Corps log, Oct. 29, 1863.

[41]*Ibid.*

[42]Mueller's testimony is from Proceedings, 154.

[43]Hall's testimony in from Proceedings, 160-61.

[44]Weigel's testimony is from Proceedings, 165.

[45]Weigel's testimony is from Proceedings, 165; Daily Log of 11th Corps, October 29-30, 1863, University of Michigan.

[46]Proceedings, 209-10.

CHAPTER NINE
"A MOST SPLENDID OFFICER"

[1]Oliver O. Howard to Krzyżanowski, March 29, 1864, *O. R.*, I, LII, I.

[2]Hebert, 260, 271-272; *O.R.*, I, XXXII, I, 32; Wittke, *Refugees*, 236-237.

[3]*Ibid.*

[4]Dyer, 456; Sandburg, II, 257; Schurz to parents, April 24, 1864.

[5]Order from Headquarters, District of Nashville, April 21, 1864.

[6]Duncan Kennedy Major and Roger S. Fitch, *Supply of Sherman's Army During the Atlanta Campaign* (Ft. Leavenworth: Army Service Schools Press, 1911), 11; George Edgar Turner, *Victory Road the Rails* (New York: Bobbs-Merrill, 1953), 208.

[7]Major and Fitch, 13; Jurczyńska, 40; Dwight Fraser to sister, April 6, 1864; Dwight Fraser, letter to Lizzie, April 25, 1864.

[8]Augustus M. Van Dyke diary, Feb. 13, 1864; Krzyżanowski to Capt. H. B. Williams, Assistant Adjutant General, Aug. 26, 1865, National Archives, RG 94, No. 159, General's papers, Box 26, #1215; "Polish Hero Received Honor," *The New American*, IV, No. 10 (Nov. 1937); Walter L. Fleming, *Civil War and Reconstruction in Alabama* (New York: Peter Smith, 1949), 361.

[9]*O.R.*, I, XXXVIII, IV, 281; *O.R.*, I, XXXVIII, IV, 307.

[10]*O.R.*, I, XXXVIII, IV, 374; *O.R.*, I, XXXIX, III, 63, 65.

[11]Thomas Speed, "Cavalry Operations in the West Under Rosecrans and Sherman," *B. & L.*, IV, 416; *O.R.*, I, XXXVIII, V, 145; Dyer, 468.

[12]Dyer, 468; Regimental Papers, 58th New York.

[13]Ksieniewicz, 77.

[14]Ksieniewicz, 76.

[15]Robert C. Black, *The Railroads of the Confederacy* (Chapel Hill: Univ.of North Carolina Press, 1952); John B. Hood, "The Defense of Atlanta," *B.&L.*, IV, 342.

[16]Paulus, "Milroy Papers," I, 374-375 and II, 374.

[17]*Ibid.*

[18]*Ibid.*

[19]"Milroy Papers," I, 394.

[20]Dyer, II, 667-668; Phisterer, *New York*, I, 271-272.

[21]Maj. Gen. Robert H. Milroy to President Lincoln, July 18, 1865, from Tullahoma, Tennessee, National Archives, Officers Papers, RG 94. Since this letter was addressed to Pres. Lincoln, some researchers believe it was actually written in 1864. However, since it refers to Missionary Ridge it would have to have been 1865.

[22]Letter, John S. Tarkington to "Dear Sir," from Indianapolis, Nov. 14, 1864, National Archives, Officers Papers.

[23]"Milroy Papers," II, 15.

[24]Haiman, *Historja Udziału*, 195; Krzyżanowski, *Wspomnienia*, 89-90.

[25]Krzyżanowski, *Wspomnienia*, 96.

[26]*Ibid.*, 83.

[27]*Ibid.*, 86.

[28]*Ibid.*, *passim*.

[29]*Ibid.*, 88.

[30]*Ibid.*, 87.

[31]James E. Sefton, *The United States Army and Reconstruction 1865-1877* (Baton Rouge: Louisiana State Univ. Press, 1967), 37; Robert S. Henry, *The Story of Reconstruction* (Gloucester: Peter Smith, 1963), 85-86.

[32]Loyal Citizens of Scottsboro, Alabama, letter to Governor Parsons, Sept. 8, 1865; Henry, 85-86.

[33]Krzyżanowski to Maj. B. H. Polk, Assistant Adjutant General, District of Middle Tennessee, June 22, 1865, National Archives, RG 393, No. 1251; Krzyżanowski to Brig. Gen. Parkhurst, Provost Marshal General, Nashville, Aug. 20, 1865, National Archives, RG 393, No. 1251; Krzyżanowski to Capt. J. F. Blickensdoerfer, Acting Assistant Inspector General, Huntsville, Alabama, Sept. 16, 1865, National Archives, RG 94, No. 159, Box 26, No. 1215.

[34]Letter to President Andrew Johnson from officers of the 135th Indiana Volunteer Infantry, June 25, 1865, National Archives, Officers Papers, RG 94, No. 159, Box 26, No. 1215.

[35]Oath of office document, National Archives, Officers Papers, RG 94.

[36]Phisterer, New York, 2502-03; Joseph F. Krzyzanowski to Mieczysław Haiman, July 8, 1938; Krzyżanowski, *Wspomnienia*, *passim*.

CHAPTER TEN
"THOSE WHO WERE FAITHFUL"

[1]Louis Seldner affidavit, Krzyżanowski pension file, National Archives.

[2]Haiman, *Historja Udziału*, 193, 241; Krzyżanowski, *Wspomnienia*, 71; Ksieniewicz, *passim*; Andrew H. Boyd, complr., *Boyd's Washington and Georgetown Directory* (Washington, DC: Hudson Taylor, 1865), 252; New York State Archives, Grand Army of the Republic, Department of New York Records, Box 60, Post 192.

[3]Minutes, Eureka Lodge No. 234, Free and Accepted Masons, Volume 1867-1869, 63; Charles H. Johnson, letter to C. W. Ksieniewicz, May 17, 1938; Frank E.

Cooley, letter to Benjamin T. Anuskiewicz, Dec. 15, 1937; Naturalization Record, I, Supreme Court, D.C., Oct. 4, 1866 to May 31, 1870, 126, RG 21, National Archives; Ksieniewicz, 79-80; Robert B. Beath, *History of the Grand Army of the Republic* (New York: Taylor & Co., Publishers, 1889), 106; F. A. Starring, letter to John A. Logan, May 11, 1870, in *Proceedings of the First Meeting of the National Encampment, Grand Army of the Republic* (Philadelphia: Merrihew & Son, Printers, 1876), 12-15, 22, 59; New York State Archives, Grand Army of the Republic, Department of New York Records, Box 60, Post 192. Kriz was elected Assistant Inspector-General in 1869, elected to the National Council of the GAR in 1870 and served as Provisional Commander for Georgia.

[4]Krzyżanowski, *Wspomnienia*, 87.

[5]John Hope Franklin, *Reconstruction After the Civil War* (Chicago: Univ. of Chicago Press, 1973), 43.

[6]Franklin, *passim.*

[7]Krzyżanowski, *Wspomnienia*, 88.

[8]Krzyżanowski, *Wspomnienia*, 87.

[9]Krzyżanowski, *Wspomnienia*, 88.

[10]Ksieniewicz, 80.

[11]W.W. Belknap, letter to Secretary of the Treasury, July 8, 1868; *Register of Officers and Agents, Civil, Military and Naval in the Service of the United States, 1869* (Washington: Government Printing Office, 1870), 60; *Register of Officers and Agents, Civil, Military and Naval in the Service of the United States, on the Thirteenth of September, 1871* (Washington: Government Printing Office, 1872), 59 lists him as Superintendent of Internal Revenue, appointed from New York, with a salary of $3,000 per annum; "Supervisors of Internal Revenue Surveyors, 1868-1871," MSS in the National Archives. A rather odd letter from Henryk Kałussowski to "Dear Romuald" dated May 21, 1869, states somewhat sarcastically of Kriz: "He is now a very high official in an administrative position for the states of Georgia, Alabama and Florida because he was a learned man from the University of Berlin. Between the two of us, his last examination, if the truth be told, he completed in Zaleski's tavern in New York, where he cleaned out Mr. Schönig of $1,500 in a game."

[12]"Supervisors of Internal Revenue Surveyors, 1868-1871"; Krzyżanowski, *Wspomnienia*, 88.

[13]Krzyżanowski, *Wspomnienia*, 90.

[14]Krzyżanowski, *Wspomnienia*, 90.

[15]Krzyżanowski, *Wspomnienia*, 90.

[16]Krzyżanowski, *Wspomnienia*, 91.

[17]Krzyżanowski, *Wspomnienia*, dialogue from 38.

[18]Krzyżanowski, *Wspomnienia*, 43.

[19]Krzyżanowski, *Wspomnienia*, 43.

[20]Krzyżanowski, *Wspomnienia*, 44.

[21]Krzyżanowski, *Wspomnienia*, 43.

[22]Krzyżanowski to Alfred Pleasonton, Commissioner of Internal Revenue, April 25, 1871; P. W. Perry, Supervisor of the Third Georgia District, to J. W. Douglas, Commissioner of Internal Revenue, Feb. 24, 1873.

[23]Krzyżanowski to Alfred Pleasonton, April 25, 1871; Table for January, February and March 1871, National Archives MSS, Department of the Treasury.

[24]National Archives, RG 92, Office of the Quartermaster General, Claims Branch, Box 13, No. B 464: 1871, June-July; letter from the Quartermaster General to the Hon. W. W. Belknap, Secretary of War, June 13 [1871]; letter, W. W. Belknap to the Commissioner of Internal Revenue, June 19, 1871; National Archives, RG 92, Office of the Quartermaster General, Claims Branch, Book B, 1871, Box 13: May 24, 1871, Case of W. Krzyzanowski; letter, W.W. Belknap to Commissioner of internal Revenue, June 19, 1871; letters, Quartermaster General to W. W. Belknap, June 5 and June 7, 1871.

[25]*Savannah Morning News,* January 16, 1871

[26]*Savannah Morning News,* January 17, 1871.

[27]*Savannah Morning News,* January 18, 1871.

[28]Krzyżanowski, letter to Alfred Pleasonton, April 25, 1871; Table for January, February and March 1871, from the National Archives MSS, Department of the Treasury.

[29]H. C. Yaryan, "Report of Investigations in Matter of Supervisor Krzyzanowski and Collector Gould," affidavit of Theodore B. Marshall and statement of W. B. Krzyżanowski, Oct. 12, 1871, Treasury Department, National Archives; *Savannah Morning News*, Jan. 2, 1871.

[30]H. C. Yaryan, "Report of Investigations in Matter of Supervisor Krzyzanowski and Collector Gould," affidavit of Theodore B. Marshall and statement of W. B. Krzyżanowski, Oct. 12, 1871, Treasury Department, National Archives; *Savannah Morning News,* March 23, 1871; *Savannah Morning News*, Jan. 2, 1871.

[31]Yaryan report, statement of Joseph A. Roberts, Oct. 16, 1871.

[32]Yaryan report, statement of Alvin B. Clark, Oct. 20, 1871.

[33]Yaryan report, statement of Alvin B. Clark, Oct. 20, 1871

[34]Yaryan report, statement of Alvin B. Clark, Oct. 20, 1871, quotation from Yaryan's comments.

[35]Yaryan report, statement of R.R. Brawley, Oct. 12, 1871, and affidavit of Theodore B. Marshall; Ledger Papers, W. B. Krzyzanowski & Co.

[36]Yaryan report, conclusions, Oct. 30, 1871.

[37]Yaryan report, conclusions, Oct. 30, 1871.

[38]Yaryan report, conclusions, Oct. 30, 1871.

[39]*Savannah Morning News,* April 8, 1871.

[40]Ksieniewicz; J. W. Douglas, letter to George S. Boutwell, Nov. 1, 1871, Revenue Correspondence, Book 31; *Savannah Morning News,* Oct. 30, 1871.

[41]J. W. Douglas, letter to George S. Boutwell, Nov. 1, 1871.

[42]"Department of the Treasury, Internal Revenue Correspondence: 1868-1873," Book 3, 426, George S. Boutwell to J. W. Douglas, Nov. 1, 1871.

[43]George S. Boutwell to Krzyżanowski, Nov. 2, 1871.

CHAPTER ELEVEN

"I FEEL THAT I HAVE DONE MY DUTY"

[1]Customs Bureau Records, Krzyżanowski's report for Nov., 1872, dated Dec. 3, 1872 [K/196-1872].

[2]Customs Bureau Records, Krzyżanowski's report for Nov., 1872, dated Dec. 3, 1872 [K/196-1872]; Joseph F. Krzyżanowski to Mieczysław Haiman, July 8, 1938; "Abstract of Accounts of Special Agents," Department of the Treasury, I, 428, statement of Krzyżanowski's accounts.

[3]Customs Bureau Records, Krzyżanowski's report for Nov., 1872, dated Dec. 3, 1872 [K/196-1872].

[4]Customs Bureau Records, Krzyżanowski's report for Jan. 1873, dated Feb. 3, 1873 [K/24-1873].

[5]*Ibid.*

[6]*Ibid.*

[7]*Ibid.*

[8]*Ibid.*

[9]*Ibid.*

[10]*Ibid.*

[11]Customs Bureau Records, Krzyżanowski's report for February, 1873, dated March 4, 1873 [K/28-1873].

[12]*Ibid.*

[13]Customs Bureau Records, Krzyżanowski's reports for April, 1873, dated May 3, 1873 [B/1-13018-1873], for March, 1873, dated April 2, 1873 [K/46-1873], for May, 1873, dated June 12, 1873 [K/83-1873], and for June, 1873, dated July 3, 1873 [B/1-22386]; Krzyżanowski to Secretary of the Treasury, June 16, 1873 [B2-17365]; Joseph F. Krzyzanowski to Mieczysław Haiman, July 8, 1938; Florence S. Hellman to Mieczysław Haiman, July 12, 1938.

[14]Customs Bureau Records, letter, Krzyżanowski to Secretary of the Treasury, June 16, 1873 [B2-17365 and K/28-1873]; letter, Krzyżanowski to Secretary of the Treasury, July 12, 1873 [A2-22073 and K/89-1873]; Ksieniewicz, 82.

[15]Customs Bureau Records, letter, Krzyżanowski to Secretary of the Treasury, Aug. 1, 1873 [L/104-1873 and A2-25091]; Krzyżanowski's report for August, 1873, dated Sept. 1, 1873 [B2-27685 and S/116-1873].

[16]Customs Bureau Records, Krzyżanowski's report for Aug. 1873, dated Sept. 1, 1873 [B2-27684 and S/116-1873]; Joseph F. Krzyzanowski to Mieczysław Haiman, July 8, 1938; Ksieniewicz, 161-164.

[17]Customs Bureau Records, Krzyżanowski's report for Sept. 1873 [A3-31189 and S/129-1873].

[18]*Ibid.*

[19]William A. Richardson to Krzyżanowski, Sept. 24, 1873, "Division of Special Agents, Record of Letters Sent," Book 10, 104.

[20]Customs Bureau Records, Phillipson to Krzyżanowski, Nov. 17, 1873 [L/151-1873], and Krzyżanowski to William A. Richardson, Secretary of the Treasury, Nov. 25, 1873 [L/151-1873 and A4-40013].

[21]Krzyżanowski to William A. Richardson, Secretary of the Treasury, Nov. 25, 1873 [L/151-1873 and A4-40013].

[22]Customs Bureau Records, Krzyżanowski to William A. Richardson, Secretary of the Treasury, Dec. 11, 1873 [L/156-1873 and A4-40883].

[23]*Ibid.*

[24]*Ibid.*

[25]*Ibid.*

[26]*Ibid.*

[27]*Ibid.*

[28]*Ibid.*

[29]*Ibid.*

[30]Customs Bureau, J. D. Cole to Krzyżanowski, Oct. 31, 1871; S. B. Baldwin to Krzyżanowski, Oct. 31, 1871; H. W. Grant to Krzyżanowski, Oct. 31, 1871.

[31]Customs Bureau Records, Krzyżanowski to William A. Richardson, Dec. 23, 1873 [L/159-1873].

[32]Customs Bureau Records, Krzyżanowski to Agent Leighton, Dec. 31, 1873 [L/162-1873]; Krzyżanowski to Secretary of the Treasury, March 19, 1874 [L/36-1874]; Krzyżanowski's report for January 1874, dated Feb. 10, 1874 [L/16-1874]; Krzyżanowski's report for February, 1874, dated March 2, 1874 [L/26-1874].

[33]*Ibid.*

[34]Customs Bureau Records, Krzyżanowski to O. D. Madge, Supervising Special Agent, April 3, 1874 [L/44-1874]; O. D. Madge to Krzyżanowski, April 23, 1874, "Abstract of Accounts," Book 10, 311.

[35]Customs Bureau Records, Krzyżanowski to O.D. Madge, May 22, 1874 [L/66-1874].

[36]Customs Bureau Records, Krzyżanowski's reports for April, 1874, dated May 2, 1874 [L/54-1874] and for May, 1874, dated May 31, 1874 [L/10-1874].

[37]Krzyżanowski to Secretary of the Treasury, May 31, 1874 [L/69-1874]; Rouček, 603; Krzyżanowski, Wspomnienia, 45.

[38]Krzyżanowski, Certificate of Appointment, dated Nov. 11, 1872, U.S. Treasury Department Files, National Archives.

[39]Letter, Krzyżanowski, to Senator George Boutwell, May 19, 1874, U.S. Treasury Department Files, National Archives.

CHAPTER TWELVE
"WITHOUT INJURY TO HIS DIGNITY"

[1]Robert G. Cleland and Glenn S. Dumke, *From Wilderness to Empire: A History of California* (New York: Alfred A. Knopf, 1959), 176, 180-181.

[2]Joseph F. Krzyżanowski to Mieczysław Haiman, July 8, 1938; Ksieniewicz, 83; letter, Fr. John B. McGloin to author, Nov. 4, 1971. The San Francisco City Directory (R. L. Polk & Co.) lists Kriz as a "barkeeper" with a dwelling on the north side of Market Street near Dupont (p. 455).

[3]Ksieniewicz, 119; Wacław Kruszka, *A History of the Poles in America to 1908*

(Washington, DC: The Catholic Univ. of America Press, 1993-2001), Vol. I, 217.

[4]Haiman, *Polish Pioneers*, 45-46, 58-61, 67-68, 74; Coleman, 33; Coleman and Coleman, 61; Chodkiewicz, 130.

[5]Haiman, *Polish Pioneers*, 58-61, 67-68, 74; Marion Read, *A History of the California Academy of Medicine 1870 to 1930* (San Francisco: Grabhorn Press, 1930), 26-28; *Langley's San Francisco Directory, 1882-3* (San Francisco: Francis, Valentine & Co., 1882), 204, 761, 766.

[6]*Langley's*, 193, 230, 511; Haiman, *Polish Pioneers*, 67; Edmund Z. Brodowski, "How Madame Modjeska's Career Was Saved by Zagloba," *Current Literature*, Vol. 46 (June 1909), 667-668.

[7]Marion M. Coleman, *Fair Rosalind: The American Career of Helena Modjeska* (Cheshire, CT: Cherry Hill Books, 1969), 1; C. Bozenta Chłapowski, "A Note from C. B. Chlapowski," *Scribner's Monthly Magazine*, XVIII (May 1879), 140-141; Henry G. Tinsley, "The Polish Colony in Southern California," *San Francisco Chronicle*, Feb. 27, 1898, 9; Helena Modjeska, *Memories and Impressions of Helena Modjeska* (New York: Macmillan, 1910), 314.

[8]Coleman and Coleman, vi, 51, 57, 40-41.

[9]Coleman, 11, 15, 18, 20-21; Tinsley, 9.

[10]Tinsley, 9.

[11]*Ibid.*

[12]Tinsley, 9; Brodowski, 668; Coleman and Coleman, 76.

[13]Tinsely, 9.

[14]Busby's quote from Tinsely, 9.

[15]Milton L. Kosberg, "The Polish Colony of California, 1876-1914" M.A. Thesis, Univ. of Southern California, June, 1952, v, 12; Tinsley, 9; Kelly, 251.

[16]Chłapowski quote from Coleman, 33; Modjeska quote from Grzeloński, *Ameryka*, 112.

[17]Johanna Tucholsky, "Henryk Sienkiewicz in the United States," *The Theatre*, VII, No. 79 (Sept. 1907), 248; Coleman, 34-35, 63, 66; Modjeska, 314; Stephen P. Mizwa, ed., *Great Men and Women of Poland* (New York: The Macmillan Co., 1942), 251.

[18]*Langley's*, 832; Kelly, 251; Modjeska, 314; Krzyżanowski's Petition for Bankruptcy, Schedule A; Mizwa, 251; David Belasco, "My Life's Story," *Hearst's Magazine*, July 30, 1914, 196.

[19]*Ibid.*

[20]*Ibid.*

[21]Conversation from Mizwa, 251 and Brodowski, 668.

[22]*Ibid.*

[23]Mizwa, 251; Kelly, 251; Brodowski, 668.

[24]Dialogue from Brodowski, 668.

[25]Brodowski, 668; Mizwa, 252; Belasco, 198.

[26]Mizwa, 252.

[27]Belasco, 198; Mizwa, 252; Coleman, 85; Coleman and Coleman, 17.

[28]Mizwa, 250; Brodowski, 667; Mabel Collins, *The Story of Helena Modjeska* (London: W.H. Allen & Co., 1883), 193; Coleman, 90; Bogdan Grzeloński, ed.

Ameryka w pamiętnikach Polaków: Antologia (Warsaw: Wydawnictwo Interpress, 1988), 200-01, gives Aug. 20, 1877 as the date for Modjeska's debut.

[29]Grzeloński, 200-01.

[30]Kelly, 250-252; Brodowski, 668; Mizwa, 258-259, 314; Grzeloński, 112.

[31]Krzyżanowski's Petition for Bankruptcy, Schedule A; Joseph F. Krzyżanowski to Mieczysław Haiman, July 8, 1938.

[32]Modjeska, 314; Kelly, 251.

[33]Henryk Sienkiewicz, *Portrait of America: Letters of Henry Sienkiewicz* (New York: Columbia Univ. Press, 1959), 97-98.

[34]Charles Morley, transl. & ed., *Portrait of America: Letters of Henryk Sienkiewicz Author of Quo Vadis?* (New York: Columbia Univ. Press, 1959), 97.

[35]Tinsley, 9; Brodowski, 667; Mizwa, 279.

[36]Tinsley, 9; Brodowski, 667; Chłapowski, 140-141.

[37]Cleland and Dumke, 182; David Lavender, *California: Land of New Beginnings* (Harper & Row Publishers, 1972), 300-01.

[38]Record of Petition for Bankruptcy, U.S. District Court for Northern California.

[39]Krzyżanowski's Petition for Bankruptcy, Schedules A and B.

[40]Record of Petition for Bankruptcy.

[40]Krzyżanowski, *Wspomnienia*, 45.

CHAPTER THIRTEEN
"WOUNDS WHICH DO NOT HEAL"

[1]Krzyżanowski to Hon. A. L. Eickhoff, Jan. 17, 1878.

[2]A. L. Eickhoff to Secretary of the Treasury John Sherman, Jan. 30, 1878.

[3]*Ibid.*, postscript of Benjamin A. Willis.

[4]John Sherman to A. L. Eickhoff, Jan. 31, 1878.

[5]Simon Wolf to John Sherman, Oct. 11, 1878.

[6]Endorsement by Carl Schurz to the letter from Simon Wolf to John Sherman dated Oct. 11, 1878.

[7]Letter, Benjamin T. Anuszkiewicz to R. Lepkowski, June 23, 1938; Register of Special Officers, April, 1869 to March, 1893, Treasury Department, 18; Grot, 104; Customs Bureau Records, Krzyżanowski to John Sherman, Oct. 23, 1878 [K/23-1878]. National Archives, RG 56, No. 287, p. 94, says "Act of June 20, 1878, appointed July 31, 1878, Ass't Agent at Seal fisheries in Alaska at $2,190 per annum plus expenses not to exceed $600 per annum." A note also indicates: "Appointment revoked by letter of Aug. 15, 78." A further entry notes that on Oct. 11, 1878, Kriz was appointed Special Inspector of Customs at Panama to reside on Isthmus at $2,500 per annum. "Reet 2999 Revised Statutes." The oath was taken Oct. 20, 1878.

[8]Customs Bureau Records, Krzyżanowski to John Sherman, Nov. 20, 1878 [K/28-1878]; Wytrwal, 373; Ksieniewicz, 84.

[9]Krzyżanowski, *Wspomnienia,* 40.

[10]*Ibid.*

[11]Division of Special Agents, Record of Letters Sent, Department of the Treasury, Series III, Book 1, 336, letter, C. F. French to Krzyżanowski, Nov. 2, 1878; Customs Bureau Records, Krzyżanowski's reports for May 1879, dated May 31, 1879 [K/40-1879] and for April 1879, dated May 5, 1879 [K/31-1879].

[12]Customs Bureau Records, Krzyżanowski to Sec. of the Treasury, June 2, 1879 [K/41-1879]; Krzyżanowski to Sec. of the Treasury, Oct. 4, 1879 [A29-7511]; Krzyżanowski to Sec. of the Treasury, Dec. 1, 1879 [A30-4305].

[13]Customs Bureau Records, Krzyżanowski reports for June, 1879, dated June 30, 1879 [K/44-1879], and for Nov. 1879, dated Dec. 2, 1879 [K/72-1879].

[14]Customs Bureau Records, Krzyżanowski's report for Nov. 1879, dated Dec. 2, 1879 [K/72-1879]; reports for July 1879, dated Aug. 2, 1879 [K/56-1879]; for Aug. 1879, dated Sept. 2, 1879 [K/60-1879], for Sept. 1879, dated Oct. 1, 1879 [K/66-1879], and for Oct. 1879, dated Nov. 5, 1879 [K/68-1879].

[15]Customs Bureau Records, Krzyżanowski's report for Jan. 1880, dated Jan. 31, 1880 [K/9-1880]; Krzyżanowski to Sec. of Treasury, Jan. 2, 1880 [K/5-1880]; Krzyżanowski to Sec. of the Treasury, Jan. 23, 1880 [K/6-1880]; Krzyżanowski to Sec. of Treasury, March 1, 1880 [K/21-1880]; Krzyżanowski to Sec. of Treasury, July 1, 1880 [K/46-1880]; Ksieniewicz, 85, cited Jan. 11, 1882 as the date of Caroline's death.

[16]Customs Bureau Records, Krzyżanowski to Sec. of Treasury, April 7, 1880 [K32-375]; Krzyżanowski to Sec. of Treasury, April 30, 1880 [K32-1880]; Krzyżanowski to Sec. of Treasury, April 24, 1880 [K/36-1880]; Krzyżanowski to Sec. of Treasury, July 1, 1880 [K/46-1880]; and Krzyżanowski's report for May 1880, dated June 1, 1880 [K/39-1880].

[17]Letter, Krzyżanowski to Emily Metzig, July 22, 1880; Customs Bureau Records, Krzyżanowski to Sec. of Treasury, July 1, 1880 [K/46-1880].

[18]Krzyżanowski referred to Emily as his niece, cousin and sister. He always felt closer to her than to his own brothers and sisters. Krzyżanowski to Emily Metzig, July 22, 1880.

[19]*Ibid.*

[20]*Ibid.*

[21]*Ibid.*

[22]Customs Bureau Records, Francis Lessen to John Sherman, June 17, 1880 [A33-4189].

[23]Customs Bureau Records, Krzyżanowski to John Sherman, Aug. 4, 1880 [A33-4189].

[24]Customs Bureau Records, Krzyżanowski to John Sherman, Jan. 1, 1881 [A33-4189].

[25]Krzyżanowski to Emily Metzig, n. d., as quoted in Grot, 89.

[26]Ksieniewicz, 169; Krzyżanowski to Emily Metzig, n. d., as quoted in Grot, 105. According to the certificate of death, Caroline died at age of 48 years, two months, of hemiplegia on Jan. 11, 1882. She lived at 157 East 76th Street in New York City where she had resided for four months. She had been stricken with an attack of hemiplegia two years before her death.

[27]*Ibid.*

[28]Krzyżanowski to Emily Metzig, April, 1882.

[29]Krzyżanowski to Emily Metzig, n. d., as quoted in Grot, 105.

[30]Krzyżanowski to Emily Metzig, n. d., as quoted in Grot, 105; Register of Special Officers, April 1869 to March 1893, 18; Abstract of Accounts of Special Agents, Department of the Treasury, II, 248, and III, 153.

[31]All references to "The Lighthouse-Keeper" are to Monica M. Gardner's translation of Henryk Sienkiewicz's short story as it appeared in *Tales From Henryk Sienkiewicz* (New York: Dutton & Co., 1931).

[32]Henry Archacki to author, Feb. 15, 1970; Chodkiewicz, 134; Von Steinwehr Post No. 192 Papers, New York State Archives, 19.

[33]Krzyżanowski to Emily Metzig, no date, in Grot, 106.

[34]Henry Archacki to author, Feb. 15, 1970; Chodkiewicz, 134; Leon Orlowski, "Henryk Korwin-Kałussowski (1806-1894) Delegate of the Polish National Government in Washington," *Bulletin of the Polish Institute of Arts and Sciences*, IV (1945-1946), 60, 62.

[35]Krzyżanowski, *Wspomnienia,* 10.

[36]Krzyżanowski, *Wspomnienia*, 25.

[37]Krzyżanowski, *Wspomnienia*, 17.

[38]Krzyżanowski, *Wspomnienia*, 17; Ksieniewicz, 89-91.

[39]*Ibid.*

[40]Krzyżanowski, *Wspomnienia*, 15.

[41]Krzyżanowski, *Wspomnienia*, passim; Sienkiewicz, 98.

[42]Florence S. Hellman to Mieczysław Haiman, July 12, 1938; Joseph F. Krzyżanowski to Mieczysław Haiman, July 8, 1938.

[43]*The Times Index-Gazetteer of the World* (London: The Times Publishing Co., 1965), 438; Wiktor A. Wojciechowski, "General Wladimir B. Krzyżanowski Civil War Hero," *Zgoda* (Kraków: Jagiellonian University, 1915).

[44]Krzyżanowski, *Wspomnienia*, 19.

[45]Krzyżanowski, *Wspomnienia*, 38.

[46]*Ibid.*

[47]Krzyżanowski, *Wspomnienia*, 41-42.

[48]Krzyżanowski, *Wspomnienia*, 45-46

[49]Krzyżanowski, *Wspomnienia, passim.*

[50]Krzyżanowski, *Wspomnienia*, 48.

[51]Krzyżanowski, *Wspomnienia*, 42.

[52]Krzyżanowski, *Wspomnienia*, 42-43.

[53]Krzyżanowski, *Wspomnienia*, 19.

[54]*Ibid.*

[55]Krzyżanowski, *Wspomnienia*, 19-20.

[56]Krzyżanowski, *Wspomnienia*, 21-22.

[57]Krzyżanowski, *Wspomnienia*, 58-59.

CHAPTER FOURTEEN

A "GENIAL AND LOYAL SPIRIT"

[1]Customs Bureau Records, Report on Daily Employment, Special Agent's Office, New York; Register of Special Officers, April 1869 to March 1893, MSS in the National Archives, p. 215; House Executive Document No. 199, 48th Congress, 2nd Session, Volume 28, 3.

[2]House Executive Document No. 93, 48th Congress, 1st Session, Volume 24, 59; Customs Bureau Records, Report of Daily Employment, Special Agent's Office, New York.

[3]Ksieniewicz, 176-177; *New York Times*, June 19, 1885.

[4]Krzyżanowski's Original Invalid Claim, April 8, 1884; Krzyżanowski's Declaration for Original Invalid Pension, March 13, 1885; "Proof of Disability" affidavit by E.W. Brueninghausen, May 26, 1885, National Archives.

[5]Customs Bureau Records, Krzyżanowski to Colonel Ira Ayer, Jr., Oct. 15, 1885 (A45-2298); Customs Bureau Records, Krzyżanowski to Ayer, Oct. 19, 1885 (A45-3803); Report of Daily Employment, Special Agent's Office, New York.

[6]Krzyżanowski, letter to Emily Metzig, n.d., in Grot, 106.

[7]Declaration for Widow's Pension by Pelagia Borkowska Krzyżanowska, Sept. 3, 1890, National Archives, states that her maiden name was Gliniecki, that she first married a man named Sick, and then took a second husband named Gustaw Rosenzweig in Warsaw on Aug. 11, 1870. The second husband was a merchant from whom she was separated and eventually divorced on June 14, 1877 in the Evangelical Lutheran Consistory. This would make Krzyżanowski her third husband. The Widow's Pension files in the National Archives (Pension Papers No. 41200, Bundle No. 25) show that Pelagia received a pension of $8 per month, the last payment being on Dec. 4, 1902, after which she was dropped from the rolls as deceased, "date unknown." An affidavit of Mary O'Neill in support of Pelagia's original pension request says that Mrs. Krzyżanowski was 42 years old (Sept. 8, 1894) and resided at 933 Folsom Street, San Francisco (Pension Series WC, No. 405,884). A letter from the Superior Court of the City and County of San Francisco to the Commissioner of the Bureau of Pensions dated Oct. 24, 1904, noted that Pelagia Maria Krzyżanowski was deceased and that her will was being contested by Aloyzy Sylvester Borkowski and Antonina Ogonowska who claimed to be her heirs. The letter included the statement that the deceased also went by the "other name" of "Palagia M. Kanoski."

[8]Division of Special Agents, Record of Letters Sent, Department of the Treasury, C.S. Fairchild letter to Krzyżanowski, Jan. 20, 1886, and C.S. Fairchild letter to Krzyżanowski, Feb. 10, 1886; Ksieniewicz, 178; Grot, 107, includes letter from Krzyżanowski to Emily Metzig, March 19, 1886.

[9]Chodkiewicz, 136; Henry Archacki, misc papers.

[10]Krzyżanowski letter to Count Plater, April 13, 1884.

[11]Chodkiewicz, 136.

[12]*Ibid.*

[13]Abstract of Accounts of Special Agents, Treasury Department, IV, p. 124; Dr. Walter J. Karwowski to author, May 13, 1975; Krzyżanowski's death certificate.

[14]Affidavit of Carl Schurz dated May 3, 1886, Krzyżanowski's pension file, National Archives; Affidavit of Dr. Vincent Żółnowski dated April 26, 1886, Krzyżanowski's pension file, National Archives; John C. Black, Commissioner of Pensions, to Dr. Vincent Zolnowski dated May 15, 1886, Krzyżanowski's pension file, National Archives; Letter, Dr. Żółnowski to Commissioner Black dated May 24, 1886, Krzyżanowski's pension file, National Archives. Interestingly, in one of his medical reports Kriz is described as having a sabre cut on the anterior surface of his left wrist about 1.5 inches long and .25 to .5 inches wide that was deep enough to reach the tendons. It was noted that he received this before coming to the U.S.

[15]Krzyżanowski's Declaration for the Increase of an Invalid Pension, Aug. 16, 1886, National Archives, cited as reasons for the claim "asthma, chronic pleuritis of the right side and dilatation of the heart"; Letter, Schurz to L.Q.C. Lamar, Sept. 28, 1886, from Frederick Bancroft, ed., *Speeches, Correspondence and Political Papers of Carl Schurz* (New York: G.P. Putnam's Sons, 1913), IV, 451; Krzyżanowski's affidavit, December 4, 1886, Pension Files, National Archives.

[16]Medical Exam for Pension Increase, Nov. 2, 1886, Pension File.

[17]Krzyżanowski's Affidavit, Dec. 4, 1886, National Archives.

[18]Carl Schurz to Mr. Hanna, Dec. 6, 1886, Krzyżanowski's Pension File.

[19]Carl Schurz to Mr. Hanna, Jan. 4, 1887, Krzyżanowski's Pension File.

[20]Customs Bureau, Report of Daily Employment, Special Agent's Office, N.Y.

[21]Affidavit of Dr. Alfred Meyer, Jan. 26, 1887, Krzyżanowski's Pension File.

[22]Customs Bureau, Report of Daily Employment, Special Agent's Office, N.Y.

[23]*Ibid.*

[24]Thomas E. Kissling, N.C.W.C. News Service Release, July 7, 1962; Henry Archacki, "Fifty Years Ago, Today!" *Nowy Świat*, Jan. 31, 1937, 21; Archacki, *Kościuszko Lodge*, 39; Rev. Felix F. Burant to Very Rev. Edward R. Gaffney, July 29, 1937; Grot, 108; Wieczerzak, 240; Post 192, GAR, papers, Feb. 1, 1887.

[25]"Bohater Wojny Domowej," 2; Archacki, misc. papers; New York State Archives, Grand Army of the Republic, Department of New York, Box 60, Post 192.

[26]*Brigadier General Wladimir B. Krzyzanowski Memorial Program* (New York: Jan. 31, 1937).

[27]Archacki, misc. papers; *Krzyżanowski Memorial Program.*

[28]*Krzyżanowski Memorial Program.*

[29]Haiman, *Polish Past*, iii; "Ameryka Składa Hołd Prochom Zasłużonego," *Dziennik Związkowy*, 9-go Października, 1937 roku, 9; Archacki, misc. papers.

[30]Archacki, misc. papers; Piekarczyk, "Polish Patriotism," 5.

[31]Krzyżanowski, *Wspomnienia*, 91.

[32]*New York State and the Civil War*, I, No. 6 (Dec. 1961), published by the New York Civil War Centennial Commission.

[33]James I. Robertson, Jr., to Henry Archacki, Jan. 19, 1961.

[34]"Bruce Catton Lauds Polish Americans for Civil War Role," *New York State and the Civil War*, Vol. 1, No. 6 (Dec. 1961), 6-7.

APPENDICES

[1]Ksieniewicz, 77-78.
[2]From *O.R.*, Series I, Volume 15, 672-73.
[3]*O.R.*,Series I, Volume 16, 311-13.
[4]*O.R.*, Series I, Volume XXV, Part 1, 666-68.
[5]*O.R.*, Series I, Volume XXXI, Part 1, 111-12.
[6]National Archives, RG 393, Pt. 2, Vol. 16, II-5314.
[7]National Archives, RG 393, Pt. 2, Vol. 18: Box 1.

Monument to the 58th New York Infantry at Gettysburg

Bibliography

Manuscript Sources

Abstract of Accounts of Special Agents, 4 vols., Department of the Treasury. Record Group 36, National Archives, Washington, D.C. Contains financial reports and accounts of Special Agents.

Alaska File of the Office of the Secretary of the Treasury, 1868-1903, Microcopy 720, rolls 2-4, National Archives, Washington, D.C., containing letters relating to Krzyżanowski's search for a federal position in San Francisco.

Anuszkiewicz, Benjamin T. Untitled, undated biographical manuscript on Gen. Krzyżanowski, 120 pages, probably dated about 1937, in the archives of the Polish Studies Program at Central Connecticut State University.

Army of the Potomac Society. Minutes, Library of Congress.

Banks, Gen. Nathaniel P. Papers, Library of Congress.

Boynton, Jonathan W.W. Reminiscences, 157th New York Infantry, U.S. Army Military History Institute, Carlisle Barracks.

Civil War Organizations Returns, Record of the Adjutant General's Office, Record Group 92, National Archives, Washington, D. C.

Daily Log of 11th Corps, April 1, 1863 to April 9, 1864, Schoff Civil War Collection, William L. Clements Library, University of Michigan.

Damkoehler, Ernst. Letters, 26th Wisconsin Infantry, in the possession of Mr. W. L. Damkoehler.

Descriptive Book, Streinwehr Post 192, Grand Army of the Republic, Albany, N.Y.

Dodge, Theodore A. Diary, 1862-1863, Library of Congress microfilm. 119th New York Infantry.

Doerflinger, Lt. Karl. Unpublished ms. in the State Historical Society of Wisconsin. 26th Wisconsin Infantry.

Eder, Franz [actual name Benno Wohlgamuth]. Diary, 119th New York Infantry, New-York Historical Society.

58th New York Volunteer Infantry File, New York State Military Museum, Saratoga, NY.

Gillis, Joseph. Letters, 82nd Ohio, courtesy of Joseph H. Gillis.

Howard, Gen. Oliver Otis. Papers, Schoff Civil War Collection, William L. Clements Library, University of Michigan.

__________. Papers, Boudoin College, Brunswick, Maine.

__________. Papers, Ohio Historical Society.

Huebschmann, Franz. Papers, Milwaukee County Historical Society. Physician, 26th Wisconsin Infantry.

Hutchinson, Ephraim M. Papers, 82nd Ohio Infantry, Civil War Times Illustrated Collection, U.S. Army Military History Institute, Carlisle Barracks.

Jacobs, Col. William H. Papers, 26th Wisconsin Infantry, Milwaukee County Historical Society.

Kałussowski, Henryk. Papers, Biblioteka Narodowy, Warsaw.
Karstin, Karl. Letters, 26th Wisconsin Infantry. Microfilm copy in the State Historical Society of Wisconsin.
Kozlay, Col. Eugene. Diary. Courtesy of Janet Kozlay.
Lackner, Francis. Diary, 26th Wisconsin Infantry, Milwaukee County Historical Society.
Małuski, Aleksander. Reminiscences, 58th New York Infantry.
Mitchell, Capt. D. W. Letters, 82nd Ohio, courtesy of Stanley R. Burleson.
Muenzenberger, Adam. Letters, 26th Wisconsin Infantry, courtesy of Mr. William Lamers.
Robinson, Col. James S. Address at Dedication of Gettysburg Monument. Gettysburg National Military Park.
_________. Papers, 82nd Ohio Infantry, Ohio Historical Society.
Roth, Wilhelm. Letters, 74th Pennsylvania Infantry, U.S. Army Military History Institute, Carlisle Barracks.
Salomon, Edward. Papers, U.S. Army Military History Institute, Carlisle Barracks.
Sanford, Addison. Papers, 82nd Ohio Infantry, Ohio Historical Society.
Schlumpf, Leonhard. Diary, 45th New York Infantry, Civil War Times Illustrated Collection, U.S. Army Military History Institute, Carlisle Barracks.
Schurz, Gen. Carl. Papers and Diary for 1862, Library of Congress.
Seymour, Capt. William J. Diary, Hays' Louisiana Infantry Brigade. U.S. Army Military History Institute, Carlisle Barracks.
Sigel, Gen. Franz. Letterbook, 1862-1865, Library of Congress.
_________. Papers, New-York Historical Society.
Steinwehr Post 192, Grand Army of the Republic. Descriptive Book, New York State Archives, Albany, New York.
Thomson, David. Papers, 82nd Ohio Infantry, courtesy of Ms. Mary A. Geiger.
26th Wisconsin Infantry, Series XII, Civil War Papers, Wisconsin Veterans Museum.
Wickesberg, Karl [Charles]. Letters, 26th Wisconsin Infantry, courtesy of Mr. Alfred Wickesberg.
Winkler, Gen. Frederick C. Papers, 26th Wisconsin Infantry, Milwaukee County Historical Society.

Newspapers

Daily National Intelligencer (Washington, D.C.)
Daily National Republican (Washington, D.C.)
Daily Tribune (New York)
Kłosy (Poland)
New York Express
New York Herald
New Yorker Staats Zeitung
New York Times
New York Tribune
Soldiers Friend and Grand Army of the Republic Weekly
Tygodnik Ilustrowany "Kraj"

Published Sources

Annual Report of the Adjutant-General of the State of New York for the Year 1900. Albany: James B. Lyon & Co., 1901.

Archer, John M. *"The Hour Was One of Horror." East Cemetery Hill at Gettysburg.* Gettysburg, PA: Thomas Publications, 1997.

Bates, Samuel P. *History of Pennsylvania Volunteers 1861-5.* Harrisburg: B. Singerly, 1869.

Battles and Leaders of the Civil War. New York: The Century Co., 1888. 4 volumes.

Battle of Chancellorsville and the Eleventh Army Corps. New York: G. B. Teubner, 1863.

Baumgartner, Richard A. *Buckeye Blood. Ohio at Gettysburg.* Huntington, WV: Blue Acorn Press, 2003.

Beath, Robert B. *History of the Grand Army of the Republic.* New York: Taylor & Co., Publishers, 1889.

Biddle, Chapman. *The First Day of the Battle of Gettysburg.* Philadelphia: J.B. Lippincott & Co., 1880.

Burnham, Stowell (1st Lt., 82nd Ohio), "Reminiscences of the Gettysburg Battle," *Lippincott's Magazine*, New Series, Vol. VI (July 1883), 54-60.

Ceremonies and Addresses at the Dedication of a Monument by the 119th Regiment, N. Y. State Vols. at Gettysburg, July 3, 1888 (Boston: Wright & Potter Printing, 1889).

Chancellorsville Source Book. Ft. Leavenworth, KS: Command and General Staff School, 1937. XI Corps, 595-686.

Coddington, Edwin B. *Gettysburg Campaign: A Study in Command.* Morningside: 1994.

Collins, Darrell L. *The Battles of Cross Keys and Port Republic.* Lynchburg, VA: H. E. Howard, Inc., 1993.

Diembach, Andrew. "An Incident at Cemetery Hill," *Blue & Gray*, 2 (July 1983), 21-22.

Dodge, Theodore A. *Addresses and Reviews.* Boston: Henry S. Dunn, 1898.

__________. "Battle of Chancellorsville, The," *Southern Historical Society Papers*, XIV (Richmond, 1886), 276-292.

__________. *The Campaign of Chancellorsville.* New York: Da Capo Press, 1999 (reprint of 1886 edition).

__________. "Gettysburg Campaign, The," *The United Service*, Philadephia, XIII, (1885).

__________. "Left Wounded on the Field," *Putnam's Magazine*, NS IV (New York 1869), 317-326.

__________. "The Romances of Chancellorsville," *Campaigns in Virginia, Maryland and Pennsylvania 1862-1863.* Boston: Papers of the Military Historical Society of Massachusetts, 1903, III, 192-218.

__________. "Was Either the Better Soldier," *Century Magazine*, XL (1890), 144-48.

Doubleday, Abner. *Chancellorsville and Gettysburg.* New York: Charles Scribner's Sons, 1882.

Fifth Annual Report of the Chief of Bureau of Military Statistics. Albany: C. Van

Benthuysen & Sons, 1868.

Fox, William F. *New York at Gettysburg.* ALbany: J. B. Lyon Co., 1900. Vol. 2.

Fuess, Claude Moore. *Carl Schurz, Reformer*. New York: Dodd, Mead & Co., 1932.

Gordon, John B. *Reminiscences of the Civil War*. Baton Rouge, LA: Louisiana State University Press, 1993.

Gottfried, Bradley M. *Brigades of Gettysburg.* Cambridge, MA: Da Capo Press, 2002.

Green, A. Wilson. "From Chancellorsville to Cemetery Hill: O. O. Howard and Eleventh Corps Leadership," in Gary W. Gallagher, ed., *The First Day at Gettysburg.* Kent, OH: Kent State University Press, 1993, 57-91.

Green, John P. "The Movement of the 11th and 12th Army Corps from the Potomac to the Tennessee," *MOLLUS-Pennsylvania* (Wilmington, NC: Broadfoot Publishing Company, 1995), I, 107-122. Reprint of the original publication in Philadelphia by Allen, Lane & Scott, 1892.

Grot, Zdzisław. "Generał Włodzimierz Krzyżanowski w świetle własnych wspomnień oraz listów pisanych do rodziny," *Kronika Miasta Poznania*, Vol. XV, No. 1 (March 31, 1937), 85-110.

Grzeloński, Bogdan, ed. *Ameryka w pamiętnikach Polaków: Antologia.* Warsaw: Wydawnictwo Interpress, 1988.

__________ and Izabella Rusinowa, *Polacy w wojnach amerykańskich, 1775-1783, 1861-1865.* Warsaw: Wydawnictwo Ministerstwa Obrony Narodowej, 1973.

Haiman, Mieczysław. *Historja Udziału Polaków w Amerykańskiej Wojnie Domowej.* Chicago: Dziennik Zjednoczenia, 1928.

Hamlin, Augustus C. *The Attack of Stonewall Jackson at Chancellorsville.* Fredericksburg, VA: Sergeant Kirkland's Museum & Historical Society, 1997.

Harrison, Noel G. *Chancellorsville Battlefield Sites.* Lynchburg, VA: H. E. Howard, Inc., 1990.

Hartwig, D. Scott, "The 11th Army Corps on July 1, 1863 — The Unlucky 11th," *The Gettysburg Magazine*, No. 2 (January, 1990), 33-49.

Hassler, Warren W. *Crisis at the Crossroads: The First Day at Gettysburg.* Gettysburg, PA: Stan Clark Military Books, 1991.

Heinrici, Max. *Das Buch der Deutschen in Amerika.* Philadelphia: Deutsch-Amerikanischer Nationalbund, 1909.

Hebert, Walter H. *Fighting Joe Hooker.* Old Saddler Books, 1987.

Hennessy, John J. *Return to Bull Run.* New York: Simon & Schuster, 1993.

__________. *Second Manassas Battlefield Map Study.* Lynchburg, VA: H. E. Howard, Inc., 1991.

Howard, Charles H. "First Day at Gettysburg," *The Gettysburg Papers.* Press of Morningside Bookshop, 1978, 310-336.

Howard, Oliver O. *Autobiography of Oliver Otis Howard.* New York: The Baker & Taylor Company, 1907. Vol. I.

Jewett, Leonidas M. "From Stafford Heights to Gettysburg in 1863," *MOLLUS-Ohio*. Cincinnati: Robert Clarke, 1903. Vol. V.

Jones, Terry L., ed., *The Civil War Memoirs of Captain William J. Seymour: Reminiscences of a Louisiana Tiger.* Baton Rouge: Louisiana State University Press, 1991.

Korn, Bertram W. *American Jewry and the Civil War.* Philadelphia: Jewish

Publication Society of America, 1961.
Krick, Robert K., *Conquering the Valley: Stonewall Jackson at Port Republic.* Baton Rouge: Louisiana State University Press, 1996.
Kross, Gary. "The XI Corps at Gettysburg July 1, 1863," *Blue & Gray Magazine*, XIX, No. 2 (December 2001). 6-24, 48-51.
Kruszka, Wacław. *A History of the Poles in America to 1908.* Washington, DC: The Catholic University of America Press, 1993-2001, 4 vols. A translation of *Historja Polska w Ameryce.* Milwaukee: Drukiem Spółki Wydawniczej Kuryera, 1905-08, 13 volumes.
Krzyżanowski, Włodzimierz B. *Wspomnienia z Pobytu w Ameryce Gen. Włodzimierza Krzyżanowskiego Podczas Wojny 1861-1864.* Chicago: Polish Museum of America, 1963.
Ladd, David L. and Audrey J. Ladd, *John Bachelder's History of the Battle of Gettysburg.* Dayton, OH: Morningside, 1997.
Lamers, William M. "A Humble Soldier Dies in Libby Prison," *Lore*, Vol. 11, No. 2 (Spring 1961), pp. 68-72. 26th Wisconsin Infantry.
__________. "Hero in Blue," *Lore*, Vol. 10, No 1 (Winter 1959), pp. 26-28. 26th Wisconsin Infantry.
Lash, Gary. *The Gibraltar Brigade on East Cemetery Hill. Fifty Years of Controversy.* Baltimore, MD: Butternut and Blue, 1995.
Ławrowski, Andrzej. *Reprezentacja Polskiej Grypy Ethicznej w Życiu Politycznym Stanów Zjednoczonych.* Warsaw: Państwowe Wydawnict-wo Naukowe, 1979.
Lee, Alfred E. "Battle of Gettysburg, The," *Report of the Ohio Gettysburg Memorial Commission* (1888), pp. 95-142.
__________. "Campaigning in the Mountain Department," *Magazine of American History*, Vol. XV (1885), pp. 391-96, 483-91, 590-95.
__________. "Cedar Mountain," *Magazine of American History*, Vol. XVI (1886), pp. 81-88, 159-67.
__________. "From Cedar Mountain to Chantilly," *Magazine of American History*, Vol. XVI (1886), pp. 266-82, 370-86, 467-82, 574-85.
__________. "Reminiscences of the Gettysburg Battle," *Lippincott's Magazine* (Philadelphia: J. B. Lippincott & Co., July, 1883), 54-60.
Legends of the Operations of the Army of the Cumberland. Washington: U.S. Government Printing Office, 1869.
Livermore, Thomas L. *Memoir of Theodore Ayrault Dodge.* Boston: Massachusetts Historical Society, 1910.
Lonn, Ella. *Foreigners in the Union Army and Navy.* Louisiana State University Press, 1951.
Madame Modjeska Countess Bozenta. Buffalo: Council on International Studies and Programs, SUNY-Buffalo, 1993.
Martin, David G. *Gettysburg July 1.* Conshohocken, PA: Combined Books, 1995.
__________. *Jackson's Valley Campaign* Conshohocken, PA: Combined Books, 1994 (Revised Edition).
__________. *The Second Bull Run Campaign.* Conshohocken, PA: Combined Books, 1997.
Meysenberg, Theodore A. "Reminiscences of Chancellorsville," *MOLLUS-Missouri.* St. Louis: Becktold & Co., 1892, I, 295-307.

Miller, Francis T. *The Photographic History of the Civil War*. New York: The Review of Reviews Co., 1912. Ten volumes.

Monfort, Elias R. "The First Division, Eleventh Corps, at Chancellorsville," *G.A.R. War Papers*, I, 60-75. Cincinnati: Fred. C. Jones Post, No. 401, Department of Ohio, n.d.

Moore, Frank. *The Rebellion Record: A Diary of American Events*. New York: D. Van Nostrand, 1868. 11 volumes.

Nachtigall, Herrmann. *Geschichte des 75sten Regiments, Pa. Vols.* Philadelphia: C. B. Kretschman, 1886.

__________. *History of the 75th Regiment, Pa. Vols.* North Riverside, IL: 1987. Transl. by Heinz D. Schwinge and Karl E. Sundstrom.

New York at Gettysburg. Albany: J. B. Lyon Company, 1900. 3 Vols.

Osborn, Hartwell. "The Eleventh Corps in East Tennessee," MOLLUS-Illinois, IV, 348-378. Chicago: Cozzens & Beaton Company, 1907.

Pennsylvania at Gettysburg. Ceremonies at the Dedication of the Monuments Erected by the Commonwealth of Pennsylvania. Vol. I (1904).

Pfanz, Harry W. *Gettysburg. Culp's Hill & Cemetery Hill.* Chapel Hill, NC: University of North Carolina Press, 1993.

__________. *Gettysburg: The First Day.* Chapel Hill, NC: University of North Carolina Press, 2001.

__________. *Gettysburg: The Second Day.* Chapel Hill, NC: University of North Carolina Press, 1987.

Phisterer, Frederick. *New York in the War of the Rebellion, 1861-1865*. Albany: J.B. Lyons & Co., 1912.

__________. *The Reminiscences of Carl Schurz*. New York: McClure & Co., 1907. 3 volumes.

Pula, James S. *The History of a German-Polish Civil War Brigade.* San Francisco: R & E Research, 1976.

__________. "The Sigel Regiment," *German-American Studies*, Vol. 8 (1974), 27-52.

__________. *The Sigel Regiment: A History of the 26th Wisconsin Volunteer Infantry, 1862-1865.* Campbell, CA: Savas Woodbury Publishers, 1997.

Reid, Whitelaw. *Ohio in the War: Her Statesmen, Her Generals, and Soldiers.* Cincinnati: Moore, Wilstack & Baldwin, 1868. 2 Vols.

Report of Major-General John Pope. Washington, DC: United States Adjutant General's Office, 1863.

Report on the New York Monuments at Chattanooga and Proceedings of Dedication of the Central Historical memorial or Peace Monument on Lookout Mountain. Albany: J.B. Lyon & Co., 1928.

Rice, Owen. "Afield With the Eleventh Army Corps at Chancellorsville," *MOLLUS-Ohio*, I, 358-391. Cincinnati: Robert Clarke & Co., 1888.

Roemer, Jacob. *Reminiscences of the War of the Rebellion 1861-1865.* Flushing, N.Y.: Published by the Estate of J. Roemer, 1897. L. A. Furney, ed.

Ropes, John C. "General Pope's Campaign in Virginia," *The Virginia Campaign of 1862 Under General Pope* (Boston: Papers of the Military Historical Society of Massachusetts, 1895), II, 73-97.

Salomon, Edward S. "Gettysburg," *MOLLUS-California*. San Francisco: Shannon-

Conmy Print Co., 1913.
Schurz, Carl. *The Reminiscences of Carl Schurz*. New York: Doubleday, Page & Company, 1909. 3 Vols.
Schwinge, Heinz D. and Karl E. Sundstrom, transl. and eds. *History of the 75th Regiment, Pa. Vols.* North Riverside, IL: Privately Printed, 1987.
Sears, Stephen W. *On Campaign with the Army of the Potomac. The Civil War Journal of Theodore Ayrault Dodge.* Cooper New York: Square Press, 2001.
Sienkiewicz, Henryk. "The Lighthouse-Keeper," in *Tales From Henryk Sienkiewicz.* New York: Dutton & Co., 1931. Translated by Monica M. Gardner.
Simonhoff, Harry. *Jewish Participants in the Civil War.* New York: Arco Publishing Company, Inc., 1963.
Sketches of War History, 1861-1865: Papers Read Before the Ohio Commandery of the Military Order of the Loyal Legion of the United States. Cincinnati: Published by the Commandery, R. Clark, 1888.
Stasic, Florian. *Polish Political Emigre;s in the United States of America 1831-1864.* Boulder, CO: East European Monographs, 2002.
__________. *Polska Emigracja Polityczna w Stanach Zjednoczonych Ameryki 1831-1864.* Warsaw: Państwowe Wydawnictwo Naukowe, 1973.
Stine, James H. *History of the Army of the Potomac.* Washington, DC: Gibson, 1893.
Svenson, Peter. *Battlefield. Farming a Civil War Battleground.* New York: Ballantine Books, 1992.
Swinton, William. *Campaigns of the Army of the Potomac. A Critical History of Operations in Virginia, Maryland and Pennsylvania From the Commencement to the Close of the War, 1861-1865.* New York: Scribners, 1882.
Taylor, Frank H. *Philadelphia in the Civil War.* Philadelphia: The City, 1913.
Teague, Charles. "Brutal Clash at Blocher's Knoll," *Gettysburg Magazine*, Vol. 32 (2005), 52-70.
Townsend, Thomas S. *The Honors of the Empire State in the War of the Rebellion.* New York: A. Lowell & Co., 1889.
Wallber, Albert. "From Gettysburg to Libby Prison," *War Papers Read Before the Commandery of the State of Wisconsin, Military Order of the Loyal Legion of the United States.* Milwaukee: Burdick & Allen, 1914. Vol. IV, pp. 191-200.
White, Gregory. *"The Most Bloody and Cruel Drama": A History of the 31st Gerogia Volunteer Infantry.* Butternut & Blue, 1997.
Winkler, Frederick C. *Letters of Frederick C. Winkler, 1862 to 1865.* Milwaukee: Privately Printed.
Young, Jesse Bowman. *Battle of Gettysburg: A Comprehensive Narrative.* New York: Harper & Brothers Publishers, 1913.

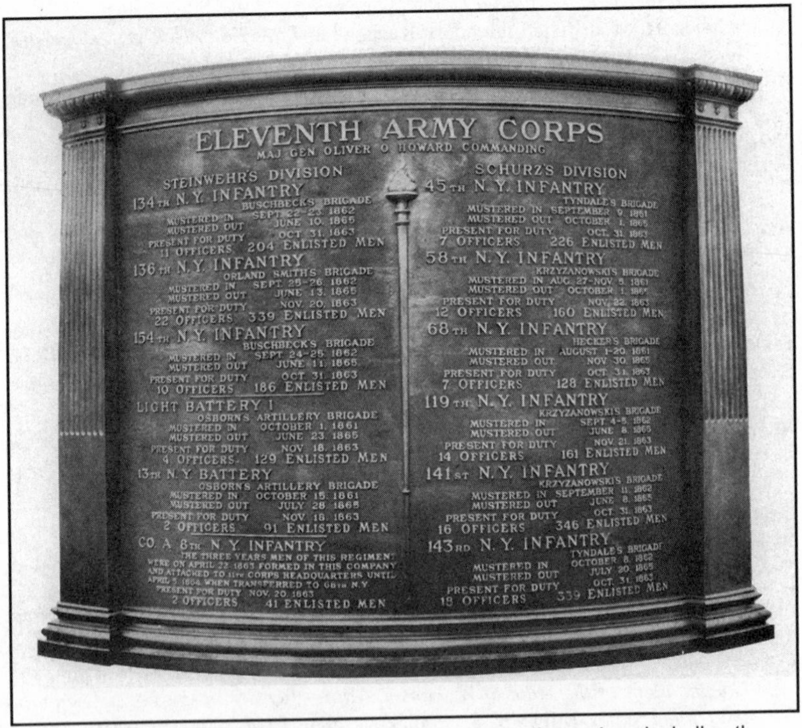

Monument to the Eleventh Corps in the Tennessee Campaigns including the 58th, 119th, and 141st New York of Krzyżanowski's brigade.

INDEX

For military units, see the index following on page 334.

Adams, George, 135.
Ahlers, N. M., 146.
Alden, A. S., 207-09, 213.
Alexander, Edward P., 64.
Allen, Julian, 31.
Ames, Adelbert, 137, 139.
Amsberg, George von, 122-24.
Anderson, Richard H., 69.
Antoniewski, Edward, 25, 136, 196.
Anuszkiewicz, Benjamin T., 263.
Archacki, Henry, 268.
Asbach, Rudolph, 132.
Association of Poles in America, 10.
Austin, James, 135.
Avery, Isaac, 125, 137.
Baetz, Henry, 130-31, 145, 196.
Banks, Nathaniel P., 52-53.
Barlow, Francis, 96, 100-01, 122, 125.
Barnes, Dixon, 57.
Barwicki, Karol, 25, 34.
Battery F, Pennsylvania Light Artillery, 51.
Baum, Adolph, 32.
Bednawski, Alexander, 224.
Beer, Adolf, 61.
Belknap. William W., 201, 204.
Benda, Frank, 131.
Bengel, Stephen, 105.
Benning, Henry, 69.
Berlandi, Philip, 131.
Bertsch, William, 62, 64.
Berwiński, Ryszard, 5.
Beurmann, Ritter und Elder von, 7.
Beutel, John, 30.
Beutel, Martin, 30.
Bielawski (or Bielaski), Kazimierz, 11-12, 15, 224, 228.
Birney, David B., 60.
Biski, Ludwik, 34.
Black, John C., 260.
Black Codes, 194.
Blenker, Ludwig, 31, 35-36, 39, 50-51.
Blickensdoerfer, J. F., 195.
Boebel, Hans, 130-31.
Boeck, Leopold, 6.
Bohlen, Heinrich, 35-37, 40, 43, 47, 51, 54.
Booth, Newton, 224.
Bories, — von, 91.
Borkowska, Pelagia, 257.
Boutwell, George S., 210, 221.
Bowen, William, 67.
Brady, James T., 166.
Bragg, Braxton, 152, 156-57, 161-62.
Branch, Lawrence O., 61, 65.
Braun, Frederick, 80, 105, 196.
Brawley, R. R., 208.
Brodowski, Edmond, 224.
Brueninghausen, E. Washington, 134, 148, 256.
Buchanan, Robert C., 69.
Buhr, Nicholas, 67, 70.
Bull Run, Second Battle of, 55-72, 269.
Burant, Felix F., 263, 266.
Burger, Christian, 165.
Burnett, Caroline Mathilda. See Krzyżanowska, Caroline.
Burnett, Enoch, 15.
Burnett, L.A., 239.
Burnett, Ward Benjamin, 15-16, 27-28.
Bushbeck, Adolf, 108, 110, 162, 168, 185.
Burnham, Stowell, 129.
Burnside, Ambrose P., 81, 83, 97, 161.
Busby, Lyman, 225.
Butterfield, Daniel, 65, 175, 180-81, 185.
Cameron, Simon, 23.
Canby, Edward, 195.
Cantey, James, 41.
Cantwell, James, 113.
Carleton, John, 24.

Carter, —, 103.
Carter, Joseph, 103.
Carterm, R.H., 239.
Cartter, D., 198.
Catton, Bruce, 270.
Central Welfare Committee, 256.
Chalaupka, George, 131, 135.
Chancellorsville, Battle of, 97-112, 269.
Chapman, Collector, 217-18.
Chattanooga Campaign, 152-161, 269.
Chechenoff, Nicoli, 217.
Chłapowski, Karol, 224-25, 227, 259.
Chopin, Fryderyk, 2.
Chopin, Michel, 2.
Cieszkowski, August, 5.
Clark, Alvin B., 208.
Cleodt, August von, 134.
Cleveland, Grover, 255.
Cluseret, Gustave Paul, 40.
Cockrell, T.G., 233.
Coles, Jacob, 135.
Collins, E., 212, 214.
Conrad, Joseph, 8, 224.
Costin, John, 129.
Couch, Darius, 100, 110.
Cross Keys, Battle of, 40-47, 269.
Czechlewski, Joseph F., 263.
Dalon, R., 167.
Davis, Jefferson, 193-94.
Democratic Society (Polish in Paris), 5.
Democratic Society of Polish Exiles in America, 10.
Derndinger, Adolf, 62.
Devens, Charles, 96, 100-01.
Dietrich, Louis, 136, 196.
Dilger, Hubert, 108, 124.
Dilpert, Gottlieb, 131.
Dmochowski, Henryk, 20.
Dodge, Theodore Ayrault, 82-85, 91-93, 100, 103, 110-11, 114-17, 119, 121, 123, 131, 146, 196.
Doerflinger, Karl, 104-05, 108.
Doles, George, 102, 123-26.
Domschcke, Bernhard, 78, 80, 120, 134, 146, 196.
Doubleday, Abner, 110, 121, 132.
Douglas, J. W., 210.
Drober, Heinrich, 131.
Dzialyński, Titus, 5.
Dzikowski, Roman, 265.
Early, Jubal, 54, 64, 124-25.
Echo z Polski, 85.
Edwards, Oliver, 59.
Eickhoff, A.L., 235-36.
Eitel, Jacob, 32, 132.
Elder, Christian, 62.
Elling, Hermann, 67.
Ellsworth, Elmer, 22.
Emancipation Proclamation, 77.
Emleben, John, 68.
Engelhard, George, 135.
Esembaux, Michael, 155.
Evans, Nathan G., 69.
Ewell, Richard S., 40, 56.
Eytinge, Rose, 230.
Fair, James, 223.
Farquier White Sulphur Springs, Skirmish at, 54.
Floyd, Edward F., 131.
Fox's Ford, Skirmish at, 54.
Franklin, William B., 56.
Frederici, Julius, 131, 135.
Freeman, Douglas Southall, 143.
Freeman's Ford, Skirmish at, 54.
Frémont, John C., 36-37, 40, 45, 49, 75.
Friedlander, Gottlieb, 80.
Fritsch, Otto von, 149, 153.
Froelich, William, 67.
Frost, Emil, 102.
Fuchs, John, 131.
Galeski, Ludwik, 34.
Garfielde, Selucius, 221.
Geary, John W., 156-59, 167-71, 173, 179, 182-85.
Gehrlein, Edward, 54.
General Krzyżanowski Memorial Committee, 263.
General Krzyżanowski Memorial March, 265.
Gerhardt, Joseph, 20, 22.
Gerke, Reinhard, 57.
Gettysburg, Battle of, 119-44, 269.
Giessinger, Jacob, 67.

Gillis, Joseph, 122, 124.
Gilsa, Leopold von, 100, 102, 137, 146.
Gordon, John B., 125, 134, 142.
Gottfried, Bradley M., 142.
Gould, John H., 207-09.
Grant, Ulysses S., 160-61, 185, 200-01, 206, 210.
Great Fall, Skirmish at, 22-23.
Greeley, Horace, 87.
Greenhut, Joseph B., 176-77.
Gregg, Maxcy, 57-61, 64-65.
Grochowski, Charles, 131.
Groveton, Battle of, 269.
Gruszka, Sylwester, 265.
Guenzert, Teodor, 32.
Gunther, C. Godfrey, 165.
Haberkorn, Emil, 67.
Häger, Franz, 131, 135.
Haiman, Mieczysław, 249.
Hall, Robert H., 170-71, 180-83.
Halleck, Henry, 88-89, 114, 151.
Hancock, Winfield Scott, 134.
Handlin, Caspar, 67.
Hartsuff, George L., 69.
Hauschildt, Henry, 122-23, 146.
Hays, Harry, 125, 133.
Hecht, Daniel, 136.
Hecker, Friedrich, 157-58, 167-71, 173-78, 180-82, 184.
Heintzelman, Samuel P., 76.
Heinzen, Karl, 50, 78.
Henkel, William, 62.
Hennessy, John J., 71.
Hill, Ambrose P., 56, 101, 136.
Hillhouse, Thomas, 29.
Hilton, Joseph, 143.
Hinterwald, Thomas, 131.
Hoefer, Peter, 65.
Hoesch, Adam, 131, 135.
Hoffenbach, John, 146.
Hoffman, Henry, 67.
Hoke, Robert, 125, 133.
Holt, Joseph, 89-90.
Hood, John Bell, 69, 188.
Hooker, Joseph, 64, 95, 97-101, 108-11, 113-14, 116-17, 151, 153, 156-59, 167-78, 180-85.
Horain, Julian, 224-25.
Howard, Charles, 168, 173-76.
Howard, Oliver Otis, 96, 100-01, 110-11, 113, 121-22, 132-35, 138, 143, 147-51, 153, 157-59, 162, 168-70, 174, 178, 185, 195.
Hübschmann, Franz, 78.
Hutchins, F., 212.
Hutchinson, D. J., 212.
Jackson, Sidney Richardson, 142.
Jackson, Thomas Jonathan "Stonewall," 56, 61, 64-65, 101.
Jacobs, Michael, 139.
Jacobs, William, 78-79, 107, 147, 152-53, 155.
Jacoby, Henry, 129.
January Insurrection, 85-88, 259.
Jaworowski, Roman (Romuald), 85, 87.
Jenkins, Micah, 156.
Jerome, Lovell, 257.
Jerzmanowski, Erazm, 256, 259-60.
Jewell, James A., 262.
Johnson, Andrew, 193-95, 198-99.
Jones, David R., 69.
Jones, P. H., 168.
Jordan, Robert, 68.
Kałussowski, Henryk, 10-13, 20, 25-27, 29, 85, 87, 247.
Kałussowski, Witold, 10, 13.
Kampf, Peter, 32.
Kargé, Joseph, 85-86.
Kearny, Philip, 61, 63-64.
Kehr, Christopher, 67.
Kemper, James, 69.
Kern, Henry, 30.
Kinkead, John H., 249.
Kinkel, Gottfried, 51.
Kinsella,. G. J., 211.
Klein, Henry, 62, 64.
Klimecki, Hieronymus, 256.
Klüfisch, Johann, 67.
Klutsch, Dominicus, 171-72.
Knoxville, Campaign, 161-62, 269.
Koenig, Emil, 79, 105, 119, 131, 164.
Koenigsberger, Wolff, Falk, & Levin, 3.
Koltes, John, 60, 65-69, 198.
Koniuszewski, —, 13.

Kościuszko, Tadeusz, 1, 17, 92, 203, 252.
Kossuth, Lajos, 7.
Koszutski, Fabron, 3.
Kötzdinger, Alois, 152.
Kovacs, Stephen, 68, 73.
Kozlay, Eugene, 29, 39, 42, 51-52.
Kozmian, Stanisław, 5.
Kramer, Albert, 175-77.
Krause, Louis, 136.
Krick, Robert K., 45-47.
Kruszewski, John, 10.
Krzyżanowska, Antoinette, 2.
Krzyżanowska, Caroline, 15-16, 73, 75, 83, 167, 215, 239-41, 243-44, 247, 257, 262.
Krzyżanowska, Justyna, 2.
Krzyżanowska, Ludwika, 1-3.
Krzyżanowska, Stanisława, 3.
Krzyżanowski, Bogumil, 2.
Krzyżanowski, Bonawentura, 2.
Krzyżanowski, Edmund, 3.
Krzyżanowski, Jakub, 2.
Krzyżanowski, Joseph, 15, 223, 250, 257, 266.
Krzyżanowski, Nemezy, 3.
Krzyżanowski, Stanisław, 1-3.
Krzyżanowski, Włodzimierz B., accused of embezzlement, 206-210; Alaska, "governor" of, 218-19, 249-50; America, impressions of, 9-10, 14-16, 241, 249; Arlington National Cemetery, 264-76; arrival in U.S., 9-10; birth, 1-2; Burnside's Mud March, 83; Chancellorsville, 97-112; Chattanooga, 152-61; Civil War, opinion on, 251-52; criticism of, for connections to Germans, 25, by Robert K. Krick, 45-47, by Theodore Dodge, 82-84, 91-93; Cross Keys, 40-46; death of, 262; drawings of, 44, 164; education, opinion on, 252; Emancipation Proclamation, 77; enlistment, 20; Farquier White Sulphur Springs, 54; 58th New York, 24-34; Fox's Ford, 54; Freeman's Ford, 54; G.A.R., 198, 223, 247; Georgia, service in, 201-210; Gettysburg, 119-45; health, 255-57, 260-62; January Insurrection, 85-88; Knoxville, 161-62; Masons, 24-25, 197-98; memoirs of, 248-54; Mierosławski Revolt, 5-7; Modjeska's career, 224-32; New Orleans, service in, 211-215; New York Casino, 223, 231-32, 235, 246; New York City, customs agent in, 255-62; Panama, 237-244; photos of, 21, 33, 39, 74, 190, 256, 270; Poles in America, 259; political ideas of, 17-19; promotion to general 88-94, 148-51; promotion to major, 23; Republican Party, 17, 200; San Francisco, 223-34; Second Bull Run, 55-72; Sienkiewicz, 232, 244-46; slavery, opinion on, 250; Turnverein, 16-17; Veteran re-enlistment, 163-64; Virginia Polish colony, 11-14; W. Krzyzanowski & Co., 206-08; Washington Territory, 15-222; Wauhatchie, 156-59; Wauhatchie court martial, 168-84; women, opinion on, 253; wounded at Gettysburg, 127, at Second Bull Run, 68.
Ku Klux Klan, 201-02, 204.
Kulinski, —, 25.
Kundel, Edward, 134,
Kunkel, John, 131.
Lackner, Franz, 130.
Lamar, L.Q., 255, 260.
Lambert, W. H., 168-69, 172.
Lamon, Ward H., 17, 24, 29.
Lane, James H., 65.
Lastofka, Wenzel, 106.
Lauber, Friedrich, 141.
Law, Evander, 156-58.
Lawton, Alexander R., 56.
Ledig, August, 67, 128.
Lee, Alfred, 117-18, 120-21, 123, 125-26, 133.

Lee, Robert E., 75, 97-98, 101, 113-14, 141-42, 145, 147, 192.
Leighton, Rufus, 215, 221.
Leski, Władysław, 27-29.
Lessen, Francis, 241.
Lew, Henry, 131.
Lichtenstein, Theodore, 31.
Libelt, Karol, 5.
Lincoln, Abraham, 51, 71, 77-78, 84, 88, 91, 96-97, 114, 117, 153, 192-93, 195, 198.
Linsbach, Paul, 132.
Livermore, Thomas L., 143.
Lockman, John T., 102, 131, 155, 164.
Logie, William T., 155, 157.
Longstreet, James, 65, 156, 161-62.
Lorsch, Peter, 106.
Ludnicki, Wincenty, 224.
Luknoski, Anna, 10.
Luniewski, C.L., 223, 233.
Lutz, Edward, 31.
Lyon, Nathaniel, 49.
Mahler, Franz, 60-61, 67, 69, 124, 127, 196.
Mahler, Louis, 127.
Mainz, C.A., 262.
Majer, Dominik, 260.
Małuski, Aleksander, 25, 31, 34, 59, 63, 85, 133.
Manning, Daniel, 255.
Manz, Louis, 106.
Marshall, J. Foster, 60.
Marshall, Theodore B., 207-08.
Marx, Karl, 6.
Mass, Godfried (Bogumił), 25, 34.
Matzdorff, Alvin, 92-93.
McClellan, George B., 34, 37, 52, 71-72, 75-76.
McCrady, Edward, 57, 60.
McCullough, John, 229.
McDowell, Irwin, 52.
McLean, Nathaniel C., 65, 69, 96, 100-01.
McNulty, J. C., 207.
Meade, George G., 117, 145, 147, 149, 152.
Meredith, Philander C., 129.
Metzig, Emily, 3, 241-42, 244, 247, 257.
Meunier, Jean Baptiste, 32, 67.
Meyer, Alfred, 262.
Meysenburg, Theodore A., 177-78.
Michel, Jacob, 106.
Mickiewicz, Adam, 244.
Mierosławski, Ludwik, 5-7.
Mierosławski Insurrection, 5-7.
Miller, Henry, 161.
Milroy, Robert H., 40, 53, 56-57, 65-67, 188-90, 192.
Modjeska, Helena, 224, 226, 228-31, 233, 238, 272.
Montez, Lola, 77.
Moore, William, 134.
Morawski, Franciszek, 5.
Morell, Louis, 131.
Morgan, Edwin D., 24, 27-29.
Morgenrot, 118.
Mueller, Rudolph, 175-76, 179.
Mueller, Valentin, 32.
Muenzenberger, Adam, 79, 81-82, 106, 111, 116, 118, 134, 146, 196.
Naylor, William A., 187.
Neuhaus, Rudolf, 67.
Neumann, Paul, 233.
Offen, John, 67.
Ohl, Martin, 22-23.
Oliver, Paul L., 171-73, 179.
O'Neal, George W., 143.
O'Neil, Edward, 102.
O'Sullivan, Timothy, 140.
Orlemann, Louis H., 107, 173, 178, 182-83.
Orr's Rifles, 60.
Ottmer, William, 132.
Otto, August, 172, 178.
Paderewski, Ignacy Jan, 1.
Pągowski, Stanisław, 1.
Panic of 1873, 223, 233.
Parkhurst, John G., 195.
Pauly, Jacob, 67.
Pawlicki, Ladislaus, 224.
Pawłowski, Ignatius, 256.
Peissner, Elias, 77-78, 84, 93, 102, 111, 196.

Pfau, Andreas, 131.
Pfeffer, Peter, 105.
Phillipson, Arena, 217.
Pickett's Charge, 141.
Piotrowski, Rudolph Korwin, 223-24, 229-30, 232-33.
Pizzala, Charles, 104, 196.
Plater, Ludwik, 259.
Pleasonton, Alfred, 204.
Polish Central Committee in the United States, 85, 87-88.
Polish Committee in San Francisco, 224.
Polish National Alliance, 259.
Polish National Museum and Treasury, 223.
Polish Society of California, 223-24.
Pope, John, 50, 52, 54, 65, 70-71, 75-76.
Porter, Fitz John, 65.
Potocki, Jerzy, 263, 265, 267.
Potter, Caroline, 266, 268.
Pułaski, Kazimierz, 1, 92.
Puls, August, 131.
Puls, Friedrich, 106.
Raczyński, Edward, 5.
Rasemann, Matthias, 135.
Raszewski, Aleksander, 85-86.
Reed, Harrison, 203.
Reynolds, John, 61, 64-65, 117, 121.
Rezac, Frank, 131.
Richardson, William A., 220, 222.
Richs, Henry, 22.
Robb, Colonel, 206.
Roberts, Joseph A., 207.
Robertson, James I., 270.
Robinson, James S., 113, 120, 128, 133, 147.
Rodder, George, 132.
Roemer, Jacob, 59-61, 69.
Rohrig, Friedrich, 131.
Roosevelt, Franklin D., 1, 265.
Root, Henry, 105.
Rosa, Rudolph, 28.
Rosecrans, William S., 38, 152, 187.
Rousseau, Lovell H., 186.
Ryan, Thomas F., 238.
Salm-Salm, Felix zu, 39, 50.
Salomon, Edward S., 97, 223, 228, 230-31, 233.
Sanguszko, Władysław, 224.
Sautter, Frederick, 62.
Schaubhut, Ernst, 154.
Schenck, Robert C., 40, 69, 215.
Schimmelfennig, Alexander, 50, 52, 56-57, 61, 69-70, 76, 88, 91, 97, 101, 110-11, 121-22, 134, 145.
Schirmer, Louis, 41, 43, 47.
Schlosser, Philip, 107.
Schlumpf, Leonhard, 38.
Schmager, Gustavus Adolphus, 30.
Schmidt, John G., 57, 59.
Schmidt, Max, 68.
Schneapper, Friedrich, 54, 67.
Schoening, Emil, 31.
Schurz, Carl, 51-56, 60-65, 70-71, 76, 78, 87-89, 95-97, 100-01, 103, 107-11, 121, 123, 125, 127, 132-34, 136, 139, 143, 147-48, 155, 157, 162, 167-80, 182-85, 188, 190, 195, 215, 235, 238, 255, 260-62.
Schwarz, Carl, 140-41.
Schwerin, Henry, 103.
Screven, Mayor., 205-06.
Sedgwick, Charles B., 27.
Seldner, Louis, 197.
Seymour, Horatio, 148.
Sherman, John, 236-38, 241, 243.
Sherman, William T., 160, 162, 185-87.
Sickles, Daniel E., 100-01, 122.
Siemon, Andrzej, 32, 62.
Sienkiewicz, Henryk, 224-25, 227, 230, 232, 238, 244-46, 249, 272.
Sigel, Franz, 49-52, 61, 64, 67, 69-70, 76, 78, 87-88, 96, 195, 259.
Sill, William J., 135.
Simonek, John, 131.
Slocum, Henry, 122, 153, 185.
Smith, Orland, 96, 157-58.
Smith, William, 125.
Snodgrass, Benjamin, 194.
Snow. —, 129.
Stahel, Julius, 36, 39-43, 46, 65-67.
Stahl, Adolph, 103.
Stampp. Kenneth M., 251.
Stanton, Edwin M., 89-91, 152.
Starke, William E., 56.
Steedman, James B., 189.
Steiger, T. Albert, 127.

Stein, Charles, 127.
Steinfeld, S., 166.
Steinwehr, Adolf von, 39-40, 100, 122, 157, 185.
Stevens, Thaddeus, 199.
Stoldt, Gustav, 131.
Stopples, François, 131, 135.
Stuart, A. C., 212.
Stuart, James E. B., 98.
Suchara, Frank, 131.
Sudnik, George, 268.
Swinarski, Herr von, 7.
Swoboda, John, 131.
Sykes, George, 69.
Sypniewski, Juliusz, 225.
Szefer, —, 3.
Szenowski, Julius, 138.
Szumowski, Jan, 32.
Szwarcenberg, —, 25.
Szyk, Arthur, 44.
Tarkington, John S., 191.
Tate, Samuel McD., 143.
Tegethoff, Anthony, 32.
Teutlin, John, 41.
Theune, Roderick, 62.
Thomain, Robert, 25.
Thomson, David, 127, 129, 133, 135, 147.
Thomas, Edward L., 62.
Thomas, George H., 151, 159, 168.
Thomas, Henry W., 142.
Thumann, Henry, 132.
Tiedemann, Frederick, 70, 149.
Tinelli, Luigi, 26, 31.
Tower, Zealous B., 69.
Trentowski, Bronisław, 5.
Trimble, Isaac, 41-43.
Trost, Emil, 135.
Trumpelmann, Otto, 135.
Tucholsky, Johanna, 227.
Tyndale, Hector, 157-58, 172, 179.
Tyssowski, Jan, 6.
Vassoldt, Sebastian, 136.
Victoran, —, 214.
Voigt, Herman, 62.
Volkhardt, John, 54.
Von Steinwehr Post, G.A.R., 247, 262.
W. Krzyzanowski & Co., 206-08.
Wade, Jenny, 140.
Wainwright, Jonathan, 265.
Wallber, Albert, 104, 106.
Warburg, Adolf C., 148.
Warren, Gouveneur, K., 65, 110.
Washburne, Elihu B., 27, 29.
Waskowicz, John, 106.
Wątroba, Piotr, 32.
Waud, Alfred A., 138.
Wauhatchie, Battle of, 156-59.
Webster, Fletcher, 69.
Webster, J. A., 217.
Weigel, Eugene, 173, 178, 182.
Wendler, Frederick, 135.
Wertheimer, Edwin, 67.
Wheeler, Joseph, 188-89.
Wickesberg, Karl (Charles), 111, 121, 130-31, 134, 155, 196.
Wiedrich, Michael, 139.
Wilcox, Cadmus, 69.
Williams, Alpheus S., 143, 185.
Willis, Benjamin A., 125-26, 139, 235-36, 259.
Wilson, Isaac, 262.
Winkler, Frederick C., 106.
Wirth, Adam, 69.
Wojciechowski, Franciszek, 224, 232.
Wolf, J., 213.
Woods, James, 168.
Wrotnowski, Stanisław, 87.
Wütschel, Franz, 40.
Wyborny, Wiktor, 32.
Yaryan, H. C., 208-09.
Young, A. B., 217.
Zbitowsky, Joseph, 131, 135.
Zetsche, Albert, 62.
Żółnowski, Wincenty, 256-57, 260.
Zuehlsdorff, Friedrich, 131.

INDEX OF MILITARY UNITS

1st Michigan Engineers and Mechanics, 187.
1st New York Infantry, 60.
1st New York Light Artillery, Battery I, 37.
1st Ohio Light Artillery, Battery I, see Dilger's Battery.
1st South Carolina Infantry, 57, 61, 64.
2nd New York Light Artillery, Battery L., see Roemer's Battery.
4th Kentucky Infantry, 195.
5th New York State Militia, 165.
6th North Carolina Infantry, 137, 143.
7th Louisiana Infantry, 138.
7th North Carolina Infantry, 65.
8th Louisiana Infantry, 138.
8th New York Infantry, 40.
8th West Virginia Infantry, 51.
9th Battery, Ohio Light Artillery, 188.
9th Louisiana Infantry, 137.
10th Battery, Indiana Light Artillery, 187.
12th South Carolina Infantry, 57, 60, 64.
13th Michigan Engineers, 189.
13th South Carolina Infantry, 59.
15th Alabama Infantry, 41.
16th Mississippi Infantry, 41-42.
17th Connecticut Infantry, 134-35.
18th North Carolina Infantry, 65.
20th Maine Infantry, 47.
21st Georgia Infantry, 41-42, 142.
23rd Georgia Infantry, 100.
26th Georgia Infantry, 143.
26th Wisconsin Infantry, 77-82, 92, 97, 101, 103-08, 111-12, 117-18, 121, 130-32, 134, 141, 145, 147, 152, 155, 160.
28th North Carolina Infantry, 65.
29th New York Infantry, 60.
31st Georgia Infantry, 143.
31st New York Infantry, 85.
33rd New Jersey Infantry, 168.
33rd North Carolina Infantry, 65.
37th North Carolina Infantry, 65.
39th New York Infantry, 26.
46th New York Infantry, 28.
52nd New York Infantry, 31.
54th New York Infantry, 42, 51-52, 54, 57, 60-62, 67, 69, 77, 164.
58th New York Infantry, recruiting of, 24-34; at Chancellorsville, 97-112; at Cross Keys, 40-47; at Farquier White Sulphur Springs, 54; at Fox's Ford, 54; at Gettysburg, 119-144; 35, 51, 81, 88, 92-93, 101, 103-05, 111, 117, 146, 148, 154-55, 163-66, 186-88, 190-91, 195-96, 270.
61st Ohio Infantry, 51.
68th New York Infantry, 67, 77, 147, 149, 155, 164, 166, 174, 187-88, 191.
74th Pennsylvania Infantry, 35, 40-42, 51, 57, 88.
75th Pennsylvania Infantry, 35, 54, 57-60, 67-68, 84, 92-93, 111, 117, 119, 122-24, 127, 155, 164, 174, 187, 191.
80th Illinois Infantry, 174.
82nd Illinois Infantry, 171, 228.
82nd Ohio Infantry, 113, 117, 120-23, 125-26, 128, 131, 133, 135, 147, 164.
106th Ohio Infantry, 188, 191.
119th New York Infantry, 77-78, 82-83, 92, 100, 102, 110, 114, 119, 121-22, 125, 131, 134, 138-39, 141, 147-48, 155, 164, 186.
133rd Indiana Infantry, 187.
133rd Missouri Infantry, 191.
135th Indiana Infantry, 188, 191, 195.
141st New York Infantry, 147, 155, 161, 186.
154th New York Infantry, 168.

Dilger's Battery, 69, 108, 123, 134.
Gibraltar Brigade, 139.
Krzyzanowski's Company, 20-23.
Roemer's Battery, 51, 57-60, 69.
Schwarze Jäger, see 54th New York Infantry.
Turner Rifles. See Krzyzanowski's Company.
Wheeler's Battery, 123.
Wiedrich's Battery, 37, 40, 137, 139.